Marketing

FOR

DUMMIES®

3RD EDITION

by Ruth Mortimer, Greg Brooks, Craig Smith and Alexander Hiam

WILEY

A John Wiley and Sons, Ltd, Publication

Marketing For Dummies®, Third Edition

Published by
John Wiley & Sons, Ltd
The Atrium
Southern Gate
Chichester
West Sussex
PO19 8SQ
England
www.wiley.com

For general information on our other products and services, please contact our Customer Care Department within the U.S. at 877-762-2974, outside the U.S. at 317-572-3993, or fax 317-572-4002.

For technical support, please visit www.wiley.com/techsupport.

Wiley publishes in a variety of print and electronic formats and by print-on-demand. Some material included with standard print versions of this book may not be included in e-books or in print-on-demand. If this book refers to media such as a CD or DVD that is not included in the version you purchased, you may download this material at http://booksupport.wiley.com. For more information about Wiley products, visit www.wiley.com.

British Library Cataloguing in Publication Data: A catalogue record for this book is available from the British Library

ISBN 978-1-119-96516-9 (pbk); ISBN 978-1-119-96649-4 (ebk); ISBN 978-1-119-96651-7 (ebk); ISBN 978-1-119-96650-0 (ebk)

Printed and bound in Great Britain by TJ International, Padstow, UK.

10 9 8 7 6 5

About the Authors

Ruth Mortimer is editor of *Marketing Week* magazine, which is the leading business magazine in its sector. She also appears regularly in national press titles such as *The Independent* and the *Daily Express*, discussing issues relating to business, marketing and branding. She also appears on TV and radio as an expert commentator in this field for multiple programmes, including several on the BBC and Sky. She has contributed to a number of *For Dummies* titles on marketing.

Before joining *Marketing Week*, Ruth was editor of global business title *Brand Strategy*, as well as a freelance journalist. She wrote for Channel 4's '4talent' service, among others, letting young people know about new talents in music, design, arts and digital techniques. Before writing about marketing for a living, Ruth was an archaeologist, working mainly in the Middle East.

Greg Brooks is Global Marketing Director at Mindshare, the global media network which works with some of the biggest advertisers in the world, such as Unilever and Nike. Previously he was Content Strategy Director at C Squared, producer of the Festival of Media, a freelance journalist and a digital media consultant with over ten years experience covering the global digital industry. He has been a regular contributor on marketing issues to titles such as *Marketing*, *New Media Age*, *Brand Strategy*, *Broadcast*, *Future Media*, *The Guardian* and Channel 4's *4Talent* online portal. He is also co-author of *Digital Marketing for Dummies*. He has worked with Sky, McDonald's, News International, BT, Red Bull, Camelot (UK Lottery operator), EnergyWatch, Visit Britain and Ofcom (UK communications regulator), advising on the future strategic use of digital media.

Craig Smith is the former editor of *Marketing*, the UK's highest circulation weekly magazine, and PPA Weekly Business Magazine of the Year, serving the marketing and advertising industries. He has worked as a business journalist for many years and is a regular commentator on marketing issues to the national press and broadcast media.

Craig works closely with industry trade bodies the Association of Publishing Agencies and Business in the Community to promote best practice in the areas of customer magazines and cause related marketing.

Alex Hiam is a consultant, corporate trainer, and public speaker with 20 years of experience in marketing, sales, and corporate communications. He is the director of Insights, which includes a division called Insights for Marketing that offers a wide range of services for supporting and training in sales, customer service, planning, and management. His firm is also active in developing the next generation of leaders in the workplace through its Insights for Training & Development. Alex has an MBA in marketing and strategic planning from the Haas School at U.C. Berkeley and an undergraduate

Publisher's Acknowledgments

We're proud of this book; please send us your comments at `http://dummies.custhelp.com`. For other comments, please contact our Customer Care Department within the U.S. at 877-762-2974, outside the U.S. at 317-572-3993, or fax 317-572-4002.

Some of the people who helped bring this book to market include the following:

Acquisitions, Editorial, and Vertical Websites

Project Editor: Simon Bell

    (*Previous Edition: Tracy Barr*)

Commissioning Editor: Claire Ruston

    (*Previous Edition: Samantha Spickernell*)

Assistant Editor: Ben Kemble

Development Editor: Kate O'Leary

Technical Editor: John Bills

Proofreader: Helen Heyes

Production Manager: Dan Mersey

Publisher: David Palmer

Cover Photos: © iStockphoto.com/Lise Gagne

Cartoons: Ed McLachlan

Composition Services

Project Coordinator: Kristie Rees

Layout and Graphics: Jennifer Creasey, Corrie Niehaus

Proofreader: Bryan Coyle

Indexer: Slivoskey Indexing Services

Publishing and Editorial for Consumer Dummies

    Kathleen Nebenhaus, Vice President and Executive Publisher

    Kristin Ferguson-Wagstaffe, Product Development Director

    Ensley Eikenburg, Associate Publisher, Travel

    Kelly Regan, Editorial Director, Travel

Publishing for Technology Dummies

    Andy Cummings, Vice President and Publisher

Composition Services

    Debbie Stailey, Director of Composition Services

Contents at a Glance

Table of Contents

Part VI: The Part of Tens.. 365

Chapter 21: Ten Common Marketing Mistakes to Avoid..........367

Chapter 22: Ten (Or So) Ways to Save Money in Marketing 371

Chapter 23: Ten (Or So) Ideas for Lower-Cost Advertising........379

Introduction

· ·

Marketing is the most important thing that you can do in business today, even if your job title doesn't have the word *marketing* in it. Marketing, in all its varied forms, focuses on attracting customers, getting them to buy and making sure that they're happy enough with their purchase that they come back for more. What could be more important? Ever try to run a business without customers?

About This Book

We wrote this book to help you do that critical job of marketing as well as you possibly can. We wrote with a variety of marketers in mind, including small business owners and entrepreneurs who wear the marketing and sales hat along with several other hats. We also wrote for managers and staff of larger organisations who work on marketing plans, product launches, ad campaigns, printed materials, websites and other elements of their organisation's outreach to customers and prospects.

We kept in mind that some of our readers market consumer products, others sell to businesses, some market physical products and others offer services. The different types of organisations have many important distinctions, but good marketing techniques can work wonders anywhere.

Marketing can be a great deal of fun – it is, after all, the most creative area of most businesses. In the long run, however, marketing is all about the bottom line; if it doesn't have the potential to translate into profits somewhere down the line, you shouldn't be doing it. So, although we had fun writing this book, and we think you can enjoy using it, we take the subject matter very seriously. Any task that brings you to this book is vitally important, and we want to make sure that the advice you get here helps you perform especially well.

Conventions Used in This Book

We refer to any organised, coordinated use of product development, price, promotion, distribution and sales as your *marketing plan*. An important distinction exists between a marketing plan and your *marketing campaign* – some people start off down the campaign route thinking that marketing is all about advertising and promotion. It isn't. We want you to have a marketing plan. Creating a plan means avoiding random or disconnected activities. It also means thinking about how everything the customer sees, whether that be your prices, premises or staff, interlinks and contributes to achieving your marketing goals. Whether you work in a large organisation or own a small business, you need a coherent, well-thought-out marketing plan!

We refer to whoever buys what you sell as the *customer*. This customer can be a person, a household, a business, a government department, a school or even a voter. We still call them your customers, and the rules of sound marketing still apply to them.

What you sell or offer to customers we refer to as your *product*, whether it's a good, service, idea or even a person (such as a political candidate or a celebrity). Your product can be animate or inanimate, tangible or intangible. But if you offer it, it's a product in marketing jargon, and using just one term for whatever the reader wants to sell saves us all a lot of time and wasted printer's ink.

We also treat person-to-person sales as one of the many possible activities under the marketing umbrella. You need to integrate selling, which is its own highly sophisticated and involved field, into the broader range of activities designed to help bring about sales and satisfy customers. We address ways of managing sales better as part of our overall efforts to make all your marketing activities more effective.

Foolish Assumptions

In writing this book, we made a few assumptions about you:

- You're clever, caring and persistent, but you don't have all the technical knowledge that you may need to do great marketing. Not yet, anyway.

- You're willing to try new ideas in order to improve sales results and grow your organisation. Marketing is challenging, after all, and requires an open mind and a willingness to experiment and try new ideas and techniques.

- You're willing and able to switch from being imaginative and creative one moment to being analytical and rigorous the next. Marketing has to take both approaches. Sometimes, we ask you to run the numbers and do sales projections. Other times, we ask you to dream up a clever way to catch a reader's eye and communicate a benefit to them. These demands pull you in opposite directions. If you can assemble a team of varied people, some of them numbers orientated and some of them artistic, you can cover all the marketing bases more easily. But if you have a small business, you may be all you have, and you need to wear each hat in turn. At least you'll never get bored as you tackle the varied challenges of marketing!

✔ You have an active interest in generating new sales and maximising the satisfaction of existing customers. This sales orientation needs to underlie everything you do in marketing. Keep in mind that the broader purpose on every page of this book is to try to help you make more and better sales happen!

How This Book Is Organised

This book is organised into parts that we describe in the following sections. Check out the Table of Contents for more information on the topics of the chapters within each part.

Part 1: Where You Are, Where You're Going

Military strategists know that great battles must be won first in the general's tent, with carefully considered plans and accurate maps, before the general commits any troops to action on the field of battle. In marketing, you don't have any lives at stake, but you may hold the future success of your organisation in your hands! We advocate just as careful an approach to analysis and planning as if you were a general preparing on the eve of battle.

In this part, we show you how to make the most of your marketing by focusing on your customers and what your organisation delivers to them and give you strong, aggressive marketing strategies that can maximise your chances of sales and success. You'll also get the help you need to put a plan of action together that you can be reasonably confident will actually work.

Part II: Creating Thinking, Powerful Marketing

Great marketing requires a wide range of special skills. If you don't already have all of them, this part shores up any gaps and helps you take advantage of specialised tools and techniques.

We cover an essential marketing skill: how to find out what you need to know in order to develop better strategies and design better ads and other elements of your marketing activity. Where can you find the best customers? What do they respond to? What is the competition up to? Imagining, communicating and researching make up the power skills of great marketers, and we want to make their insights available to you!

We share with you that most precious and hard-to-capture of marketing skills: the marketing imagination. When marketers can bottle up a little of this magic and work it into their marketing plans, good things begin to happen. We also address another fundamental marketing skill: communicating with customers. Good ideas plus clear, interesting communications add up to better marketing.

Part III: Advertising Everyone Can Do

Advertising is the traditional cornerstone of marketing. Back in the early days of marketing, firms combined advertisements with sales calls and great things happened to their revenues. In this part, we show you how to create compelling, effective ads, brochures and fliers on paper – the traditional medium of marketing. You can run full-page, colour ads in national magazines if you have a big budget, or you can place small, cheap black-and-whites in a local newspaper – and either one may prove effective with the right creativity and design. Everyone can access radio and TV these days, too, regardless of budget, if you know how to use these media economically and well. However, you may also want to use perhaps the simplest – and most powerful – form of advertising: the simple sign – from signs on buildings, vehicles and doors to posters at airports and advertising hoardings next to main roads. You can put advertising to good use in your business in so many different ways.

Part IV: Powerful Alternatives to Advertising

Digital marketing – search, display, social media and mobile – is becoming more important in a global economy, so we cover the basics in this section. We offer advice on getting your company website to appear when people search online for your product or similar ones, ensure that you always reach the right customers with powerful emails and even give you some tips on social marketing using social networks. Many marketers also value the power of publicity and we discuss how to help the media cover your stories to get more exposure at far less cost than if you'd advertised. Special events also provide you with a powerful alternative or supplement to ad campaigns and can bring you high-quality sales leads.

Part V: Connecting With Your Customers

The classic marketing plan has seven components (the 7 Ps – see Chapter 1), but much of what marketers do (and what is covered throughout Parts II to IV) falls into the fourth P: promotion. In this part, we go deeper into the other Ps: product design and branding, pricing and discounting to create incentives for purchase; the aggressive use of distribution strategies to place your product in front of consumers when and where they're most likely to buy; and selling and servicing customers. We draw your attention to the all-important product and make sure yours is naturally brilliant enough to shine out and beckon customers to you. We also encourage you to examine your distribution, sales and service because these can make or break a marketing plan (and a business), too.

Part VI: The Part of Tens

The Part of Tens is a traditional element of *For Dummies* books, and it communicates brief but essential tips that didn't fit easily into the other parts. We recommend that you look at this part whenever you need insights or ideas because it encapsulates much of the essential philosophy and strategies of good marketing practice. And reading this part also helps you avoid some of the dead ends and traps that await the unwary marketer.

Icons Used in This Book

Look for these symbols to help you find valuable stuff throughout the text:

This icon flags specific advice that you can try out in your marketing plan straight away. The icon uses a pound sign for the filament of the light bulb because the acid test of any great idea in business rests in whether it can make you some money.

Sometimes, you need the right perspective on a problem to reach success, so this icon also flags brief discussions of how to think about the task at hand. Often, a basic principle of marketing pops up at this icon to help you handle important decisions.

All marketing is real-world marketing, but this icon means that you can find an actual example of something that worked (or didn't work) in the real world for another marketer.

In marketing, lone rangers don't last long. Successful marketers use a great many supporting services and often bring in graphic artists, ad agencies, digital agencies, research firms, package designers, retail display designers, publicists and many other specialists. You can't do it all. Sometimes, the best advice we can give you is to pick up the phone and make a call. And this icon marks a spot where we give you leads and contacts.

You can easily run into trouble in marketing because so many mines are just waiting for you to step on them. That's why we've marked them all with this symbol.

When we want to remind you of essential or critical information you need to know in order to succeed, we mark it with this icon. Don't forget!

Where to Go from Here

If you read only one chapter in one business book this year, please make it Chapter 1 of this book. We've made this chapter stand alone as a powerful way to make the most of your marketing by upgrading or enhancing the things that you do to make profitable sales. We've packed the rest of the book with good tips and techniques, and it all deserves attention. But whatever else you do or don't get around to, read the first chapter with a pen and action-list at hand!

Or maybe you have a pressing need in one of the more specific areas covered by the book. If fixing your website is the top item on your to-do list, go to Chapter 10 first. If you need to increase the effectiveness of your sales force, try Chapter 20 instead. Or are you working on a letter to customers? Then Chapters 6 and 14 on marketing communications and direct mail can really help out your project. Whatever you're doing, we have a feeling that this book has a chapter or two to help you out. So don't let us slow you down. Get going! It's never too early (or too late) to do a little marketing.

Part I
Where You Are, Where You're Going

'It was a marketing company's suggestion, and it's also a great help to the school finances.'

In this part . . .

Management's job is to see the company not as it is, but as it can be. Helping you recognise that vision is the purpose of this part. Whatever your current business or service is and does, this part helps you to imagine and plan what it may be best become in the next quarter and year. How do you do that?

You need, first, to understand your marketing programme – the integrated ways in which you reach out to motivate customers and win their loyal support. Next, we highly recommend that you come to grips with the big strategy questions in a marketer's life – who are we and what makes us so special that our sales and profits deserve to grow? Finally, we also recommend that you write down your big picture insights to help organise and simplify later decisions about the details of marketing. A plan, even a simple one-page plan, can help you a lot as you make marketing decisions throughout the coming year.

Chapter 1

Making the Most of Your Marketing

In This Chapter

▶ Focusing your marketing by understanding your customers

▶ Clarifying what your marketing is trying to achieve

▶ Leveraging your marketing with focus and control

▶ Identifying your customer touchpoints

▶ Maximising the appeal of your product, service or business

*E*ven though you're reading Chapter 1 of a book called *Marketing For Dummies*, you're probably already 'doing' quite a bit of marketing, maybe without even knowing it. If you have a product or service that's selling, know who your best customers are and what they want, and have plans to develop new products for them or to find more customers, then you're already addressing some of the fundamentals of marketing. Many companies, and even some of the biggest ones, mistake marketing for advertising. But promotion is just one aspect of marketing; many of the other elements that go into doing good marketing are things that you may think of as essential and everyday parts of doing business, such as setting prices and getting your product into the hands of your customers.

You may be good at doing some or all of these things, but unless you're co-ordinating all of these activities under a formal marketing framework, your efforts aren't nearly as efficient or effective as they could be. Your marketing activity (by which we mean everything about your business that makes a difference to your customers) is crucial because it's what gets your business from where it is now to where you want it to be. In this chapter, we go over lots of simple, quick steps you can take to make progress with your marketing activities.

Your Marketing Strategy: A Map to Success

Any marketing you do needs to be based on a *marketing strategy*, which is the big-picture idea driving your success. In order to make your marketing strategy happen, you need to work out how you're going to achieve it, which involves writing up a *marketing plan*.

We like to use a simple analogy to stress the importance of doing all this in a co-ordinated way, which involves a destination, a starting point and a map. Your marketing strategy is your destination – where you want to be by a certain time. Your marketing plan is your map, which tells you where you are now, and sets the best course to get to your destination. This analogy is effective because it demonstrates the importance of getting everything working together. You can have a destination and try to feel your way to it, but you'll get there quicker and more efficiently if you know where you're starting from, what the most direct route is and what obstacles lie in your way. Our map analogy has a final part: you can plan the most perfect route to your destination, but unless you start putting one foot in front of the other you'll never get there!

Knowing Your Customer

Many definitions of marketing have been created by experts with too much time on their hands. The Chartered Institute of Marketing (CIM), the international body for marketing and business development, defines marketing as 'the management process responsible for identifying, anticipating and satisfying customer requirements profitably'. Wow. We prefer our own, simpler version – 'selling more stuff to more people'. We're being a little unfair to the wordier version, because it does reflect one of the more important changes in modern marketing. You don't get very far in business these days by just making stuff and then finding people to buy it. Instead, you've got to find out what customers want from you and then create a product to meet those needs. This view is the difference between being what the experts call product-orientated and customer-orientated.

Whether you're product- or customer-orientated, however, the first and most important principle of marketing is this: know your customer. When you understand how customers think and what they like, you can develop products or services that meet those needs and come up with appropriate and appealing ways to communicate them.

The ultimate campaign

Old Spice aftershave is a brand with a lot of history that has recently been given a very modern makeover. As a result, it saw its sales double in summer 2010 by using a clever combination of marketing methods to reposition the 73-year-old brand as relevant for men today.

Old Spice's owner, Procter & Gamble, began with a TV ad airing during the Super Bowl in February 2010. The very silly ad featured a bare-chested, attractive, deep-voiced man who promised women that he was 'the man your man could smell like'. It spoofed serious, over-the-top fragrance ads with the man appearing on a posh boat, dripping in diamonds.

The company didn't just use TV. The ad was uploaded to video site YouTube, where it was viewed by millions of people. The Old Spice man utilised social networks like Twitter and Facebook and offered funny updates about his manliness.

Five months later, when the Old Spice man already had a significant following, the company then got him to 'answer' his fans' questions on Twitter and Facebook. The brand produced 180 videos of the Old Spice man answering real-time questions in less than two days.

This was a bold move in a traditional area like selling fragrance, where most ads tend to be beautiful, posed shots in glossy magazines. But it paid off. More than 35 million people watched the videos in their first week online and sales went up by 107 per cent in a month.

This campaign is notable because it was less about spending vast amounts of money on expensive TV ads and more about amazing strategic marketing, using multiple communication methods. It captured shoppers' imaginations and made them reconsider buying a long-established product that had fallen out of favour. And the enormous rise in sales tells a story we can all understand.

You need to understand your customer on two levels: the rational, functional dimension of making a purchase decision, and the irrational, emotional dimension. Every purchase, whether of a fizzy drink, a software program, a consulting service, a book or a manufacturing part, has both rational and emotional elements. So to truly know your customer, you need to explore two primary questions:

- **How do they feel about your product?** Does it make them feel good? Do they like its personality? Do they like how it makes them feel about themselves?

- **What do they think about your product?** Do they understand it? Do they think its features and benefits are superior to those of the competition and can meet their needs? Do they think that your product is good value given its benefits and costs?

Sometimes, one of these dimensions dominates for the customer you want to sell to. In other instances, all dimensions are equally important. Which is true of your customers? Depending on your customers, you need to take one of the three following approaches:

- **Informational approach:** The approach you use if your customers buy in a rational manner. This is the case for many business-to-business (B2B) marketers. This approach involves showing the product and talking about its benefits. Comparisons to worse alternatives are a great idea when using an informational approach. Use this approach when you think buyers are going to make a careful, thoughtful, informed purchase decision or when you have strong evidence in favour of their buying *your* product or service instead of others.

- **Emotional approach:** This approach pushes emotional instead of rational buttons. For example, a marketer of virus-scanning software may try to scare computer users by asking them in a headline, 'What would it cost you if a virus destroyed everything on your computer right now?' That emotional appeal can be much more powerful than a pile of statistics about the frequency and type of viruses on the web. Use an emotional approach when your customers have strong feelings you can tap into and relate to your product or service, or when you think people are going to make an impulsive decision.

- **Balanced mix:** This approach uses a combination of informational and emotional appeals. We'd choose this approach to sell anti-virus software, and many other products, because it engages both the rational and emotional sides of the buyer's mind. For example, after a scare-tactic (emotional) headline asking, 'What would it cost you if a virus destroyed everything on your computer right now?' we'd follow up with a few statistics such as, 'One out of every ten computer users suffers a catastrophic virus attack each year.' The facts reinforce the nervous feelings the headline evoked, helping move the prospect toward purchase.

Decide which of these three approaches to use and then use it consistently in all your communications. When in doubt, use the balanced mix to hedge your bets.

Getting focused

You begin to organise and focus your marketing activities when you define as clearly as possible who you're targeting with your marketing. Your marketing may include sales, service, product design and packaging, all marketing and media communications and anything else that helps win loyal customers. Marketing can encompass tens to hundreds of contributing elements, so you need a clear focus to keep them all on target. Remember that your target is a clearly defined customer.

To help you focus, write a detailed description of this customer, as if you were developing their character for use in a novel or screenplay you plan to write. (The plot of this story is, of course, that the character falls in love – with your product.)

When you try to identify distinct groups of customers to whom your product or service may appeal, you're using segmentation, and the cake can be cut in any number of ways. If your customers are other businesses, then you can group them by the type of product or service they offer or by the industry sector they're in. If your customers are people, the common ways to define them are by demographics (age and location), socio-economic status or by attitude and behaviour. Whichever way you try to identify the group or groups of customers most likely to buy from you, the objective is the same: to create a specific product and tailored marketing message that will have the best effect on them.

You further increase your focus when you decide whether your target customers prefer marketing that takes a rational, information-based approach, an emotional, personality-based approach, or a balanced mix of the two. By simply being clear about whom to target and whether to market to them in an informational or emotional manner, you've taken a great leap in providing a clear focus. You know whom to target, and you have an important clue as to how to target them and communicate with them in every element of your marketing.

Another aspect of your customer focus is whether you want to emphasise attracting new customers, or retaining and growing existing customers. One or the other may need to dominate your marketing, or perhaps you need to balance the two. Marketing to new prospects is usually a different sort of challenge to communicating with and satisfying existing customers, so knowing what is most important helps you to improve the effectiveness of your marketing.

As a marketer, you face a great many decisions. Marketing tends to be fragmented, so that marketing efforts spring up with every good idea or customer demand, rather like rabbits. In most organisations, hundreds of marketing rabbits are running around, each one in a slightly different direction from any other. Focus gets every element of your marketing moving in the right direction.

Finding out why customers like you

In marketing, always think about what you do well, and make sure you build on your strengths in everything you do.

You can't be all things to all customers. You can't be the best on every rational and emotional dimension. If you try to meet the competition on their ground, you remain in second place. So now we want you to clearly and succinctly define (notes, please!) what your special strength or advantage is. Start your sentence like this: 'My product (or service) is special because. . . .'

The way you complete that sentence reflects whatever it is that's outstanding about your product or business. Use this strength-based method to add an additional degree of focus to your marketing. Take a minute to think about what makes your firm or product special and different, and why customers have been attracted to that excellence in the past. Then make sure your marketing leverages that strength wherever possible.

For example, if you're known for good customer service, make sure to train, recognise and reward good service in your employees and to emphasise good service in all communications with your customers and prospects. A photo of a friendly, helpful employee could be featured in your advertising, in brochures and on your web page, because friendliness personifies your excellence in customer service. You can also quote customer testimonials that praise your service. You may want to offer a satisfaction guarantee of some sort, too. Focus on your strength in all that you do and your marketing becomes more profitable.

Working out the best way to find customers

We periodically survey managers of successful businesses to ask them about their marketing practices. And the first and most revealing question we ask is, 'What is the best way to attract customers?' Now, the interesting thing about this question is that the answer differs for every successful business. So, you need to answer this question yourself; you can't look up the answer in a book.

Take a look at the following list to see some of the most common answers – things that businesses often say are most effective at bringing in the customers:

- **Referrals:** Customers sell the product (see coverage of word of mouth in Chapter 15 for how to stimulate them).

- **Trade shows and professional association meetings:** Contacts sell the product (see Chapter 16).

- **Sales calls:** Salespeople sell the product (see Chapter 20).

- **TV, radio or print ads:** Advertising sells the product (see the chapters in Part III).

- **Product demonstrations, trial coupons or distribution of free samples:** Product sells itself (see Chapters 17 and 18).

- **Websites, social media and newsletters:** Internet information sells the product (see Chapter 10).

- **Placement and appearance of buildings/shops:** Location sells the product (see Chapter 19).

As the preceding list indicates, each business has a different optimal formula for attracting customers. However, in every case, successful businesses report that one or two methods work best – their marketing is therefore dominated by one or two effective ways of attracting customers. These businesses put one-third to two-thirds of their marketing resources into the top ways of attracting customers and then use other marketing methods to support and leverage their most effective method. Successful businesses don't spend any time or money on marketing activities inconsistent with their best method or that rob resources from it.

You need to find the one best way to attract customers to your business. If you already know that way, you may not be focusing your marketing around it fully. So you need to make another action note and answer another question: what is your best way to attract customers and how can you focus your marketing to take fuller advantage of it?

When you answer this question, you're taking yet another important step toward highly focused marketing that leverages your resources as much as possible. Your marketing can probably be divided into three lists of activities:

- ✔ Works best
- ✔ Helpful
- ✔ Doesn't work

If you reorganise last year's budget into these categories, you may well find that your spending isn't concentrated near the top of your list. If not, then you can try to move your focus and spending up. Think of this approach as a *marketing pyramid* and try to move your spending up it so that your marketing resources are concentrated near the top where you get the most successful results. What does your marketing pyramid look like? Can you move up this pyramid by shifting resources and investments to higher-achieving marketing activities?

Defining Your Marketing Methods

Peter Drucker, who passed away in 2005 and was one of few justly famous management gurus, defined marketing as the whole firm, taken from the customer's point of view. This definition is powerful, because it reminds you that your view from the inside is likely to be very different from the customer's view. Your own view is totally irrelevant to customers. The success of any business comes down to what customers do and they can only act based on what they see. That's why marketing and advertising gurus often say, 'perception is everything'. You must find ways to listen to your customers and to understand their perceptions of your firm and offerings, because your customers (not you) need to define your marketing methods.

This section requires you to think about and write down some ideas, so get out a pencil and paper, smartphone or iPad to jot down notes while you're reading.

Finding your customer touchpoints

From the customer's point of view, identify the components of your marketing. (The components include everything and anything that the customer sees, hears, talks to, uses or otherwise interacts with.) Each customer interaction, exposure or contact is what we call a touchpoint, where good marketing can help build customer interest and loyalty.

We want to warn you that, if you have a marketing plan or budget already, it probably doesn't reflect this customer perspective accurately. For example, in many firms, the marketing department is separate from product development, yet customers interact with your products so, to them, this is a key component of your marketing.

Similarly, some of the people who sell your product may not be in your plan or even on your company's payroll. A salesperson in the field, a distributor, a wholesaler or anyone else who sells, delivers, represents, repairs or services your product is on the marketing frontline from the customer's perspective. All of these people may be seen to represent or even *be* the product, from the customer's point of view. Are they all representing your firm and product properly – with the focus and professionalism you want? Are they available when and where needed? Are they likeable? Is their presentation and personality consistent with your strategy for your marketing? If not, you must find ways to improve these people's impact on the customer, even though you may not have formal authority over them.

Analysing your seven Ps

In marketing, points of contact between the customer and your communications, products and people are the only things that really matter. These interactions with you constitute your marketing, from the customer's point of view. These are *touchpoints*, and we find that most of them aren't itemised in a firm's marketing budget or plan.

When does your customer interact with your people or product, or information about your people or product? Take a few minutes to make up your master list of touchpoints, which will form the basis of a more extensive and accurate marketing plan. To help you create this list, we suggest you use the seven Ps of marketing: product, price, place, promotion, people, process and physical presence. Now think about your touchpoints using these seven Ps.

There used to be just four Ps of marketing (product, price, place and promotion), which are sometimes referred to as the *marketing mix*. Every marketing expert seems to have his or her own set of Ps, and wants to interfere with what is a very useful framework for trying to target a specific group of customers with a specific product. All these different ideas are okay – marketing is about challenging orthodoxy, after all. But don't get too hung up on which set of Ps is the right one. The list we give here is the most up to date and covers all the key touchpoints.

Product

What aspects of the product itself are important and have an influence on customer perception or purchase intentions? Include tangible features that relate to how well the product is meeting current and future customer needs, and intangibles like personality, look and feel and also packaging. Remember that first impressions are important for initial purchase, but performance of the product over time is more important for repurchase and referrals.

List the aspects (both rational features and emotional impressions) of your product that influence customer perception.

Price

What does it cost the customer to obtain and use your product? The list price is often an important element of the customer's perception of price, but it isn't the only one. Discounts and special offers are part of the list of price-based touchpoints, too. Don't forget any extra costs the customer may have to incur, such as the cost of switching from another product to yours. This can really affect the customer's perception of how attractive your product is. (If you can find ways to make switching from the competitor's product to yours easier or cheaper, you may be able to charge more for your product and still make more sales.)

List the aspects of price that influence customer perception.

Place

When and where is your product available to customers? Place is a big influence because most of the time, customers aren't actively shopping for your product. Nobody runs around all day, every day, looking for what you want to sell. When someone wants something, they are most strongly influenced by what is available. Getting the place and timing right is a big part of success in marketing and often very difficult. When and where do you currently make your product available to customers?

List the aspects of place (in both time and space) that influence accessibility of your product.

Promotion

This fourth P incorporates any and all ways you choose to communicate to customers. Do you advertise? Send mailings? Hand out brochures? Promotion includes all aspects of communicating with customers: advertising, personal selling, direct marketing, sales promotion and public relations. Do distributors or other marketing partners also communicate with your customer? If so, include their promotional materials and methods because they help shape the customer's perception, too. What about other routine elements of customer communication, such as bills? Routine admin forms part of the impression your marketing communications make as well.

List all the ways you have to promote your offering by communicating with customers and prospects.

People

Almost all businesses offer a variety of human contacts to customers and prospective customers, including salespeople, receptionists, service and support personnel, collections, and sometimes shipping, billing, repair or other staff, too. All these points of human contact are important parts of marketing, even though they may not all be working well to help keep your marketing focused and effective right now. People need to be trained and motivated to put across the right image for your marketing and that's down to you, not them.

List all the points of human contact that may be important to the success of your marketing.

Process

You need to think not only about the point when customers buy your product, but everything that happens before and after that. These are the processes through which you connect the product with the customer. Are you identifying prospective customers properly and professionally? Do you keep them informed about deliveries and can you avoid delays? Do you have a proper complaints procedure to alert you to dissatisfaction early on? All these issues aren't as back-office as many companies believe, and they all affect the way your customers perceive your business.

List all the processes involved in delivering your products and services to the customer.

Physical presence

Not all businesses make a tangible product and this latest addition to the list of marketing Ps covers those organisations and the image they portray to customers. Physical presence means your company's premises and vehicles, and even the appearance of your staff. If you offer services rather than tangible products, you need to provide prospective customers with an image communicating what your organisation represents (you do anyway, you probably just haven't thought about it or formally planned it).

List all the physical spaces viewed by your customers, from your reception area through to your delivery vehicles and drivers.

Adding to your list

You need to find efficient, effective ways to positively influence customer perception. You want to use elements of your marketing to motivate customers to buy and use your product (service, firm or whatever). The list of your current touchpoints for each of your seven Ps is just a starting point on your journey to an optimal marketing mix.

Now ask yourself what else can be added. Think about each of the Ps and try to add more possible touchpoints. Look to competitors or successful marketers from outside your product category and industry for some fresh ideas. The longer your list of possibilities, the more likely you are to find really good things to include in your marketing.

For example, the energy drink Red Bull uses student ambassadors to talk about the product to other students and to run marketing activities such as sampling campaigns on university campuses. The company makes heavy use of advertising as well, but finds that using students to target other students is an effective way of communicating credibly with its core audience.

Can you think of one or more new ways to reach and influence your customers and prospects in each of the seven Ps? If so, add them to your list as possibilities for your future marketing activity.

Determining what works best for each P

Within each of the seven Ps of marketing, one or two things have the biggest impact and give you the most improvement for your effort. Make your best guess or do some research to find out what works best.

Observe the results from different activities in an experimental way and then focus on those activities that produce the best results. Or you can ask customers or industry experts their opinion to find out what elements of each of the Ps have the biggest impact on your customers and their purchase decisions.

Should you concentrate your resources on a bigger presence at industry trade shows or build up your website? Should you use print advertising or hire a public relations consultant to get editorial coverage? The answers to these questions depend on what works best for your marketing strategy, customers and industry.

Deciding which P is most important

Ask yourself which of the seven Ps needs to be most important in your marketing. If you've already identified what customers like about you (for example, your special quality or a distinct point of difference from competitors), this may point you toward one of the Ps.

The company that sells the quality of its service, for example, obviously needs to emphasise people and processes in its marketing and business plan. In contrast, the company whose products are technically superior needs to make sure its marketing investments focus on maintaining the product edge.

Don't be tempted to make price the main focus of your marketing. Many marketers emphasise discounts and low prices to attract customers. But price is a dangerous emphasis for any marketing activity; you're buying customers instead of winning them. That approach is a very, very hard way to make a profit in business. So, unless you actually have a sustainable cost advantage (a rare thing in business), don't allow low prices, coupons and discounts to dominate your marketing. Price reasonably, use discounts and vouchers sparingly and look for other things to focus on in your marketing.

Catching the uncontrolled Ps

You can easily lose control of one or more of the seven Ps. In fact, you may never have had control of them in the first place! Small companies often have to use intermediaries or part-time sales staff, while big companies have so many employees that aligning them all behind the image they want to portray to customers can be difficult. Does your marketing display this kind of inconsistency and does it also miss opportunities to get the message across fully and well? If so, you can increase your marketing effectiveness by eliminating these pockets of inconsistency to prevent out-of-control marketing. Given the reality that some of your touchpoints may be partially or fully uncontrolled right now, draw up a list of inconsistent and/or uncontrolled elements of your marketing. You'll probably find some in each of the seven Ps – these inconsistencies are common. If you can make even one of the elements work better and more consistently with your overall marketing plan and its focus, you're improving the effectiveness of your marketing. Use Table 1-1 to draw up your list.

Table 1-1	Getting Your Marketing in Focus
Customer Focus	
Define your customers clearly: Who are they? Where and when do they want to buy?	
Are they new customers, existing customers or a balanced mix of both?	
Understand what emotional elements make them buy: What personality should your brand have? How should customers feel about your product?	
Understand what functional elements make them buy: What features do they want and need? What information do they need to see in order to make their decision?	
Product Attraction	
What attracts customers to your product?	
What is your special brilliance that sets you apart in the marketplace?	
Do you reflect your brilliance through all of your marketing efforts?	
Most Effective Methods	
What is the most effective thing you can do to attract customers?	
What is the most effective thing you can do to retain customers?	
Which of the seven Ps (product, price, place, promotion, people, process, physical presence) is most important in attracting and retaining customers?	
Controlling Points of Contact	
What are all the ways you can reach and influence customers?	
Are you using the best of these right now?	
Do you need to increase the focus and consistency of some of these points of contact with customers?	
What can you do to improve your control over all the elements that influence customer opinion of your product?	
Action Items	
Draw up a list of things you can do based on this analysis to maximise the effectiveness of your marketing.	

Clarifying Your Marketing Expectations

When you make improvements to your marketing, what kind of results can you expect? As a general rule, the percentage change in your marketing activity will at best correspond with the percentage change you see in sales. For example, if you only change 5 per cent of your marketing from one year to the next, you can't expect to see more than a 5 per cent increase in sales over whatever their natural base would be.

Projecting improvements above base sales

Base sales are what you can reasonably count on if you maintain the status quo in your marketing. If, for example, you've seen steady growth in sales of 3 to 6 per cent per year (varying a bit with the economic cycle), then you may reasonably project sales growth of 4 per cent next year, presuming everything else stays the same. But things rarely do stay the same, so you may want to look for any threats from new competitors, changing technology, shifting customer needs and so on, and be careful to adjust your natural base downward if you anticipate any such threats materialising next year. Your base, if you don't change your marketing, may even be a negative growth rate, because competitors and customers tend to change even if you don't.

When you have a good handle on what your base may be for a status quo sales projection, you can begin to adjust it upward to reflect any improvements you introduce. Be careful in using this tactic, however, because some of the improvements are fairly clearly linked to future sales, while others aren't. If you've tested or tried something already, then you have some real experience upon which to project the improvement's impact. If you're trying something that is quite new to you, be very cautious and conservative about your projections at first, until you have your own hard numbers and real-world experience to go on.

Planning to fail, understanding why and trying again

Start small with new ideas and methods in marketing so that you can afford to fail and gain knowledge from the experience and then adjust and try again. Effective marketing formulas are usually developed through a combination of planning and experimentation, not just from planning alone. In marketing, you don't have to feel bad about making mistakes, as long as you recognise what went wrong and take away useful lessons.

We're positive pessimists in relation to marketing. Our philosophy is, 'what can go wrong, will go wrong . . . and we'll be fine!' We advise you to avoid being too heavily committed to any single plan or investment. Keep as much flexibility in your marketing as you can. For example, don't buy ads too far in advance even though doing so makes them cheaper, because if sales drop, you don't want to be stuck with the financial commitment to a big ad campaign. Favouring monthly commissions for salespeople and distributors is also wise, because then their pay is variable with your sales and goes down if sales fall, which means you don't have to be entirely right about your sales projections.

Flexibility, cautious optimism and contingency planning give you the knowledge that you can survive the worst. That way, you have the confidence to be a creative, innovative marketer with the courage to grow your business and optimise your marketing. And you can afford to profit from your mistakes.

Don't expect to solve all your company's problems through your marketing. If the product is flawed from the customer's perspective, the best thing you can do as a marketer is to present the evidence and encourage your company to improve the product. Marketing can't make a dog win a horse race, so don't let others in your company try to tell you otherwise.

Finding More Ways to Maximise Your Marketing Impact

We want to end this chapter by sharing our conviction that you can improve your marketing and increase the sales and profits of your business in an infinite number of ways. The preceding sections look at some of the most important ways to focus your marketing, but we want to encourage you to keep searching for more ideas and to implement as many good ideas as you can.

Here, for example, are some additional ways to make the most of your marketing:

- ✔ **Talk to some of your best customers:** Do they have any good ideas for you? (Ignore the ideas that are overly expensive, however. You can't count on even a good customer to worry about your bottom line.)

- ✔ **Thank customers for their business:** A friendly 'Thank you' and a smile, a card, note, email, message on Facebook or polite covering letter stuffed into the invoice envelope are all ways to tell your customers you appreciate their business, and people tend to go where they're appreciated and may spread the news – Word of Mouth (WOM) is a powerful tool.

- ✔ **Change your marketing territory:** Are you spread too thinly to be visible and effective? If so, narrow your focus to your core region or customer type. But if you have expansion potential, try broadening your reach bit by bit to grow your territory.

- ✔ **Get more referrals:** Spend time talking to and helping out people who can send customers your way. Always make sure you thank anyone who sends you a lead. Positive reinforcement increases the behaviour.

✔ **Make your marketing more attractive (professional, creative, polished, clear, well written and well produced):** Often, marketing activities can work better simply by upgrading the look and feel of all the communications and other components. (Did you know that the best-dressed consultants get paid two to five times as much as the average in their fields?)

✔ **Be pleasant, to attract and retain business:** Make sure your people have a positive, caring attitude to customers. If they don't, their negativity is certainly losing you business. Don't let people work against your marketing – spend time making sure they understand that they can control its success. Use training and good management to help them take a positive, helpful and productive approach to all customer interactions.

✔ **Offer a memorable experience for your customer or client:** Make sure that doing business with you is a pleasant, memorable experience. Plan to do something that makes it memorable (in a good way, please!).

✔ **Know what you want to be best at and invest in being the best:** Who needs you if you're ordinary or average? Success comes from being clearly, enticingly better at something than any other company or product. Even if only a small thing makes you special, know what it is and make sure you retain that excellence. It is why you deserve the sale.

✔ **Try to cross-sell additional products (or related services) to your customer base:** Increasing the average size of a purchase or order is a great way to improve the effectiveness of your marketing. But keep the cross-sell soft and natural. Don't sell junk that isn't clearly within your focus or to your customer's benefit.

✔ **Debrief customers who complain or who desert you:** Why were they unhappy? Could you have done something simple to retain them? (But ignore the customers who don't match your target customer profile because you can't be all things to all people.) A well-handled complaint can teach you a lot and may even turn an angry customer into one of your most loyal – research reveals that customers who've been 'turned around' will even become ambassadors for your business, and spread the word about how good your service is.

Every time you put your marketing hat on, seek to make at least a small improvement in how marketing is done in your organisation and for your customers.

Marketing activity needs to constantly evolve and improve. Most companies fall far short of their full potential, which is why for every hundred businesses, only a few really succeed and grow. The others don't have the right marketing needed to maximise their success. Think big in your marketing. You can always do something more to improve your effectiveness and your results.

Chapter 2

Clarifying Your Marketing Strategy

· ·

In This Chapter

▶ Thinking about a market expansion strategy

▶ Targeting your customers

▶ Deciding what your market share should be

▶ Rethinking your strategy as you go forward

▶ Keeping your strategy in mind by writing it down

· ·

S trategies are the big-picture insights that guide your marketing activity and make sure all its elements add up to success. A good strategy gives a special kind of high-level direction and purpose to all you do. This chapter shows you how to take your focus to an even higher level, by centring your marketing on a single, core strategy that gives you an overarching goal.

Benefitting from a Core Strategy

Key to using a core strategy is making sure that your strategy is the hub around which all your marketing activities rotate.

In Figure 2-1, you can see how a strategy provides an organising central point to a range of marketing activities. This example is for the gift shop at an art gallery; its strategic goal is to get gallery visitors to come into the shop and make a substantial purchase. Gift-shop staff use a variety of tactics for their marketing, each of which is clearly helpful in achieving the strategy or the goal.

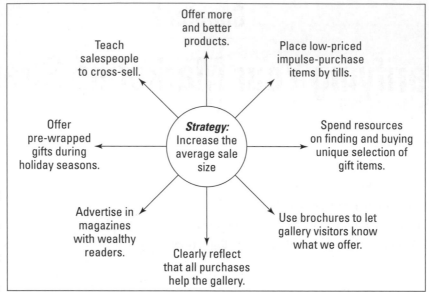

Figure 2-1:
A strategy
wheel for a
gallery's gift
shop.

As you create your own core strategy, make sure you can draw a solid arrow from your chosen strategy to each of the activities on the rim. Also try to explain in simple words how the activity helps implement your strategy and achieve your strategic goal. If the link to the big-picture strategy isn't clear, modify or eliminate the activity.

If you have more than one strategy, draw more than one wheel. But avoid too many or your resources get spread so thinly that you can't achieve *any* of your goals. Also, try to select strategies that have some synergy. The strategy wheels need to belong on the same wagon or they can't move you forward.

Expanding with a Market Expansion Strategy

Market expansion is the most common strategy in marketing and the idea is disarmingly simple. Just pick some new territory and head out into it. Oh, and don't come back until you've struck gold.

The market expansion strategy has two variants: you can expand your market by finding new customers for your current products (often this means going into new geographic territory to do so), or you can try to sell new products to your existing customers and market.

Expanding sales within your territory

The drinks company Innocent is expanding its market without expanding its geographic territory. In fact, as the company makes fresh fruit smoothies, expanding geographically is difficult, as the nature of its products mean they don't store or ship particularly well. Innocent's expansion plans are based on increasing the range of products it offers. As well as offering single-serve smoothies, it sells family-size packs, fruit-flavoured waters, smaller cartons and squeezy fruit purees for kids and even little snack-sized 'veg pots'. With a larger product line, Innocent can occupy more shelf space in the supermarkets, cafes and sandwich bars where it sells and get a larger 'share of throat' as a result. The bigger pack sizes means the smoothies can make it into people's fridges at home, pushing out traditional rivals such as standard fruit juices. The fruit waters and

purees for kids take the brand into school lunchboxes. Meanwhile, the pots of vegetables take the company into the lunch or dinner savoury food market. So it stands to reason that Innocent's sales goals can be increased to reflect its market expansion strategy. But by how much? The answer to that question depends not only on the increase in Innocent's potential market due to its product expansion, but also on the strategic risks of growing its market. The main risks are that new sales won't really be new, but may be replacement sales for its original smoothies and that customers won't like the new products as much as the old. Innocent needs to make sure it keeps product quality high and that any new elements of its range are different enough from its original product line not to cannibalise its sales.

If you choose to adopt a market expansion strategy as your main focus – the hub of your marketing wheel – make sure most of your marketing activity is working toward this goal. For example, if you seek publicity, make sure most of it is about your new product or in your new market, not about the old. All of your resources may be needed to effectively expand your market. And the faster you get through the transition and achieve your growth goal, the better, because extra costs are usually associated with any expansion.

Risk increases if you experiment with new products – defined as anything you're not accustomed to making and marketing. So you need to discount your first year's sales projections for a new market by some factor to reflect the degree of risk. A good general rule is to cut back the sales projection by 20 to 50 per cent, depending upon your judgement of how new and risky the product is to you and your team.

Risk also increases if you enter any new market – defined as new kinds of customers at any stage of your distribution channel. You should also discount those sales projections by 20 to 50 per cent if you're entering a new market to reflect your lack of familiarity with the customers.

What if you're introducing a new product into a new market? *Start-up firms* –
those just setting out in business – often run both these risks at once, and
need to discount sales projections even further to reflect them. Sometimes a
market expansion strategy is so risky that you really shouldn't count on any
revenues in the first year. Better to be conservative and last long enough to
work out how to correctly handle the marketing than to over-promise and
have your marketing die before it succeeds.

Specialising with a Market Segmentation Strategy

A *market segmentation strategy* is a specialisation strategy in which you target
and cater to (specialise in) just one narrow type or group of customers. If
you're in the consulting business, you can specialise in for-profit businesses
or not-for-profit businesses. You can even design and market your services
to individuals – as, for example, a career development consultant does. Each
of these types of customer represents a subgroup, or segment, of the larger
consulting industry. And you can drill down even further to define smaller
segments if you wish. You can specialise in consulting to the healthcare
industry, or to manufacturers of boxes and packaging, or to start-up firms
in the high-tech sector. Certain consultants use each of these strategies to
narrow down their markets.

A segmentation strategy has the advantage of allowing you to tailor your product
and your entire marketing effort to a clearly defined group with uniform, specific
characteristics. For example, the consulting firm that targets only the healthcare industry knows that prospective clients can be found at a handful of
industry conferences and that they have certain common concerns around
which consulting services can be focused. Many smaller consulting firms
target a narrowly defined market segment in order to compete against larger,
but less specialised, consulting firms.

Specialising to outdo the competition

Use the segmentation strategy if you think your business can be more profitable
by specialising in a more narrowly defined segment than you currently service.
This strategy works well when you face too many competitors in your broader
market and you can't seem to carve out a stable, profitable customer base of
your own. Also use the specialisation strategy if it takes better advantage of
things you're good at. This strategy sits well with the idea of focusing better,
based on your unique qualities (see Chapter 1).

Adding a segment to expand your market

If you're running out of customers and market and need to expand (see the 'Expanding with a Market Expansion Strategy' section earlier in this chapter), targeting a new segment is one way of doing so. For example, a consultant specialising in coaching executives in the healthcare industry could decide to start offering a similar service to not-for-profit organisations. A different approach and different marketing may be needed because the two industries are different in many ways and have only partial overlap (much of the healthcare industry is not-for-profit, but many not-for-profit organisations are not hospitals). But by specialising in two segments instead of just one, the consulting firm might be able to grow its total sales significantly.

Developing a Market Share Strategy

Another common and powerful strategy is to increase your market share through your marketing activities. In essence, this means taking some business from your competitors. *Market share* is, very simply, your sales as a percentage of total sales for your product category in your market (or in your market segment if you use a segmentation strategy too).

Calculating your share of the market

If you sell £2 million worth of inflatable paddling pools and the world market totals £20 million per year, then your share of the global inflatable paddling pool market is 10 per cent. The calculation is almost that simple. Or is it? Not quite. To accurately identify your market share, you need to consider what units to use to measure sales, the total sales in your market, your product category and more. The following sections explain.

Choosing a unit

What unit should you measure sales in? Sterling, euros, dollars, units, containers or grams are fine, as long as you use the same unit throughout. You can calculate your share of the European market for fibre optic cable in metres sold, so long as both your sales and wider industry sales are measured in metres sold, and euro sales or metric tonnes aren't mixed into the equation by mistake. Just pick whatever seems to make sense for your product and the information you have access to.

For example, if you're a distributor of premium chocolate biscuits to UK supermarkets and grocery shops, you can buy a market intelligence report on the biscuit sector (the figures we use here are from a Mintel report) to discover that the British biscuit market was worth £2.2 billion in 2011. If your sales are £78 million, then your market share is 78 ÷ 2200 or 3.5 per cent.

The report may also tell you that Brits spend £348 million of that £2.2 billion on savoury biscuits, a market segment that doesn't compete directly with you, in which case you can calculate your market share of the £1.9 million that is solely sweet biscuits. This would suggest that your market share is now 4.1 per cent of the market, based on this narrower definition. Which calculation is right?

Defining your product category

What is your product category? This may be the most important strategic question you ever ask or answer. If you sell premium biscuits, are you competing with the mass-market biscuit brands such as McVitie's and Fox's, or not? Should you count these products' sales in your market share calculations and try to win sales from them?

Ask your customers. Are they choosing among all the biscuit options or just some of them? What matters is *customer perception*: how the customers see the category. So watch your customers or ask them to find out what their purchase options are (see Chapter 4 if you want to conduct a formal study). Get a feel for how customers view their choices – then include all the likely or close choices in your definition of the market. With biscuits, you may find that a majority of consumers do sometimes buy both mass-market biscuits such as digestives, as well as posher premium biscuits for a special occasion. And you may also find that you must, as a distributor, fight for grocery shelf space and room on supermarket aisles against the mass-market brands. So you probably do need to use total biscuit market sales (including savoury versions) as your base, not sweet biscuit sales alone.

Researching the total sales in your market

To calculate market share, you need to estimate the total sales in your market. Doing so requires some research on your part. (Sorry, you can't avoid the research.) While you're at it, why not try to get some historical data – the sales in your market for the past five or ten years, for example? This information allows you to look at the growth rate of your market – which is an indicator of its future potential for you and your competitors.

Such data is most easily obtained from industry trade associations or marketing research firms, many of which track sales by year in different product categories. Many companies offer these market reports, but some of the best known are Mintel (www.mintel.com), Euromonitor (www.euromonitor.com) and Datamonitor (www.datamonitor.com). Market reports will cost you between £200 and £20,000, depending on the source, geographic scope and size of the report. A cheaper option for more rudimentary data is the trade magazines for the industry of your choice (that generally cover industry size and trends at least once a year). *Marketing Week*, for example, publishes analysis and research on a different consumer goods sector every week. Trade magazines are often the best source for the business-to-business marketer.

Such data is increasingly available on the web, too. For keyword searches, enter the name of your product combined with 'sales figures' or 'market size' into a search engine such as Google and see what you can find. Sites with marketing information abound.

Using the napkin method for estimating market share

Take a look at this simple method for estimating market size and share that you can sketch on the back of a napkin if you haven't the time or money for fancier approaches:

1. **Estimate the number of customers in your market (how many people in your country are likely to buy toothpaste or how many businesses in your city buy consulting services?).**

2. **Estimate how much each person buys a year, on average (six tubes or fifteen hours of consulting service).**

   You can check your sales records, or ask some people what they do, to improve this estimate.

3. **Now, just multiply the two figures together to get the total size of the annual market and then divide your unit sales into it to get your share.**

Setting market share goals

Market share gives you a simple way of comparing your progress with that of your competitors from period to period. If your share drops, you're losing; if your share grows, you're winning – the calculation's that simple. Most marketing plans are thus based at least partly on a *strategic market share goal*, such as: 'Increase share from 5 to 7 per cent by introducing a product upgrade and increasing our use of trial-stimulating special offers.' A biscuit wholesaler, for example, whose product competes primarily with premium biscuit brands and secondarily with mass-market biscuit products, may develop strategic goals that look something like this:

- ✔ Increase value sales of our products to end consumers of biscuits from 3.5 to 8 per cent.

- ✔ Protect our share of the premium biscuit market by keeping it at 15 per cent or higher.

- ✔ Differentiate our product even more from McVitie's, Fox's and other mass-market biscuit brands by emphasising what makes our product special to avoid having to compete directly against much larger marketers.

Post mortems on last year's marketing plan should always be based on an examination of what market share change accompanied it. If you don't already do routine post mortems, or careful analyses of what happened and why it differed from your plans, you should. If the past period's marketing doubled your market share, seriously consider replicating it. But if share stayed the same or fell, you're ready for something new. So, whether you make share gain the focus of your marketing or not, at least keep it in mind and try not to lose any share.

Deciding whether you should invest in growing your share

In addition to its use as a benchmark, market share may also give you insights into the realities of your potential success or at least into the future profitability of your product and business. Many experts believe that market share is a good long-term predictor of profitability, arguing that market-share leaders are more profitable and successful than other competitors. This belief is taken so seriously in some companies that brands with low market share are dropped so as to focus spending on those brands with a chance at category leadership.

If this theory is correct, you need to build market share aggressively. We favour share-growth strategies because some good studies are showing that high-share businesses have higher returns on investment, on average. The Strategic Planning Institute (a consulting firm in Cambridge, USA) has extensive data on market share and financial returns in its PIMS (Profit Impact of Marketing Strategy) database. We like its database because it looks at *business units* (divisions or subsidiaries in a single market) rather than whole companies and is thus more marketing orientated. And those business units with higher market shares have higher pre-tax *returns on investment* (or ROI; the percentage yield or the amount earned as a percentage of the amount invested). The relationship is roughly as shown in Table 2-1.

Table 2-1	Profiting from Market Share
Market Share (%)	*ROI (%)*
Less than 7	10
7 to 15	16
15 to 23	21
23 to 38	23
38 or more	33

Also impressive is some PIMS data suggesting that a gain in market share seems to lead to a corresponding gain in ROI (although the ROI gain is a half to a quarter as large on a percentage basis). You can visit `http://pimsonline.com` for more details of its research on effective marketing strategies.

Oh, by the way, we must warn you that loss of share leads to loss of ROI. So defending existing market share is a good strategy. You can accomplish this by keeping your brand's image well polished, by innovating to keep your product fresh and by designing good marketing campaigns in general. We generally advise marketers to defend leading shares, and to try to grow their low shares into leading positions. For example, if you're a strong third-place finisher in the share race, you should probably consider investing in a growth effort in order to leapfrog the number-two player and get within striking distance of the number-one slot.

But not all studies say the same thing about market share. If you're a small firm with a narrow market niche, trying to grow your share by expanding aggressively can get you in trouble. Balance share growth with the need to avoid excessive risks.

Achieving your market share goals

How can these market share goals be achieved? Consider the biscuit wholesaler example (see the 'Setting market share goals' section earlier in this chapter). For starters, a distributor needs retail shelf space, so you may need to push to win a larger share of shelf space from retailers, especially if you're dealing with large supermarkets. To earn the right to this shelf space, you may need to produce some consumer advertising or publicity, provide the stores with good point-of-purchase displays or signs, improve your product packaging or do other things to help ensure that consumers take a stronger interest in buying your products.

This plan needs to revolve around the goal of increasing share by 1½ percentage points. Each point of share is worth £22 million in annual sales (1 per cent of the total sales in the market), so a plan that involves spending, say, an extra £250,000 to win a 1.5 per cent share gain can provide an extra £33 million if it works. But will it work? To be cautious, the marketer may want to discount this projection of £33 million in additional sales by a risk factor of, say, 25 per cent, which cuts it back to a projected gain of £24.75million.

Now consider timing. Remember that the plan can't achieve the full gain in the first month of the year. A sales projection starting at the current level of sales in month one and ramping up to the projected increase by, say, month six, may be reasonable. Dividing your market share by 12 to find the monthly value of the risk-discounted 1.5 share point increase gives you the value of extra monthly sales for the sixth month and beyond. Lower increases apply to earlier months when the marketing is just starting to kick in. But the marketing expenses tend to be concentrated in the early months, reflecting the need to invest in advance in order to grow your market share.

Perhaps the most important research you can do for the market share strategy is to simply study your closest and/or most successful competitors. What do they do well? How do they take business from you now? What new initiatives are they trying this year? The better you understand your competitors, the more easily you can take customers away from them. Talk to customers, suppliers, distributors and anyone else with good knowledge of your competitors' practices, and gather any online information about them from their websites. Also collect your rivals' marketing materials and brochures, and keep track of any information you come across on how they market. For example, if your rivals are picking up good business by having a stand at a trade show you don't attend, consider getting a booth next time to make sure you're able to compete against them there.

Revising Your Strategy over the Life of the Product Category

Every *product category* – the general grouping of competitive products to which your product belongs (be it merchandise or a service) – has a limited life. At least in theory, and usually in all-too-real reality, some new type of product comes along to displace the old. The result is a never-ending cycle of birth, growth and decline, fuelled by the endless inventiveness of competing businesses. Categories of products arise, spread through the marketplace, then decline as replacements arise and begin their own life cycles. Marketing works differently depending on where in its life cycle your product is. In this section, we show you a practical version of the life-cycle model that helps you choose the most applicable of three powerful marketing strategies.

To use the life-cycle model, you need to look at the long-term trend in the overall market, as indicated by the sales of your brand and those of its major competitors.

Interpreting and predicting market growth

Over a long period of time, sales (in sterling, units or as a share of the potential market) will

✔ Follow a sigmoid growth curve (like a stretched-out, right-leaning S, or sigma, in shape).

Having trouble visualising that image? See the bottom half of Figure 2-2 for a picture of this life-cycle curve. Because of this characteristic pattern, products generally go through a series of four life-cycle stages.

✔ Level off to grow at the rate at which the customer base grows.

✔ Fall off when a replacement product enters the market.

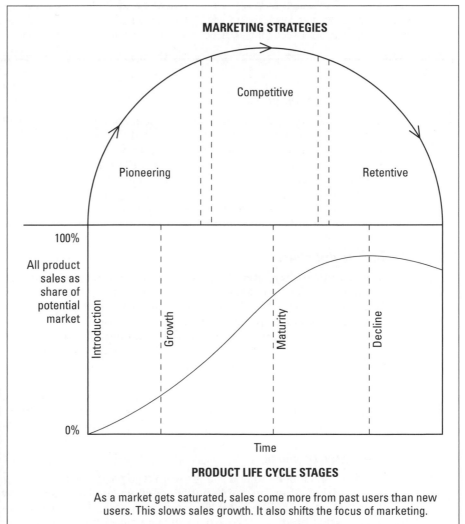

Figure 2-2:
Growth rates and market conditions over the product life cycle.

Stimulating a second childhood

Sometimes markets seem to have matured and then are revived with a new growth phase by creative marketers. The market for television sets was originally assumed to be limited to one TV per household, as it was presumed that watching TV was a family activity. While some homes have had two or more TVs for years, only since the rapid growth of multi-channel TV have marketers really started to push the idea that you can have more individual choice over what you watch when you have multiple TVs in the home and subscriptions to services like Sky. With online TV accessed through computers taking off too and 3D TVs aimed at sports lovers, now there can be even more TV channels used at the same time in any one residence.

The introduction phase

Sales start slowly because a new product concept takes time to gain momentum and catch on. That situation makes the introductory phase of the life cycle a tough one for marketers. You have to educate consumers about the advantages of the new product. The more unfamiliar the product is, the more change the product demands from its users and the longer this introductory phase takes. In the introduction phase, marketers emphasise coaching prospective customers about their exciting new product. Here, marketers worry less about competition than about converting the dubious to their cause.

The growth phase

After a while – often after 10 to 20 per cent of the potential market is reached – the idea gains momentum. The life cycle enters its growth stage. Consumers accept the product and begin to adopt it in greater numbers. Growth rates shoot upward. Unfortunately, the obvious success of the new product attracts more competitors – the number of rival products always grows during the growth phase, so the market leaders generally lose market share. But still, the rapid growth usually enriches all viable competitors and everybody is happy. In this phase of the life cycle, marketers jockey for position by trying to maximise their share of distribution and consumption (getting people to use more of their product, more often), hoping to emerge in maturity as one of the leaders.

The maturity phase

A sad thing happens to end the growth-stage party: marketers begin to run out of market. After most able-bodied people who like to skate have bought their first pair of in-line roller skates, for example, the nature of the roller skate market has to change. Now you can't get rich just by spreading the good news about this new product. You have to wait until people are ready to replace their old skates and then you have to fight tooth-and-nail with competitors to make the sale. At best, you keep most of your old customers and pick up a share of the new people who have thoughtfully managed to be born and grow up with a proclivity for roller-skating. The days of heady growth are over because your market is becoming *saturated*, meaning that most potential customers have already found out about and started using the product. In-line roller skates reached this point a few years ago and the mobile phone market is pretty much there now.

When a market is saturated, you can no longer grow just by finding new customers. Your ambitions are limited by the rate at which customers replace the product and your ability to steal customers from your competitors. Competitive, share-orientated marketing is the way to go, and you need to focus on refining your points of difference from competitors and communicating them clearly to customers.

The death phase

Finally, so the product life-cycle model says, people stop replacing their old products with similar new ones because something even better has come along. Where once CDs replaced LP records, now the CD market itself is over-whelmed by a burgeoning music download market. Most products eventually enter a decline stage in which sales fall, profits evaporate and most of the competitors exit. Sometimes you can make good money by hanging on to serve the die-hard loyals, but often this stage is a waste of time. Best to make hay while the sun shines and then switch your product line into some hot new growth markets.

Reincarnation: Life after the death phase

Some marketers refuse to give up. They think a dose of imagination and some clever marketing can revive a dying product. And sometimes these marketers are right. Cadbury marketers noted back in 2007 that significant demand existed for its Wispa bar, which had been discontinued four years previously. The company saw that thousands of consumers had joined groups on Facebook asking for the bar to be sold again. So it harnessed this free publicity and created a whole marketing campaign around the demand for the Wispa, resulting in a relaunch for the product. Once it was back on the shelves, the company carried out a marketing campaign to tell consumers that if they wanted the reintroduction to be permanent, they needed to keep buying. And when Cadbury saw another group on Facebook asking for sub-brand Wispa Gold to come back too, it reintroduced that bar too. It even invited the person running the Facebook group to press the button to restart the production line. This whole campaign was an excellent piece of marketing. The company found a ready-made audience for its product on Facebook allowing it to create the impression that remaking the Wispa was a matter of great public demand rather than a corporate decision. And it involved interested fans when it did come back by getting them involved with the production process and reaping even more good PR material as a result. Behold: life after death.

Choosing your life-cycle strategy

In the upper half of Figure 2-2 is the advertiser's version of the life cycle with its helpful emphasis on what to do to win sales. We've redrawn it slightly (usually the model looks like half of a wagon wheel) to make it tie into the product life-cycle drawing. Put the two together, and you have that finest of combinations: situation diagnosis plus practical prescription.

The advertising life-cycle model says that products go through three stages, each requiring a different marketing strategy: *pioneering* (use it when the majority of prospects are unfamiliar with the product), *competitive* (use it when the majority of prospects have tried at least one competitor's product) and *retentive* (use it when attracting new customers costs more than keeping old customers). By tying these to the life-cycle model, you can choose the right strategy based on the current growth rate trend in your market. Table 2-2 shows the strategic objectives of each of these stages.

Table 2-2	What to Do in Each Product Stage	
Pioneering	*Competitive*	*Retentive*
Educate consumers	Build brand equity	Retain customers
Encourage trial usage	Position against competitors	Build relationships with customers
Build the distribution channel	Capture a leading market share	Improve quality
Segment market to better serve specific needs	Improve service	Upgrade product

Everything about your marketing follows from these simple strategies. And you can tell when you need them by looking at where you are in your product's life cycle, which makes your strategic thinking fairly simple.

For example, if you're marketing a radical new product that has just begun to experience accelerating sales, then you know you're moving from the introduction to the growth stage of the product life cycle. Table 2-2 indicates that a pioneering strategy should apply. And the table tells you that you need to educate consumers about the new product, encourage them to try it and make sure that the product is widely distributed. Now you have a clear strategic mandate as you move on to define your marketing activity.

How should you price this pioneering product – high or low? Well, the price should be low enough to keep from discouraging new customers, so the high end of the price range may be a mistake. On the other hand, no mandate exists to compete head-to-head on price (that would be more appropriate to the competitive strategy later on). So the best time to use low prices is probably in special offers to stimulate trial. In fact, perhaps free samples are appropriate now, especially if coupled with a moderately high list price.

What about your advertising? It certainly needs to be informative, showing potential consumers how to benefit from the product. Similarly, you know you need to encourage distributors to stock and push the product, so special offers to the trade and a strong sales effort (through your own salespeople or through reps or distributors) should get a fair share of your marketing budget.

All these conclusions are fairly obvious – if you stay focused on the strategic guidelines in the model. And that is the beauty of strategy – it makes the details of your tactics so much clearer and simpler.

Designing a Positioning Strategy

A positioning strategy takes a psychological approach to marketing. This strategy focuses on getting customers or prospects to see your product in a favourable light. The positioning goal you articulate for this kind of strategy is the position your product holds in the customer's mind.

When you go to the trouble of thinking through your positioning statement, you have – a positioning statement. So what? You can't use the statement to sell products. But you can use a positioning statement to design all your marketing communications. Everything you do in your marketing, from the product or service's packaging to its advertising and publicity, should work together to convince customers of the points your positioning statement contains. So put the statement up over your desk and refer to it to make sure that you communicate the right information and feelings to get the point across and help customers think about your product in the right way.

For example, you may decide to emphasise speed and reliability if you're advertising a courier service. You may even make a grid or positioning map, with one axis representing a range from low to high speed and the other from low to high reliability, and then stake out the quadrant where both are as high as your goal, as Figure 2-3 shows.

Figure 2-3:
A positioning map for a courier service.

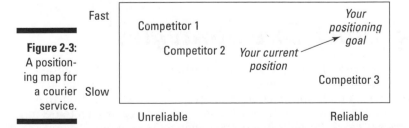

Here are some of the more common options for a positioning strategy:

- **You may position against a competitor.** A finance brand might say: 'Our interest rates are lower than Citibank's.' (This tactic is a natural in a mature product category, where the competitive strategy applies.)

- **You may emphasise a distinctive benefit.** A food brand might say: 'The only peanut butter with no harmful transfats.' (This positioning strategy can be combined with a pioneering strategy or a competitive one.)

- **You can affiliate yourself with something the customer values.** A toothpaste brand may say: 'The toothpaste most often recommended by dentists.' (Doing so allows some of the virtues of this other thing to rub off on your brand.) A celebrity endorser, an image of a happy family playing on the beach, a richly appointed manor house set in beautiful gardens, a friendly giant – all have been used to position products favourably in consumers' minds.

You can write down your positioning strategy in big print and pin it above your desk to make sure that you actually stay focused on its execution. Handing out copies of your positioning statement to your ad agency, distributor, PR firm, salespeople and anyone else who works on or in your product marketing also pays off.

Writing a positioning statement is pretty easy. First you need to decide:

- What type of customer you target.
- What you do for that customer.
- How you do it.
- Why you do it better than your competitors.

Next, you need to fill in the following with your own words:

- Our product offers the following benefit:
- To the following customers (describe target segment):
- Our product is better than competitors in the following manner:
- We can prove we're the best because of (evidence/differences):

Considering Other Core Strategies

Do other winning marketing strategies exist? Certainly. In fact, strategy, like everything in marketing, is only limited by your imagination and initiative. If you can think of a better approach to strategy, go for it. This section goes over a few examples of other strategies that marketers have proven to be effective in recent years. Perhaps one of them may work for you.

Simplicity marketing

Apple launched its 3G iPhone in summer 2008 to a UK market that hadn't snapped up the first release of the handset a year previously. The new marketing campaign to promote the handset featured advertising spots that showed off the product's ease of use in a direct attempt to show how the iPhone could enhance the lives of its owners in a simple way. It focused particularly on how the Internet was easy to use on the handset (since a common complaint is that mobile phones access the web in a much more complicated way than using a computer). Apple managed to generate a huge swell of anticipation and interest ahead of its release using this technique, with sales far outstripping those of the iPhone's first release. It has since carried on this strategy for the release of the iPhone 4 and its iPad tablet computer.

Use this strategy in your business to position yourself as simpler, easier to understand and easier to use or work with than the competition. According to research firm Datamonitor, so-called *simplicity positioning* is a new opportunity. This firm predicts that, as people are offered more and more choice in every aspect of their lives, they're going to be increasingly attracted to simple brands that are easy to buy and use. In fact, Datamonitor's studies indicate that many customers are willing to pay a premium in order to avoid complexity and make purchase decisions simply and quickly. Could this approach be useful to customers in your market? Look for technologies or processes that can make your customers' lives simpler and easier.

Quality strategies

Most marketers grossly underrate quality. All else being anywhere near equal, a majority of customers choose the higher-quality option. But be careful to find out what your customers think quality means – they may have a different view from you. Quality as an end in itself can be a wasteful and unsuccessful strategy if your customers plan to replace the product every couple of years. A mobile phone company that made a durable mobile that could last 20 years is adding cost all round with no benefit to people keen to change their phone frequently – quality should mean better than the competition, not better than is required. Also, be careful to integrate your quality-based marketing messages with a genuine commitment to quality in all aspects of your business.

You can't just say you're better than the competition; you really have to deliver. But if customers see you as superior on even one dimension of quality, by all means emphasise this in your marketing. Quote customer testimonials praising your quality, describe your commitment to quality in your marketing materials and make trial usage easy for prospective customers so that they can experience your quality, too. Also, make sure your pricing is consistent with a high-quality image. Don't focus on advertising big discounts, as these signal cheapness, not quality.

Reminder strategies

A reminder strategy is good when you think people would buy your product if they thought of it – but might not without a reminder. Many routine purchases benefit from this strategy.

The theme of an ad from the Scottish Dairy Marketing Company (SDMC) and DairyCo (formerly the Milk Development Council in the UK) is quite simply to remind people to drink more milk – 'Milk. Got the White Stuff?' The campaign has for the past few years used celebrities, such as tennis player Andy Murray and TV presenter Myleene Klass, posed wearing milk moustaches. The campaign for milk has been expanded by the Milk Marketing Forum online to create Facebook campaigns and apps to promote milk as a healthy drinking option for young people. The same strategy is also used by dairy promotion bodies on the other side of the Atlantic, with the phrase 'Got Milk' accompanying the moustached famous faces in the US.

Point-of-purchase marketing (POP) is often an effective way to implement the reminder strategy. POP marketing simply means doing whatever advertising is necessary to sway the consumer your way at the time and place of their purchase. For retail products, this strategy often means a clever in-store display or sign to remind the consumer.

Writing Down Your Strategy

What is your marketing strategy? Is your strategy a pure version of one of the strategies reviewed in this chapter, or is it a variant or even a combination of more than one of them? Whatever it is, take some time to write your marketing strategy down clearly and thoughtfully. Put your strategy in summary form in a single sentence. (If you must, add some bullet points to explain it in more detail.)

Looking at an example

Here's what one company's marketing strategy looks like:

> Our strategy is to maximise the quality of our security alarm products and services through good engineering and to grow our share of a competitive market by communicating our superior quality to high-end customers.

What you have here is a nice, clear statement of strategy. Now you know what the big-picture game plan is and can set to work designing good products and packaging, friendly services and impressive ads that communicate your quality to consumers.

Dusting it off and reading it, for goodness sake

Is your strategy obvious in all you do? When you adopt a specific marketing strategy, you must actually read it from time to time and check that you're following it. We're often amazed at the lack of relationship between companies' strategies and their actions.

For example, take the case of a car parts manufacturer emphasising efficiencies as a way to win contracts from the big car-makers. Efficiencies include quicker order turnaround, computer systems to manage orders and inventories better, and substitutable component parts to simplify repairs. Companies such as Ford or Toyota want to buy from suppliers who make good component parts quickly, reliably and cheaply. But this particular firm isn't consistent in communicating its efficiency strategy to its customer base. The firm purchases very handsome full-colour brochures illustrating its marvellous efficiency; however, it hires an inexpensive direct-mail service to send these brochures to its entire customer list. The result is that many of the labels have errors in them and the envelopes are so light and cheap that a significant number tear during mailing. The impression made is a poor one and quite inconsistent with the intended strategy.

After you develop a marketing strategy, make sure you follow it. You may need to write your strategy down and display it so that you (and others) can't forget it. In fact, we highly recommend that you do some formal planning to figure out exactly how you'll implement your strategy in all aspects of your marketing. Chapter 3 shows you how to develop a plan as painlessly as possible.

Chapter 3

Writing a Marketing Plan

● ●

In This Chapter

▶ Avoiding common marketing errors

▶ Writing a powerful executive summary

▶ Clarifying and quantifying your strategic objectives

▶ Gaining an advantage through your situation analysis

▶ Defining your marketing mix

▶ Projecting and controlling revenues and expenses

● ●

*Y*ou don't have to write a marketing plan to use this book or even to benefit from this chapter. But you may want to, because doing so isn't as hard as you may think and, most important, a good plan increases the odds of success. In fact, most of the really successful businesses we know – small or large, new or old – write a careful marketing plan at least once a year.

Marketing combines lots of activities and expenditures in the hope of generating or increasing sales and maintaining or increasing market share. You won't see those sales numbers rise without a coherent plan linking a strategy based on the strengths of your position to your sales and marketing activities. Marketing can get out of control or confused in a hurry unless you have a plan. Every successful business needs a marketing plan. (Yes, even if you're in a small or start-up business. In fact, especially if you are; you don't have the resources to waste on unplanned or ineffective marketing.)

Identifying Some Planning Rules and Tips

Marketing plans vary significantly in format and outline from company to company, but all have core components covering:

- ✔ **Your current position:** In terms of your product, customers, competition and broader trends in your market.

- ✔ **For established businesses, what results you achieved in the previous period:** In terms of sales, market share and possibly also in terms of profits, customer satisfaction or other measures of customer attitude and perception. You may want to include measures of customer retention, size, frequency of purchase or other indicators of customer behaviour, if you think them important to your new plan.

- ✔ **Your strategy:** The big picture that will help you get improved results.

- ✔ **The details of your marketing activities:** Including all your company's specific activities, grouped by area or type, with explanations of how these activities fit the company's strategy and reflect the current situation.

- ✔ **The numbers:** Including sales projections and costs. Consider whether knowing these additional numbers would help your business: market share projections, sales to your biggest customers or distributors, costs and returns from any special offers you plan to use, sales projections and commissions by territory or whatever helps you quantify your specific marketing activities.

- ✔ **Your learning plans:** You may want to test the water or experiment on a small scale if you have a new business or new product or if you're experimenting with a new or risky marketing activity. You need to determine what positive results you want to see before committing to a higher level. Wisdom is knowing what you don't know – and planning how to work it out.

The more unfamiliar the water, the more flexibility and caution your plan needs. If you're a start-up, for example, consider a plan with a timeline and alternatives or options in case of problems. Especially if you're writing a marketing plan for the first time, make flexibility your first objective. Avoid large advance purchases of media space or time, use short runs of marketing materials at the copy shop over cheaper off-set printing of large inventories and so on. (We cover details such as these in Parts III and IV.) Optimising your plan for flexibility means preserving your choices and avoiding the commitment of resources. Spending in small increments allows you to change the plan as you go.

If your business has done this all before, however, and your plan builds on years of experience, you can more safely favour *economies of scale* over flexibility. (Advertising, for example, is cheaper and more efficient if you do it on a large scale, because you get bigger discounts on design of ads and purchase of media space or airtime.) If you know a media investment is likely to produce leads or sales, go ahead and buy media in larger chunks to get good rates. You don't have to be as cautious about testing mailing lists with small-scale mailings of a few hundred pieces. A good in-house list supplemented by 20 per cent or fewer newly purchased names probably warrants a major mailing without as much emphasis on advance testing. Adjust your plan to favour economies of scale if you feel confident that you can make sound judgements in advance.

But always leave yourself at least a *little* wiggle room. Reality never reflects your plans and projections 100 per cent of the time. Aim for an 80 per cent match in marketing, and plan accordingly.

The following sections share a few other suggestions to follow if you want to increase your marketing plan's chances of success.

Avoiding common mistakes

Marketing campaigns end up like leaky boats very easily, so be sure to total up your costs fully and carefully. Each activity seems worthy at the time, but too many of them fail to produce a positive return – creating holes in the bottom of your boat: too many of those holes, and the water starts rising. To avoid the costly but all-too-common mistakes that many marketers make, follow these suggestions:

- ✔ **Don't ignore the details:** You build good plans from details like customer-by-customer, item-by-item or territory-by-territory sales projections. Generalising about an entire market is hard. Your sales and cost projections are easier to get right if you break them down to their smallest natural units (like individual territory sales or customer orders), do estimates for each of these small units and then add those estimates up to get your totals.

- ✔ **Don't imitate the competitors:** Even though everyone seems to market their products in a certain way, you don't have to imitate them. High-performing plans clearly point out what aspects of the marketing are conventional and why – and these plans also include some original, innovative or unique elements to help differentiate your company from and outperform the competition. Your business is unique, so make your plan reflect your special talents or advantages.

- ✔ **Don't feel confined by last period's budget and plan:** Repeat or improve the best-performing elements of the past plans, but cut back on any elements that didn't produce high returns. Every plan includes some activities and spending that aren't necessary and can be cut out (or reworked) when you do it all over again next year. Be ruthless with any underperforming elements of last year's plan! (If you're starting a new business, at least this is one problem you don't have to worry about. Yet.)

- ✔ **Don't engage in unnecessary spending:** Always think your plan through and run the numbers before signing a contract or writing a cheque. Many of the people and businesses you deal with to execute your marketing activities are salespeople themselves. These people's goal is to get *you* to buy their ad space or time, use their design or printing services or spend money on fancy websites. They want your marketing money and they don't care as much as you do whether you get a good return or not. You have to keep these salespeople on a tight financial rein.

Breaking down your plan into simple sub-plans

If all your marketing activities are consistent and clearly of one kind, a single plan is fine. But what if you sell services (like consulting or repairs) and also products? You may find that you need to work up one plan for selling products (perhaps this strategy aims to find new customers) and another plan for convincing product buyers to also use your services. Follow the general rule that if the plan seems too complicated – divide and conquer! Then total everything up to get the big picture with its overall projections and budgets.

If you have 50 products in five different product categories, writing your plan becomes much easier if you come up with 50 sales projections for each product and five separate promotional plans for each category of product. (Believe it or not, this method sounds tricky but will make life much simpler.) We've included some methods to break down your planning, making it easier and simpler to do:

- ✔ Analyse, plan and budget sales activities by sales territory and region (or by major customer if you're a business-to-business (B2B) marketer with a handful of dominant companies as your clients).

- ✔ Project revenues and promotions by individual product and by industry (if you sell into more than one).

- ✔ Plan your advertising and other promotions by product line or other broad product category, as promotions often have a generalised effect on the products within the category.

- ✔ Plan and budget publicity for your company as a whole. Only budget and plan publicity for an individual product if you introduce it or modify it in some way that may attract media attention.

- ✔ Plan and budget for brochures, websites and other informational materials. Be sure to remain focused in your subject choices: one brochure per topic. Multipurpose brochures or sites never work well. If a website sells cleaning products to building maintenance professionals, don't plan for it to broker gardening and lawn-mowing services to suburban homeowners as well. Different products and customers need separate plans.

Remember that every type of marketing activity in your plan has a natural and appropriate level of breakdown. Find the right level, and your planning will be simpler and easier to do.

Writing a Powerful Executive Summary

An executive summary is a one-page plan. This wonderful document conveys essential information about your company's planned year of activities in a couple of hundred well-chosen words or less. If you ever get confused or disorientated in the rough-and-tumble play of sales and marketing, this clear, concise summary can guide you back to the correct strategic path. A good executive summary should be a powerful advertisement for your marketing, communicating the purpose and essential activities of your plan in such a compelling manner that everyone who reads it eagerly leaps into action and does the right things to make your vision comes true.

Draft the executive summary early in the year as a guide to your thinking and planning. But revise this document often, and finish it only after finishing all the other sections, because it needs to summarise them.

Help yourself (and your readers, if others in your company are going to be involved in approving or implementing the plan) by giving an overview of what's the same and what's different in this plan, compared with the previous period's plan. Draft a short paragraph covering these two topics.

Summarise the main points of your plan and make clear whether the plan is:

- **Efficiency orientated:** For example, your plan introduces a large number of specific improvements in how you market your product.

- **Effectiveness orientated:** For example, your plan identifies a major opportunity or problem and adopts a new strategy to respond to it.

Make sure that you summarise the bottom-line results – what your projected revenues will be (by product or product line, unless you have too many to list on one page) and what the costs are. Also show how these figures differ from last year's figures. Keep the whole summary under one page in length if you possibly can.

If you have too many products to keep the summary under a page, you can list them by product line. But a better option is to do more than one plan. If a plan can't be neatly summarised in a page, it probably needs more thought. We've worked with many businesses in which marketing prepares a separate plan for each product.

Divide and conquer.

Clarifying and Quantifying Your Objectives

Objectives are the quantified, measurable versions of your strategies. For example, if your strategy involves raising the quality of service and opening a new territory in order to grow your sales and market share, you need to think through how you'll do all that and set a percentage increase goal for sales and a new, higher goal for market share. These numbers become your objectives. The objectives flow from your thinking about strategies and tactics, but put them up near the front of your plan to help others quickly understand what you're saying.

What objectives do you want your plan to help you accomplish? Will the plan increase sales by 25 per cent, reposition a product to make it more appealing to upmarket buyers, introduce a direct marketing function via the Internet or launch a new product? Maybe the plan will combine several products into a single family brand and build awareness of this brand through print and radio advertising. This approach could gain market share from several competitors and cut the costs of marketing by eliminating inefficiencies in coupon processing, media buying and sales force management. Address these sorts of topics in the objectives section of the plan. These points give the plan its focus.

If you write clear, compelling objectives, you'll never get too confused about what to write in other sections – when in doubt, you can always look back at these objectives and remind yourself what you're trying to accomplish and why.

Try to write this part of the plan early, but keep in mind that you'll rewrite it often as you gather more information and do more thinking. Objectives are such a key foundation for the rest of the plan that you can't ever stop thinking about them. However, for all their importance, objectives don't need a lot of words – half a page to two pages, at most. (Paradoxically, we have to tell you more about these short upfront sections than about the longer, detail-orientated sections in the back because planners find the short sections more conceptually challenging.)

Preparing a Situation Analysis

The context is different for every marketing plan. A *situation analysis* examines the context, looking at trends, customer preferences, competitor strengths and weaknesses and anything else that may impact sales. The question your situation analysis must answer is, 'What's happening?' The answer to this question can take many forms, so we can't give you an easy formula for preparing the situation analysis. You should analyse the most important market changes to your company – these changes can be the sources of problems but also potential opportunities. (See Chapter 4 for formal research techniques and sources.)

What are the most important changes that have occurred since you last examined the situation? The answer depends on the situation. See the difficulty? Yet somehow you have to gain enough insight into what's happening to see the problems and opportunities clearly.

Seeing trends more clearly than others do

Your goal is to see the changes more clearly than the competition. Why? Because if your situation analysis isn't as accurate as the competition's, you'll lose market share to them. If your analysis is about the same as your competition's, then you may hold even. Only if your situation analysis is better than your rivals' can you gain market share on the competition.

What you want from your situation analysis is:

- ✔ **Information parity:** When you know as much as your leading competitors. If you don't do enough research and analysis, your competitors will have an information advantage. Therefore, you need to gain enough insight to put you on a level playing field with your rivals. That includes knowing about any major plans they may have. Collect rumours about new products, new people and so on. At a minimum, do a weekly Internet search for any news about them. You can also customise web pages such as Google News to highlight any stories about specific brands or businesses and have them delivered to your email inbox. Also, follow your competitors' tweets on Twitter and search rival company and product names to see what other people are saying about them. In addition, check out how your rivals' products and services fare on Facebook brand fan pages.

- ✔ **Information advantage in specific areas:** This refers to insight into the market that your competitors don't have. Information advantage puts you on the uphill side of an uneven playing field and that's an awfully good place from which to design and launch a marketing campaign. Look for new fashions, new technologies, new ways to segment the market – anything that you can use to change the rules of the game even slightly in your favour.

Most marketing plans and planners don't think about their situation analysis in this way. We're telling you one of our best-kept secrets because we don't want you to waste time on the typical *pro forma* situation analysis, in which the marketer rounds up the usual suspects and parades dull information in front of them without gaining an advantage from it. That approach, although common, does nothing to make the plan a winner.

Using a structured approach to competitor analysis

What kinds of information can you collect about your competitors? You can gather and analyse examples of competitors' marketing communications. You may have (or be able to gather) some customer opinions from surveys or informal chats. You can group the information you get from customers into useful lists, such as discovering the three most appealing and least appealing things about each competitor. You can also probably get some information about how your competitors distribute and sell, where they are (and aren't) located or distributed, who their key decision-makers are, who their biggest and/or most loyal customers are and even (perhaps) how much they sell. Gather any available data on all-important competitors and organise the information into a table for easy analysis.

Building a competitor analysis table

Develop a format for a generic competitor analysis table. Make entries on the following rows in columns labelled for Competitor #1, Competitor #2, Competitor #3 and so on:

- ✔ **Company:** Describe how the market perceives it and its key product.

- ✔ **Key personnel:** Who are the managers, and how many employees do they have in total?

- ✔ **Financial:** Who owns it, how strong is its *cash position* (does it have spending power or is it struggling to pay its bills?), what were its sales in the last two years?

- ✔ **Sales, distribution and pricing:** Describe its primary sales channel, discount/pricing structure and market share estimate.

- ✔ **Product/service analysis:** What are the strengths and weaknesses of its product or service?

- ✔ **Scaled assessment of product/service:** Explore relevant subjects such as market acceptance, quality of packaging, ads and so on. Assign a score of between 1 and 5 (with 5 being the strongest) for each characteristic you evaluate. Then add the scores for each competitor's row to see which seems strongest, overall.

- ✔ **Comparing yourself to competitor ratings:** If you rate yourself on these attributes, too, how do you compare? Are you stronger? If not, you can include increasing your competitive strength as one of your plan's strategic objectives.

Explaining Your Marketing Strategy

Many plans use this section to get specific about the objectives by explaining how your company will accomplish them. Some writers find this task easy, but others keep getting confused about the distinction between an objective and a strategy. The objective simply states something your business hopes to accomplish in the next year. The strategy emphasises the big-picture approach to accomplishing that objective, giving some good pointers as to what road you'll take.

An objective sounds like this: 'Solidify our leadership of the home PC market by increasing market share by 2 points.'

A strategy sounds like this: 'Introduce hot new products and promote our brand name with an emphasis on high quality components, in order to increase our market share by 2 points.'

Combining strategies and objectives

Some people view the difference between objectives and strategies as a pretty fine line. If you're comfortable with the distinction, write a separate *Strategy* section. If you're not sure about the difference, combine this section with the objectives section and title it *Objectives and Strategies*; what you call the points doesn't matter, as long as they're good. For more details about how to develop and define marketing strategies, see Chapter 2.

Your strategies accomplish your objectives through the tactics (the seven Ps) of your marketing plan. (See Chapter 1 for a discussion of the seven Ps, sometimes also known as the *marketing mix*.) The plan explains how your tactics use your strategies to accomplish your objectives.

Basing your strategy on common sense

This advice isn't easy to follow and make concrete. Unlike a mathematical formula or a spreadsheet column, no simple method exists to check a marketing strategy to make sure that it really adds up. But you can subject a marketing strategy to common sense and make sure that it has no obvious flaws – as outlined in the following sections.

Strategy fails to reflect limitations in your resources

Don't pull a Napoleon. If you're currently the tenth-largest competitor, don't devise a plan for becoming number one by the end of the year simply based on designing all your ads and mailings to claim you're the best. Make sure that your strategy is achievable. Would the average person agree that your strategy sounds attainable with a little hard work? (If you're not sure, find some average people and ask them.) And do you have enough resources to execute the strategy in the available time?

Strategy demands huge changes in customer behaviour

You can move people and businesses only so far with marketing. If you plan to get employers to give their employees every other Friday off so those employees can attend special workshops that your firm sponsors, well, we hope you have a back-up plan. Employers don't give employees a lot of extra time off, no matter how compelling your sales pitch or brochure may be. The same is true of consumer marketing. You simply cannot change strongly held public attitudes without awfully good new evidence.

A competitor is already following the strategy

This assumption is a surprisingly common error. To avoid this mistake, include a summary of each competitor's strategy in the *Strategy* section of your plan. Add a note explaining how your strategy differs from each of them. If you're marketing a computer installation and repair service in the Liverpool area, you really need to know how your strategy differs from the multiple competitors also trying to secure big corporate contracts in that area. Do you specialise in certain types of equipment that others don't? Do you emphasise speed of repair service? Are you the only vendor that distributes and supports CAD/CAM equipment from a leading maker? You need a distinctive strategy to power your plan. You don't want to be a 'me-too' competitor.

Strategy requires you to know too much that you don't already know

You can't use some brilliant strategies for your business because they require you to do too many things you don't know anything about. For example, a growing need exists for computer skills training, but if your business is in selling and servicing computer equipment, that doesn't automatically give you experience in developing, selling or delivering computer courses. Strategies that involve doing a lot of things you have little or no expertise in are really start-up strategies, not marketing strategies. If you want to put a minority of your resources into trying to start a new business unit, go ahead. But don't put your entire marketing plan at risk by basing it on a strategy that takes you into unfamiliar waters.

Is your strategy snappy?

In 2009, Cisco, best known for making large scale corporate technology products, wanted to get in on the consumer video market. The company spent $590 million (in a stock deal) acquiring a company that made an inexpensive video camera called the Flip.

Cisco, already a leader in the communication market for large corporations, wanted to adopt the same position in the consumer communications market. The thinking appeared sound. People were becoming more 'digital', taking more photos and more video, and increasingly sharing it with their friends and family online, using sites like YouTube.

So far, so good. However, Cisco fundamentally misjudged the market. People did want to take more video and photos and share them with their friends and family, but they didn't want to have multiple devices to do it. Mobile phones were becoming more and more sophisticated all the time. Cisco found itself competing not only with dedicated video device manufacturers, but also with the might of the world's mobile phone manufacturers, from Apple's iPhone to the plethora of Google Android powered phones made by Samsung and others.

On 12 April 2011, Cisco finally admitted defeat and stopped making the Flip Video device, issuing a rather sad statement saying it would be 'exiting aspects of its consumer business'. The company had got its timing wrong and was overtaken by its competitors' technology, which fitted better into the way people were living their lives.

Summarising Your Marketing Mix

Your *marketing mix* is the combination of marketing activities you use to influence a targeted group of customers to purchase a specific product or line of products. Creating an integrated and coherent marketing mix starts, in our view, with an analysis of your *touchpoints* (see Chapter 2) – in other words, how your organisation can influence customer purchases. And the creative process ends with some decisions about how to use these touchpoints. Usually you can come up with tactics in all seven of the marketing Ps: product, price, place (or distribution), promotion, people, process and physical presence.

Prioritising your touchpoints and determining cost

Prioritise by picking a few primary touchpoints – ones that will dominate your marketing for the coming planning period. This approach concentrates your resources, giving you more leverage with certain components of the mix. Make the choice carefully; try to pick no more than three main activities to take the lead. Use the other touchpoints in secondary roles to support your primary points. Now begin to develop specific plans for each, consulting later chapters in this book as needed to clarify how to use your various marketing components.

Say that you're considering using print ads in trade magazines to let retail store buyers know about your hot new line of products and the in-store display options you have for them. That's great, but now you need to get specific. You need to pick some magazines. (Call their ad departments for details on their demographics and their prices – see Chapter 7 for how.) You also need to decide how many of what sort of ads you'll run, and then price out this advertising campaign.

Do the same analysis for each of the items on your list of marketing components. Work your way through the details until you have an initial cost figure for what you want to do with each component. Total these costs and see if the end result seems realistic. Is the total cost too big a share of your projected sales? Or (if you're in a larger business), is your estimate higher than the boss says the budget can go? If so, adjust and try again. After a while, you get a budget that looks acceptable on the bottom line and also makes sense from a practical perspective.

A spreadsheet greatly helps this process. Just build formulas that add the costs to reach subtotals and a grand total, and then subtract the grand total from the projected sales figure to get a bottom line for your campaign. Figure 3-1 shows the format for a very simple spreadsheet that gives a quick and accurate marketing campaign overview for a small business. In this figure, you can see what a campaign looks like for a company that wholesales products to gift shops around the UK. This company uses personal selling, telemarketing and print advertising as its primary marketing components. The company also budgets some money in this period to finish developing and begin introducing a new line of products.

This company's secondary influence points don't use much of the marketing budget when compared with the primary influence points. But the secondary influence points are important, too. A new web page is expected to handle a majority of customer enquiries and act as a virtual catalogue, permitting the company to cut back on its catalogue printing and postage costs. Also, the company plans to introduce a new line of floor displays for use at point of purchase by selected retailers. Marketers expect this display unit, combined with improved see-through packaging, to increase turnover of the company's products in retail stores.

Overview of Campaign to Target Retail Store Buyers

Components	Direct Marketing Costs (£)
Primary influence points:	
– Sales calls	£265,100
– Telemarketing	162,300
– Ads in trade magazines	650,000
– New product line development	100,000
	Subtotal: £1,177,400
Secondary influence points:	
– Quantity discounts	£45,000
– Point-of-purchase displays	73,500
– New Web page with online catalogue	15,000
– Printed catalogue	30,500
– PR	22,000
– Packaging redesign	9,200
	Subtotal: £195,200
Projected Sales from This Programme	£13,676,470
Minus Campaign Costs	– 1,372,600
Net Sales from This Marketing Campaign	**£12,303,870**

Figure 3-1:
A campaign budget, prepared on a spreadsheet.

Creating marketing plans for multiple groups

If your marketing plan covers multiple groups of customers, you need to include multiple spreadsheets (such as the one in Figure 3-1) because each group of customers will need a different marketing mix.

For example, the company whose wholesale marketing campaign you see in Figure 3-1 sells to gift shops. But the company also does some business with stationery shops. And even though the same salespeople call on both, each of these customers has different products and promotions. They buy from different catalogues. They don't use the same kinds of displays. They read different trade magazines. Consequently, the company has to develop a separate marketing campaign for each customer, allocating any overlapping expenses appropriately. (For example, if you make two-thirds of your sales calls to gift shops, then the sales-calls expense for the gift shop campaign should be two-thirds of the total sales budget.)

Exploring Your Marketing Components

In this part of your plan, you need to explain the details of how you aim to use each component of your marketing mix. Devote a section to each component, which means that this part of your plan may be quite lengthy (give it as many pages as you need to lay out the necessary facts). The more of your thinking you get on paper, the easier implementing the plan will be later – as will rewriting the plan next year.

Although this portion is the lengthiest part of your plan, we're not going to cover it in depth here. You can find details about how to use specific components of a marketing mix, from product positioning to web pages to pricing, in Chapters 7 to 20 of this book.

At a minimum, this part of the plan should have sections covering the seven Ps – the product, pricing, place (or distribution), promotion, people, process and physical presence. But more likely, you'll want to break these categories down into more specific areas. You can even get as detailed as this book does, having a section corresponding to each of Chapters 7 to 20, for example.

Don't bother going into detail in your marketing plan on components that you can't alter. Sometimes, the person writing the marketing plan can't change pricing policy, order up a new product line or dictate a shift in distribution strategy. Explore your boundaries and try to stretch them, but you need to admit they exist or your plan can't be practical. If you can only control promotion, then this section of the plan should concentrate on the ways that you'll promote the product – in which case, never mind the other Ps. Acknowledge in writing any issues or challenges you have to cope with, given that you can't change other factors. Now write a plan that does everything you can reasonably do given your constraints. (A section called *Constraints* ought to go into the *Situation Analysis*, if your company or department has such constraints.)

Managing Your Marketing

The management section of the plan simply ensures that enough warm bodies are in the right place at the right time to get the work done. This section summarises the main activities that you, your employees or your employer must perform in order to implement the components of your marketing mix. The section then assigns these activities to individuals, justifying the assignments by considering issues such as an individual's capabilities and capacities, and how the company will supervise and control that individual.

Sometimes this section gets more sophisticated by addressing management issues, such as how to make the sales force more productive or whether to decentralise the marketing function. If you have salespeople or distributors, develop plans for organising, motivating, tracking and controlling them. Also create a plan for them to use in generating, allocating and tracking sales leads. Start these subsections by describing the current approach and do a strengths/weaknesses analysis of that approach, using input from the salespeople, reps or distributors in question. End by describing any incremental changes/improvements you can think to make.

Make sure that you run your ideas by the people in question *first* and receive their input. Don't surprise your salespeople, sales reps or distributors with new systems or methods. If you do, these people will probably resist the changes, and sales will slow down. So schmooze and share, persuade and propose, and enable them to feel involved in the planning process. People execute sales plans well only if they understand and believe in those plans.

Projecting Expenses and Revenues

Now you need to put on your accounting and project management hats. (Perhaps neither hat fits very well but try to bear them for a day or two.) You need these hats to:

- ✔ Estimate future sales, in units and by value, for each product in your plan.

- ✔ Justify these estimates and, if they're hard to justify, create worst-case versions, too.

- ✔ Draw a timeline showing when your marketing incurs costs and when each component begins and ends. (Doing so helps with the preceding section and also prepares you for the unpleasant task of designing a monthly marketing budget.)

- ✔ Write a monthly marketing budget that lists all the estimated costs of your activity for each month of the coming year and breaks down sales by product, territory and month.

If you're a start-up or small business, we highly recommend doing all your projections on a *cash basis*. In other words, put the payment for your year's supply of brochures in the month in which the printer wants the money, instead of allocating that cost across 12 months. Also factor in the wait time for collecting your sales revenues. If collections take 30 days, show money coming in during December from November's sales, and don't count any December sales for this year's plan. A cash basis may upset accountants, who like to do things on an accrual basis – see *Accounting For Dummies* by John A. Tracy (Wiley) if you don't know what that means – but cash-based accounting keeps small businesses alive. You want a positive cash balance (or at least to break even) on the bottom line during every month of your plan.

If your cash-based projection shows a loss in some months, fiddle with the plan to eliminate that loss (or arrange to borrow money to cover the gap). Sometimes a careful cash-flow analysis of a plan leads to changes in underlying strategy. One B2B company made its primary marketing objective the goal of getting more customers to pay with credit cards instead of on invoices. The company's business customers co-operated, and average collection time shortened from 45 days to under 10, greatly improving the cash flow and thus the spending power and profitability of the business.

Several helpful techniques are available for projecting sales, such as build-up forecasts, indicator forecasts and time-period forecasts. Choose the most appropriate technique for your business based on the reviews in this section. If you're feeling nervous, just use the technique that gives you the most conservative projection. Here's a common way to play it safe: use several of the techniques and average their results.

Build-up forecasts

These predictions go from the specific to the general, or from the bottom up. If you have sales reps or salespeople, ask each one to project the next period's sales for their territories and justify their projections based on what changes in the situation they anticipate. Then aggregate all the sales force's forecasts to obtain an overall figure.

If you have few enough customers that you can project per-customer purchases, build up your forecast this way. You may want to work from reasonable estimates of the amount of sales you can expect from each shop carrying your products or from each thousand catalogues sent out. Whatever the basic building blocks of your marketing, start with an estimate for each element and then add these estimates up.

Indicator forecasts

This method links your forecast to economic indicators that ought to vary with sales. For example, if you're in the construction business, you find that past sales for your industry correlate with *gross domestic product* (known as

GDP or national output) growth. So you can adjust your sales forecast up or down depending on whether experts expect the economy to grow rapidly or slowly in the next year.

Multiple scenario forecasts

You base these forecasts on what-if stories. They start with a straight-line forecast in which you assume that your sales will grow by the same percentage next year as they did last year. Then you make up what-if stories and project their impact on your plan to create a variety of alternative projections.

Try the following scenarios if they're relevant to your situation:

- ✔ What if a competitor introduces a technological breakthrough?
- ✔ What if your company acquires a competitor?
- ✔ What if the government deregulates/regulates your industry?
- ✔ What if a leading competitor fails?
- ✔ What if your company has financial problems and has to lay off some of its sales and marketing people?
- ✔ What if your company doubles its ad spending?

For each scenario, think about how customer demand may change. Also consider how your marketing would need to change in order to best suit the situation. Then make an appropriate sales projection. For example, if a competitor introduced a technological breakthrough, you might guess that your sales would fall 25 per cent short of your straight-line projection.

The trouble with multiple scenario analysis is that . . . well, it gives you multiple scenarios. Your boss (if you have one) wants a single sales projection, a one-liner at the top of your marketing budget. One way to turn all those options into one number or series of numbers is to just pick the option that seems most likely to you. That's not a very satisfying method if you aren't at all sure which option, if any, will come true. So another method involves taking all the options that seem even remotely possible, assigning each a probability of occurring in the next year, multiplying each by its probability and then averaging them all to get a single number.

For example, the 'cautious scenario' projection estimates $5 million, and the 'optimistic scenario' projection estimates $10 million. The probability of the cautious scenario occurring is 15 per cent, and the probability of the optimistic scenario occurring is 85 per cent. So you find the sales projection with this formula: $[(\$5,000,000 \times 0.15) + (\$10,000,000 \times 0.85)] \div 2 = \$4,630,000$.

Time-period projections

To use this method, work by week or month, estimating the size of sales in each time period and then add up these estimates for the entire year. This approach helps you when your marketing activity or the market isn't constant across the entire year. Ski resorts use this method because they get certain types of revenue only at certain times of the year. Marketers who plan to introduce new products during the year or to use heavy advertising in one or two *pulses* (concentrated time periods) also use this method because their sales go up significantly during those periods. Entrepreneurs, small businesses and any others on a tight cash-flow lead need to use this method because it provides a good idea of what cash will be flowing in by week or month. An annual sales figure doesn't tell you enough about when the money comes in to know whether you'll be short of cash in specific periods during the year.

Creating Your Controls

This section is the last and shortest of your plan but, in many ways, is the most important. This section allows you and others to track performance.

Identify some performance benchmarks and state them clearly in the plan. For example:

- ✔ All sales territories should be using the new catalogues and sales scripts by 1 June.
- ✔ Revenues should grow to £75,000 per month by the end of the first quarter if the promotional campaign works according to plan.

These statements give you (and, unfortunately, your employers or investors) easy ways to monitor performance as you implement the marketing plan. Without these targets, nobody has control over the plan; nobody can tell whether or how well the plan is working. With these statements, you can identify unexpected results or delays quickly – in time for appropriate responses if you've designed these controls properly.

A good marketing plan gives you focus and a sense of direction, and increases your likelihood to succeed, but writing a good one takes time and many businesses don't have a lot of that to spare. A sensible rule is to spend time on your marketing plan, but not so much that you don't have a chance to look up and see whether the market has changed since you started writing it. If the plan you wrote at the start of the year is no longer relevant because business conditions have changed quickly, tear it up and start again – don't stick rigidly to something that's no longer relevant just because it's there.

Using Planning Templates and Aids

Referring to model plans can help you in this process. Unfortunately, most companies don't release their plans; they rightly view them as trade secrets. Fortunately, a few authors have compiled plans or portions of them, and you can find some good published materials to work from.

Several books provide sample marketing plans and templates. These texts show you alternative outlines for plans, and they also include budgets and revenue projections in many formats – one of which may suit your needs pretty closely:

- ✔ *The Marketing Kit For Dummies*, by Greg Brooks, Ruth Mortimer and Alex Hiam (Wiley), includes a five-minute marketing plan worksheet if you're the impatient sort

- ✔ *The Marketing Plan*, by William Cohen (Wiley), is a practical step-by-step guide that features sample plans from real businesses

Part II
Creative Thinking, Powerful Marketing

'And as they move so slowly, people can actually read the message.'

In this part . . .

Famous scientist Albert Einstein once said that imagination is more important than knowledge. But still, knowledge can be useful too. In Part II we help you ground your marketing efforts in both. We share ways of increasing your knowledge of your customers, competitors, and market, and we also help you turn your imagination into profitable marketing ideas and actions.

Several basic skill sets underlie everything else you do in marketing. Great marketing demands skills in analysis, so we show you how to do some simple market research in this part. But great marketing also requires creativity and imagination, and we devote an entire chapter to helping you dip into this free and easy-to-leverage asset of your business. A little imagination can increase the return on a marketing or advertising effort by a factor of ten, so please make sure that you tap into the power of your marketing imagination!

The third essential skill is communication, the key to almost every aspect of marketing. In this section of the book, we help you translate the insights from your research and creativity into really powerful marketing communications, no matter which of the many media you choose to communicate though (which we talk about in later sections of this book).

Chapter 4

Researching Your Customers, Competitors and Industry

*W*hat makes your product or service better or worse than that of your competitors? That question, and more like it, can help you tighten up your strategy, make more accurate sales projections and decide what to emphasise (visually or verbally) in your marketing communications. A little research can go a long way toward improving the effectiveness of your marketing.

One per cent of companies do 90 per cent of all market research. Big businesses hire research firms to do extensive customer surveys and to run discussion groups with customers. The marketers then sit down to 50-page reports filled with tables and charts before making any decisions. We don't recommend this expensive approach, which can lead to analysis paralysis. In other words, marketers spend more time poring over the mountains of data in front of them than actually acting upon them.

Instead, in this chapter, we want to help you adopt an inquisitive approach by sharing relatively simple and efficient ways of learning about customers, competitors and the environment. As a marketer, you need to challenge assumptions by asking the questions that lead to useful answers – something you can do on any budget. In the end, not only will you know what you need to know about your customers and competitors, but you'll also better understand your own business.

Understanding Why Research Matters – and Knowing What to Focus On

Many large companies do research, in part, to cover the marketer's backside if the resulting campaign subsequently fails – 'Well, it's not our fault; this is what the research told us to do!' – and more than half of all market research expenditure just builds the case for pursuing strategies the marketers always planned to do anyway. These marketers use research in the same way a drunk uses a lamppost – for support rather than illumination. Other businesspeople refuse to research anything at all because they know the answers already – or think they do. Gut instinct will only get you so far before the ideas, customers or both run out.

Many companies use focus groups for research. A *focus group* is a group of potential or actual customers who sit behind a one-way mirror discussing your product while a trained moderator guides their conversation and hidden video cameras immortalise their every gesture and phrase. Of course, you don't have to be so formal with your research techniques. You can always just ask your customers what they think of your product or service directly; the resulting information's not as impartial, but it may tell you everything you need to know without having to pay professional researchers.

So, what are good reasons to do research? Doing research to cover your backside or to bolster your already-decided-upon plans is a waste of time and money. Basically, if you can get a better idea or make a better decision after conducting market research, then research is worth your while. You should embrace research because it's the first step to making your company customer-orientated rather than product-orientated. In other words, asking what your customers want from your business is a better starting point than merely trying to sell them what you've already got. It makes for a more profitable business. If you can find out where your customers are, what they want and how best to reach them, then you're on the right path to doing better business.

Research for better ideas

Information can stimulate the imagination, suggest fresh strategies or help you recognise great business opportunities. So always keep one ear open for interesting, surprising or inspiring facts. Don't spend much money on this kind of research. You don't need to buy in an expensive trend-watching service to keep a businesslike eye on new consumer developments that may affect your market. Instead, take subscriptions for a diverse range of publications, read free blogs on the Internet such as Trendwatching (www.trendwatching.com) and make a point of talking to people of all sorts, both in your industry and beyond it, to keep you in the flow of new ideas and facts. You can also ask other people about their ideas and interests.

Every marketer should carry an ideas notebook with them wherever they go and make a point of collecting a few contributions from people every day. This habit gets you asking salespeople, employees, customers and complete strangers for their ideas and observations. You never know when a suggestion may prove valuable.

Research for better decisions

Do you have any issues that you want more information about before making a decision? Then take a moment to define the situation clearly and list the options you think are feasible. Choosing the most effective advertising medium, making a more accurate sales projection or working out what new services your customers want are all examples of important decisions that research can help you make.

Suppose, for example, that you want to choose between print ads in industry magazines and email advertisements to purchased lists. Figure 4-1 shows what your notes may look like.

Research for your strengths and weaknesses

Perception is everything. What customers think of your product or service is ultimately what determines the success of your business, which is why you need to make a habit of asking them, on a regular basis, what they love and what they hate about it.

So how do you find out what customers think? By asking customers to rank you on a list of descriptors for your business/product/service. The scale ranges from 1 to 10 (to get a good spread), with the following labels:

1	*2*	*3*	*4*	*5*	*6*	*7*	*8*	*9*	*10*
Very bad		Bad		Average		Good		Very good	

If you collect a rating of all the descriptive features of your product from customers, many of those ratings will prove quite ordinary. Consider the type of responses you'd get for a bank branch. The list of items to rate in a bank may include: current accounts, savings accounts, speed of service and the friendliness of banking staff, along with many other things you'd need to put on the list in order to describe the bank in detail. You're likely to discover that some items, like current accounts and saving accounts, get average ratings. The reason is that every bank offers those and, in general, each one handles such accounts in the same way. But a few of the features of a particular bank may be exceptional – for better or for worse.

Decision	Information Needs	Possible Sources	Findings
Choose between print ads in industry magazines and email advertisements to purchased lists	How many actual prospects can print ads reach?	Magazines' ad salespeople can tell us.	Three leading magazines in our industry reach 90 per cent of good customers, but half of these are not in our geographic region. May not be worth it?
	What are the comparable costs per prospect reached through these different methods?	Just need to get the budget numbers and number of people reached and divide available money by number of people.	Email is a third of the price in our market.
	Can we find out what the average response rates are for both magazine ads and emails?	Nobody is willing to tell us, or they don't know. May try calling a friend in a big ad agency; they may have done a study or something.	Friend says response rates vary wildly, and she thinks the most important thing is how relevant the customer finds the ad, not the medium used.
	Have any of our competitors switched from print to email successfully?	Can probably get distributors to tell us this. Will call several and quiz them.	No, but some companies in similar industries have done this successfully.

Conclusions?

Seems like we'll spend less and be more targeted if we design special emails and send them only to prospects in our region. Don't buy magazine ad space for now; we can experiment with email, instead. But we need to make sure the ads we send are relevant and seem important, or people just delete them without reading them.

Figure 4-1:
Analysing the information needs of a decision.

Bright spark

Research can help you discover weaknesses and turn them into strengths. Comet, the chain of electrical stores, had been losing sales for several years to supermarkets and general retailers as they entered the market. It decided that some flashy destination stores would fix the problem and set about overhauling the layout, product ranges and signage to differentiate them from Comet's new competitors.

The size and design of the stores wasn't the main solution to the problem, though. A simple and,

at £20,000, inexpensive research programme discovered that Comet's customers felt that its greatest weakness was the quality of its staff. This was a twofold problem as they also felt that the most important aspect of customer satisfaction was, you guessed it, the quality of the staff. Comet accepted the truth and acted on it by changing its criteria for customer satisfaction. Soon after, it achieved a record trading performance.

Notable negatives, such as long queues at lunchtime when people rush out to do their banking, stand out in customers' minds. They remember those lines and tell others about them. Long queues at lunchtime may lead customers to switch banks and drive away other potential customers through bad word of mouth. On the flip side, notably good customer service sticks in customers' minds, too. If that same branch has very friendly staff and express queues for simple transactions during busy periods, this warmth and efficiency can build loyalty and encourage current customers to recruit new customers through word of mouth.

With this information, you know what things your customers think you do brilliantly and what features you need to do some work on. You should now improve on the worst-on-the-list features to make them average, at least, and emphasise the high-rated items by talking them up in marketing and investing even more in them to maximise their attractiveness.

Here are a few tips to keep in mind as you gather customer ratings:

✔ Draw a graph of all the features of your product, rated from negative to neutral to positive. A graph will give you a visual image of how your customers perceive your business's strengths and weaknesses. You'll find that most features cluster in the middle of the resulting bell curve, failing to differentiate you from the competition. A few features stick out on the left as notably negative; other features, hopefully, stand out on the right as notably positive.

✔ Offer customers a reward for filling in a survey sheet (that's how important survey sheets are). You can offer a free prize draw for the returned survey sheets, a reduction on current fees or a discount on future products. Whichever option you choose, let your customers know that their views matter to you; that alone can improve your customer-service scores.

✔ If you want to get fancy, you can also ask some customers to rate the importance of each item on the list to them, personally. If you're lucky, your brilliant areas are important to them and your bad areas aren't.

Planning Your Research

Start research with a careful analysis of the decisions you must make. For example, say you're in charge of a two-year-old software product that small businesses use to manage their invoicing. As the product manager, what key decisions should you be making? The following are the most likely:

✔ Should we launch an upgrade or keep selling the current version?

✔ Is our current marketing plan sufficiently effective or should we redesign it?

✔ Is the product positioned properly or do we need to change its image?

So before you do any research, you need to think hard about those decisions. Specifically, you need to:

✔ Decide what realistic options you have for each decision.

✔ Assess your level of uncertainty and risk for each decision.

Then, for any uncertain or risky decisions, you need to pose questions whose answers can help you reduce the risk and uncertainty. And now, with these questions in hand, you're ready to begin your research!

When you work through this thinking process, you often find that you don't actually need research. For example, maybe your boss has already decided to invest in an upgrade of the software product you manage, so researching the decision is pointless. Right or wrong, you can't realistically change that decision. But some questions do make it through the screening process and turn out to be good candidates for research. For these research points, you need to pose a series of questions that have the potential to reduce your decision-making uncertainty or to reveal new and exciting options for you as a decision-maker.

Take the question, 'Is the product positioned properly or do we need to change its image?' To find out whether repositioning your product makes sense, you may ask how people currently perceive the product's quality and performance, how they view the product compared with the leading competitor's and what the product's personality is. If you know the answers to all these questions, you're far better able to make a good decision.

You need to start by defining your marketing decisions very carefully. Until you know what decisions you must make, market research has little point. See Figure 4-2 for a flowchart of the research process.

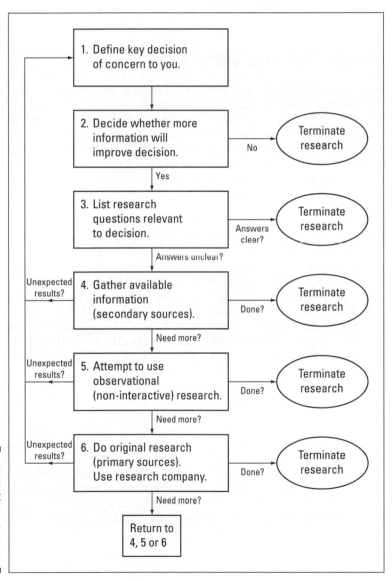

Figure 4-2: Follow this market research process to avoid common errors.

Carrying Out Primary Research

Primary research gathers data from people by observing them to see how they behave or by asking them for verbal or written answers to questions. You can, and should, ask your customers all the time whether they are happy with the service they get from your company, but taking some time out to question your assumptions about how customers view your product or service can yield some valuable insights.

Observing customers

Going 'back to the floor' has become something of a phenomenon of modern business, to the extent that the BBC made a popular TV series of the same name. The experiences of a senior manager who's thrown back into the thick of things alongside general workers can make hilarious viewing. But how and why did these executives become so disengaged from the basics of their business in the first place? Getting and staying close to your customers, as well as the front-line staff who deal with them every day, is one of the most valuable ways to spend your time.

Consumers are all around you – shopping for, buying and using products. Observing consumers, and discovering new and valuable information by doing so, isn't hard. Even business-to-business (B2B) marketers (who sell to other businesses instead of individual consumers) can find plenty of evidence relating to their customers at a glance. The number and direction of a company's lorries on various roads can tell you where their business is heaviest and lightest, for example. Despite all the opportunities to observe, most marketers are guilty of Sherlock Holmes's accusation that 'you have not observed, and yet you have seen'. Observation is the most underrated of all research methods.

Find a way to observe one of your customers as she uses one of your products. Professional research firms can provide a location for customers to visit and use your products or can even put their people into the homes of willing customers. We want you to observe, not just watch. Bring along a pad and pencil, and take care to notice the little things. What does the customer do, in what order and how long do they spend doing it? What do they say, if anything? Do they look happy? Frustrated? Disinterested? Does anything go wrong? Does anything go right – are they surprised by how well the product performs? Take detailed notes and then think about them. We guarantee that you'll end up gaining at least one insight into how to improve your product.

Asking questions

Survey research methods are the bread and butter of the market research industry, and for a good reason. You can often gain something of value just by asking people what they think. If your product makes customers happy, those customers come back. If not, goodbye. Because recruiting new customers costs on average ten times as much as retaining existing ones, you can't afford to lose any. You need to measure and set goals for customer satisfaction.

The survey methods do have their shortcomings, however. Customers don't always know what they think or how they behave – and even when they do, getting them to tell you can be quite costly. Nonetheless, every marketer finds good uses for survey research on occasion.

Measuring customer satisfaction

Try to design a customer satisfaction measure that portrays your company or product in a realistic light. You can measure customer satisfaction with survey questionnaires or with the rate of customer complaints; measures combining multiple sources of data into an overall index are best.

Your customer satisfaction has to be high, relative to both customer expectations and competitors' ratings, before it has much of an effect on customer retention rates. So make sure that you ask tough questions to find out whether you're below or above customers' current standards. To gauge customer satisfaction, ask your customers revealing questions, similar to those in the following list:

1. **Which company (or product) is the best at present?**

   Provide a long list, with instructions to circle one, and give a final choice, labelled Other, where respondents can write in their own answer.

2. **Rate [your product] compared with its competitors:**

Far worse		*Same*				*Far better*
1	2	3	4	5	6	7

3. **Rate [your product] compared with your expectations for it:**

Far worse		*Same*				*Far better*
1	2	3	4	5	6	7

You can get helpful customer responses by breaking down customer satisfaction into its contributing elements. (Focus groups or informal chats with customers can help you come up with your list of contributing elements.) For example, you can ask the following questions about a courier company:

1. **Rate Flash Deliveries compared with its competitors on speed of delivery:**

Far worse   *Same*   *Far better*

1   2   3   4   5   6   7

2. **Rate Flash Deliveries compared with its competitors on reliability:**

Far worse   *Same*   *Far better*

1   2   3   4   5   6   7

3. **Rate Flash Deliveries compared with its competitors on ease of use:**

Far worse   *Same*   *Far better*

1   2   3   4   5   6   7

4. **Rate Flash Deliveries compared with its competitors on friendliness:**

Far worse   *Same*   *Far better*

1   2   3   4   5   6   7

You can find useful guidelines on how to design a questionnaire on the website of the Market Research Society (www.mrs.org.uk), within the Frequently Asked Questions and Information Resources section. The site also includes advice on how to select a research agency and lists sources of statistical and demographic information.

Customer satisfaction changes with each new interaction between person and product. Keeping up with customer opinion is a never-ending race and you need to make sure that you're measuring where you stand relative to those shifting customer expectations and competitor performances.

Avoiding the traps

As you conduct a customer survey, avoid these all-too-common traps, which can render your research practically useless:

✔ **Make sure your survey (or surveyor, for that matter) doesn't fluff up customer satisfaction to conceal problems:** In bigger companies, we sometimes see people pressurising customers to give them good ratings because it helps their own prospects. One of the authors recently bought car insurance over the phone from an enthusiastic salesperson who unashamedly asked them to give her a high rating on a survey so that she could win the monthly customer service bonus. You might award her ten out of ten for effort, but this was probably not what the company had in mind when it set up the survey. Design your customer service measure to find areas of the business you can improve, which means asking questions that expose any weak spots. The more 'honest' your questions are, the more meaningful the responses will be.

✓ **Watch out for over-general questions or ratings:** Any measure based on a survey that asks customers to 'rate your overall satisfaction with our company on a 1-to-10 scale' isn't much use. What does an average score of 8.76 mean? This number seems high, but are customers satisfied? You didn't really ask customers this question. Even worse, you didn't ask them if they're more satisfied with you than they used to be or if they're less satisfied with competitors than with you. Ask a series of more specific questions, such as 'Was doing business with us convenient and easy?'

✓ **Don't lose sight of the end goal – customer satisfaction:** You may need to find out about a lot of other issues in order to design your marketing plan or diagnose a problem. None of what you find out matters, however, unless it boils down to increased customer satisfaction in the long run. Whatever else you decide to research, make sure you keep one eye on customer satisfaction: it's the ultimate test of whether your marketing is working!

Using the answers

When you've gathered the data, make sure that it gets put to good use rather than becoming a pile of questionnaires gathering dust in the corner. So which parts of the information you've amassed should you include as action points in your next marketing plan?

Even the most rudimentary piece of research can throw up a range of different, and sometimes contradictory, findings. One customer may think the most important thing is for you to lower your prices; another may be prepared to pay more for greater staff expertise. You probably can't achieve both of these goals simultaneously. Here are a few strategies that can help you focus your response:

✓ **Your own instinct should allow you to sort the good research results from the bad:** This doesn't mean ignoring what you don't want to hear, but it does mean you shouldn't unquestioningly react to everything the research tells you. When Sony asked people whether they'd like a portable device so they could listen to music on the move, the company found no demand existed. People didn't know that they wanted music on the move because it wasn't available to them yet. Sony went ahead and launched the Walkman anyway, because the company felt it had a great product innovation. You needn't always believe the expression 'the customer is always right' but one that you can heed when doing any research is 'they don't know what they don't know'.

✓ **Concentrate on just one of the strengths and one of the weaknesses:** If your product or service has a unique feature, you need to exploit it to the full. If you have a real problem that may drive valuable customers away, you need to put it right fast.

> ✔ **Pay attention to your most valuable customers:** You can't please all
> of the people all of the time, so don't try. One of the hidden benefits of
> observing and asking questions of customers is that doing so can help
> distinguish your most valuable customers from those you'd be better off
> without (yes, they really do exist). By looking at survey responses, you'll
> soon be able to spot ideas and customers that generate additional value
> and those that simply want more for less. Surveys help you to establish
> priorities for your business that will keep profitable customers loyal.

The life cycle of any piece of research should last no longer than your next
marketing plan – any longer and the market or competition will have moved
anyway. (We talk more about rewriting your marketing plan in Chapter 3.)

Introducing a Dozen Ideas for Low-Cost Research

You don't have to spend thousands of pounds researching ideas for a new
ad campaign (or anything else). Instead, focus on ways of gaining insight or
checking your assumptions using free and inexpensive research methods.
But how can you do useful research without a lot of time, money and staff to
waste? This section shares ideas to get you off on the right foot.

Watching what your competitors do

When you compare your marketing approach to your competitors', you
easily find out what customers like best. Make a list of the things that your
competitors do differently to you. Does one of them price higher? Does another
one give away free samples? Do some of them offer money-back guarantees?
How and where do they advertise? Make a list of at least five points of difference.
Now ask ten of your best customers to review this list and tell you what they
prefer – your way or one of the alternatives. Keep a tally. You may find that
all your customers vote in favour of doing something different to the way you
do it now. Don't discount something just because your rivals have been doing
it; if your customers want that service or feature, simply find a way of doing it
differently and better.

Creating a customer profile

Take photographs of people you think of as your typical customers. Post
these pictures on a bulletin board and add any facts or information you can
think of to create profiles of your 'virtual' customers. Whenever you aren't

sure what to do about a certain marketing decision, you can sit down in front of the bulletin board. Use it to help you tune into your customers and what they do and don't like. For example, make sure the artwork and wording you use in a letter or ad is appropriate for the customers on your board. Will these customers like it or is the style wrong for them?

Entertaining customers to get their input

Invite good customers to a lunch or dinner, or hold a 'customer appreciation' event. Entertaining your customers puts you in contact with them in a relaxed setting where they're happy to chat and share their views. Use these occasions to ask them for suggestions and reactions. Bounce a new product idea off of these customers or find out what features they'd most like to see improved. Your customers can provide an expert panel for your informal research, and you just have to provide the food! They may even become more vocal advocates of your products to friends and family because they feel their advice is taken seriously.

Using email for single-question surveys

If you market to businesses, you probably have email addresses for many of your customers. Try emailing 20 or more of these customers for a quick opinion on a question. Result? Instant survey! If a clear majority of these customers say they prefer using a corporate credit card to being invoiced because the card is more convenient, well, you've just gained a useful research result that may help you revise your approach.

Don't email customers with questions unless they're happy to be approached. You don't want to be treated as an email spammer!

Watching people use your product

Be nosy. Find ways to observe people as they shop for and consume your product or service. What do they do? What do they like? What, if anything, goes wrong? What do they dislike? You can gain insight into what your consumers care about, how they feel and what they like by observing them in action. Being a marketing peeping Tom provides you with a useful and interesting way to do research – for free. If you're in a retail business, be (or ask someone else to be) a *secret shopper* by going in and acting like an ordinary customer to see how you're treated.

If you have an online business, you can take part in usability testing that will do everything from tracking where consumers click and get stuck on your website to monitoring where their eyes move across a screen and how their heart rate and electrical impulses change when they encounter your online marketing or use your online product. This information, gathered by companies such as Bunnyfoot (www.bunnyfoot.com), Foviance (www.foviance.com) and Webcredible (www.webcredible.co.uk), can be hugely revealing.

Establishing a trend report

Email salespeople, distributors, customer service staff, repair staff or willing customers once a month, asking them for a quick list of any important trends they see in the market. You flatter people by letting them know that you value their opinion and email makes giving that opinion relatively easy for them. A trend report gives you a quick indication of a change in buying patterns, a new competitive move or threat, and any other changes that your marketing may need to respond to. Print out and file these reports from the field and go back over them every now and then for a long-term view of the effectiveness of your marketing strategies.

Researching your strengths

Perhaps the most important element of any marketing plan or strategy is clearly recognising what makes you especially good and appealing to customers (we talk more about identifying your strengths in Chapter 1). To research the strengths that set you apart from the competition, find the simplest way to ask ten good customers this simple but powerful question: 'What's the best thing about our [fill in the name of your product or service], from your perspective?' (Or you can undertake the more detailed survey we describe in the 'Research for your strengths and weaknesses' section earlier in this chapter.)

The answers to this question usually focus on one or, at most, a few features or aspects of your business. Finding out how your customers identify your strengths proves a great help to your marketing strategy. After you know what you do best, you can focus on telling the story about that best attribute whenever you advertise, create publicity or communicate with your market in any way. Investing in your strengths (versus your competitors' strengths or your weaknesses) tends to grow your sales and profits most quickly and efficiently.

Analysing customer records

Most marketers fail to mine their own databases for all the useful information they may contain. Studying your own customers with the goal of identifying three common traits that make them different or special is a good way to tap into this free data – because you already own it!

A computer shop we frequent went through their records and realised that its buyers are:

- ✔ More likely to be self-employed or entrepreneurs than the average person.
- ✔ More sophisticated users of computers than most people.
- ✔ Big spenders who care more about quality and service than price.

This shop revised its marketing goal to find more people who share these three qualities. What qualities do your customers possess that make them special and what would constitute a good profile for you to use in pursuing more customers like them?

Surveying your own customers

You can gather input from your own customers in a variety of easy ways because your customers interact with your employees or firm. You can put a stamped postcard in shipments, statements, product packages or other communications with your customers. Include three or fewer simple, non-biased survey questions, such as, 'Are you satisfied with this purchase? No = 1 2 3 4 5 = Yes.' Also leave a few lines for comments, in case the customers have something they want to tell you. You generally get low response rates with any such effort, but that doesn't matter. If someone has something to tell you, they let you hear about it, particularly when it's negative. But even a 5 per cent response rate gives you a steady stream of input you wouldn't otherwise have.

Testing your marketing materials

Whether you're looking at a letter, web page, press release or ad, you can improve that material's effectiveness by asking for reviews from a few customers, distributors or others with knowledge of your business. Do they like the material? Do they like it a lot? If the responses are only lukewarm, then you know you need to edit or improve the material before spending money on publishing and distributing it. Customer reviewers can tell you quickly whether your marketing communications have a real attention-generating, wow factor.

Big companies do elaborate, expensive tests of ads' readability and pulling power, but you can get a pretty good idea for much less money. Just ask a handful of people to review a new marketing material while it's still in draft form.

Interviewing defectors

You can find out far more from an angry customer than you can from ten happy ones. If you have a customer on the phone who wants to complain, look on them as an opportunity, not a call to be avoided. If you can find out what went wrong and fix it, that customer may well become one of your greatest advocates.

You can easily overlook another gold mine: company records of past customers. Work out what types of customers defect, when and why. If you can't pinpoint why a customer abandoned ship, try to make contact and ask them directly.

Tracking these lost customers down and getting them on the phone or setting up an appointment may prove difficult. Don't give up! Your lost customers hold the key to a valuable piece of information: what you do wrong that can drive customers away. Talk to enough of these lost customers and you may see a pattern emerge. Probably three-quarters of them left you for the same reason (which might be pricing, poor service, inconvenient hours and so on – that's for you to find out).

Plug that hole and you lose fewer customers down it. Keeping those customers means you don't have to waste valuable marketing resources replacing them. You can keep the old customers and grow every time you add a new one.

Asking your kids

Seriously, consider this tactic! Get your children – or any kids on hand – to think about your market for a few minutes; they'll probably have a unique and more contemporary view than you. Ask them simple questions such as, 'What's going to be the next big thing in [name your product or service here]?' 'What's in and what's not this year?' Kids know, and you don't. In any consumer marketing, you need to make sure that you're cool and your competitors aren't. Since kids lead the trends in modern society, why not ask them what those trends are? Even in B2B and industrial markets, young people and their sense of what's going on can be helpful. They might offer you early indicators of shifts in demand or new technologies that could have an impact all the way up the line, from consumers to the businesses that ultimately serve them.

Finding Free Data

Whatever aspect of marketing you're looking at, further information is available to you – and it won't cost a penny. Some of that data can give you just what you need to get started on your research project. So, before you buy a report or hire a research firm, dig around for some free (or at least cheap) stuff.

A world of free data exists out there, if you know where to look for it. Also keep in mind that free data generally falls into a category known as *secondary data* – meaning the information has already been collected or published by someone else – so you get it second-hand. While this data's useful stuff, remember that it isn't specific to your company and your competitors can easily access it too.

Getting info from the web

Throughout this book, we include numerous websites, as these are the quickest and easiest places to find free information. For instance, the Internet Advertising Bureau (IAB) and the Interactive Media in Retail Group (IMRG) have more data on how many customers are connected to the Internet and who shop online than we can possibly include here or even in Chapter 10 on e-marketing. Look out for these website references but, more importantly, remember that Internet search engines, such as Google, make finding free data simple – and the more you use them, the easier it is to filter out all the sites you're not interested in.

Say you want to set up a website where customers can buy your products directly. You want to know how many people have access to the Internet in the UK and how many are prepared to use their credit card details to buy things. You may also want to find a website developer who can create a secure and fully transactional site for you. Already you have three questions that need answers and you haven't even started your search.

Go to the Google search engine (www.google.co.uk) type in the key words 'internet access', and you'll get a list of 238 million sites, most of them trying to sell you something. You can narrow the information down by being more specific. The phrase 'online shoppers' will return just over 37.5 million sites; this number is better, but still too many. Type in 'online shoppers market size', however, and you get just 5.2 million suggestions, which is better again.

Explore these results but if you don't find the information you need, the IAB or IMRG have the answers to all three questions. You only need a bit of practice to be able to find relevant information on the web quickly and easily.

Hooking up with a librarian

Libraries are an undervalued national treasure and librarians are trained to archive information as well as know how to access it. Your local library is a good starting place, but you can also get a wealth of market information from university libraries and specialist business libraries.

You can find a lot of what you might need, including industry guides, through the Business and IP Centre at the British Library (www.bl.uk). You can make enquiries by phone on 020 7412 7454 or online through the website.

Tapping into government resources

Often, the best source of free information is national and local government. Many governments collect copious data on economic activity, population size and trends within their borders. In Britain, the UK Statistics Authority, now an independent, non-ministerial body accountable directly to Parliament, and its executive arm, the Office for National Statistics (ONS), are the best general sources of data on a wide range of demographic and economic topics.

We're always amazed at the sheer range and quantity of information available on the UK Statistics Authority website, and you probably will be too. Of course, we don't know whether you need to know crime statistics in a certain London borough, but if you do, this is the right place! Described as the 'home of official UK statistics', you can access the ONS at www.statistics.gov.uk.

Much of the UK population data is based on the Census. Although the Census only takes place every ten years, the information is very detailed and, usefully, can be broken down by neighbourhood. The statistics on inflation and prices, consumer spending, business investment – in fact, anything financial – are more up to date, usually to the last full quarter.

Getting media data

If you're doing any advertising, ask the magazine, newspaper, website or radio station you buy advertising space from to give you information about their customer base – snippets about the people exposed to your ads. This information can help you make sure you reach an appropriate audience. You can also use the exposure numbers to calculate the effectiveness of your advertising.

If you've yet to decide where to advertise, or even in which media, some useful media websites can give you the numbers on how many and what kind of consumers each title or station will deliver. You can trust these sources because, in most cases, they were set up and are supported by the media owners operating in that area to provide an independent verification of sales and audience profiles so that advertisers can see what they're getting – and hopefully buy more. For this reason, the latest data, for occasional users like you, is free.

The Audit Bureau of Circulations (ABC; www.abc.org.uk) has data on magazines, national and local newspapers and exhibition visitors and their associated websites. You can find out how many people are reading the titles, where they live and what type of consumers they are; for B2B magazines, you can find out what sector they work in and what their job titles are. Most of the different media have organisations providing this sort of data: for TV, see BARB (www.barb.co.uk); for radio, see RAJAR (www.rajar.co.uk); and for outdoor media such as posters, see POSTAR (www.postar.co.uk).

Chapter 5

Harnessing Creativity in Your Business

In This Chapter

▶ Achieving breakthroughs by being creative

▶ Making meetings and teams more creative

▶ Recognising your creative style to avoid creative process failures

▶ Applying your creativity to advertising and brand-building

*O*kay, time to be creative. Ready, set, go. Come up with any good ideas yet? No? Then try again. Now do you have some good ideas? What? No?

If you can't be spontaneously creative, don't be alarmed. Most people face this problem. When a need arises to be creative in marketing, many people find that they require some help. This chapter helps you put the processes in place to generate some unusually creative – and hopefully profitable – ideas.

Taking in the Creative Process at a Glance

If you think of creativity as generating wild and crazy ideas, you're right but only partly so. You have to do some open-minded thinking to come up with creative concepts (and we tell you how in the following sections). But to actually make any money from your creativity, you need to have a mix of activities that includes not only exploring new ideas but also developing the best of them into practical applications for your ads, products, sales presentations or other marketing activities. Here's a simple four-step process for turning ideas into action:

1. **Initiate:** In this step, you recognise a need or opportunity and ask questions that begin the creative process. For example, you may take a look at your delivery vehicle(s) and ask yourself if you can find a way to make them stand out and communicate what your business is all about. The creative brief that we discuss later on in this chapter is useful at the initiate stage.

2. **Imagine:** In this stage of the creative process, you engage in the imaginative, uninhibited thinking that taps into your artistic side. The techniques that we cover in the 'Brainstorming' section later in this chapter are good for this stage; your goal is to see how many wild ideas you can generate.

3. **Invent:** Now you need to get more practical. Take a critical look at all those wild ideas and choose one or a few that seem most promising. Work on these ideas to see how to make them more practical and feasible. You can't put flashing lights all over your company vans to catch attention; the effect's certainly creative but falls foul of road traffic law. Does another fun, engaging but workable idea from stage 2 suggest itself? The smoothie company Innocent made a statement when it started out by using vans covered in artificial grass and flowers. Not only was doing so an eye-catching way to stand out from other companies, it also reinforced the concept behind the business – fresh, natural drinks sold in a fun, friendly manner – in a memorable way.

4. **Implement:** Finally, you need to complete the creative process by pursuing successful adoption or implementation of your new idea or design. You may have a great design for a new company vehicle, but does a company exist that can actually transfer your ideas onto the real thing? Just how, for instance, do you get a phone number and web address onto fake grass?

Finding Out What You Need To Change

When you have a stunning, timeless, classic success in marketing, leaving it alone is the smartest move. But how many of those kinds of concepts can you think of? A tin of Heinz Baked Beans, the Apple computer logo, a Porsche sports car, a Swiss army knife and the Michelin Man? Actually, even these marketing icons have experienced many subtle changes over the years but the companies they represent are careful to protect the brand heritage they possess. So if you're not changing many of the aspects of your marketing, you need to ask yourself – why not?

Harnessing creativity in your business allows you to do things differently. This means not only differently from before but also differently from your competition. Once you start thinking about creativity and change, you may find yourself surprised by how much of what you do has remained the same over time. You don't want to allow others to catch up, or for your marketing to become stale, so you need to start a creative overhaul of your business.

Undertaking the marketing audit: More fun than it sounds

To find out what your next marketing project should be, do a quick marketing creativity audit right now. Respond to each of the situations in Table 5-1 as honestly as you can, circling 1 if your answer is 'rarely', 5 if your answer is 'frequently' and the numbers in-between if your answer is somewhere between these extremes.

Table 5-1	Marketing Creativity Audit
Marketing Creativity Actions	*Rating (1 = rarely, 5 = frequently)*
We make improvements to the selection, design, packaging or appearance of our product(s).	1 2 3 4 5
We experiment with prices, discounts and special offers to achieve our marketing goals.	1 2 3 4 5
We find new ways to bring our product(s) to customers, making buying or using the product(s) more convenient or easier for them.	1 2 3 4 5
We update and improve our brand image or the ways we communicate that brand image.	1 2 3 4 5
We try creative new ways of communicating with customers and prospects.	1 2 3 4 5
We improve the look and feel of our sales or marketing materials.	1 2 3 4 5
We listen to customer complaints or objections, and we find creative ways to turn those complaints into our next business opportunities.	1 2 3 4 5
We change our marketing message.	1 2 3 4 5
We reach out to new types of customers to try to expand or improve our customer base.	1 2 3 4 5
We share creative ideas and have freewheeling discussions with all those people who are involved in marketing our product(s).	1 2 3 4 5

Add up all the numbers you circled to get a score between 10 and 50. See where your score falls in the range following this paragraph to find out what your Marketing Creativity Score means. Depending on your answers, you can rate your marketing creativity as very low, low, medium or high. You need to be at least in the medium range, if not at the high end, to gain any benefits from creativity.

- 10–19 = very low
- 20–29 = low
- 30–39 = medium
- 40–50 = high

You can't leave anything alone in marketing. This audit may reveal aspects of your marketing that nobody has looked at or tried to improve for the past few years. If you can identify any unchanging elements of your sales, service, advertising, mailings or anything else that touches the customer, you have just found your next marketing project. Now jot down three to six things that you tend to take for granted. You've just made your creative to-do list.

Picking your creative role

In marketing (and in business, in general) you have to actually do something practical and effective with your creative ideas to profit from your imagination. You need to make a focused effort to invent useable ways in which to implement what you imagine.

Four steps are involved in the creative process (see the preceding section), which rely on different types of behaviour. You may be especially suited to one or two of the steps, but possibly not to all of them. Work out which steps you are best and worst at, and then find people to help you fill your creative gaps. Read the following list of styles to see which suits your temperament best:

- **Entrepreneur:** The entrepreneur senses a need or problem and asks tough questions to initiate the creative process. ('Why do we do it this way? It seems so inefficient.') This style proves valuable in stage 1 of the creative process, Initiate.

- **Artist:** The artist is highly imaginative and a free thinker. When given a focus by the entrepreneur's initiating question, the artist can easily dream up many alternatives and fresh approaches from which to choose. ('We could do this, or this, or this, or . . .') The artist comes to the fore in stage 2 of the creative process, Imagine.

- **Inventor:** The inventor has a more practical sort of imagination and loves to develop and refine a single good idea until he can make it work. ('Let's see. If we adjust this, and add that, it will work much better.') The inventor is most productive in stage 3 of the creative process, Invent.

> ✓ **Engineer:** The engineer's style is practical and businesslike. Engineers are particularly good at getting closure on a project by taking an untested or rough invention the rest of the way and making it work smoothly and well. ('Great ideas, but let's come up with a firm plan and budget so we can get this thing started.') Engineers make sure the process reaches the essential stage 4, Implement.

Whichever one of these creative roles most closely represents your approach to work, recognise that a single role alone can't make good, creative marketing happen. Be prepared to adjust your style by wearing some of the other creative hats at times, or team up with others whose styles differ from your own. That way, you have the range of approaches that you need to combine in order to harness the power of creativity for all your marketing efforts.

Generating Great Ideas

Creativity is the most fundamental and powerful of all the marketing skills. You can always find a better way to do something. And if things aren't going well – sales are slow, the boss rejects your proposals, customers complain about service or your mailings don't get a good response – taking some time out for creativity is crucial. Having the right creative idea at the right moment can turn the marketing tide your way. But generating that creative spark takes a little time, a little work and a few strategies.

Finding the time to think

To be creative, you first need to give yourself permission to be creative in your work. Creativity requires letting your mind's engine sit in idle mode. You can't be creative if you're busy returning emails or phone calls or rushing to finish your paperwork for the day. If the hands are busy, the mind is distracted from creativity and your imagination may not be able to work. So, for starters, we must ask you to budget time for creativity.

How much time? Well, if creativity is the most powerful and profitable of the marketing skills, how often do you think you should use it? One hour a month, week or day, or one day a week? You need to decide exactly how much creativity time you need, based on what your product or company demands. We don't know how much creativity your business needs or how many opportunities you may capture by being innovative, but we do know that you need to commit some time and effort to using your imagination when you're at work.

We urge you not to think about creativity as something you wheel out from time to time when business is slow. Make it something you do all the time.

Becoming an ideas factory

Once you've found the time, what do you do with it? You can profitably apply creativity in every aspect of marketing, from finding new customers to developing new products. Having a purpose is the important thing, but after that the only rule is that there are no rules.

Try soaking up information, questioning issues, tossing ideas back and forth with an associate and then setting the whole thing aside to incubate in the back of your mind while you do something else. Plan to work in different ways when you're working on creative ideas. Set up a large flip chart and start listing crazy concepts for your next mailing. Ask someone to help you find 20 words that rhyme with your company's or brand's name in the hope that this list may lead you to a clever idea for print or radio advertising. Cut out faces from magazines to try to find one that expresses an appealing new personality that can represent your product, and consider how that face might influence everything you then do.

Open yourself up through new and different ways of working, asking questions and exploring your marketing problems and opportunities.

You can start coming up with more ideas almost immediately, simply by changing the way you approach your work. Here's a list of fundamentals to think about; obsessing about just a few of them will make you a more creative marketer:

- **Seek ways to simplify:** Can you come up with a simpler way to explain your product or your business and its mission? Life is complicated enough for your customers. Most marketing and advertising is, too. Simplify everything to attract attention and zap the key idea into the customer's mind.

- **Think like a customer:** Doing so should be easy, shouldn't it? After all, you are a consumer. So why do you change when you go to work? You stop thinking about what you want (like a customer) and start thinking about what you do (like a businessperson). You need to think about what your customers like and might dislike about your business on a constant basis.

- **Tinker with everything:** Look at every aspect of what your company does and find a way to change it – for the better, obviously. We explore the idea of change later in this chapter, because this concept is so important and because so few marketers really embrace the idea of disrupting what their company does in order to make it do it better.

✔ **Try to cut your prices:** If you can't, then you're already charging the right price; now congratulate yourself and change something else. If you can cut prices, why haven't you? Or, to rephrase this question, how long will it be before someone else does? You may not think of pricing as creative but, as with all other aspects of your marketing, thinking about how to do it differently can yield startling results, especially if you haven't thought about pricing at all for a while.

✔ **Separate yourself from the competition:** If you're doing things in the same way as your rivals, why will customers come to you? You need to offer something different and something you'll be remembered for. You don't need to spend a lot – what about striking outfits for your customer-facing staff (as long as your employees like the idea, too)?

✔ **Borrow great ideas from other businesses:** You need to show an interest in what other companies, totally outside your field, do and say. If you can find an idea that's working in another market, but no one is doing in yours, ask yourself how you can apply it to your business.

✔ **Find new places to advertise:** Can you think of places to put messages to your customers that nobody in your industry has used before?

✔ **Get other people to put the word out for you:** Some people call this approach public relations (PR) and that's what it amounts to. Good marketers are natural publicists – always finding ways to get their business written or talked about by others. We cover PR in Chapter 15.

These activities spur you to engage your imagination in new and unusual ways. A useful insight emerges from half an hour spent on one of these approaches surprisingly often.

Encouraging group creativity

Being creative on your own is hard enough. But often in marketing, and work in general, you have to get a group or team of people to come up with some creative concepts.

Most groups of people, when confined to a conference room for a morning, do little more than argue about stale old ideas. Or even worse, somebody suggests an absolutely terrible new idea and the rest of the group jumps on it and insists the suggestion is great . . . thus eliminating the need for *them* to think. If you hope to get a group to be creative, you need to use structured group processes. Doing so means you have to talk the group into going along with an activity such as brainstorming. Sometimes the group initially resists, but be persistent; ask them what they have to lose by generating ideas for half an hour. We bet that after they try one brainstorming technique, they see how productive the group becomes and want to try more new ways of working.

We describe some of the best group creativity techniques later in this section. We know that all these techniques work; as we work for magazines such as *Marketing Week*, we've used them ourselves to generate new content and product ideas and seen other companies use them profitably as well.

Note that these techniques generally produce a list of ideas – hopefully a long and varied list. But still, it's just a list. So be sure to schedule some time for analysing the list in order to identify the most promising ideas and then develop those ideas into full-blown action plans.

Brainstorming

Brainstorming is a great way to increase the number and variety of ideas. The goal of brainstorming is to get people to generate a very long list of unusual ideas beyond their normal thought patterns or experience. To brainstorm, you first state the problem and then ask participants to offer solutions. Any solution that comes to mind is fine; the more creative the better. Each solution is written down or recorded.

You may need to encourage your group by example. If you've stated the problem as 'Think of new ideas for our exhibition stand', you can brainstorm half a dozen ideas to start with, just to illustrate what you're asking the group to do. Your ideas might include: a stand shaped like a giant cave, decorated to look like an outdoor space complete with blue sky and white clouds overhead; a revolving stand; or a display area where you offer tea and strawberries to visitors.

These ideas aren't likely to be adopted by the average company – they may not be any good – but they do illustrate the spirit of brainstorming, which is to set aside your criticisms and have some fun generating ideas. The rules (which you must tell the group beforehand) are as follows:

- ✔ **Quantity, not quality, is what matters:** Generate as many ideas as possible.

- ✔ **No member of the group can criticise another member's suggestion:** No idea is too wild and, if appropriate, you can even go as far as keeping a water gun to hand to squirt any naysayers.

- ✔ **No one person 'owns' any of the ideas:** Everyone builds off each other's ideas.

Don't let your group just go through the motions of brainstorming. To really get in the spirit of the exercise, they have to *free associate*. This means allowing their minds to wander from current ideas to whatever new concepts first pop up, no matter what the association between the old and new idea may be.

Question brainstorming

Question brainstorming is another way to generate novel questions that can provoke your group into thinking more creatively. This technique follows the same rules as brainstorming, but you instruct the group to think of questions rather than ideas.

For example, if you need to develop an exhibition stand that draws more prospects in, the group may think of the following kinds of questions:

- ✔ Do bigger stands draw in more people than smaller ones?
- ✔ Which stands drew the most people at the last trade show?
- ✔ Are all visitors equal or do we want to draw only certain types of visitors?
- ✔ Will the offer of a resting place and a free coffee do the trick?

After getting these questions from the group, you get the job of answering them and seeing how those answers can help you create a new and successful exhibition stand.

Wishful thinking

Wishful thinking is a technique suggested by Hanley Norins, of ad agency Young and Rubicam. It follows the basic rules of brainstorming, but with the requirement that all statements start with the words *I wish*.

The sort of statements you get from this activity often prove useful for developing advertising or other marketing communications.

If you need to bring some focus to the list to make it more relevant to your marketing, just state a topic for people to make wishes about. For example, you can say, 'Imagine that the Exhibition Fairy told you that all your wishes can come true as long as they have to do with the company's stand.'

Analogies

Analogies are a great creativity device. You may not think we're serious because the idea sounds so trivial. But we define creativity as making unobvious combinations of ideas. A good analogy is just that.

To put analogies to work for you, ask your group to think of things similar to the subject or problem you're thinking about. For example, you may ask a group to brainstorm analogies for your product as a source of inspiration for creating new advertisements about that product. At first, group members will come up with conventional ideas but they'll soon run out of these obvious answers and must create fresh analogies to continue.

Analogies are evident everywhere in advertising. A press ad for the haemorrhoids treatment cream Preparation H was one of the best we've seen. The ad was simply a picture of a bicycle with a jagged saw blade where the saddle should be – an image so striking, you could almost feel it. Although the ad was from Japan, it would have worked equally well anywhere. Communicating your message quickly, cleverly and effectively is the trick of a good analogy. So what is your product or service similar to, or what is the customer need it meets?

Pass-along

Pass-along is a simple party game that can also help a business group break through its mental barriers to reach free association and collaborative thinking.

Say a team of marketing and salespeople meets to generate new product concepts for the product-development department of a bank. Now, that sounds like a tough assignment – what can possibly be new in banking? You may be surprised by what you come up with if you play pass-along:

1. **You, the creative marketer, pick a subject and pass the paper to the first person.**

   Imagine that your subject is how to make your customers' personal finances run better.

2. **This person writes something about the topic in question on the top line of a sheet of paper and passes it to the next person.**

3. **The next person writes a second line beneath the first.**

4. **Go around the table or group as many times as you think necessary. In general, try to fill up a full page of lined paper.**

If people get into the spirit of the game, a line of thought emerges and dances on the page. Each previous phrase suggests something new until you have a lot of good ideas and many ways of thinking about your problem. Players keep revealing new aspects of the subject as they build on or add new dimensions to the lines above. You may end up with a list of ideas similar to those in Figure 5-1.

One idea leads to another. So even if the first idea isn't helpful, new ideas generated from it can produce useful thoughts. For example, banks probably can't get into the lottery business (there must be a law against that). But after the members of this group thought along those lines, they came up with some practical ways of increasing their customers' wealth, such as plans that can help them transfer money to savings automatically each month.

As this simple example illustrates, generating novel ideas doesn't take long, even in a mature industry like banking, as long as you use creativity techniques.

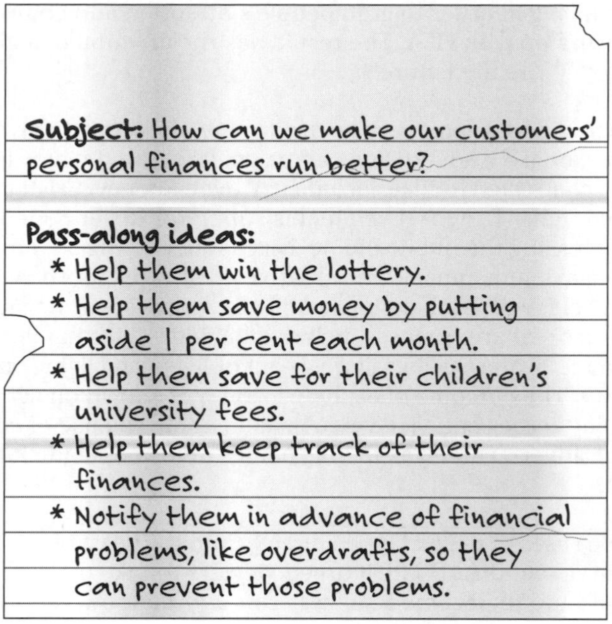

Subject: How can we make our customers' personal finances run better?

Pass-along ideas:
* Help them win the lottery.
* Help them save money by putting aside 1 per cent each month.
* Help them save for their children's university fees.
* Help them keep track of their finances.
* Notify them in advance of financial problems, like overdrafts, so they can prevent those problems.

Figure 5-1:
A list generated by a game of pass-along.

Applying Your Creativity

Advertising – whether in print, TV, radio, outdoors, at point of purchase or elsewhere – is a key area of application for creativity. If you work in the advertising industry or use ads in your marketing, you're dependent on creativity for your success. Why? Because if your ads just say what you want people to remember, people won't pay any attention to them. Too many other ads compete for consumers' attention. Only the most creative ones cut through the clutter, attract attention and make a permanent mark on consumer attitudes.

Think of the role of creativity in advertising as a vehicle for building relationships between your brand and your prospects. We find this a particularly powerful way to think about advertising's role in marketing. Marketers use creativity to add something special and unique, to accentuate a brand's differences, in order to help that brand stand out in consumers' eyes.

In 2010, sportswear company Nike wanted to steal a march on its big rival Adidas and hog the limelight around the FIFA World Cup, being held in South Africa for the first time. Adidas was an official sponsor of the tournament – even providing the match balls for every game. Every time a match was played, the TV cameras zoomed in on an Adidas ball, which was picked up by the referee as he led the teams out onto the pitch. This provided Adidas with the perfect piece of marketing in every game that was played.

Nike had to think big in order to grab people's attention and compete against Adidas's sponsorship with FIFA. The result was the creation of a global TV campaign called 'Write the Future'.

In the lead up to the tournament, Nike used social networks to give sneak previews of its global TV advertising campaign. It featured major footballing stars who were contracted to Nike, including: Wayne Rooney, Cristiano Ronaldo, Ronaldinho and Didier Drogba. Even tennis superstar Roger Federer was involved. After teasing the public online, Nike launched the TV advertising worldwide for maximum impact. The creative ad showed footballers taking actions on the field, with each action leading to a positive or negative consequence; success or failure. Success included having babies named after you and being knighted by the Queen; failure meant oblivion and living on a caravan site in obscurity. The outcome of each decision was shown on screen with heroes becoming zeroes and vice versa in an instant. The use of comedy throughout the advert, as well as the big names involved, made it an instant hit worldwide.

The creative idea used in the ad tapped directly into the heart of the Nike brand, which uses the slogan 'Just Do It!' It urged viewers to take their destiny into their own hands and to become a success through their own efforts.

And it worked for Nike. Product orders were up by 7 per cent, 12 million people viewed the advert on YouTube the day it was aired on TV and Nike's 'buzz', the measure of how much people are talking about the brand, was twice that of Adidas during the tournament.

Writing a creative brief

Advertising benefits from the use of a *creative brief*, an information platform on which to do your creative thinking. A creative brief lays out the basic purpose and focus of the ad, and provides some supporting information that provides helpful grist for your creative mill.

Leading advertising agencies design the creative brief with three key components:

> ✔ **Objective statement:** What the advertising is supposed to accomplish. Make the goals or objectives clear and specific. A single objective is easier to accomplish than many. The objective statement also includes a brief description of who the ad is aimed at because this target group's actions determine if you accomplish an objective.

Think about the task of designing a new package for one of your product lines. If you write a creative brief first, you have to define what the packaging should accomplish and what sort of customers you want to aim the design at. The objective statement demands that you make these decisions.

✔ **Support statement:** The product's promise and the supporting evidence to back up that promise. You use this point to build the underlying argument for the persuasive part of your ad. The support statement can be based on logic and fact, or on an intuitive, emotional appeal. Either way, you need to include a basis of solid support.

You have to review (and maybe do some creative thinking about) the evidence available to support your product's claims to fame. What may make you stand out from rival products on the shelves? If you aren't sure, then use the demands of the support statement to do some research and creative thinking. Make sure that you have your facts at hand so that your ideas for packaging design can communicate this evidence effectively.

✔ **Tone or character statement:** A distinct character, feel or personality for the ad. You choose whether the statement should accentuate the brand's long-term identity or put forth a unique tone for the ad itself that dominates the brand's image. The choice generally flows from your objectives. A local retailer's objective may be to pull in a lot of shoppers for a special bank holiday sale. The retailer should give the event itself a strong identity, so defining an appropriate tone for the ad with that goal in mind is necessary. In contrast, a national marketer of a new health-food line of soft drinks should build brand identity rather than focus on any specific occasion, so the creative brief needs to concentrate on that brand in words or images.

To go back to our package design analogy, at this point you need to define the tone of your packaging. Think about your product's overall image and how the packaging's tone and use of language can reflect that image. The tone or character statement requires this step.

The creative brief is useful for any marketing material or for any situation in which you must design something creative to communicate and persuade. Figure 5-2 shows an example of a creative brief for a new coffee shop's local advertising.

After you fill in the three sections of the creative brief to your satisfaction, you're ready to start brainstorming or using any other creativity tools you care to try. The creative brief gives you a clear focus and some good working materials as you apply your creativity to developing a great ad or other promotional piece.

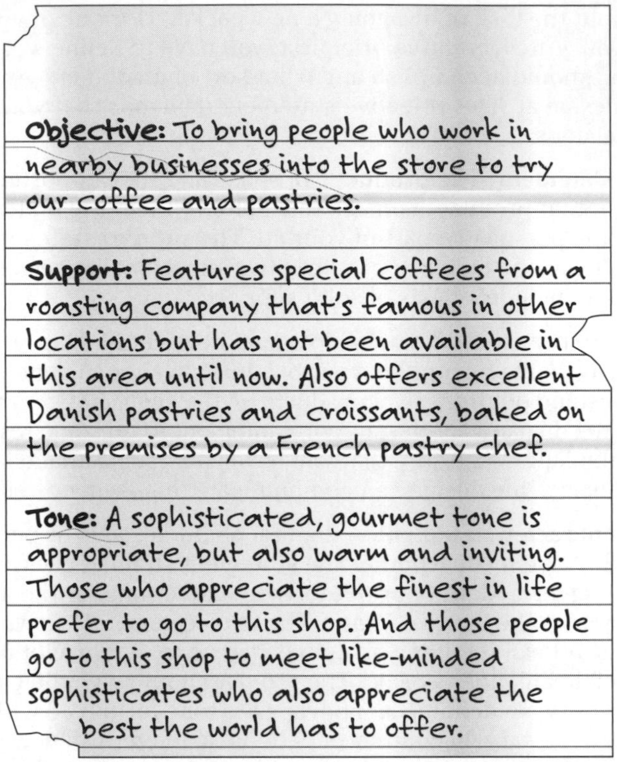

Objective: To bring people who work in nearby businesses into the store to try our coffee and pastries.

Support: Features special coffees from a roasting company that's famous in other locations but has not been available in this area until now. Also offers excellent Danish pastries and croissants, baked on the premises by a French pastry chef.

Tone: A sophisticated, gourmet tone is appropriate, but also warm and inviting. Those who appreciate the finest in life prefer to go to this shop. And those people go to this shop to meet like-minded sophisticates who also appreciate the best the world has to offer.

Figure 5-2:
A sample creative brief.

Using creativity to forge brand image

Creating a strong, appealing brand image is one of the most important things you can do in marketing. Creativity is the key to doing just that. As the preceding section, 'Writing a creative brief', explains, advertising communicates the all-important brand image or personality to the consumer. Sometimes advertising focuses on that image; by doing so, it provides a common focus for all other design decisions, from the look of products to packaging to special events and other marketing communications.

Chapter 6

Making Your Marketing Communications More Powerful

*Y*ou communicate constantly in marketing. In fact, most of what marketers do is communication of one sort or another. But what's the difference between good and bad marketing communications? *Impact* is the single most important difference. Good communications have the *desired* impact; bad communications don't. The key to this idea is the word 'desired'. You can easily make an impact for all the wrong reasons. A famous adman once said of his advertising: 'When I want a high recall score, all I have to do is show a gorilla in a jockstrap.' He knew that the pursuit of impact for its own sake was a pointless exercise, as it didn't meet any of his client's goals.

In this chapter, we help you make your marketing communications more powerful by showing you some of the best ways to increase the impact of your message. With more effective communication, you can build sales and attract new or better customers.

As you read this chapter, ask yourself: what are my goals and how well am I achieving them right now? Doing so will help you decide whether your communications are sending out the right message and how to change them for the better. You need to continually evaluate your marketing to improve the results in line with your objectives.

Establishing Communication Priorities

Which is more important – getting noticed or getting noticed for the right reason? Of course, the correct answer is both. A powerful ad is nothing if customers don't remember what it was trying to tell them and which brand it was promoting. Equally, a turgid explanation of why your product is worth buying won't grab the customer's attention for long enough to even begin to get that message across. So you need to combine stopping power with persuasion. Customers don't believe you're the best just because you tell them so; you actually have to be the best or find a different message that will sell your product.

Creating an eye-catching and persuasive ad isn't enough. Your ad also has to be clear. Often the most exciting and creative ads fail to actually make the sale because they're not simple and clear enough. For example, one Burger King TV ad campaign boasted that Burger King's fries had beaten McDonald's in a taste test. But consumers didn't pick up the nuances; they just noticed the mention of McDonald's. Rumour has it that sales went up at McDonald's instead of Burger King. Oops.

Clarity is the first job of the marketer. Creativity, excitement and persuasion are actually secondary to clarity. Is that clear? Good! The following sections cover what you need to know to make your marketing endeavours successful.

If you can communicate more effectively and persuasively than your competitors, then consider your marketing communications a success; if not, you're throwing precious marketing pounds away and you probably won't convince many people to buy your product.

Strengthening your marketing communications

Communication goes on in many different ways, at many points of influence and wherever you have some exposure to your markets. You need to craft a compelling message to send out through all influence points, from advertising to packaging and point-of-sale. Follow these steps to create a compelling marketing message:

1. **Position the product in your customers' minds.**

   You need the right positioning strategy as a foundation and then you build on this with products that follow through on the promises you make. A *positioning strategy* is a detailed (but readable) statement of how you want customers to think and feel about your product (or service). Your customers don't need to know every detail of your strategy, but you and everyone who works in your organisation should know what it is. You can describe your positioning with attributes and adjectives (such as 'fast', 'helpful' or 'sexy'). You can also describe your positioning with comparisons to competitors ('faster than a BMW') or with metaphorical comparisons ('faster than a speeding bullet'). See Chapter 2 for details if you don't already have a clear positioning strategy taped to the wall above your desk.

2. **Craft a *basic appeal*: a motivating message that gets your positioning across.**

   Here, you need to work out what you can say that clearly conveys your positioning strategy. Take the basic statement of how you want people to think of your product and convert it into a message that may actually convince them. For example, if you want to introduce a new, healthier kind of pizza made only of organic and low-fat ingredients, your positioning statement could be: 'healthier pizza that doesn't sacrifice taste'. Okay, now craft the basic appeal that will convince others to see the pizza that way. Here's a possibility with appeal: 'Instead of fighting to keep your kids from eating the unhealthy junk-food pizzas they love, why not give them healthy pizzas that actually taste even better?'

3. **Find a creative big idea: something that packages your appeal in a message so compelling that people stop in their tracks.**

   The message should persuade people of your point or convince them to give your product or service a try. It should do so creatively or it will be boring and nobody will pay attention. For example, suppose you're doing marketing for a pizza restaurant chain whose basic positioning is 'organic and low-fat, so it's healthy and it also tastes good'. Now you need to use a simple appeal to parents, convincing them of this positioning strategy: 'Instead of fighting to keep your kids from eating the unhealthy junk-food pizzas they love, why not give them healthy pizzas that actually taste even better?' Now, what creative idea can you come up with to turn this appeal into a compelling communication? Here are some suggestions:

   - Mother goes to chemist's to get prescription for child. She's shocked when the pharmacist reads the doctor's note, pulls a freshly-baked pizza out of a big oven, boxes it, hands it over the counter and says, 'Give him a piece of this, day or night.'

   - A huge crowd of kids stare longingly through the window of a sweet shop and the viewer wonders what has drawn their attention – it turns out to be the newest flavour of the low-fat, organic pizza.

   - A journalist is interviewing swimmers on a remote tropical island where longevity is the highest in the world. In response to the question, 'What is the secret of your amazing health and long life?' a tanned and fit grandmother says: 'We don't do anything special, we just order a lot of pizza.' She then dives off a cliff into a tropical pool. The pizza, of course, is from a little old hut sporting your brand's logo, with a crowd of village children in the doorway, hands out, happily receiving slices of the magical pizza.

4. **Develop, edit and simplify your creative idea until you've made it transparently clear and it fits the medium in which you want to communicate it.**

   Note that your choice of marketing medium is partially determined by your message and by the creative idea you select to get it across. To tell a story, you might plump for television advertising if your budget is large. If you want to spend less, a video playing on your website or a radio ad version of the story will cut your costs (see Chapter 9). A really low-cost option is to commission a cartoonist to do a series of drawings in comic-strip format that you can turn into a print ad or flier or place on your website.

These steps, done well, create a compelling marketing message and communicate that message persuasively. This task is a challenging but vital one – crafting the compelling message you need for all your marketing communications.

Deciding whether to appeal to logic or emotions

You face a choice in many marketing communications: should you build your appeal and communication strategy around a strong factually-based claim, backed by irrefutable evidence, or make an emotional appeal that feels right to the customer but cannot be proven?

You need to make this choice based on the product you're marketing and who you're marketing it to because everyone makes decisions in both ways, depending on the situation. People usually make an emotional decision about who they want to marry but rational decisions about what jobs to search for and which employment offers to accept. Similarly, in purchase decisions, sometimes the emotions prevail and other times the logical parts of our minds dominate.

To complicate matters even further, people are inconsistent about when they use which mode. Some people make highly emotional decisions about major purchases such as cars and houses; others approach the decision carefully and rationally, comparing statistics and running the numbers. Which camp do you fall into? If you've ever bought a car, try to recall why you bought it. If you say, 'Because I liked it' or 'Because I felt good about being seen driving it' or something similar, your emotions probably dominated your purchase decision. If, however, you say things like 'Because it has a higher resale value and *What Car?* rated it highly on reliability and running costs', then you made a logical or rational decision.

Have you heard the one about the Škoda?

Have you seen any of the rmemorable advertising for Škoda cars? One TV spot showed a group of dedicated cake-makers handcrafting a car out of confectionery, accompanied by the song 'My Favourite Things' from *The Sound of Music*.

But only a few years ago, it was unlikely that anyone would admit to the Škoda being their favourite brand of car. So how did the marketers manage to change the car's image? We're sure you can remember the decades of jokes about Škodas: What do you call a Škoda with no roof? A skip. Why do Škodas have heated rear windows? To keep your hands warm when you're pushing them.

Even though Volkswagen bought the East European car manufacturer in the 1990s and improved the products on offer, the stigma attached to the Škoda brand remained until the early 2000s. The cars might have been very well made but, for many people, the brand still stood for poor quality.

Instead of relying on a message that told consumers how good the Volkswagen-designed cars now were (the rational message), the marketers took the brave but original step of confronting people's prejudices head on. The 'It's a Škoda. Honest' ads included one featuring a confused car park attendant apologising to a driver whose car had been 'vandalised' with a Škoda badge, the idea being that the cars were so good, no one could believe they were Škodas. Perception of the brand and sales shot up immediately in the UK.

The marketers followed up the 'Honest' campaign with a new set of ads proclaiming: 'Škoda. It might earn you more respect than you think.' Over several years, the humorous ads were able to evolve the image of Škoda even further to the stage where the most recent ads play on an emotional image of the car having the attributes of powerful animals.

Each person tends toward one end or the other of this range and makes decisions more rationally or more emotionally. So you can pitch your marketing communications at the rational buyer or at the emotional buyer. You can even segment your market based on this difference, and design separate marketing campaigns for each!

When you design your communications, emphasise strongly one or the other way of thinking. When you waffle, trying to appeal to both sides of the brain at once, you weaken your message. Your job, as the communicator, is to get into the customer's head and sense which is the hotter button – the emotional or rational one.

So, which camp do your customers and prospects fall into? You probably know already, but if you don't, asking your customers or carrying out some specific research is the way to go (see Chapter 4 for more on researching your customers).

Using Four Easy Strategies to Strengthen Your Appeal

You want to help people see what makes your product great. You want to get these people to come into a shop, send an email, click on a website 'buy' button or make a phone call to purchase it. But you can't just tell potential customers that your product is great because they won't pay any attention; they've heard that one before. First, you need an appealing message. The message must sell itself!

What can you communicate that appeals to the consumer's basic motives and desires and does so with enough strength to move them to action? You can use one or more of the strategies listed in the following sections to improve the impact of your appeal.

Most appeals are ineffective. Achieving the kind of impact you want as a marketer isn't easy.

Image strategy

An *image strategy* shows people your product and its personality – it presents a good image of your brand, product, service or business. For example, a health spa may develop a sophisticated logo and colour scheme and work sophistication into everything it produces, from its print ads and website to its decor, towels, robes and bottled water. What's your image? And do you communicate that image in an appealing way through all points of contact with your customers and prospects?

Information strategy

An *information strategy* communicates facts that make your business appealing. For example, a van hire company may want to let prospects know the range of vans it has available, that they're maintained in immaculate condition and their rental terms are excellent. The facts should make the sale. If you know you're particularly strong in a certain area, communicate the facts of your brilliance instead of wasting effort on more ordinary details. What information can you communicate that will appeal to customers and prospects?

Motivational strategy

A motivational strategy builds a compelling argument or feeling that should inspire prospects to take action and make a purchase.

One advertising campaign for the Weightwatchers clubs, which ran over the post-Christmas period, featured real customers telling viewers how much weight they'd lost, how easy it was and how great they felt as a result. Prospects often experience strong emotional responses to these stories – particularly if they've just over-indulged during the festive celebrations – so this approach should lead to new sales. What motivation can you provide that can move prospective customers to make a purchase now?

Demonstration strategy

A *demonstration strategy* leverages the fundamental appeal of the product itself simply by making that product available to prospects. Sampling is when you get handed a product to taste or try as you're walking through a shopping centre or when a sachet of coffee gets posted through your door. Sometimes marketing really is as easy as making the product available to people – such as when a car dealership offers free test-drives of an exciting new model. Does your product have fundamental appeal that you can take advantage of by making it more accessible to prospects?

Catching Your Customers' Eyes and Pulling Them In

Stopping power is the ability of an ad or other marketing communication to stop people in their tracks, make them sit up and take notice. Communications with stopping power generate 'What did you say?' or 'Did you see that?' responses. These communications generate a high level of attention.

Pulling power is the ability of marketing communications to draw people to a place or event. Marketers use publicity, personal selling, direct mail, price-based promotions and point-of-purchase spending to exercise effective pulling power.

Stopping power

Most efforts to communicate fail as a result of the high level of clutter in the marketing environment. Most ads go unnoticed by most of the people they target.

To witness how 'blind' people are to ads, ask a friend to recall five ads they saw on television last night (and they probably saw dozens). Watch their reaction. A puzzled look may cross your friend's face as she tries desperately to remember what she knows she must have seen. Then she may say, 'Oh, yeah. I saw that funny ad where this bloke . . . .' Your friend may come up with several ads that way, if last night's crop of advertising was fairly good; and of these, she may remember the brand name of one or two – but rarely all.

If you repeat the same exercise, but ask your friend about print ads in magazines, newspapers, brochures or junk mail letters, you may well draw a complete blank. Many people don't recall even one ad in a magazine they read yesterday unless you actively prompt them. Asking about radio ads will elicit the same response.

This simple activity puts the importance of stopping power into perspective. You can be sure that thousands of other marketing messages bombard your customer, along with your own. For that reason, your ads need to have much more stopping power than most if you hope to get a significant number of people to remember and think about your product!

According to Hanley Norins, who spent a lot of time training the staff at advertising agency Young and Rubicam to make better ads, seven principles apply in making an ad or any marketing communication a real stopper. We've modified those principles through our own experience, coming up with the following list. Your ad must do the following:

- **Have intrinsic drama that appeals to everyone:** The ad should attract many people outside of the target audience. If kids like an ad aimed at adults or vice versa, that ad fulfils this principle.

- **Demand participation from the audience:** The ad needs to draw people into some action, whether that means calling a number, going to a shop, laughing out loud or just thinking about something. A 'stopper' ad should never permit the audience to play a passive role.

- **Force an emotional response:** This principle should hold true even if you're making a rational appeal. The heart of the ad must still contain some basic human need, something about which people feel passionate.

- **Stimulate curiosity:** The audience should want to know more. This desire gets them to stop, study the ad and follow up with further information searches afterward.

✔ **Surprise its audience:** A startling headline, an unexpected visual image, an unusual opening gambit in a sales presentation or a weird shop window display – all have the power to stop people by surprising them.

✔ **Communicate expected information – in an *detcepxenu* way:** (*Hint:* Try reading that mystery word backwards.) A creative twist, or a fresh way of saying or looking at something, makes the expected unexpected. You have to get the obvious information in: what the brand is, who it benefits and how. But don't provide the information in an obvious way or the communication doesn't reach out and grab attention and the audience just ignores your ad.

✔ **Occasionally violate the rules and personality of the product category:** The product has to stand out. People notice things that don't follow expected patterns (and patterns certainly exist in marketing). One way is to make your ad distinctly different from what consumers have come to expect in your product's category. If you market office-cleaning services, for example, you no doubt make up fliers with your price list and a few client testimonials. Yawn! To complement this ordinary marketing effort, send a sponge in the mail to prospective clients with your name and phone number on one side and, on the other, the message, 'Just in case you still insist on doing the cleaning without our help.'

Take a look at Hanley Norins's *The Young and Rubicam Traveling Creative Workshop* (Prentice Hall) for further inspiring ideas.

Pulling power

Smaller or local marketers usually concern themselves with pulling power. After all, somebody has to actually sell a product at the ground level – in the local market and customer by customer. And so, at this level, you just need to draw in those customers. Pulling power is everything.

Local marketing communications are unique as a result of their pull orientation:

✔ Local communications tend to be part of a short-term, tactical effort, rather than a long-term campaign. Don't feel you have to do anything permanent. Short, powerful bursts usually have more pulling power.

✔ You can do local communications on a shoestring budget – far smaller than the millions spent by national or multinational advertisers. Keep it simple!

✔ Local communications should get customers into the shop, make the phone ring, attract more people to your website or accomplish some other pull-orientated tactical goal. If your marketing communication isn't pulling, then pull it.

Sex, anyone?

Advertising research reveals another secret of stopping power: sex. As the header for this sidebar illustrates, even the word catches your eye. So to create an ad with stopping power, just give it some sex appeal.

However, here's the hitch. The same research that shows sex-based ads have stopping power also shows that they don't prove very effective by other measures. Brand recall – the ability of viewers to remember what product the ad advertised – is usually lower for sex-orientated ads than other ads. So, although these ads do have stopping power, they don't seem to have any other benefits and they may fail to turn that high initial attention into awareness or interest. Sex-based ads don't change attitudes about the product: in short, they sacrifice good communication for raw stopping power.

The only exception to the rule that sexy ads are bad communicators is when sex is relevant to the product. If you're marketing a lingerie shop, running some print ads of scantily clad, attractive female models in the Sunday newspapers certainly makes sense. But leave sexy models out of ads for hardware shops, lawn-care services or office supplies because they have no obvious relevance.

David Ogilvy, the adman who founded Ogilvy and Mather, one of the largest advertising agencies in the world, found out that sex doesn't always sell well the hard way. The first ad he produced featured an attractive, naked woman next to an oven. Ogilvy later admitted that the ad failed because the sexy woman had nothing to do with the appeal of the oven – he should have included a beautiful cake or a golden roast chicken because those items are actually relevant to the product.

For maximum pulling power, give people a strong reason to act. Tell consumers your location and that you have what they need. Ask potential customers to visit, call, return a coupon or visit your website. And keep inviting these people, always in new and creative ways, so they never forget you.

Part III
Advertising Everyone can Do

'Are you sure this stunt is going to sell our
custard pies, Colin?'

In this part . . .

Advertising can be fun and we're going to ask you to have some serious fun. It also needs to be creative and have that special spark to work really well.

In Part III, we outline the essentials of effective, eye-catching, mind-altering communications that can build your brand or reputation, attract great leads, or actually make a sale. The essence of great advertising communications remains the same across all the dozens of possible media – from the lowly business card or the simple brochure to the sophisticated print ad, local television spot ad or Internet ad campaign.

You also have a lot of media choices – probably more than you realise – because you can always advertise in alternative ways and advertising doesn't have to be as expensive as most people assume.

So, read on to find out how you can pump up your marketing communications and put advertising to better effect in your business. (By the way, this last sentence is a *call to action*, to use an ad copywriter's term that we discuss later on. You always want to tell people what you expect them to do as a result of seeing your ad).

Chapter 7

Brochures, Press Ads and Print

· ·

In This Chapter

▶ Recognising the elements of printed advertising

▶ Understanding design and layout issues

▶ Designing with type

▶ Designing the simplest print product of all – brochures

▶ Placing and testing your print ad

· ·

Most marketers budget more for print advertising than any other type – the exception being the major national or multinational brands that market largely on television. But for most local and regional advertising, print probably provides the most flexible and effective all-around marketing medium, although Internet advertising is fast eating into this lead.

Print advertising also integrates well with many other marketing media. You can use written brochures and other sales support materials (which have many design elements in common with print advertising) to support personal selling (see Chapter 14) or telemarketing (see Chapter 15). Similarly a print ad in a magazine can generate leads for direct marketing (see Chapter 14). Print ads also work well to announce sales promotions or distribute coupons. (We cover the use of print ads for promotions in Chapter 18.)

Anyone with a basic computer and inkjet printer can now set up shop and create his own fliers, brochures, business cards and ad layouts. In fact, Microsoft Office includes a number of excellent templates that simplify layout and allow you to bang out a new brochure or other printed marketing piece in as little as an hour. Print advertising and print-based marketing are the backbone of most marketing campaigns, even in today's high-tech world.

Designing Printed Marketing Materials

Many marketers start with their printed marketing materials (such as ads, brochures or downloadable PDF product literature on their websites) and then work outward from there to incorporate the appeal and design concepts from their printed materials or ads into other forms of marketing. (A common look and feel should unite your print ads, brochures and website.)

Brochures, *tear sheets* (one-page, catalogue-style descriptions of products), posters for outdoor advertising, direct mail letters and catalogues all share the basic elements of good print advertising: good copy and visuals alongside eye-catching headlines. All good marketers thus need mastery of print advertising as an essential part of their knowledge base. This section covers the essentials.

When designing anything in print, remember this: your ad's purpose is to stimulate a sale. Think ahead to that goal. What will people see when they make that purchase? If your product sells in shops, create signs, packaging, displays or coupons that echo the ad's theme and remind the buyer of it. If you're selling online, make sure you provide a web address on your print ads that helps the consumer to find the product you're advertising. If you make the sale in person, supply the salespeople or distributors with catalogues, order forms, PowerPoint presentations or brochures (see the 'Producing Brochures, Fliers, and More' section later in this chapter) that are consistent with your design, to remind them of the ad that began the sales process. If you intend contacting the customer after the sale, ensure that any mailings continue the look and feel of the ad that began the sales process.

Dissecting printed materials

Before you can create great printed marketing materials, you need to dissect an ad, brochure, tear sheet or similar printed marketing matter and identify its parts. Inside most printed marketing materials, you'll find parts and each part has a special name:

- **Headline:** The large-print words that first attract the eye, usually at the top of the page.
- **Subhead:** The optional addition to the headline to provide more detail, also in large (but not quite as large) print.
- **Copy or body copy:** The main text, set in a readable size.
- **Visual:** An illustration that makes a visual statement. This image may be the main focus of the ad or other printed material (especially when you've designed an ad to show readers your product), or it may be secondary

to the copy. Such an image is also optional. After all, most classified ads use no visuals at all, yet classifieds are effective for the simple reason that people make a point of looking for them (instead of making a point to avoid them, as many people do with other types of ads!).

✔ **Caption:** Copy attached to the visual to explain or discuss that picture. You usually place a caption beneath the visual, but you can put it on any side or even within or on the image.

✔ **Logo:** A unique design that represents the brand or company (like Nike's swoosh). Register logos as trademarks.

✔ **Signature:** The company's trademarked version of its name. Often, advertisers use a logo design that features a brand name in a distinctive font and style. The signature is a written equivalent to the logo's visual identity. Here's how a furniture maker called Heritage Colonial Furniture may do it:

HERITAGE

Colonial Furniture®

✔ **Slogan:** An optional element consisting of a (hopefully) short phrase evoking the spirit or personality of the brand. For example, when you think of sportswear company Nike, you immediately conjure up its famous slogan summing up the brand in three short words: 'Just Do It'. The creation of this slogan, voted one of the top five ad slogans of the twentieth century by *Advertising Age* magazine, is designed to emphasise the characteristics of the brand – Nike represents achievement, whether that means winning, taking part or just enjoying yourself. The slogan is broad enough to work in tandem with the theme of any advert – such as athletes running their hardest or footballers attempting to score a goal. The furniture maker Heritage Colonial, used earlier, could use 'Bringing the elegance and quality of early antiques to the modern home' as its slogan.

The shorter and snappier the slogan, the more likely it is to be recalled by the consumer.

Figure 7-1 shows each of these elements in a rough design for a print ad (a brochure's layout is a bit more complicated and is covered at the end of this chapter). We use generic terms in place of actual parts of an ad ('headline' for the headline, for example) so that you can easily see all the elements in action. This fairly simple palette for a print ad design allows you endless variation and creativity. You can say or show anything, and you can do so in many different ways. (And you can use this layout for a one-page marketing sheet to include in folders or as handouts at trade shows even if you aren't buying space to run the ad in a magazine or newspaper.)

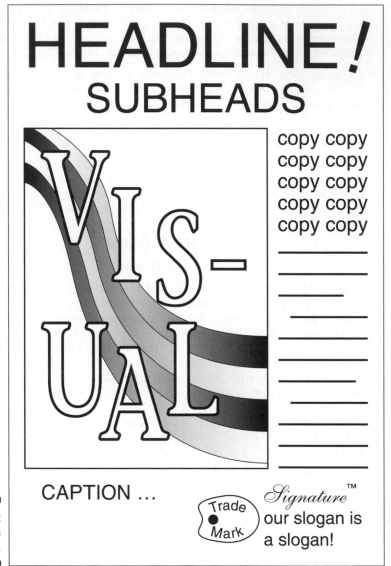

Putting the parts together: Design and layout

Design refers to the look, feel and style of your ad or other printed marketing materials. Design is an aesthetic concept and, thus, putting it into precise terms is difficult. But design is vitally important: it has to take the basic appeal of your product and make that appeal work visually on paper (see Chapter 6 for details of how to develop this appeal). Specifically, the design needs to overcome the marketer's constant problem: nobody cares about your advertising. So the design must somehow reach out to readers, grab their attention, hold it long enough to communicate the appeal of the product you're advertising and attach that appeal to the brand name in the readers' memories.

A memorable photograph is often the easiest way to grab attention. Depending on your brand or product, you could choose options such as an interesting face, a photo of a child or a beautiful scene; as long as you can make the image relevant in some way to your product, pretty much anything that grabs attention goes.

Great advertising has to rise off the page, reach out and grab you by the eyeballs. In the cluttered world of modern print-based marketing, this design goal is the only one that really works. So we want you to tape up a selection of ads from the same publication(s) that yours will go in (or use samples of competitor brochures or catalogue sheets or whatever exactly it is you'll be designing in print). Put up a draft of your design along with these benchmarks. Step back – a long way back. Now, does your ad grab the eye more than all the others? If not . . . back to the drawing board!

Understanding the stages in design

Designers often experiment with numerous layouts for their print ads or other printed materials before selecting one for formal development. We strongly recommend that you do the same or insist that your designer or agency does the same. The more layouts you look at, the more likely you are to get an original idea that has eye-grabbing power. But whether you design your own print materials or have experts do the work for you, you want to be familiar with the design stages. These are:

- ✔ **Stage 1. Thumbnails:** The rough sketches designers use to describe layout concepts are called *thumbnails*. They're usually small, quick sketches in pen or pencil. You can also use professional design and layout packages like Quark XPress or InDesign to create thumbnails.

- ✔ **Stage 2. Roughs:** Designers then develop thumbnails with promise into *roughs* – full-size sketches with headlines and subheads drawn carefully enough to give the feel of a particular font and *style* (the appearance of the printed letters). Roughs also have sketches for the illustrations. The designers suggest body copy using lines (or nonsense characters, if the designer does the rough using a computer).

Are you using an ad agency or design firm to develop your print ads or other printed marketing materials? Sometimes clients of ad agencies insist on seeing designs in the rough stage, to avoid the expense of having those designs developed more fully before presentation. We recommend that you ask to see rough versions of your designs, too, even if your agency hesitates to show you its work in unfinished form. After the agency realises that you appreciate the design process and don't criticise the roughs simply because they're unfinished, you can give the agency more guidance and help during the design process.

✔ **Stage 3. Comprehensive layout:** Designers then develop chosen roughs into a *comp* (short for *comprehensive layout*). A comp should look pretty much like a final version of the design, although designers produce a comp on a one-time basis, so it may use paste-ups in place of the intended photos, colour photocopies, typeset copy and headlines. Designers used to assemble comps by hand, but now most designers and agencies do their comps on computer. A high-end PC and colour printer can produce something that looks almost like the final printed version of a four-colour ad or other printed marketing material. Designers refer to a computer-made comp as a *full-colour proof*.

✔ **Stage 4. Dummy:** A *dummy* is a form of comp that simulates the feel – as well as the look – of the final design. (Every design should have a feel or personality of its own, just as products should have a personality. Often you can create the best personality for your ad simply by carrying over the brand identity you've created for the product. Consistency helps.) Dummies are especially important for brochures or special inserts to magazines, where the designer often specifies special paper and folds. By doing a dummy comp, you can evaluate the feel of the design while you're evaluating its appearance.

Designing and submitting your ads the old-fashioned way

The traditional way to submit a design to a printing firm was to generate what printers call *camera-ready artwork*, a version of the design suitable for the printer to photograph with a large-scale production camera in order to generate *colour keys* (to convert colours to specific inks) and *films*, clear sheets for each layer of colour to be printed. You (or the designer) would produce this camera-ready art by making a *mechanical* or *paste-up*, in which typeset copy, visuals and all the other elements of the design were transferred on to a foam-core board, using a hot wax machine.

The hot wax machine heated wax and spread it on a roller so that you could roll a thin layer of warm wax onto the back of each element. The wax stuck each piece neatly to the board, allowing those pieces to be peeled off easily, in case you wanted to reposition anything. When you had everything the way you wanted it, this is the point at which you would send the artwork off to the printer.

Designing and submitting your ads on a computer

If you're quick and able on a computer and like to work in design and layout programs (such as Adobe InDesign or Quark XPress), you can do the same kind of creative rough designing simply by searching for images on the web. (To find an image, try specifying an image search in Google, but remember not to use copyrighted images in your final design without permission or payment. Plenty of royalty-free image websites are available. Websites such as www.iStockphoto.com or www.Shutterstock.com offer monthly subscription services at reasonable rates that give you access to thousands of photos to use in your marketing. Copy the chosen images onto your computer and you can click and drag them into different programs and pages.

Invest a bit of time and effort in honing these computer-based design techniques. Look up the latest *For Dummies* books on how to use Quark Xpress, Adobe InDesign or any other design and layout program of your choice, or just work in Microsoft Word, which is pretty impressive in its latest incarnations as a basic design program itself. Also, take a look at the growing number of great-looking ad templates you can find online and then adapt them in any of the common graphic design programs. As an example, see many options at www.iStockphoto.com or www.mycreativeshop.com.

When your preliminary design is ready for the printer, you (or the ad agency) can send the design over the web using desktop publishing software. You can even do the colour separations for four-colour work on your PC and send those colour separations, too. (Ask the printer for instructions to make sure that you submit the design in a format that their system can use.) The printer then makes plates for printing the design straight from the file that you've emailed to them. (*Plates* are metal or plastic sheets with your design on them – the printer applies the ink to the plates when the printing press does its thing.)

Until recently, electronic submission to printing firms generally had to be executed in a professional software package like Quark XPress, but increasingly, printers are accepting Word files or PDF files generated by Acrobat (lots of people prefer this route because it reduces the chances of incompatibility problems). And if you're designing in a recent version of Word, you'll find that creating a PDF file can be done from your program.

Finding your font

A *font* is a particular design's attributes for the *characters* (letters, numbers and symbols) used in printing your design. *Typeface* refers only to the distinctive design of the letters (Times New Roman, for example). Font, on the other hand, actually refers to one particular size and style of a typeface design (such as 10-point, bold, Times New Roman).

The right font for any job is the one that makes your text easily readable and harmonises with the overall design most effectively. For a headline, the font also needs to grab the reader's attention. The body copy doesn't have to grab attention in the same way – in fact, if it does, the copy often loses readability. For example, a *reverse font* (light or white type on dark paper) may be just the thing for a bold headline, but if you use it in the body copy, too, nobody reads your copy because doing so is just too hard on the eye.

Choosing a typeface

What sort of typeface do you want? You have an amazing number of choices because designers have been developing typefaces for as long as printing presses have existed. (Just click on the font toolbar in Microsoft Word to see an assortment of the more popular typefaces.)

A clean, sparse design, with a lot of white space on the page and stark contrasts in the artwork, deserves the clean lines of a *sans serif typeface* – meaning one that doesn't have any decorative *serifs* (those little bars or flourishes at the ends of the main lines in a character). The most popular body-copy fonts without serifs are Helvetica, Arial, Univers and Avant Garde. Figure 7-2 shows some fonts with and without serifs.

Figure 7-2:
Fonts with and without serifs.

A richly decorative, old-fashioned sort of design, in contrast, needs a more decorative and traditional serif typeface, such as Century or Times New Roman. The most popular body-copy fonts with serifs include Garamond, Melior, Century, Times New Roman and Caledonia.

Table 7-1 shows an assortment of typeface choices, in which you can compare the clean lines of Helvetica, Avant Garde and Arial with the more decorative designs of Century, Garamond and Times New Roman.

Table 7-1	Popular Fonts for Ads
Sans Serif	*Serif*
Helvetica	Century
Arial	Garamond
Univers	Melior
Avant Garde	Times New Roman

In tests, Helvetica and Century generally top the list as most readable, so start with one of these typefaces for your body copy; only change the font if it doesn't seem to work. Also, research shows that people read lowercase letters about 13 per cent faster than uppercase letters, so avoid long stretches of copy set in all capital letters. People also read most easily when letters are dark and contrast strongly with their background. Thus, black 14-point Helvetica on white is probably the most readable font specification for the body copy of an ad (or other printed marketing materials), even if the combination does seem dull to a sophisticated designer.

Generalising about the best kind of headline typeface is no easy task because designers play around with headlines to a greater extent than they do with body copy. But, as a general rule, you can use Helvetica for the headline when you use Century for the body, and the other way round. Or you can just use a bolder, larger version of the body copy font for your headline. You can also reverse a larger, bold version of your type onto a black background for the headline. Use anything to make the headline grab the reader's attention, stand out from the body copy and ultimately lead their vision and curiosity into the body copy's text. (Remember to keep the headline readable – nothing too fancy, please.)

Sometimes the designer combines body copy of a decorative typeface, one with serifs, like Times New Roman, with headers of a sans serif typeface, like Helvetica. The contrast between the clean lines of the large-sized header and the more decorative characters of the smaller body copy pleases the eye and tends to draw the reader from header to body copy. This book uses that technique. Compare the sans serif bold characters of this chapter's title with the more delicate and decorative characters in which the publishers set the text for a good example of this design concept in action.

Making style choices within the typeface

Any typeface gives the user many choices and so selecting the typeface is just the beginning of the project when you design your print. Other questions include: how big should the characters be? Do you want to use the standard version of the typeface, a lighter version, a **bold** (or darker) version or an *italic* version (one that leans to the right)? The process is easier than it sounds. Just look at samples of some standard point sizes (12- and 14-point text for the body copy, for example, with 24-, 36- and 48-point for the headlines). Many designers make their choice by eye, looking for an easy-to-read size that isn't so large that it causes the words or sentences to break up into too many fragments across the page – but not so small that it gives the reader too many words per line. Keep readability in mind as the goal.

Figure 7-3 shows a variety of size and style choices for the Helvetica typeface. As you can see, you have access to a wonderful range of options, even within this one popular design.

Figure 7-3:
Some of the many choices that the Helvetica typeface offers designers.

Helvetica Light 14 point

Helvetica Italic 14 point

Helvetica Bold 14 point

Helvetica Regular 14 point

Helvetica Regular 24 point

Helvetica Regular Condensed 14 point

Helvetica Bold Outline 24 point

Keep in mind that you can change just about any aspect of type. You can alter the distance between lines – called the *leading* – or you can squeeze characters together or stretch them apart to make a word fit a space. Assume that anything is possible. Ask your printer or consult the manual of your desktop publishing or word-processing software to find out how to make a change.

While anything is possible, be warned that your customers' eyes read type quite conservatively. Although most of us know little about the design of typefaces, we find traditional designs instinctively appealing. The spacing of characters and lines, the balance and flow of individual characters – all these familiar typeface considerations please the eye and make reading easy and pleasurable. So, although you should know that you can change anything and everything, you must also know that too many changes may reduce your design's readability. Figure 7-4 shows the same ad laid out twice – once in an eye-pleasing way and once in a disastrous way.

<table>
<tr><td>

WHEN LIFE GIVES YOU LEMONS...

What should you do? Juggle them? Make lemonade? Open a farm stand? Or give up and go home to Momma?

WHO KNOWS? It's often hard to come to grips with pressing personal or career problems. Sometimes it's hardest to see your *own* problems clearly. Fortunately, JEN KNOWS. Jen Fredrics has twenty years of counseling experience, a master's in social work, and a busy practice in personal problem solving. Call her today to find out how to turn your problems into opportunities.

And next time, when life gives you lemons, you'll know just what to make. An appointment.

</td><td>

WHEN LIFE GIVES YOU LEMONS...

What should you do? Juggle them? Make lemonade? Open a farm stand? Or give up and go home to Momma?

WHO KNOWS? It's often hard to come to grips with pressing personal or career problems. Sometimes it's hardest to see your own problems clearly. Fortunately, JEN KNOWS. Jen Fredrics has twenty years of counseling experience, a master's in social work, and a busy practice in personal problem solving. Call her today to find out how to turn your problems into opportunities.

And next time, when life gives you lemons, you'll know just what to make. An appointment.

</td></tr>
</table>

Figure 7-4:
Which copy would you rather read?

Don't just play with type for the sake of playing (as the designer did in the left-hand version of the classified ad in Figure 7-4). Stick with popular fonts, in popular sizes, except where you have to solve a problem or you want to make a special point. The advent of desktop publishing has led to a horrifying generation of advertisements in which dozens of fonts dance across the page, bolds and italics fight each other for attention and the design of the words becomes a barrier to reading, rather than an aid.

Choosing a point size

When designers and printers talk about *point sizes*, they're referring to a traditional measure of the height of the letters (based on the highest and lowest parts of the biggest letters). One *point* equals about $\frac{1}{72}$ of an inch, so a 10-point type is $\frac{10}{72}$ of an inch high, at the most.

Personally, we don't really care – we've never measured a character with a ruler. We just know that if the letters seem too small for easy reading, then we need to bump the typeface up a couple of points. Ten-point type is too small for most body copy but you may want to use that size if you have to squeeze several words into a small space. (But why do that? You're usually better off editing your body copy and then bumping up the font size to make it more readable!) Your eye can't distinguish easily between fonts that are only one or two sizes apart, so specify a larger jump than that to distinguish between body copy and subhead or between subhead and headline.

Producing Brochures, Fliers and More

You can get your print design out to the public in an easy and inexpensive way, using brochures, fliers, posters and many other forms – your imagination is the only limit to what you can do with a good design for all your printed materials. Your word-processing or graphics software, a good inkjet or laser printer and the help of your local photocopy or print shop (which should also have folding machines) allows you to design and produce brochures quite easily and also come up with many other forms of printed marketing materials. In this section, however, we focus largely on a basic brochure, because this form is easy, a business staple and effective at marketing your company.

You can also do small runs (100 or less) straight from a colour printer. Buy matte or glossy brochure paper designed for your brand of printer and simply select the appropriate paper type in the print dialog box. Today's inexpensive inkjet printers can produce stunning brochures. But you have to fold these brochures yourself and the ink cartridges aren't cheap. So print as needed or try contacting your local copy shop. Kall Kwik and many other copy shops now accept emailed copies of files and can produce short runs of your brochures, pamphlets, catalogue sheets or other printed materials on their colour copiers directly from your file.

Many brochures foolishly waste money because they don't accomplish any specific marketing goals; they just look pretty, at best. To avoid creating an attractive, but pointless, brochure that doesn't achieve a sales goal, make sure that you know:

- ✔ Who will read the brochure.
- ✔ How they will get the brochure.
- ✔ What they should discover from and do after reading the brochure.

These three questions focus your brochure design and make it useful to your marketing.

Marketers often order a brochure without a clear idea of what purpose the brochure should serve. They just think a brochure is a good idea: 'Oh, we need them to, you know, put in the envelope along with a letter, or, um, for our salespeople to keep in the boots of their cars; maybe we'll send some out to our mailing list or give them away at the next trade show.'

With this many possibilities, the brochure can't be properly suited to any single use. It becomes a dull, vague scrap of paper that just talks about the company or product but doesn't hit readers over the head with any particular appeal and call to action, something that's become increasingly important as consumers can look up information about your company online at any time.

Listing your top three uses

Define up to three specific uses for the brochure. No more than three, though, because your design can't accomplish more than three purposes effectively. The most common and appropriate uses for a brochure are:

- ✔ To act as a reference for or describe technical details of the product for sales prospects.

- ✔ To support a personal selling effort by lending credibility and helping overcome objections (to find out more about sales, read Chapter 20).

- ✔ To generate leads through a direct-mail campaign (we talk about direct-mail campaigns in Chapter 14).

Say you want to design a brochure that does all three of these tasks well. Start by designing the contents. What product and technical information must be included? Write the information down and collect necessary illustrations, so that you have the *fact base* (the essential information to communicate) in front of you.

Writing about strengths and weaknesses

After you create your fact base (see the preceding section), organise these points in such a way that they highlight your product's (or service's) greatest strengths and overcome its biggest challenges. Don't know what your product's strengths and weaknesses are? List the following, as they relate to sales:

- ✔ The common sales objections or reasons prospects give for not wanting to buy your product.

- ✔ Customers' favourite reasons for buying, or the aspects of your product and business that customers like most.

With your fact base organised accordingly, you're ready to begin writing. Your copy should read as if you're listening to customers' concerns and answering each concern with an appropriate response. You can write sub-heads in the format: 'Our Product Doesn't Need XXX' and 'Our Product Brings You XXX' so that salespeople or prospects can easily see how your facts (in copy and/or illustrations) overcome each specific objection and highlight all the major benefits.

Incorporating a clear, compelling appeal

Add some basic appeal (see Chapter 6), communicated in a punchy headline and a few dozen words of copy, along with an appropriate and eye-catching illustration. You need to include this appeal to help the brochure stand on its own as a marketing tool when it's sent out to leads by post or passed on from a prospect or customer to one of his professional contacts.

The appeal needs to project a winning personality. Your brochure can be fun or serious, emotional or factual – but it must be appealing. The appeal is the bait that draws the prospect to your hook, so make sure your hook is well baited!

Putting it all together

When you have all the parts – the appeal, the fact base and the design – you're ready to put your brochure together. The appeal, with its enticing headline and compelling copy and visual, goes on the front of the brochure – or the outside when you fold it for mailing, or the central panel out of three if you fold a sheet twice. The subheads that structure the main copy respond to objections and highlight strengths on the inside pages. You then organise the fact base, for reference use, in the copy and illustrations beneath these subheads.

Although you can design a brochure in many ways, we often prefer the format (along with dimensions for text blocks or illustrations) in Figure 7-5. This format is simple and inexpensive because you print the brochure on a single sheet of 490mm × 210mm paper that you then fold three times. The brochure fits in a standard DL (110mm × 220mm) envelope or you can tape it together along the open fold and mail it on its own. This layout allows for some detail, but not enough to get you into any real trouble. (Larger formats and multi-page pieces tend to fill up with the worst, wordiest copy, and nobody ever reads those pieces.)

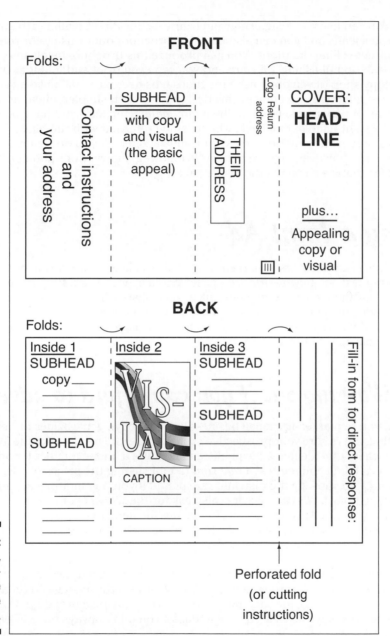

FRONT

Folds:

Contact instructions
and
your address

SUBHEAD
with copy
and visual
(the basic
appeal)

THEIR
ADDRESS

Logo Return
address

COVER:
HEAD-
LINE

plus…
Appealing
copy or
visual

BACK

Folds:

Inside 1
SUBHEAD
copy
SUBHEAD

Inside 2
VIS-
UAL
CAPTION

Inside 3
SUBHEAD
SUBHEAD

Fill-in form for direct response:

Perforated fold
(or cutting
instructions)

Figure 7-5:
A simple,
multi-
purpose
brochure
layout.

You can use the design shown in Figure 7-5 for direct mailings to generate sales leads and you can also hand the brochure out or use it for reference in direct-selling situations. You can produce this brochure using any popular desktop publishing software and you can even print and fold it at the local copy shop (if you don't need the thousands of copies that make off-set printing cost-effective). To convert this design to an even simpler, cheaper format, use A4 paper and eliminate the *return mailer* (the left-hand page on the front, the right-hand on the back, which can be returned with the blanks filled in to request information or accept a special offer). If you do remove the return mailer, however, be sure to include follow-up instructions and contact information on one of the inside pages!

Placing a Print Ad

This section covers a marketing speciality called *media buying*, with an emphasis on buying print ad space. Media agencies and the marketing departments of big companies have specialists who do nothing but buy media and some brokers specialise in it for mid-sized or smaller marketers. But if you're a smaller-scale marketer, you can easily work out how to buy media space on your own.

Working out if you can afford to advertise

If you're marketing a small business, start by buying magazines or newspapers that you're sure your prospective customers read. Then look for the information in them that identifies the publisher and gives a phone number for advertisers to call. Call and request a *rate card* (a table listing the prices of ads by size and also showing the discount rate per ad if you buy multiple ads instead of just one). With a magazine, also ask for the *schedule* or *forward features list*, which tells you when ads for each issue need to be placed and what the topics of future issues will be. Alternatively, you can get information for advertisers on the websites of many publications.

After you've collected a selection of rate cards from magazines or newspapers, take a hard look at the pricing. How expensive is the average ad (in the middle of the size range for each publication)? This may be a broad number and should always be treated as negotiable: you don't always have to pay rate card prices!

If a single ad costs 5 per cent or more of your marketing budget for the entire year, throw the rate sheets away and forget about advertising in those publications. Your business isn't currently operating on a large enough scale to be able to do this kind of advertising.

Instead of blowing that much money on a single ad, spread it over more economical forms of advertising and marketing, such as brochures, mailings, search engine advertising and emails. If you operate on too small a scale or budget to afford advertising, try turning that ad design into a good flier and mailing it instead. You can send the flier to 200 names and see what happens – that approach is a lot less risky and expensive than buying space in a magazine that goes to 200,000 names. You can also search for smaller-circulation publications with a more local or specialist readership, where the rates may be much cheaper.

Finding inexpensive places to advertise

Many local businesses buy ad space in theatre programmes. What does this cost? About £450 for a quarter-page colour ad for three months in one theatre in a small town, to £750 for the same in a well-known theatre in a big town. Compare that price to a full-colour ad in a national newspaper, which can cost up to £60,000. That's a big difference! If buying ads in the best publications to reach your market is too expensive, you can always find smaller-circulation publications that charge less.

One great way to advertise for less is to take advantage of the tens of thousands of newsletters published by professional groups and interest groups. You can buy ad space in 10 or 20 such newsletters for far less money than buying one ad insertion in a national daily newspaper. But you may have to be creative and persistent, because opportunities to advertise in newsletters aren't as obvious as with larger and more professional publications.

Professional associations' monthly newsletters provide an excellent opportunity for small-budget advertising. Professionals are people who have buying power, so even if you don't sell a product aimed at the people the newsletter is written for, they may still respond to your ad. Some insurance agents have advertised successfully in newsletters that go to doctors, for example. Increasingly, newsletters are published in web versions in addition to – or even instead of – print versions. With a web publication, you can take advantage of the larger reach of the Internet to reach more people while paying the lower price of a small publication.

Also explore local newspapers. You can find hundreds of newspapers and weeklies with *circulation* (readership) only in the tens of thousands, which means their rates for ads are one-fifth to one-tenth the price of a national newspaper. Of course, you don't reach as many people, either – advertising tends to be priced on a *cost per thousand readers* basis (the cost of buying that ad divided by the number of readers who read the publication, then multiplied by 1,000). You generally get as much exposure as you're willing to pay for. But by buying ads in small-circulation publications, you avoid taking huge risks and you minimise your investment. If an ad pays off, you can try running it in additional publications. But if the ad doesn't produce the results you want, you can afford to write off the cost without feeling too much pain.

Keep the scale of your print advertising (and indeed any advertising) at a level you're comfortable with, even if your ad doesn't produce any sales. Although that outcome is certainly not your goal, zero sales are always a possibility and you want to base your buying decision on that possibility.

Selecting the ad size

What size ad should you buy? The answer depends in part on the design of your ad. Does the ad have a strong, simple visual or headline that catches the eye, even if it only takes up a third of a page? Or does the ad need to be displayed in a larger format to work well?

In addition to your (or your designer's) judgement about the specifics of your ad, also take into account some general statistics on what percentage of readers *notice* an ad based on its size. As you may expect, the rate goes up with size – bigger ads get more notice (all other things being equal), according to a study by US research company, Media Dynamics (see Table 7-2).

Table 7-2	Selecting the Right Size
Size of Ad	*Index (recall scores)*
Page, colour	100
2-page spread, colour	130
⅔-page vertical, colour	81
½-page horizontal, colour	72

Remember: the bigger the ad, the bigger the impact. But also consider the fact that the percentage of readers noticing your ad doesn't go up *in proportion* to the increase in size. Doubling the size of your ad gives you something like a quarter more readers, not twice as many, which is partly why the cost of a full-page ad isn't twice the cost of a half-page ad.

If you're watching your pennies, a full-page ad is often your best choice. Even though a large ad costs more, it is sufficiently more noticeable than smaller sizes, which means you'll reach more readers and, thus, bring the cost per exposure down a bit. However, remember that while a full-page ad is more economical, it's also more risky, because you'll have blown more money if it doesn't work. You may want to test a new design with a quarter-page, inexpensive ad and, if that pays off, buy a full-page ad next time.

Testing and improving your print ad

Is anybody actually reading your ad? A *direct-response ad*, one that asks readers to take a measurable action such as calling, texting from a mobile phone or going to a shop, gives you a clear indication of that ad's effectiveness within days of its first appearance. Say you expect to receive a lot of enquiries and orders over the telephone during the week the issue with your ad goes on sale. If you don't receive those calls, you know you have a problem. Now what?

Troubleshooting your ad

What if you want to know more about why that direct-response ad didn't get the desired level of response? Or what if you want to study an *indirect-response ad* – one that creates or strengthens an image or position in order to encourage sales? Much brand advertising is indirect, leaving it to the retailer or local office to close the sale. No phones ring, whether consumers liked the ad or not, so how do you know whether the ad worked?

To get this sort of information, you can go to a market research firm and have your ad tested for effectiveness. In fact, if you plan to spend more than £100,000 on print ads, you can probably consider the £1300 or so needed to hire a research firm to pretest the ad money well spent. *Pretesting* means exposing people to the ad in a controlled setting and measuring their reactions to it.

To test an ad's effectiveness, use one of the free techniques described in Chapter 4: you can assemble your own panel of customers and ask them to rate your ad and give you feedback about why they do or don't find that ad appealing. This feedback can give you good ideas for a new, improved version next time. You can also tap into the large-scale studies of ad readership done routinely by some research firms. Just subscribe to the study, and the firm feeds you detailed data about how well each ad you publish works.

A number of commercial media research services can give you information on issues such as what your competitors are up to in terms of advertising and how much they're spending. Kantar Media (www.kantarmedia.com/en/our-expertise/intelligence) and Nielsen (www.nielsen.com/uk) are the best known of these companies.

Using these services, you can find out exactly what your competitors are up to, where they're spending their advertising money and how much they're spending, allowing you to plan your own campaigns accordingly.

Other services such as GfK NOP Media (www.gfknop.com) can help you to find out to what extent consumers notice or read an ad and to measure the level of interest the ad generated.

Say that GfK NOP data shows that readership of your ad falls a little lower than average and that, although many people note the ad, few read enough to get the point or even the brand name. Should you kill this ad and start over?

The answer depends on what's wrong with the ad. Sometimes using the data provided by these research companies can help you find a problem that can be fixed without starting from scratch. Maybe your headline and photo work well, but the body copy flunks with consumers. You can try rewriting and shortening the copy, or changing the layout or choice of fonts. Perhaps the body copy is in reverse font, which consumers find hard to read. Often, switching the text to dark letters on a white or light background can help, without the need for any other changes!

Or maybe you need to switch from a black-and-white or two-colour visual to a four-colour one. Sure, you have to pay more, but the resulting ad may yield a better return, despite its higher price. Studies show that consumers recall full-colour ads better than two-colour ads, which in turn outperform mono ads. So, as with size, more is better in relation to colours. However, you need to run the numbers to see how the extra costs and extra readers affect your cost per thousand figure. As with all print ad decisions, you should be able to reduce the options to reasonable estimates of costs and returns and then pick the highest-yielding option.

Getting ad analysis for free

Maybe you don't really need to spend good money on a research service to find out if your ads are working. Here are some alternatives:

- Run three variations on the ad and see which one generates the most calls or website visits (offering a discount based on a code number or using different phone numbers on different ads tells you which responses come from which ad and which media work best).

- Do your own ad tests. Ask people to look at your ads for 20 seconds, and then quiz them about what they remember. If they missed much of the ad, you probably need to rewrite it.

- Run the same ad (or very similar ones) in large and small formats and see which pulls in the largest number of consumers.

 Any experiments you can run as you do your marketing give you useful feedback about what is and isn't working. Always think of ways to compare different options and see how those options perform when you advertise, giving you useful insight into ad effectiveness.

Considering some brilliant examples

Marketers generally assume that they have to work hard with colours and text to make their ads noticeable and persuasive. Statistically, they're right. But don't discount the power of imaginative design to simplify the task. You can do a simple two-colour ad that actually works better than other, more elaborate ads.

Two famous press campaigns prove that simple can be best. One from *The Economist* uses the same white and red design that the magazine has been using in its poster advertising for the past few years. The press ad consists of a black-and-white Albert Einstein mask with a dotted line around it – the idea being that readers can cut out and wear the mask to look intelligent, or they can buy the magazine. Only two colours and two words are on the page – '*The Economist*'.

Another ad, this one from Volkswagen, uses more words but even less colour. Their full-page 'Word Search' ad plays on the simple puzzle idea but with a twist. The design is in the shape of a car (the Golf) created from black letters on the white page, while in the top left-hand corner is a list of phrases, such as 'power-assisted steering' and 'engine immobiliser'. The strapline says 'Full of hidden extras', inviting the reader to look for the hidden words inside the car. Great print advertising doesn't have to be expensive; it just has to be clever.

Chapter 8

Signs, Posters and More

- -

In This Chapter

▶ Finding successful signs for your business

▶ Using flags, banners and awnings

▶ Designing billboards and other large signs

▶ Utilising transport advertising

▶ Opting for bumper stickers, umbrellas and shopping bags

- -

*O*utdoor advertising refers to a wide variety of advertising. The most obvious types (but not necessarily most important for you) are large (to very large!) signs and posters, including roadside billboards, but we also include signs, flags and banners in this medium. Outdoor advertising also includes what the experts call *ambient advertising*, which means putting an ad in an unexpected place to catch people by surprise.

All these methods try to communicate your message through public display of a poster, sign or something of similar design requirements. For this reason we incorporate signs, flags, banners, bumper stickers, transit advertising and even T-shirts in this chapter, along with the traditional poster formats. These media are more powerful than many marketers realise and some businesses succeed by using no other advertising. In this chapter, you find out how to design for and use outdoor advertising (the term we use to indicate outdoor signs and banners, plus related displays like posters and signs, which, just to keep you on your toes, can be displayed indoors as well as out).

Whenever you review your marketing, do an audit of your signs, posters, T-shirts and other outdoor ads. How many do you have displayed? Are they visible, clear and appealing? Are they in good repair? And then ask if you can find an easy way to increase the number and impact of these signs. You can never do too much to make your brand identity and marketing messages visible.

Introducing the Essential Sign

Signs (small, informational outdoor ads or notices) don't show up in the index or table of contents of most books on marketing. *Signs* are displays with brand or company names on them and sometimes a short marketing message or useful information for the customer, too. In our experience, every marketer needs to make good use of signs.

Signs are all over the place; if you're in an office right now, look out of the nearest window and you can probably see a handful with ease. Signs are undeniably important. Even if they serve only to locate a shop or office, signs do a job that marketers need done. If your customers can't find you, you're out of business. So why do those marketing experts who write the books tend to ignore signs so completely?

The Outdoor Media Centre (www.outdoormediacentre.org.uk) is the best starting place when looking to learn about outdoor advertising in the UK. It has links to all the major outdoor advertising specialist agencies, loads of data about the performance of outdoor advertising, plenty of case studies and should either answer, or provide a link to the answer for, any question you have about outdoor advertising. While the Outdoor Media Centre can help with some general guidance, when evaluating signs, we can't send you to the experts as easily as we can with radio, TV, print or other outdoor media. You'll probably end up working with a local sign manufacturer, unless you're planning a big campaign, and you and your designer will have to specify size, materials, copy and art. Fortunately, you're not all on your own; you can find some guidance and help. First, you need to remember a few things:

✔ The Outdoor Media Centre has a good round-up of information and regulations relating to outdoor advertising, and links to relevant websites. Most basic signs are normally permitted, while others will require planning application consent from your local authority.

✔ If you rent retail or office space, your landlord may have put some restrictions regarding signs into your lease. Research these possible constraints, and talk to those who feel they have authority over your sign and seek their approval based on a sketch and plan before you spend any money having signs made or installed.

✔ Consult your local or regional business telephone listings when you need to have a sign made. You should find several options. You may want to talk to a good design firm or experienced designer for a personal reference, too. Modern high-street copy shops also now provide cheap high-tech solutions for smaller or temporary signs.

✔ To stand out next to those shiny, high-tech signs and project a quality image, have your sign designed and painted by an artist or consider hiring a cabinet-maker, stained glass artist or oil painter. Most signs have little real art about them so unusual and beautiful ones tell the world that your company is special. A really special sign, well displayed in a high-traffic area, can have more power to build an image or pull in prospects than any other form of local advertising.

Appreciating what your sign can do

Signs have limited ability to accomplish marketing goals but perhaps not as limited as you think. As well as displaying the name of your business, you can include a phone number, website address or email contact details so that, even when your premises are closed, potential customers know how to get in touch with you. And you can say what your business does – a butcher doesn't have to be just a 'butcher', he can be a 'family-owned, free-range butcher'. With signs, as with all marketing communications, the way you say it is what counts!

Every morning on our way to work, we pass Munson's coffee shop. We couldn't begin to tell you how many other shops we must pass or what they're called, but we remember Munson's (and go in occasionally) because of the chalk board they put on the pavement outside the shop. No matter how early we are, a new piece of homespun philosophy is always written on the board – for example 'We are here to clear the path for the children behind' – intriguing people and enticing customers in for a drink or snack. This board offers cheap, easy and effective marketing – it's a sign (literally!).

Aside from their practical value (letting people know where you are), signs can and should promote your image and brand name. An attractive sign on your building or vehicle can spread the good word about your business or brand to all who pass by. Don't miss this brilliant opportunity to put your best foot forward in public.

Many commercial signs are in poor condition. Signs sit out in the weather, and when they fade, peel or fall over, they act as negative advertising for your business. Don't let your signs give the public the impression that you don't care enough to maintain them (they may even think you're going out of business!). Renew and religiously maintain your signs to get the maximum benefit from them.

Writing good signs

As a marketer, you need to master the strange art of writing for signs. Too often, the language marketers use on signs is ambiguous. The sign doesn't say anything with enough precision to make its point clear. Keep in mind the suggestions outlined in the following sections.

Make sure your sign says what you want it to

One of our favourite stories about how to easily turn a bad sign into a good one comes from the marketing consultant Doug Hall. A friend of his put up a sign that read 'Seasons in Thyme – Epicurean Food & Wine'. Do you have any idea what that company does? Doug changed his friend's sign to 'Seasons in Thyme RESTAURANT. Casual, Elegant, Island Dining'. For the first time in all his years in business, the owner received some customers who said they came in because they'd seen the sign.

Before you approve any design, review the copy to make sure that the writing provides a model of clarity. Try misinterpreting the wording. Can you read the sign in a way that makes it seem to mean something you don't intend to say? And try thinking of questions the sign doesn't answer that seem obvious to you – remember that the consumer may not know the answers. For example, some people have a terrible sense of direction, so a sign on the side of a shop leaves them confused about how to enter the premises. Solution? Put an arrow and the instructions 'Enter from Front' on the sign.

Use a header to catch your customer's eye

Marketers design some signs to convey substantial information – directions, for example, or details of a shop's merchandise mix. Information-heavy signs are often too brief or too lengthy. Divide the copy and design into two sections, each with a separate purpose, as follows:

- **Have a header:** The first section resembles the header in a print ad (see Chapter 7), and you design it to catch attention from afar and draw people to the sign. Given this purpose, brevity is key – and don't forget the essential large, catchy type and/or visuals.

- **Communicate essential information:** The second section of the sign needs to communicate the essential information accurately and in full. If the first section does its job, viewers walk right up to the sign to read the part with all the important information, so you don't need to make that type as large and catchy. The consumer should be able to easily read and interpret the wording and type used for the information and this section needs to answer all likely viewer questions.

Most signs don't have these two distinct sections, and so they fail to accomplish either purpose very well – they neither attract people very strongly nor inform them fully. Unfortunately, most sign-makers have a strong urge to make all the copy the same size. When pressed, the sign-makers sometimes make the header twice as big as the rest of the copy, but going further than that seems to upset them. Well, to get a good sign, you may have to upset some people. As in many aspects of marketing, if you want above-average performance, you have to swim against the current!

You may have to make your sign bigger to fit the necessary words on it in a readable font. So be it. The form of the sign must follow its function.

Be creative!

Consider adding a beautiful photograph to your sign to give it more of the eye-catching appeal of a good print ad. Most sign-makers and printers can include photos now, but few marketers take advantage of this option.

Another problem is that marketers write the copy on most signs in the most tired and obvious manner. Tradition says that a sign, unlike any other marketing communication, must simply state the facts in a direct, unimaginative way. One reason for this lack of creativity is that most marketers assume people *read* signs. The conventional wisdom is that your customers and prospects automatically find and read your signs.

Try walking down an average high street and later listing all the signs you remember seeing. Some stand out, but most go unseen. And we bet you can't re-create the text of the majority of those signs your eye bothered to linger on long enough to read. To avoid having yours being lost in this sea of similar signs, you have to make it stand out!

Whenever you find other marketers making silly mistakes, you can turn their errors into your opportunities. Signs permit innovation in two interesting areas. You can be innovative with the copy and artwork, just as you can in any print medium, from a magazine ad to a roadside billboard. But you can also innovate in the form of the sign itself. Experiment with materials, shapes, lighting, location and ways of displaying signs to come up with some novel ideas that help your sign grab attention. Signs should be creative and fun. (So should all marketing, for that matter.)

Here are some of the many variations in form that you can take advantage of when designing a creative sign:

- Vinyl graphics and lettering (quick and inexpensive but accurate to your design)
- Hand-painted (personal look and feel)

✔ Wood (traditional look; routing or hand carving enhances the appeal)

✔ Metal (durable and accurate depictions of art and copy, but not very pretty)

✔ Window lettering (hand-painted or with vinyl letters/graphics)

✔ Light boxes (in which lettering is back-lit; highly visible at night)

✔ Neon signs (high impact)

✔ Magnetic signs (for your vehicles)

✔ Electronic displays (also known as *electronic message repeaters*; movement and longer messages, plus a high-tech feel, make these displays appropriate in some situations)

✔ Flat-panel TV screens (with shifting sign content and images or video; the price of these TVs has been coming down in recent years)

✔ Pavement projection (a unit in the shop window moves and spins a logo or message at the feet of passers-by at night)

Discovering Flags, Banners and Awnings

Movement is eye-catching. So think of flags as more dynamic kinds of sign, and try to find ways to use them to build brand awareness, to make your location(s) more visible or to get a marketing message displayed in more forms and places than you could otherwise. Cloth-based forms of advertising can be surprisingly reasonable, which is why outdoor messages on canvas or synthetic cloth make up an important part of many marketing campaigns.

It's a wrap

Only the size of the building you can hang it from and your budget limit how big or imaginative you can get with a banner. Many big organisations commission temporary *building wraps* nowadays, which cover the whole or a large part of their premises. When London was bidding to win the 2012 Olympics, the group leading the bid revealed the biggest building wrap in Europe – two banners covering the roof of what was then the Millennium Dome, which could be seen from planes as they flew into London. Thanks to its innovative thinking (including this stunt), London won the 2012 Olympic Games. You may not be able to do anything on this scale, but this example does show that sticking to stock formats isn't necessary.

Flagging down your customers

Did you know that Shakespeare used flags to advertise? In Elizabethan times the Globe Theatre in London had a small tower with a flagpole for advertising the next play to be shown – they were even colour coded, black for a tragedy and white for a comedy. Today theatres, galleries and museums are still some of the biggest users of flags and banners because they can adorn their buildings with colourful displays that promote forthcoming events – the temporary nature of the medium suits the rotation of the plays and exhibitions. Do you have a similar short-term message that you could get across on a flag or banner?

A number of companies specialise in making custom-designed flags and banners. Of course, you see tacky paper banners – often produced by the local copy shop – hanging in the windows of shops on occasion. But we're not talking about those banners (because they probably don't help your image). We mean a huge, beautiful cloth flag flapping in the breeze. Or a bold 3 × 5-foot screen-printed flag suspended like a banner on an office or trade-show wall. Or a nylon table banner that turns the front and sides of a table into space for your marketing message.

Consider using a flag or banner as a sign for your shop or business. Doing so will help you stand out because so few marketers take advantage of this way to use a banner. A flag or banner is less static and dull than the typical metal or wooden sign. Cloth moves, and even when it isn't moving, you know it has the potential for movement. This gives the banner a bit of excitement and helps it seem decorative and festive. People associate flags and banners with special events because these decorations are traditionally used in that context, instead of for permanent display.

Flag companies give you all these options and more. These businesses regularly sew and screen large pieces of fabric, and they can also supply you with all the necessary fittings you need to display flags and banners. In recent years, silk-screening technology and strong synthetic fibres have made flags and banners brighter and more permanent, expanding their uses in marketing.

You can find suppliers of a full line of stock and custom products by searching online, looking in your local *Yellow Pages* or in the directory sections of trade magazines such as *Marketing Week* (www.marketingweek.co.uk). Whoever you contact, ask to see their custom flag and banner price list, which includes a lot of design ideas and specs, and photos of effective banners made for previous clients.

Utilising canopies and awnings

If appropriate for your business, consider using an awning and canopy. For retailers, awnings and canopies often provide the boldest and most attractive form of roadside sign. Office sites may also find them valuable.

Awnings combine structural value with marketing value by shading the interior and can even extend the floor space of your shop by capturing some of the pavement as transition space. An awning can perform all of the functions of a sign in a highly visible but not intrusive way. Conveniently, a row of awnings doesn't look as crass and commercial as huge signs because your eye accepts them as a structural part of the building. So a row of awnings provides you with the same amount of advertising as a big sign but without looking pushy.

Putting up Posters: Why Size Matters

If you're planning to use posters to advertise, one of the first things to think about is how much time customers will have to read your ad and how far away they'll be. This information will help you decide how much you can say in your ad and how to say it.

Here's a simple exercise to help you understand the design requirements for a large-format poster. Draw a rectangular box on a sheet of blank paper, using a ruler as your guide. Make the box 12 cm wide and 6 cm high – the proportion of a standard *48-sheet* poster (we talk more about poster formats later in this section). Although a poster is large (over 6 metres wide in this instance), from a distance it will look as small as that box on your sheet (see Figure 8-1). Now hold your paper (or Figure 8-1) at arm's length and think about what copy and artwork can fit in this space while remaining readable to passers-by at this distance. Not much, right? Now imagine they're driving past it in a car. Next imagine them staring at it for minutes while waiting for the 8.30am train from Dorking to Waterloo. Sometimes you need to limit your message to a few, bold words and images to avoid your poster becoming a mess that no one can read. At other times you can afford to include more detail. The people waiting for that train may even be grateful for the distraction!

The problem with outdoor advertising, in general, is that viewers have to read the ad in a hurry, and often from a considerable distance. So the ad has to be simple. Yet people who walk or drive the same route view the same ad daily. So that ad has to combine lasting interest with great simplicity.

With all these constraints, you see the difficulty of designing effective outdoor ads. Make your message fun, beautiful or at least important and clear, so that people don't resent having to see it often.

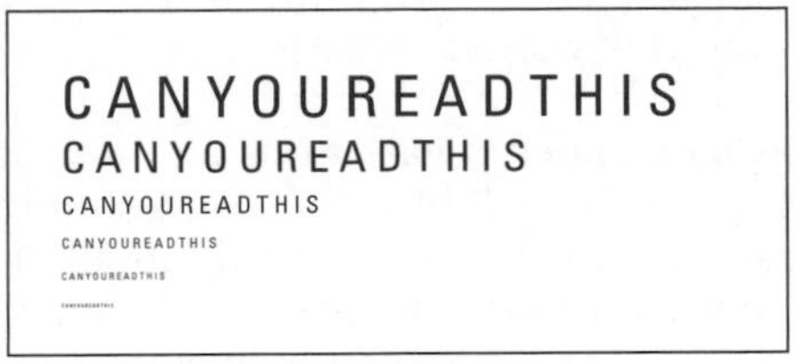

Figure 8-1:
From a distance, a large road-side poster looks no bigger than this image.

CANYOUREADTHIS
CANYOUREADTHIS
CANYOUREADTHIS
CANYOUREADTHIS
CANYOUREADTHIS

Deciding on outdoor ad formats

Four different sectors exist in the outdoor market: roadside, transport, retail/point-of-sale/leisure and 'non-traditional':

- **Roadside:** You can choose anything from phone booths to 96-sheet ads, which at 40-feet wide by 10-feet high are the largest of the standard poster formats. Special versions, such as a real car stuck to a billboard, and banners count as roadside ads, too.

- **Transport:** While it includes standard poster sites in stations, airports and on trains and tubes, transport is a wide-ranging outdoor sector that also covers (literally) bus-sides, taxis and trucks. For that reason, this medium has its own lexicon of jargon, from *L-Sides* to *T-Sides* and the enticingly named *Super Rears*. All that really matters is that these terms describe ways of advertising on the outside of buses, which we cover later in this chapter. This method is effective for reaching people 'dwelling' longer in front of ads.

- **Retail/point-of-sale/leisure:** If you sell your products through retailers, outdoor ads near those outlets can make a lot of sense. As well as poster sites at supermarkets, the retail sector includes shopping centres, cinemas, gyms and petrol stations, and can include ads on trolleys and screens. These types of ad are good for reaching those people with their minds already in 'shopping' mode.

- **Non-traditional formats and ambient:** This is also a sector, but no one's come up with a straightforward name for it, which just proves its diversity. Think petrol pump nozzles, takeaway lids, ticket backs, beer mats, floor stickers – in fact, think anything at all. We talk about some of the more popular ambient formats, as well as the truly outlandish, later in the chapter.

You can find the proportions and relative sizes of some standard outdoor formats offered by Clear Channel UK at their web site (`www.clearchannel.co.uk/useful-stuff/billboard-poster-sizes`).

You can also explore the growing number of variations on these standards. Do you want your message displayed on a lobby floor, on a shopping trolley or alongside the noticeboards at leisure centres? Or how about on signs surrounding the arenas and courts hosting athletic events? You can use all of these options and more, by directly contacting the businesses that control such spaces or using one of a host of ad agencies and poster contractors that can give you larger-scale access.

Maximising your returns

Outdoor advertising costs vary widely depending on what formats you use. As an example, a 48-sheet roadside poster will cost you around £400 per panel for a two-week period – the standard time for an outdoor campaign. You're unlikely to buy just one poster site, and even more unlikely to find an outdoor advertising company that will sell you one. Poster space is typically sold by a pre-determined group of panels in one area, or a national campaign. So, if you want to advertise on 25 48-sheet sites for two weeks, you'll pay approximately £10,000. Seventy sites will cost £28,000.

Postar (`www.postar.co.uk`) offers data on outdoor advertising effectiveness, but as you'll have to pay a subscription fee, we suggest you also go direct to the outdoor advertising companies for rate cards and data. You can find the main poster companies through the Outdoor Media Centre website (`www.outdoormediacentre.org.uk`) too.

Delivering Messages on the Move: Transport Advertising

Transport advertising is any advertising in or on railway or underground systems, airports, buses, taxis, on the sides of vans or lorries, and more. Although transport advertising is a form of outdoor advertising, this term is misleading because you set up some transit ads indoors: ads at airport terminals, ads displayed within Tube carriages and so on.

Transport ads work well if you get the people in transit to take an interest in your product, from consumer items to business services. We've seen transit ads generate sales leads for local estate agents and for international consulting firms. Yet few marketers make use of them. Consider being an innovator and trying transit ads, even if your competitors don't.

Standard options – the ones most easily available through media buying firms and ad agencies – include bus shelter panels, bus and taxi exterior signs, posters and back-lit signs in airports.

Transport advertising offers one definite advantage: it typically delivers high frequency of viewer impacts in a short period of time. Public transport vehicles generally travel the same routes over and over, and so almost everyone along the route sees an ad multiple times.

Bus advertising

Shelter panels are 6-sheet (120 cm x 180 cm) posters, which appear on bus shelters. In many cities, the site owners have back-lit some of the shelter panels for night-time display. A two-week showing typically costs anywhere from £250 upwards, depending upon the area.

Well-accepted standards exist for *bus advertising* in the UK, largely due to the fixed available space on any single- or double-decker bus – although some companies now also offer the option of full-bus branding. Check out www.cbsoutdoor.co.uk/en-gb/Our-Media/Bus/ to view bus ad options, offered by outdoor specialist CBS Outdoor.

Combinations of different transport media can be very effective, linking up bus shelters, buses and taxis to make your ad visible to people throughout their journey. Check here for the huge list of possible bus, tube, tram and other transport advertising formats offered by CBS Outdoor: http://www.cbsoutdoor.co.uk/Our-Media/Campaign-Support/Production-Library/Production-Library/#BusProduction.

Taxi advertising

Taxi advertising provides you with a route to target local customers and high-value businesspeople. You can advertise on the outside, inside and on the back of receipts; you can even cover the whole cab. A company called Cabvision actually sells ads on its in-taxi TV channel – £40 per cab per month for a 10-second slot, in case you were wondering. A fully covered taxi costs from £2,500 for 12 months, but just advertising on the sides is obviously cheaper. Contact a company that specialises in this form of advertising, such as VeriFone Media (www.verifonemedia.co.uk).

Airport advertising

Airport advertising is taking off fast. If you want a relatively well-to-do audience with a rich mix of tourists and professional travellers, enquire about airport advertising options with international site owners and domestic specialists such as JCDecaux (www.jcdecauxairport.co.uk) or Airport Partners Advertising (www.airportpartners.co.uk).

A note about your own vehicles

Does your company have its own vehicles on the road? If so, are you using them for outdoor advertising? Most marketers say either 'no' or 'sort of' when we ask them this question. Small, cheap, magnetic signs on the doors don't count; nor does a painted name on the door or side panel of a van or lorry. If you pay for as much display space as even a standard-sized van offers, you'd probably hire a designer or agency and put great care into your message. In fact, you're paying for the exterior space on your vehicles; the cost just doesn't show up in the marketing budget. So why not cash in on this investment more fully by treating that lorry or van as a serious advertising medium? Mount frames for bus-sized posters and display a professionally designed ad that you change monthly or weekly. Or hire a competent airbrush painter to do a more permanent, custom job on each vehicle.

Freight company Eddie Stobart uses branded vehicles to great effect. You'll have seen the dark green lorries with yellow and red lettering on the motorway, but did you know that each one carries a different woman's name. Its branding is so good that an Eddie Stobart fan club exists, where you get your own personalised membership card, lapel badge and complete fleet list telling you the name of every vehicle. A different company, coincidentally using similar colours, is the Foxtons chain of estate agents. Since 2001 Foxtons has branded its entire fleet of company cars in striking limited edition liveries, from 'Italian Job' to 'Urban Graffiti'. You can use your vehicles as more than just a form of transport, too; all you require is a little imagination.

Being Innovative with Ambient Media – Your Ad in Unusual Places

Ambient or *non-traditional advertising* does exactly what it says on the tin (or takeaway lid, egg or petrol pump nozzle). In fact, we can't really tell you what ambient media is, as the concept covers so much and changes so rapidly. We can tell you what it isn't, which is any of the traditional outdoor advertising opportunities. Ambient is one of the fastest-growing sectors within outdoor advertising because you can create a lot of impact for relatively little outlay. The nature of ambient advertising also means it can offer you precise targeting by area or by audience type.

We like to divide ambient advertising into two parts: the uncontroversial and the unconventional. *Uncontroversial* includes all forms of outdoor advertising that are really just poster ads in disguise, and which are in almost constant use by some fairly major advertisers. These ads appear on petrol pump nozzles, floor stickers in supermarkets and train stations, and posters in public conveniences. *Unconventional* includes everything else. In our time we've heard about ads that appear on pretty much everything you can imagine, and a lot of what you probably wouldn't. These unconventional places include Tube maps and tickets, tattoos, urinal stickers and even on cows standing by the side of major roads.

Just because the concept's different doesn't mean ambient advertising is a great idea for your product or service. Only use ambient advertising when you know that the idea is a good fit for your brand or you're prepared to take a gamble with the investment (most of the wilder ideas have pretty poor audience measurement, so the choice is based more on whether it feels right to you).

Here are some of the most interesting ambient media ideas we've encountered and some of the companies that have used them effectively:

- **Rubbish skips:** Directory enquiries service 118 118 used skips to communicate the idea of people throwing away their old telephone directories.

- **Petrol pump nozzles:** Good for targeting drivers with impulse buys, and used by food and drink brands such as Polo and Red Bull.

- **Takeaway lids:** Full-colour Adlids have been used by a host of organisations, from Blockbuster video ('Here's just four of our new takeaways', plus a money-off coupon) to Her Majesty's Revenue and Customs.

- **Chalk ads:** Sometimes known as vandaltising, chalk-drawn ads on pavements have been used by companies such as Gossard to advertise a new range of underwear. Be careful, though: this idea is less popular with local councils, despite the fact that the ads eventually wash away.

- **Car park tickets:** A great way to reach people just before they go shopping. This method has been used by retailers such as Sainsbury's and Specsavers.

- **Shopping trolleys and floor posters:** We group these together as they offer the same great benefits to you if your products are found on supermarket shelves. Did you know that 75 per cent of purchasing decisions are made in-store and over 90 per cent of advertising budget is spent out of store? Trolleys and floor posters act as reminders to shoppers that your product exists, and can even direct them to the right shelf.

- **Adwalker wearable ads:** These modern 'sandwich boards' involve people wearing interactive screens. They can be used not only to advertise your services but also to get potential customer information. Brands such as Nivea, Yahoo! and Sony have used this approach to engage customers on the street and at airports.

- **ForeheADS:** Why use your head when you can use someone else's? This is a wacky idea, which involves renting out the foreheads of cash-strapped students, who must be seen out in public for at least three hours a day to earn their fee. Companies including *FHM* magazine and CNX have used ForeheADS to carry their logos in the form of temporary tattoos.

Advertising on T-shirts to Shopping Bags: Small but Effective

Broadly defined, a sign may include any public display of your brand or marketing message. To us, a message on a T-shirt is just as legitimate as one on a poster. And a T-shirt ad is often a lot easier and cheaper to make. The following sections share simple, small-scale ways to get your message across.

Embellishing T-shirts, umbrellas and bumper stickers

Sometimes you can get people to advertise your company on their vehicles or bodies for free (see 'Praising T-shirts' in the nearby sidebar). Your customers may think of a nice T-shirt as a premium item or gift for them, but you can see that T-shirt as a body billboard! Isn't it nice that people are willing to go around with your advertising messages on their clothes (or even on their bodies – temporary tattoos are also a marketing option)? Don't overlook this concept as a form of outdoor advertising. In fact, use it as much as you can. People happily display marketing messages if they like them.

Similarly, umbrellas can broadcast your logo and name and a short slogan or headline, although only in especially wet or overly sunny weather.

Praising T-shirts

Sometimes you just need a cheap T-shirt. We have drawers stuffed full of them, and many of those shirts feature artwork promoting a company or brand name. If you can make a T-shirt appropriate to your brand, by all means use T-shirts as a premium item!

Even a good-quality T-shirt is pretty cheap, so you can easily implement a quality premium strategy with this medium. You achieve quality by using a heavy, all-cotton fabric and sporting a compelling design developed by a real designer.

Oh, and you need to use an experienced, quality-conscious silk-screener to put that fine design on those good T-shirts.

T-shirt buyers are frustrated by the poor selection of shirts available in the shops. A lack of exciting new designs, not a lack of drawer space, holds these customers back. So you just need to put a cool design on your T-shirt to get your target audience to want it. Customers can't get enough of this premium item as long as your design is fresh and good. No, we don't really want another cheap pen with some company's name on it. But we're happy to get another good T-shirt or two. We may even pay you for it – if it's good enough.

To find companies providing customised T-shirts, try searching online, your local *Yellow Pages* for listings of silk-screening businesses near you (generally listed under 'Printing') or take a look at the back of a trade magazine such as *Marketing Week*.

Don't overlook bumper and car-window stickers. If you make them clever or unique enough, people eagerly seek those stickers out. Don't ask us why. But because people do, and because producing bumper stickers is cheap, why not come up with an appealing design and make stickers available in target markets as giveaways on shop counters or at outdoor events?

Commercial or brand-orientated bumper stickers are used by people who think the brand is so cool that it enhances the car. Achieving coolness and desirability is very difficult for most marketers, however. An alternative is to keep your brand identity small, and use an appealing message instead. A clever joke, an inspiring quote or something similar is appealing enough to get your message displayed. And for mugs, window stickers and other premium items, the secret is to have a great visual design or other picture that people enjoy or to offer a humorous cartoon.

You can even include a nice sticker in a direct-mail piece, where that sticker can do double duty by both acting as an incentive to get people to retain and read the mailing and giving you cheap outdoor advertising when they display the sticker on their vehicles. (Contact local print shops, sign-makers or T-shirt silk-screeners; any of these businesses may also produce bumper stickers.)

Bagging it up

Big stores believe in the importance of shopping bags as an advertising medium. But many other businesses fail to take advantage of the fact that shoppers carry bags around busy shopping centres and high streets, and also on trains and buses, giving any messages on the bags high exposure.

To use bags effectively, you need to make them far easier to read and much more interesting than the average brown paper or white plastic shopping bag. Remember, you're not just designing a bag – you're designing a form of outdoor advertising. So apply the same design principles. Come up with a *hook*: a striking image or attention-getting word or phrase that gets everyone looking at that bag. Try alternative colours or shapes. (By the way, most bag suppliers can customise their bags – check with suppliers in your local area. If no suppliers near you can do so, contact printers and silk-screeners instead.)

If you offer the biggest, strongest bag in a shopping area, you can be sure that shoppers stuff everyone else's bags into yours, giving your advertising message the maximum exposure. Of course, bigger, stronger bags cost more, but these days, with environmental concerns relating to plastic bags, you may win more customers with a heavy-duty plastic bag for multiple uses or you could even invest in a cotton or recyclable version. After all, if you have an ad message you can get across with a bag, compare the cost of a better bag to other media. Pretty cheap, right? So why not go for it?

 If you aren't in the retail business, you may think that this idea doesn't apply to you. Wrong! Plenty of store managers view bags as an irritating expense rather than a marketing medium. Offer to supply them with better bags – or more environmentally-friendly ones – for free, in exchange for the right to print your message on the bags. Result: a new marketing medium for your campaign. A specialist such as PromotionalBags.co.uk (`www.promotionalbags.co.uk`) can help you design and create bags with your brand on them.

Considering a Few Commonsense Rules for Outdoor Advertising

Depending on whether you're advertising on roadside or transport sites, follow these commonsense rules when designing your poster to make sure that it catches and holds customers' attention:

✔ If your poster site is by the side of a main road, people will have just a few seconds to see and understand your ad. Keep the image simple and use as few, large words as possible. Make sure that you use colours that contrast, so they can be seen from a good distance.

✔ Think like a bored passenger. When you advertise on interior Tube panels, inside taxis or on train platform posters, you can afford to use more complex visuals and a greater number of words.

✔ Consider layering the message so that you provide a clear, large-scale, simple message for first-time viewers, but also a more detailed design and message for repeat viewers to find within the poster.

✔ Humour and word play work well for posters. Try to use them in your ad to build viewer involvement.

✔ Show your logo. Whether you're just using posters or are including other media in your marketing campaign, don't forget the logo! Using your logo consistently on everything you do will improve recognition of your business and achieve better results from your advertising.

Chapter 9

TV and Radio Ads (Or Your Own Show!)

In This Chapter

▶ Designing ads for radio

▶ Creating great video ads for little cash

▶ Harnessing the emotional power of television

▶ Advertising online

▶ Brushing up on branded content

*R*adio and television are well-established, extremely powerful marketing media, while video (especially if shot in digital format) is a hot new item for streaming-video messages on your website. Video can also offer marketing messages on television screens and computers on your stand at a trade show.

The problem with radio and TV is that the costs associated with producing and broadcasting ads have traditionally been quite high, making these media too expensive for smaller marketers. We want to encourage you to be open-minded about radio, video and TV because new and easier ways to produce in these media are emerging all the time, along with a growing number of low-cost ways to broadcast your ads. Every year brings more radio and television stations, including those appearing online, on mobile phones and on cable and satellite TV channels. Digital radio is also available that you can listen to through a digital set, digital TV or your laptop.

Even if you don't use these commercial media, you can possibly find more modest ways in which to share your ads with prospects. In fact, increasingly marketers use websites that communicate using digital video, PowerPoint or radio-style voice-overs. Modern technology is making these media more flexible and affordable for all marketers.

Creating Ads for Radio

Conventional wisdom says you have only three elements to work with when you design for radio: words, sound effects and music. In a literal sense, that wisdom's true, but you can't create a great radio ad unless you remember that you want to use those elements to generate *mental images* for the listener. And that means you can often perform the same basic plot on radio as on TV. Radio isn't really as limited as people think but is now rarely used to its full advantage. Society's love affair with radio has been eclipsed by its love of TV and films.

When creating radio ads, favour direct action goals over indirect ones. Sometimes you may want to use radio just to create brand awareness *(indirect-action advertising)*, but in general, the most effective radio ads call for direct action. Give out a web address (if the listener can remember that address easily) or a freefone number in the ad.

Put your brand name into your radio ad early and often, regardless of the story line. If you fail to generate the desired direct action, at least you build awareness and interest for the brand, which supports other points of contact in your marketing campaign. Radio is a great support medium and not enough marketers use it that way. You may as well fill the vacuum with *your* marketing message!

Here's a simple rule that can help you avoid confusion in your radio ad: ensure that your script identifies all sound effects. Sound effects are wonderful and evocative, but in truth, many sound very similar. Without context, rain on the roof can sound like bacon sizzling in a pan, a blowtorch cutting through the metal door of a bank vault or even an alien spaceship starting up. So the script must identify that sound, either through direct reference or through context. You can provide context with the script, the plot or simply through other sound effects. The sounds of eggs cracking and hitting a hot pan, coffee percolating and someone yawning, all help to identify that sizzle as the breakfast bacon, rather than rain on the roof or a blowtorch.

Buying airtime on radio

We often find ourselves urging marketers to try radio in place of their standard media choices. Why? Because, although local retailers frequently use radio to pull people into stores for sales or special offer periods, many other marketers overlook radio as a viable medium. Those advertisers don't realise how powerful radio can be and may not be aware of its incredible reach. In the UK, around 47.6 million people (91.7 per cent of the population) tune into digital and non-digital radio every week. We bet your target audience is in there somewhere! (Also consider radio not just for advertising but for editorial publicity. Many radio talk shows will be willing to invite you on as a guest if you pitch your expertise well and have a unique angle to discuss.)

RAJAR (Radio Joint Audience Research) is the UK's audience measurement system for commercial radio stations and the BBC. Every quarter, RAJAR releases detailed listening figures for all the UK's national and local radio stations, which you can access at www.rajar.co.uk. You can also get in touch with the Radio Advertising Bureau (RAB), which does a good job of promoting radio as an advertising medium and is a great source of campaign data and ideas for creative radio advertising (www.rab.co.uk).

Experts often talk about how the traditional media environment is fragmenting, with fewer people watching TV and more people accessing entertainment online and through their mobile phones. While radio will be affected by this development, in many ways it will also benefit. Radio fits with people's increasingly mobile lives. It allows people to listen to it while doing other things – like cleaning, driving, sitting on the bus or getting stuck in a traffic jam! Those people can only welcome the distraction of your well-crafted radio ad.

You can also target radio advertising quite narrowly – both by type of audience and by geographic area. This fact helps make radio a very good buy. The general lack of appreciation for this medium also helps by keeping ad prices artificially low.

Radio airtime is cheaper and may be more cost-effective than TV airtime, but the biggest advertisers can reach a larger total audience by using TV, so this medium's not ideal for everyone. For some younger audiences, web advertising may be even more suitable. It all depends which people you're trying to reach and how they use media.

Targeting advertising via radio

We like the fact that radio stations make a real effort to target specific audiences – after all, most advertisers try to do the same thing. You can get good data, both demographic and lifestyle- or attitude-orientated information, on radio audiences. And you can often find radio stations (or specific programmes on those stations) that reach a well-defined audience, rich in those people you want to target, making radio an even better buy.

You can get details of radio station formats and audience characteristics for all UK commercial radio stations from the communications regulator Ofcom, just by going to the Radio Broadcast Licensing section of its website, at www.ofcom.org.uk.

And here's another option for radio advertising that you may not have considered. How about running ads over the internal broadcasting systems used in many shops? This opportunity gives you another great way to target a particular audience going about a particular task – for instance, you could advertise your brand of tiles to DIY shoppers using Tiles FM. *In-store radio* is an entirely different medium from a buying perspective because the shop, or more usually a specialist media owner, develops and controls the programming. As a result, most marketers don't know how to use in-store radio. But an ad agency may be able to help you gain access and some media-buying firms handle this kind of advertising, too.

So remember: don't overlook radio! It can give you better reach, better focus on your target market and greater cost-effectiveness than other media. Like TV, radio can *show* as well as tell – you just have to use the listener's imagination to create visual images. And if you manage to create a really good script, we guarantee you can catch and hold audience attention.

If you're planning to make radio a big part of your marketing plan, *An Advertiser's Guide to Better Radio Advertising* by Andrew Ingram and Mark Barber from the RAB (Wiley) is dedicated to telling you how to do it better.

Finding Cheaper Ways to Use the Power of Video

If you're thinking of skipping this section, consider this: video can cost £1000 per minute to produce – or even £10,000 if you're making a sophisticated national TV ad – setting aside the cost of the airtime to actually air the ad! But video can cost £50 a minute or even less.

Do you have access to a high-quality, handheld digital video camera? Well, that camera (when combined with a good microphone) is actually capable of producing effective video for your marketing, especially for use on the web, where low-resolution video files are usually used, making camera quality less important. Just think of all those videos getting millions of viewers on YouTube; the quality isn't great but people keep watching because they're interested in the content.

Many marketers don't realise that the limiting factor in inexpensive or home-made video is usually the sound quality, not the picture quality. So as long as you plug in a remote microphone and put it near anyone who's speaking, you can probably make usable video yourself.

Here are some tips if you decide to shoot video yourself:

- ✔ Write a simple, clear script and time it before you bother to shoot any video.

- ✔ Clean up the background. Most amateur efforts to shoot video presentations or ads for marketing are plagued by stuff that shows up in the background. Eliminate rubbish bins, competitors' signs and anything else unsightly.

- ✔ Use enough light and try to have multiple light sources. A digital video camera is just a fancy camera and it needs light to work. Normal indoor lighting is too dim for quality video. Instead, add more lights, including bright floodlights and open windows. And make sure light shines from both sides so that you fill the shadows. (Shadowed areas get darker in the video.)

- ✔ Shoot everything more than once. Editing is easy (well, easier) as a result of the many software programs you can use on your own computer to edit video. But editing is much easier if you have lots of footage to select from. Always repeat each short section several times, then, in editing, choose the version that came out best. That approach is how they make films stars look good and it can work well for you, too! If you have more than one camera, you could even edit shots from different angles.

- ✔ You can produce radio ads or sound-only messages for your website using the same digital recording and editing capabilities as you use to do home-made digital video. The key is a quiet environment and a good microphone for recording. Or you can go into a production studio's sound booth and let the technicians there worry about the technical aspects.

- ✔ If you want actors, consider recruiting them locally and even asking people to volunteer. We hate to promote this idea, but if you're still a small organisation, avoiding paying Equity rates for your actors makes things considerably cheaper. Paying union rates and residuals is appropriate for major or national campaigns but can be prohibitively expensive for small marketers. However, employees can make great brand ambassadors, too.

For information on editing and production, check out the many *For Dummies* books that can help you better understand what's involved or hire a media production firm that can do high-quality work at moderate rates. With plenty of smaller production firms around, try interviewing some in your area and getting samples of their work plus price quotes – you may find that by the time you master the software and come up to speed, you're spending as much doing your own work!

Designing Ads for TV

Television is much like theatre. TV combines visual and verbal channels in real-time action, making it a remarkably rich medium. Yes, you have to make the writing as tight and compelling as good print copy, but the words must also sound good and flow with the visuals to create drama or comedy.

TV ads must use great drama (whether funny or serious), condensed to a few seconds of memorable action. These few seconds of drama must etch themselves into the memory of anyone who watches your ad.

You can't reduce a great film to a formula. You must have a good script with just the right touch of just the right emotion. Great acting. Consistent camera work and an appropriate set. The suspense of a developing relationship between two interesting characters. Achieving this level of artistry isn't necessary to make a good TV ad, but to stand out yours certainly needs to be higher than average, and if you can create truly great TV, your ad pays off in spades.

TV looks simple when you see it, but don't be fooled – it's not simple at all. Hire an experienced production company to help you do the ad or do what many marketers do and hire a big ad agency (at big ad agency prices) to design and supervise its production. This choice costs you, but at least you get quality work. Just remember that *you* ultimately decide whether the script has that star potential or is just another forgettable ad. Don't let the production company shoot until they have something as memorable as a classic film (or at least close).

If you work for a smaller business and are used to shoestring marketing budgets, you may be shaking your head at our advice. You think you can do it yourself. But why waste even a little money on ads that don't work? If you're going to do TV, do it right. Either become expert yourself or hire an expert. Without high-quality production, even the best design doesn't work. Why? Because people watch so much TV that they know the difference between good and bad ads and they don't bother to watch anything but the best.

If you're on a shoestring budget and can't afford to hire an expert or don't have the time to become one yourself, consider the following bits of advice:

- ✔ **Forgo TV ads and put your video to work in more forgiving venues.** Simple video can look great in other contexts, like your website or a stand at a trade show, even if it would look out of place on television. (See the 'Cheaper Ways to Use the Power of Video' section earlier in this chapter.)

- ✔ **Consider doing a self-made *spoof ad*.** Make fun of one of the silly TV ad genres, such as the one where a man dressed in black scales mountain peaks and jumps over waterfalls to deliver a box of chocolates to a beautiful woman. Because the whole point is to make a campy spoof, you don't want high production values. You can follow this strategy on your own pretty easily, but you still need help from someone with experience in setting up shots and handling cameras and lights. Make sure you upload a version of the ad to YouTube or give people the power to share it from your website. You can give your spoof ad extra exposure if you make it easy for people to pass on to each other.

✔ **Find a film student at a nearby college who's eager to help you produce your ad.** To budding film-makers, your video is an opportunity to show they can do professional work. For you, using a student may be an opportunity to get near-professional work at a very low price. But make sure the terms are clear upfront. Both the student and their tutor need to clarify (in writing) that you'll own the resulting work and use it in your marketing.

Getting emotional

TV differs from other media in the obvious way – by combining action, audio and video – but these features make TV different in less obvious ways as well. Evoking emotions in TV and video is especially easy, just like in traditional theatre. When planning to use TV as your marketing tool, always think about what emotion you want your audience to feel.

Select an emotional state that fits best with your appeal and the creative concept behind your ad. Then use the power of imagery to evoke that emotion. This strategy works whether your appeal is emotional or rational. Always use the emotional power of TV to prepare your audience to receive that appeal. Surprise, excitement, empathy, anxiety, scepticism, thirst, hunger or the protective instincts of the parent – you can create all of these emotional states and more in your audience with a few seconds of TV. A good ad creates the right emotion for your appeal. The classic Hamlet cigar ad always aimed for a strictly emotional appeal ('Happiness is a cigar called Hamlet'). Even though that ad hasn't been on the box for years, we bet many of you can still hear the music as you read that line.

Some marketers measure their TV ads based on warmth. Research firms generally define warmth as the good feelings generated from thinking about love, family or friendship. Although you may not need to go into the details of how researchers measure warmth, noting *why* people measure it can help you. Emotions, especially positive ones, make TV ad messages far more memorable. Many marketers don't realise the strength of this emotional effect because you can't pick it up in the standard measures of ad recall. In day-after recall tests, viewers recall emotional-appeal TV ads about as easily as rational-appeal ads. But in-depth studies of the effectiveness of each kind of ad tend to show that the more emotionally charged ads do a better job of etching the message and branding identity in viewers' minds.

So when you think TV advertising, think emotion. Evoking emotion is what TV can do – often better than any other media, because it can showcase the expressiveness of actors and faces – and emotion makes for highly effective advertising.

Showing your message

Be sure to take full advantage of TV's other great strength: its ability to show. You can demonstrate a product feature, show a product in use and do a thousand other things just with your visuals.

Actually, in any ad medium, you want to show as well as tell. (Even in radio, you can create mental images to show the audience what you want them to see; see 'Creating Ads for Radio' earlier in this chapter.) The visual and verbal modes reinforce each other. And some people in your audience think visually while others favour a verbal message, so you have to cover both bases by using words and images in your advertising. But in TV, you have to adapt this rule: the TV ad should *show* and tell (note the emphasis on showing). Compare this scenario with radio, where you show by telling; or print, where the two modes balance each other out, so the rule becomes simply to show and tell.

Because of this emphasis on showing, TV ad designers rough out their ideas in a visually-orientated script, using quick sketches to indicate how the ad will look. You – or preferably the competent agency or scriptwriter you hire – need to prepare rough storyboards as you think through and discuss various ad concepts. A *storyboard* is an easy way to show the key visual images of film, using pictures in sequence. The sketches run down the centre of a sheet of paper or poster board in most standard storyboard layouts. On the left, you write notes about how to shoot each image, how to use music and sound effects, and whether to superimpose text on the screen. On the right, you include a rough version of the *script* (the words actors in the scenes or in a voice-over say). See Figure 9-1 for an example storyboard.

Considering style

You can use a great variety of styles in TV advertising. A celebrity can endorse the product. Fruit modelled from clay (claymation) can sing and dance about it. Animated animals can chase a user through the jungle in a fanciful exaggeration of a real-life situation. Imagination and videotape know no limits, especially with the growing availability of high-quality computerised animation and special effects at a reasonable cost. But some of the common styles work better – on average – than others in tests of ad effectiveness. Table 9-1 shows styles that are more and less effective.

VIDEO		AUDIO
Lightning and thunder. Rabbit pops out of top hat. Zoom in.		Surprise!
Cut to dark room. Lights come up on birthday party. Zoom in on cake.		Many voices: Surprise!
Cut to dark; sudden flash of lightning illuminates new product. Zoom in.		Even more voices: SURPRISE!
Inset product in slide.	(SLIDE) Company name and logo	ANNCR: Until you try the new *** from ***, you don't know what a surprise is!

Figure 9-1:
Roughing out a TV ad on a story-board.

Table 9-1   It Don't Mean a Thing If It Ain't Got That Swing

More Effective Styles	*Less Effective Styles*
Humorous commercials	Candid-camera style testimonials
Celebrity spokespeople	Expert endorsements
Commercials with children	Song/dance and musical themes
Real-life scenarios	Product demonstrations
Brand comparisons	

Most studies show that the humour and celebrity endorsement styles work best. So try to find ways to use these styles to communicate your message. On the other hand, making ads that are the exception to the rule may give you an edge, so don't give up hope on other styles.

For a great example of exceptions to the rule, consider the Cadbury's iconic ad featuring a drumming gorilla. On the face of it, this scenario doesn't have a great deal to do with chocolate. However, this ad has great standout value, uses music (retro Phil Collins) and imagery (gorilla and purple background) together in a very powerful way. Despite not being obviously to do with chocolate, it's easily one of the most memorable ads of the past few years.

Buying airtime on TV

Which television stations work best for your ad? Should you advertise on a national (*terrestrial*) or digital channel? Should the ad run in prime time, evening or late night-time slots? What programmes provide the best audience for your ad?

The UK's main provider of TV audience measurement is BARB (Broadcasters' Audience Research Board; www.barb.co.uk). BARB is a not-for-profit organisation owned jointly by the BBC, ITV, Channel 4, Five, BskyB and the Institute of Practitioners in Advertising (IPA). It keeps track of how many people are watching which channel (and TV programme) by installing homes around the country with a little black box that sits on top of the TV. Although BARB is not for profit, you can't get this data for free. An annual subscription will cost you upwards of £6840, so consider whether you really need that depth of data. For instance, if you're trying to sell gardening products to amateur gardeners and know that you're only interested in home-improvement TV programmes, the channels themselves can give you the viewing figures you need.

Some of BARB's biggest customers are the ad and media-buying agencies, so if you're using an agency to buy your airtime or create your ad, asking them for media data before getting out your own credit card is worthwhile.

Working out the cost of a TV ad

Several different factors affect how much you'll pay for a TV advertising campaign.

The first, and most important, bit of jargon you need to know is *TVRs*, which means television ratings. Audience delivery is measured in TVRs, which can be confusing but has the merit of giving you an idea of how many people in a particular target audience will see your ad. Knowledge of target audiences is important to avoid wasting money advertising to people who're unlikely to buy your product. A TVR is defined as the percentage of a particular audience that has seen a piece of TV content (although they may have spent an ad break talking to their partner or making the tea, so this figure is always an approximation). So, for example, if *Coronation Street* achieved a Housewives TVR of 20 in Yorkshire, this means that 20 per cent of all housewives in the Yorkshire region watched the soap opera.

You can actually get a TVR for your ad that's higher than 100 per cent, which means that a viewer may see your ad more than once and each viewing is counted separately. The actual number of times viewers are exposed to a commercial break is called *impacts*. If you think that repeat viewing is important to your campaign, these can be useful programmes or times of the day to target.

Identifying your target audience

You can choose any of the target audiences, shown in the following list, that are commonly sold by broadcasters. Heavy TV viewers such as housewives or general audiences are usually cheaper to buy because they're easier to reach than audiences such as upmarket men.

Adults

16- to 34-year-old adults

ABC1 (upmarket) adults

Men

16- to 34-year-old men

ABC1 men

Women

16- to 34-year-old women

ABC1 women

Housewives

Housewives and children

ABC1 housewives

Children

Timing your broadcast

The size and type of audience likely to see your ad is governed by the time of day it appears – so that factor will also affect how much you pay. Broadcasters call these *dayparts*, and they're broadly timed as follows:

Daytime 6am–5.29pm

Early peak 5.30–7.29pm

Late peak 7.30–11pm

Night-time 11.01pm–5.59am

Some broadcasters may break down these day-parts even further, adding in such elements as 'breakfast time' or 'lunchtime' during the day. The highest price you'll usually pay is for the highest audience – in peak time, between 5.30pm and 11pm, although again this timing can vary.

Remembering other factors

You also need to factor in a few other variables to the cost of your ad:

- ✔ **The length of your commercial:** Airtime is sold in multiples of 10 seconds, with 30 seconds being the most common ad length.

- ✔ **What time of year you need to advertise:** If you're in the business of selling Christmas gifts, you'll pay considerably more for airtime than if you can advertise in the cheaper months of January, February, March and August.

- ✔ **Size of the region you advertise in:** Prices also vary by *macro region*, which reflects the size of the local population and relative demand. The highest advertiser demand is for London, which makes it the most expensive. If you operate outside London, however, targeting the precise areas where you're based, such as Yorkshire or Tyne-Tees, may be more cost-effective. Some TV macro regions can even be split into *micro regions*. So if your business is in the East Anglia area, for instance, you can buy just that small part of the larger Anglia macro region, giving you tighter targeting and better value for money. TV marketing body Thinkbox (www.thinkbox.tv) provides a good explanation of how the regions are broken down; click on 'Planning', then 'Targeting', then 'Regional TV'.

Because of the complexity of some of these calculations, think hard about using a media agency to plan and buy the airtime. You can let a media agency know what you're trying to achieve with your ad and what type of people you need to target and then let their experts do the rest. Many of these agencies buy up chunks of airtime in advance, so you benefit from an agency-wide deal and don't have to negotiate individually with the TV sales houses. Media agencies can also advise you on TV opportunities you may not have previously considered.

Making your own TV (or radio) programme

A lot of TV and radio ads exist out there and yours is in constant danger of becoming just one of the many that people are exposed to and, increasingly, try to avoid. You don't want your ad to be the one that makes the viewer leave the room to make the tea. The following sections give you a few alternative strategies to consider.

Using advertiser-funded programming (AFP)

The experts have come up with a new term, *branded content*, to describe something that's not quite an ad but which can be used to communicate a commercial message. In TV and radio, branded content means creating your own show (or at least, segment of a show) – the official term for which is *advertiser-funded programming* or *AFP*. This type of communication is becoming increasingly frequent, although many restrictions are still in place about what you can or cannot say about your product. But asking your agency, or the radio stations and channels themselves, about these opportunities is worthwhile because they allow your message to stand out from the clutter of all the other ads.

Screened on Five, Chinese Food in Minutes is just one recent example of AFP. It features chef Ching-He Huang preparing Chinese dishes that bring food most commonly eaten in restaurants into people's own kitchens. Chinese Food in Minutes is funded by the food company Sharwoods.

This type of communication is generating a lot of excitement because it allows advertisers to give viewers something they want (entertainment) rather than something many of them don't (ads).

The real benefit of AFP is that you can give viewers *relevant content* or information that's close to your product or service. Sharwoods uses the show to promote its own products to the audience, as well as suggest new occasions and recipes for which they're ideal.

The recent change in rules about product placement means that companies can get closer to the editorial agenda of a show than ever before. Brands can now use product placement in shows – except news or children's programmes – as long as they meet Ofcom's rules (check them out at `http://consumers.ofcom.org.uk/2011/02/product-placement-on-tv/`).

While Heinz nearly got fined by the TV regulators for showing recipes using baked beans and spaghetti hoops when it ran a show called *Dinner Doctors* on Five in 2003, it is notable that Sharwoods now hosts a section called 'Sharwoods Recipes' on Five's *Chinese Food in Minutes* website. Over 1.3 million people clicked through from Five to Sharwoods's own site and the brand's sales went up by 4 per cent year-on-year. Far more scope for brands to get involved with TV exists these days.

Sponsoring a TV or radio programme

If AFP is still at a relatively early stage, then sponsorship must be centre stage. Alright, you don't quite get your own TV or radio programme, but if you find a show that's a good fit with your product, this route's almost as good (and a lot less risky).

TV and radio sponsorship is growing fast in the UK as advertisers try to avoid the dual issues of ad clutter and digital personal video recorders (PVRs) such as Sky+, BT Vision and TiVo, which allow viewers to skip through the ad break. You don't need us to tell you that TV and radio sponsorship is growing – you'll have seen it for yourself. TV sponsorship is already believed to be worth more than £200 million and this figure is set to increase.

Turn on your telly and you'll see *The TV Book Club*, brought to you by Specsavers and *The X Factor*, sponsored by TalkTalk. These brands are clearly relevant to the programmes they sponsor.

While TalkTalk's sponsorship of *The X Factor* is rumoured to be worth around £20 million over three years, you don't need to pay anything like this amount. You can find relevant programmes at less popular times of the day or on digital channels for a sponsorship price of around £150,000.

Advertising on interactive TV

Interactive TV advertising has more in common with traditional spot TV advertising, but we include it here because, if you can get viewers to press the red button on their remote control, you can take them away from the mainstream TV environment and into your own dedicated space. This ability represents both the opportunity presented by and the main problem with this medium.

Interactive TV advertising gives you a lot of opportunities to do things a traditional 30-second spot won't. You can give additional product information, issue a call to action (such as requesting a brochure) or capture your prospective customers' data. You can even fulfil a transaction entirely using interactive TV ads. An additional cost for constructing the microsite and capturing the data (upward of £100,000) is entailed, though, on top of the cost of the airtime for the ad itself. The benefit of interactive TV ads is that you get real, measurable customer transactions resulting from your investment – something that traditional TV advertising can't always deliver.

The drawback is that the viewer is actually watching TV to see a certain programme and so may not want to be distracted by going off into an advertiser controlled environment in case they miss the start of the next part of the show. This market is still developing and trials of 'red button' advertising that loads information 'behind' the viewed show, to be watched later, seems promising.

Advertising online

Television is no longer confined to the box in the corner of the living room; it also appears on your computer. You may think the computer is a relatively small market but nearly 6 billion video viewing sessions occurred online in

March 2011 in the US alone. Meanwhile, according to a 2011 Accenture study, viewing video on laptops is up by 35 per cent, use of desktop computers has risen by 28 per cent and internet-enabled TV is up by 26 per cent.

Multiple TV streaming and download channels are now available for all the main broadcasters on terrestrial television and web-only channels such as Babelgum and Joost also exist. Google TV and a new service called YouView are also planning launches into this area in 2012 so it's likely to get more crowded in future. As these are still relatively new media channels, you may find opportunities to get involved with sponsorship or advertising at a lower cost than with normal TV. And if you're targeting young people who use the web a lot, this medium may be the best place to promote your products or services.

Even if you don't have the budget or know how to appear on an online TV channel, why not consider using video site YouTube? (See more on other types of social marketing in Chapter 12.) You can post a version of your ad on the site, create a little trailer to promote your product or even just come up with a humorous spot to generate interest. If your product needs some explaining or assembling, why not create a 'how-to' video? You may be surprised by how many people find a demonstration useful and how offering one may bring publicity to your company through sites such as YouTube and www.videojug.com.

Even huge brands use YouTube to generate interest in their products and marketing. The American Super Bowl, during which the biggest and most expensive ads are shown each year, even has its own branded channel on YouTube! People can see the ads, post their own spoofs and leave comments. YouTube offers a tool for research, feedback and promotion all in one. Just make sure that you monitor any responses to your promotional work carefully!

Part IV
Powerful Alternatives to Advertising

'In your marketing plan, you said you wouldn't spend unnecessarily. I thought that only applied to your business!'

In this part . . .

In marketing, the goals never really change. This year's crop of marketers are no more nor less eager to find new customers and grow our revenues than were last year's or last decade's marketers.

But the means of achieving these goals can and do change. You should always look for alternatives and fresh approaches. You especially have to stay on top of your game in today's advertising because entirely new ways of communicating with customers and prospects have emerged in the last couple of decades. Marketers no longer need to feel confined to traditional advertising. Corporate websites, social networks, e-mail, paid listings on search engines and many more innovations are transforming marketing.

In addition, we highly recommend that you explore the power of publicity and of events in your marketing area. Sometimes, these approaches can be more effective than anything else in the entire field of marketing, yet marketers traditionally give them little thought and funding in most companies.

You can, in fact, design an effective marketing programme for any business that completely skips conventional advertising and substitutes one or more of the many alternative media instead.

Chapter 10

Digital Marketing

· ·

· ·

*W*hat does digital marketing make you think of? Websites and the Internet, yes. But digital or e-marketing includes online advertising, email and also using text, pictures or even video to reach customers through their mobile phones. These digital tools have opened up lots of new ways to help you sell your products or services. Even better, a lot of these tools are cheaper and certainly more cost-effective than traditional advertising using press or TV.

Nearly every month it seems a new way to communicate with customers using digital media emerges. The market is indeed rapidly evolving but for most marketers, waiting a while before jumping in to the newest techniques is safest, as they can be untried and possibly aggravating to the very people you're trying to win over if you don't execute them well. However, if used properly, many of these techniques can prove immensely valuable and have been particularly effective in opening up markets for smaller businesses.

According to the communications regulator Ofcom, 74 per cent of UK homes are now online using broadband, and more than 27 per cent of UK adults now own a smartphone that can access the Internet. These figures mean that, however much or little you spend on digital marketing, you have to find a space for it in your marketing budget. For that reason, this chapter covers just what you need to know to begin your digital adventures.

Reaching Out with a Website

Digital marketing changes fast and often and changing with it is essential. To be a part of the revolution, you need to create a website for your business.

The same Ofcom Communications Report that monitors broadband usage also shows that watching television is the dominant regular media activity, both for those aged 16–24 and those aged 75+, but there is significant variation across other measures. The most marked difference between the age groups is in use of the Internet via a computer or laptop – 83 per cent of 16–24 year olds said they did o regularly, compared to just 13 per cent of those aged 75 and over.

You'd certainly advertise on TV if your budget stretched to it, but not every-one's does, so you need to have a presence on the other most-used medium. Importantly, advertising online is something you can afford to do. In fact, you can't afford not to!

Gaining a web presence is relatively easy. Sometimes doing so can be as simple as getting a listing on an online business directory covering your area, so that when consumers key in your company name or look for the type of services you offer using a search engine such as Google, they can find your address and phone number. We strongly believe that every business – including yours – needs a website, even if all it does is provide your contact details and opening hours. You can think of your website as a shop window where potential customers from all over the world can look at the products or services you offer. You can even turn this site into an actual shop. Having a transactional website can be one of the lowest-cost ways to expand geographi-cally without having to move out of your neighbourhood (it's not called the World Wide Web for nothing, you know!).

A good website can bring in customers who would never find your product or service were it not for the Internet. So spending some time and money creating a decent website to attract them is worthwhile.

You need a unique and memorable website address and an easy to use and appealing design (doubly so, if you intend creating a *transactional site* where customers can buy products or services using a credit or debit card). The following sections cover what you need to know. Of course, you also need to think about how customers will find your site out of the millions in existence, which we cover in Chapter 11.

Choosing a web address

First you need to find and register a web address (also known as a *domain name* or *URL*). Unless you're starting a business from scratch, you probably already have a web address in mind that you want to use. Your web address should be as close as you can possibly get to the name of your business or, if you need a site for each of your products and services, it should relate closely to them. You may think this detail sounds obvious, but we see too many web addresses falling into the trap of having little to do with the parent business (usually because the most obvious name is being used by someone else; see 'Checking your name's availability' later in this chapter).

As you search for potential web addresses, keep the following points in mind to ensure you end up with the best name for your site:

- ✔ **A good address relates to your business or product:** The web address www.streetpavedwithgold.com is available to register, along with all of the other main name extensions. The address is catchy and amusing. Should you rush off and register it? Not if it fails this first test: does the name relate to your product or service? Remember, being relevant is better than being clever.

- ✔ **A good name is memorable:** Customers should be able to remember your web address easily. That doesn't mean you have to register any-thing stunningly cool or clever – and besides, if the web address is obscure, people are less likely to remember it. Using your company name makes the site memorable to anyone who knows the name of your business. You can easily remember that IKEA's web address is www.ikea.com. But you can just as easily combine two or three easy words and make a string into a memorable address. An online competitor to IKEA in the UK is the very simply named www.thisisfurniture.com.

- ✔ **A good name isn't easily confused with other addresses:** If consumers can easily mix up your site with similar addresses, some will go to the wrong site by accident. If your company name is a common word or is similar to others, add an extra term or word to your web address to distinguish it. For example, Triumph is a brand name that the lingerie maker and the motorcycle manufacturer have equal claim to. Although customers are unlikely to mistake one brand for the other, they could easily find themselves on the wrong website. As a result, the motorbike brand trades from www.triumphmotorcycles.com while Triumph International uses www.triumph.com.

- ✔ **A good name doesn't violate trademarks:** You don't want to bump into someone's trademark by accident. Legal rights now favour the trademark holder rather than the domain-name holder – putting an end to the ugly practice of 'cyber-squatting' that existed a few years ago. To be sure that you don't inadvertently step on someone else's toes, check any web address against a database of trademarks. The Intellectual Property Office provides a searchable database at www.ipo.gov.uk but if you think you may run into a problem, ask a lawyer to do a more detailed analysis. We cover trademark law in Chapter 17.

Checking your name's availability

Picking a name is the easy part. The tricky part is finding out whether that name's available and then getting creative if you find out it's not.

Check a domain name's availability by typing it into the web browser to seeing if someone already has it. If you want to check out if a domain name is available in a number of extensions, sites exist to help you.

Any good provider of web services will have its own site that allows you to check on the availability of a web address. One such provider is `www.network solutions.com`, the administrator of the *.com* domain name extension, but you can just type in 'domain names' and pick any of the companies that offer registration services. The service you need will be on the homepage of any of these sites; just remember to check your preferred address against all of the main extensions – *.com*, *.co.uk*, *.net* or *.org* are among the most desirable, as people remember them first.

Interestingly, `www.networksolutions.com/whois/index.jsp` gives you information on who owns a domain name, so if a URL fits your business perfectly, you could always offer that person some money to hand it over!

In the best of all possible worlds, your web name search will reveal that your name is free. If that's the case, thank your lucky stars, jump up and down and make a few happy noises. Then register your name. The section 'Registering your site name' tells you how. But, as few of us live in the best of all possible worlds, you're more likely to find that your name is already taken. In that case, don't despair. You still have options and, depending on which avenue you take, you may still get to use your name.

If someone has registered the name you want with one or most of the main extensions, but left the more obscure *.biz, .org.uk* or even *.me.uk* extensions, seeking another name is wisest because customers could forget your extension and go to someone else's site instead. If the other businesses using the extensions are selling similar products to yours, in the same country, people may be confused, so choosing another name is crucial.

When the web's an important sales route for your business, aim to own most or all of the possible extensions and versions of your web address.

If the person who owns the rights to your web address isn't willing to sell it, consider going back to the drawing board and finding another name that isn't being held hostage. Many online operators are looking to make easy money by buying up web addresses for the purpose of selling them at a profit.

Other routes can help you secure the name you want. Many sites that were registered in the frenzy of the dotcom boom eventually come back on to the open market because they were never used or because the original registrar forgot to re-register. When this happens, the web address becomes *detagged*. Alternatively, if you believe you have a stronger or more legitimate claim to a web address than someone else, you can use a disputes resolution service, or even legal action, to make them give the name up. For information on detagging and disputes, visit Nominet at www.nominet.org.uk, which is officially recognised as the *.uk* name registry by the industry and government.

Registering your site name

After you ensure that your web address is available, you're ready to register your name. Doing so is inexpensive, and the process is simple. The example we give here is based on the provider easily.co.uk, which charges £25 to register a *.com*, *.org* or *.net* address for two years, or £8.99 to register a .uk address. All you need to do is type in the domain name you want, and the site tells you which extensions are available (if any aren't, you can also see who owns them). Highlight all the extensions you want and then get out your credit card. The process is as easy as that – and easily.co.uk will even email you a reminder when the address needs to be renewed.

You can use any provider to register your web address and some are half as cheap as the example we give here. The only thing to stop you going for the cheapest price is to consider whether you also want the provider to *host* the site (meaning to provide the server space where your site resides on the web). You can transfer web addresses to another provider after the event, but it' is simpler (and sometimes cheaper) to find the right provider for your needs in the first place.

If consumers may get confused by alternate spellings or mis-spellings of your domain name, register them too. Registering a name is cheap, so don't lose a prospective customer just because they can't spell your name. You can always redirect them from a mis-spelt URL to your website – if you don't, your competitors may view this mistake as an easy way to steal potential customers from you.

Creating a Compelling Website

Designing good web pages is a key marketing skill, because your website is at the centre of all you do to market online. Also, increasingly, websites are at the heart of companies' marketing – businesses put their Internet addresses on every marketing communication, from company pens to letterheads and business cards, and in ads, brochures and catalogues. Serious shoppers will visit your website to find out more about what you offer, so make sure your site is ready to close the sale. Include excellent, clear design, along with plenty of information to answer likely questions and move visitors toward a purchase. Websites have earned their place in the core of any marketing activity. If you're a consumer-orientated marketer, you want your website to be friendly and easily navigated, as well as to do the following:

- ✒ Engage existing customers, giving them reasons to feel good about their past purchases and connect with your company and other consumers (at least to connect emotionally, if not in actual fact).

- ✒ Share interesting and frequently updated information about your products or services, industry and organisation on the site, so the consumer can gain useful knowledge by visiting it.

- ✒ Maintain a section of the site or a dedicated site for business-to-business (B2B) relationships that matter to your marketing (such as distributors, stores and sales reps).

Finding resources to help with design

You can easily create a basic website – one that includes your contact details plus a few pages showing what your business does – on your own. Doing so is the simplest and cheapest route to create a web presence, if all you need is to let customers know where to find you and why they should get in touch. If your needs are more advanced and you want customers to be able to buy direct from your site, for example, skip down to the section on 'Hiring a professional designer'. This section doesn't cover how to use authoring languages or do any of the programming. That information would fill an entire book, not a chapter, let alone a section. If you decide to create a sophisticated website yourself, you can find excellent books that do go into all the details.

If you want to create your own web pages, we recommend, in particular, *Creating Web Pages All-in-One Desk Reference For Dummies* by Richard Mansfield and Richard Wagner (Wiley). It goes a bit deeper than the also good *Creating Web Pages For Dummies* by Bud E. Smith and Arthur Bebak (also by Wiley). These two titles cover the range in both price and detail, so take your pick. If you like tinkering, you can certainly build your own web pages using web authoring software such as FrontPage or Dreamweaver and contract with a web provider to put them up.

You can find a provider to host your site quite easily, and searching the web is the best place to start. Just pick one that offers the fee structure, services and flexibility you want at the right price – and change providers if they don't satisfy.

Consider using your domain name and provider to create your own email addresses, too. An example is jane@janesmithflowers.com if your website is www.janesmithflowers.com. Having your email reflecting your own website URL looks so much more professional than going through a public domain does. An email like jane@janesmithflowers.com looks much better than using janesmithflowers@yahoo.co.uk.

Hiring a professional designer

If you aren't a do-it-yourselfer, a very easy way to create good web pages is available: find an expert who can do it for you under contract.

Good website design is harder than it looks and going to a reputable design firm and asking them to do it for you is probably best. We recommend a business relationship (spelled out on paper in advance) that specifies that you, not they, own all content and designs at the end (so that you can switch to another vendor if it doesn't work out or they go bust) and also specifies an hourly rate and an estimate of the site's size and complexity, with a cap on the number of billable hours needed to design it.

You can expect to pay anything from £750 for a basic brochure-style website of ten pages to upwards of £50,000 for a Flash-animated fully transactional (or e-commerce) one. That's quite a range, even for custom-designed pages, so here's a basic list of what you can expect to get, and for what price:

✔ If you have no budget at all – not even £25 – you can always use a free blog site service such as Wordpress, Tumblr or Blogger to make a very basic updatable site. This option allows you to post stories and makes your contact details available for Internet users. But bear in mind that this site will look very homemade and amateur, so is probably only an option if you really have no other alternatives and are prepared to update it regularly.

✔ You can get a simple template-style website for as little as £50 from some of the web providers that register domain names and host websites, or with web authoring software programs like FrontPage and Dreamweaver. Some programs are quite good, but people often recognise these one-size-fits-all designs, which may lower their opinion of your site design.

✔ For a basic, custom-designed site, where you provide a company logo, images and copy, plan to spend around £750 to £1500. A dedicated *Content Management System* (*CMS*) costs around £2000 to £2500. You can get a web designer to arrange web hosting set up, too. A basic hosting plan costs around £50 to £100 per year, which includes domain name registration.

✔ A more advanced site with a custom look built around your logo, and which contains navigation suited to the service or product that you're offering, will cost from £3500 upwards (although here the price starts climbing depending on what bells and whistles you want to add on). The customised graphics and stock photography necessary for these sites can also drive up your costs, but if your online presence needs this unique, professional look to set you apart from your competitors, then the money may well be worth it.

Beyond the cost of the site, you also need to be aware of additional costs that you may incur – or that you should budget for – in order to enhance the professional appearance and functionality of your website:

✔ Consider an online shopping trolley, for an extra £300 to £500 on top of your bespoke site design. Many basic hosting plans include a shopping trolley, so you can implement this feature fairly easily by using theirs (but you lose out on the custom-look website). Assume that you'll be adding products over time, so select a shopping trolley that gives you room to grow.

✔ Consider streaming video, animation and database management. You can use these technologies as important delivery methods, like showing a speaker in action, demonstrating a new product or providing services, and supporting the consumer online.

✔ Build some room for photography into your budget because sites with relevant images – especially of real people – are graphically more appealing and hold the visitor's attention longer. We highly recommend using photographs in most sites.

✔ Get your contractor to provide monthly maintenance (web designers charge around £70 per hour) because keeping your site working is the same as ensuring your car is roadworthy

✔ Plan to spend your own time keeping your site content fresh, which will help to attract new customers and retain existing ones.

Developing a registration service

Many sites used to have a registration system for consumers to complete to gain access to the website. Now nearly all sites give free access to everyone and, in the case of sites with content such as stories or video, they make their money through advertising instead.

Don't create a site that needs the user to register to gain access to basic information – after all, you want to sell something to them, so why stop them from looking at the produce? We know that creating a free registration hurdle in order to collect their information for future marketing purposes is tempting, but in the long run, this tactic is the wrong way to go about getting hold of this valuable data.

Instead, a handy trick is to offer some extra content – the latest product updates, exclusive content or a weekly newsletter – in order to get your customers to sign up with their details. All online businesses want to find out who their customers are because this information allows them to target them more effectively with products and services; these days, however, accessing customer details is more likely to put off Internet users than bring you any benefit unless you're offering something extra.

Driving traffic with content

Most websites are really just huge, interactive advertisements or sales promotions. After a while, even the most cleverly designed ad gets boring. To increase the length of time users spend with your materials and to ensure high involvement and return visits, you need to think like a publisher and not just an advertiser. For this reason, we consider web content to be the hidden factor for increasing site traffic. Unless you have valuable and appealing content, you may have difficulty building up traffic on your site.

Make sure you offer information and entertainment. People like to use the web for research. Often, that research relates to a purchase decision. To be part of that research and purchase process, put useful, non-commercial information on your site. B&Q, the home improvement retailer, strikes a nice balance between online sales and DIY adviser. Its site, at www.diy.com, lists all its major product lines as you'd expect, but also offers a useful 'DIY advice' area that provides step-by-step instructions on everything from designing your own garden to tiling a wall. Professional services firms can get in on the act, too. If you're a law firm, why not offer some simple, downloadable legal guides for the public? Keep these updated so that people always have a reason to visit.

Tracking Your Site's Traffic

The web offers an unmatched ability to evaluate how effectively your marketing is working and to capture information on the people who are visiting your site. Compared with other media, digital marketing is entirely transparent – meaning you can see how many visitors you get and, if they register for more information on your site, who they are. Make the most of this rare opportunity to measure the impact of your expenditure.

Google Analytics is the most widely used analytics service online because it's free and offers lots of data on your website's traffic – such as visitors' geographic location, what they view on your site and how long they stay there. Visit www.google.com/analytics/.

You can evaluate performance of web advertising every day or week, and get statistics on each and every ad that you run. So use this data intelligently to experiment and adjust your approach. Aim to increase both the quantity and the quality of clicks week by week throughout your marketing campaign and track the impact on enquiries and sales.

Paying attention to your site's visitors

Each time someone visits your website, they're exhibiting interest in you and your products (or they're lost, which is less likely if your site is aptly named and clearly designed so that no one can confuse it with unrelated types of business). And someone exhibiting interest makes them interesting to you. So whatever you do, however you go about setting up a site, make sure that you capture information about your visitors in a useful form that gets sent to you regularly.

Ask your web provider what kinds of reports they can offer you – probably more than you imagined possible. With these reports in hand, you can track traffic to your site. You probably notice that you, unlike the giants of the web, don't have as much traffic as you may want. Sure, millions of people use Google to do searches or go to eBay to bid on auctioned products. But the average website only has a few dozen visitors a day. For an effective site, you need to build up this traffic at least into thousands of visitors per day, at least. How? By making sure it gets noticed in search engines. See Chapter 11 for more on getting picked up by search engines.

Designing and Placing a Banner Ad

A lot has changed in just a few years in Internet advertising. You can see how quickly things have moved on just by looking at what's happened to the most common form of online advertising – the *banner ad*. A banner used to be the only format for online advertising. That traditional format still exists, but for many marketers 'banner' has become a generic term for a whole host of different online ad formats.

We've jumped from one-size-fits-all banners, through as many different types of ad formats as you could wish for, and have come out at the other end with a selection of standard sizes that fit the needs of most advertisers. The *Universal Advertising Package (UAP)*, as its creators at the Internet Advertising Bureau (IAB) call it, comprises a banner (running across the top of a web page), skyscraper, large rectangle and regular rectangle. You can find out all about the technical specifications for UAP formats at the IAB's website (`www.iabuk.net`).

UAP formats make the whole process of buying online advertising much more cost-effective. You should pay less for the production of an online campaign if you don't have to re-create your ad for each website you advertise on, and you can compare costs of online ad space more easily if you're comparing like with like – rather than apples with oranges, as was the case before.

Hiring a web media service

Companies providing *web media services* (meaning web page design) can also design and place banner ads and pop-up ads for you. Searching for agencies or individuals to do this work for you can be a long and random process, however. If you're lucky enough to know a competent web designer or programmer, seriously consider using their services – they can create custom banners to your specification quite easily because they're such a small ad format.

If you have more ambitious plans for rich media online ads, however, you'll need to study the extensive field. We recommend you go straight to the Internet Advertising Bureau website (www.iabuk.net) and visit the membership directory section. In this section, you'll find companies offering every kind of web media service, from ad server and online campaign analysis to website design. Listed under 'creative agencies' alone are 50 suppliers, from Advertising.com to Zenith Optimedia.

While the larger (and more expensive) agencies are well represented in the IAB membership, finding cheaper, local assistance is possible if you're prepared to put in the leg work. The best place to start this research is to Google for relevant services in your area or to check local directories such as the *Yellow Pages* or its online incarnation, www.Yell.com.

Creating your own banner ad

Creating your own banner ads is a relatively easy process, particularly if you've designed your own website and are familiar with HTML coding. Basic banner ads can be created using off-the-shelf design software such as Photoshop or Paint Shop Pro. Not surprisingly, the web is a good starting point for finding templates for banner ads. Because the format is now so common, a lot of sites allow you to use their standard designs for free. One of the best known is AdDesigner.com (you can guess the web address), which makes designing a professional looking animated banner ad within minutes easy. We can't see why any marketer planning a small-scale online campaign would take anything other than the DIY route, given the high standards of these templates, but if you're really not keen on having a go, searching for one of the many factory-orientated banner ad designers that can make you an ad quickly and for less than £50 is just as simple.

Focusing on a simple design

The best design for starters is a banner that flashes a simple one-line offer or headline statement, shows an image of your logo or product and then switches to a couple more lines of text explaining what to do and why to do it ('Click here to take advantage of our introductory offer for small business owners and get 20% off your first order of . . . ').

You want your ad to be simple and bold – able to attract the viewer's attention from desired information elsewhere on the screen for long enough to make a simple point.

This ad style delivers a clear marketing message using both print and illustration. Make sure that, if prospects click on the banner, they go directly to a page on your website that supports the product or service with more information and offers several easy purchase options.

Being positively creative with your ad

Online advertising, done well, can do many more tasks for you than a TV ad, press ad or poster. For a start, users who click on your ad can be delivered directly to your transactional website. Job done (well, almost – see 'Creating a Compelling Website' earlier in this chapter). An online ad can be tactical, by alerting customers to a special offer, or it can help with brand-building, by raising awareness of your product or service without a clear call to action. Unlike TV or press ads, you (or the size of your budget) control how intrusive your ad becomes.

Why would you want any web user to miss an ad you're paying good money for? Obviously, you wouldn't. So be careful about the gimmicks your ad uses. Case in point: bells-and-whistles online advertising gimmickry (or *rich media*, as the experts call it). With this type of media, you can buy an ad that totally obscures a page someone's trying to view, that chases their cursor around the screen, and basically forces them either to pay attention or close it. That technology runs contrary to every other trend in the advertiser–customer relationship, which is why this tactic has fallen out of favour in recent years. Instead, create some eye-catching online ad designs that integrate with the web page they appear on and don't irritate potential customers.

Placing your banner ads

Designing the banner is just the beginning because you then have to buy space to display it from publishers. If you poke around on large sites like Yahoo! or Google, you can find sections devoted to advertisers like you, where you can explore ad buying options and rates and ask for help from a salesperson. Alternatively, you can go to an online media-buying agency and hire them to do the placement. These agencies take a small commission but probably more than make up for this loss by knowing where to place the ads to target your core customer base, negotiating better rates and avoiding some of the inflation of exposure numbers that can happen when you have to rely on the publisher's accounting.

Placing a banner ad typically costs between £1 and £5 per thousand viewers, depending on where it's placed – not bad if you have an ad that actually generates some responses. But watch the banner ad closely and pull or modify it, or try running it elsewhere, if the click rate is too low to justify the cost. You may have to try a few versions to get it right, but with the rapid feedback possible on the web, this experimentation can take place fairly quickly and inexpensively.

If you're planning to do things on a smaller scale, simply find the sites you wish to advertise on, ring them up and negotiate a good rate.

Interpreting click statistics

You may find click-through statistics a useful and easy-to-get indicator of how well an ad or search-engine placement is performing. If you get a lot of people clicking through to your site from an ad or placement, that ad is clearly doing its job of attracting traffic for you. So, all else being equal, more clicks are better. However, all else isn't equal all of the time. Here are a few wrinkles to keep in mind when interpreting click rates:

- ✔ When a pop-up ad appears, the companies you buy the ad space from usually report it as a click. But don't believe the numbers because you have no indication that someone actually read or acted on that pop-up – they may have just closed it without looking. Dig deeper into the statistics from whoever sold you that pop-up ad to find out how it actually performed. You can probably get some more detailed data if you ask, but you need more than the simple click count.

- ✔ Some ads have multiple elements that load in sequence, creating a countable click with each loading, so that one ad may generate several click-through counts. This counting method may lead you to think that the more complex ad is better, but the higher number can be an artifact of the way those who sell ad space on the web count the clicks. (Ask your provider if it can sell web ad space to you, or visit a really popular site and look for the section offering ad space to advertisers.)

- ✔ Quality is more important than quantity. Who are these people who clicked to your site? That information is harder to obtain but more important. Getting 10,000 clicks in a week is nice – but do they include relevant and active prospects? Only by digging into detailed reports on who goes where and looks at what on your website, plus information on what types of emailed questions you receive and the average order size per week, can you really begin to evaluate the quality of those clicks. See the 'Paying attention to your site's visitors' section earlier in this chapter for details on how to find out who's visiting your site.

If you're generating poor quality traffic, experiment with putting ads in other places or redesign your ads to specifically focus on your desired target. Keep working on it until you achieve the best click-through rates, regardless of numbers.

You can evaluate web advertising performance every day or week, and get statistics on each and every ad that you run. So use this data intelligently to experiment and adjust your approach. Aim to increase both the quantity and the quality of clicks week by week throughout your marketing campaign and track the impact on enquiries and sales.

Getting Others to Do the Work: Affiliate Marketing

Affiliate marketing is another term for 'finder's fees' or 'lead fees'.

Affiliate marketing programmes work by rewarding websites that deliver users to other websites. Affiliate programmes are usually used by online retailers who pay the referring website a fee for every consumer that completes a certain function, such as purchasing or signing up for something. Although early affiliate deals rewarded on a click basis, so that every click that went through to the destination was paid for, this system has changed in recent years and nearly always uses a performance-based remuneration model – so, as an advertiser, you only pay if you make money. Brilliant!

Carried out correctly, affiliate marketing can be a remarkably effective method for advertisers to get people to their site to buy things. Its payment by results nature also means that you haven't got anything to lose by getting involved.

Getting started

Unless you're a big company with lots of time and resources to spare to develop your own programme, seek to join an existing affiliate network. A number of these networks exist in the UK and all have different affiliate member websites and focuses, so matching your business to the network that can deliver you the best results is important.

To begin with, here's a list – in no particular order – of the bigger networks active in the UK today:

    www.tradedoubler.com.uk

    www.affiliatefuture.co.uk

    www.affiliatewindow.com

```
www.buy.at

www.paidonresults.com

www.webgains.com

www.linkshare.co.ukm/uk

www.uk.cj.com
```

We won't go through every option that every affiliate network offers you or you'll be reading forever. But different networks can deliver a variety of results, and, as the list above suggests, there's a lot of scope for shopping around, although almost all networks will have strengths and weaknesses in different areas.

Every network will also likely show you the three arms of its business on its homepage: merchants (advertisers), affiliates (publishers) and agencies. In this case, you're the advertiser, so check out what the network has to offer for you. You never know, you may even want to join a programme yourself as a publisher and make some extra money!

Choosing a network

Picking your way through the different affiliate network offerings can be a bit of a minefield, but when you're engaging any agency for outsourced work, try to get as much information about them as possible.

Use the checklist below to help you select an affiliate partner:

- ✔ Ask the network about their expertise in your chosen sector and ask them to back it up with examples and case studies, if possible.

- ✔ Get them to show you a client list and any testimonials that they have.

- ✔ Ask them about the size and breadth of their network. Is it only UK based? What are the demographics?

- ✔ Check out the top ranking affiliate networks from a search engine results page, using the search term 'affiliate marketing'. Search is a key part of affiliate marketing and the result may say a lot about the network.

- ✔ Have an immediate conversation about pricing and costs. You're better off knowing what you're dealing with at the outset.

- ✔ Come into the process with your eyes wide open. These people want to sell you the affiliate marketing dream, so don't get carried away with the hype. If their claims sound too good to be true, they may well be.

- ✔ Ask them what support and services they offer to advertisers.

- ✔ Find out which networks your competitors use. Being in the same network as a competitor can drive up the price of your affiliate marketing as your rival may offer a better commission deal to publishers than you do. Publishers will then try harder on behalf of your competition than for you and force you into a bidding war.

✔ Find out what measurement technology the network uses to track clicks to your site.

✔ Discover the publishers' payment basis.

Going through this checklist means you've applied due diligence to the process and will thus know less chance exists of anything going wrong when you begin using affiliate marketing.

Entering the Blogosphere

You have your website and have set up an online advertising programme and also maybe an affiliate programme; now you're ready to enter the Blogosphere! We don't mean outer space but the online world of blogs.

At its most basic, blogging is a way of recording thoughts, collecting links and sharing ideas and content with other people via a very simple website. In effect, blogs are online journals for individuals or organisations. A blogging craze is currently sweeping the world, with hundreds of millions of people writing them on a daily basis.

Although still behind the US, blogging has become massively popular in the UK. Some are political in nature, such as Guido Fawkes (http://order-order. com) and others focus on technology, like www.mashable.com.

Anyone who's anyone is blogging – from David Cameron to London Underground Tube drivers. Some blogs have also turned their authors into mini-celebrities. 'Perez Hilton' is the world's most famous celebrity blogger, reporting on the underbelly of Hollywood, and is now a media mogul in his own right with everything from a clothing range to a TV show.

If you want people to keep coming back to look at your blog, you need to keep it up to date, interesting and relevant. Boring blogs are a turn-off!

Blogger, Tumblr and Wordpress are just three of the free blogging tools available to you. Moving your blog from one tool to another isn't always easy, so make your decision carefully.

Many companies now use blogs to communicate with their customers with varying degrees of success. These are known as corporate blogs, and yours will fall into this category (albeit on a smaller scale). The Innocent drinks blog (www.innocentdrinks.co.uk/blog) (www.guinnessblog.com) is perhaps the most engaging of the corporate offerings as it details everything from information about the brand's charity campaigns to insights into the brand behind the scenes, along with the people who make up the company. Companies are increasingly starting to view blogging as a crucial communications tool and so, you too need to follow the guidelines below to ensure that your company gets the most out of this medium. Follow these guidelines:

- Be open and honest. Hiding the truth on the Internet is impossible and if you try to mislead consumers via your blog you'll regret it because negative sentiment goes just as far online as goodwill.

- Keep your blog up to date, relevant and interesting. No -one wants to read a blog from two years ago; it looks like your company gives up on things when they become too much trouble.

- Be clear about the aims of your blog from the outset and stick to them.

- Do let bloggers comment on what you write and make sure you don't over-react if or when they post anything negative about your company. If you really want a conversation with customers, be prepared for people to tell you their truth, not just yours.

- If negative posts do appear, react in an open and honest way. Blogs are a very useful way of developing your product or service to better meet the needs of your customers.

- Avoid 'corporate speak'. Blogs are about presenting a side to the business not encompassed in the official website, so don't weigh them down with jargon.

- Don't try to sell to your audience; that's a job for an official website. If you make your blog a sales pitch, people simply won't visit it.

- Make sure that, if more than one person is blogging on behalf of the company, everyone's clear on what constitute acceptable topics for discussion and the right tone and style so that the blog remains consistent rather than appearing confused.

Nowadays, blogging isn't simply an activity that's carried on through a brand's own website. You can also talk to customers through various social media tools (see Chapter 12 for details), including Facebook, Twitter and LinkedIn. Each of these social networks has a different character and tends to be appropriate for different types of conversation with consumers. But all offer a similar 'conversation' opportunity to blogging and sometimes reaching people in places where they're already spending time, such as Facebook, is easier. Bear in mind, though, that the above rules about not selling to people, choosing the correct tone and being interesting still apply!

Using Email for Marketing

Email is a powerful digital marketing tool. This medium may seem a bit old hat in a world of Facebook and Twitter, but you can create yourself, or hire a designer to create, a professional email that looks like a well-designed web page, with animation and clickable buttons linking to your site. Now, all you have to do is blast out your message to millions of email addresses and surely you can make millions overnight!

Not so fast! Okay, so you have this great marketing message or sales pitch, and you want to send it to everyone in the world who has an email address. You can actually do that, but we don't advise doing so. The more specific and targeted your use of email for marketing, the better. In fact, since the introduction of legislation in the UK, Europe and the US, marketers must be careful to avoid violating all sorts of restrictions on *spam*, or junk emails. We help you stay on the sunny side of the law in this section.

Sending only good emails

The best email is a personal communication with a customer you know (and who wants to hear from you), sent individually from you with an accurate email return address as well as your name, title, company name, full mailing address and phone number. The email may read as follows:

> Dear So-and-so
>
> I wanted to follow up after your purchase of (your product) on (date) to see how it's working out for you and to thank you for your continuing business. If you have any concerns or questions, please let me know by return email, or feel free to call me directly on 0123 123 1234.
>
> Best wishes
>
> Your Name

Your customer is going to receive, open, read and appreciate an email like this one. She may even respond to it, especially if the customer has any current concerns or questions or has another order on its way. Even if she doesn't reply to it, she still appreciates that email. And that message doesn't irritate anyone or look like spam.

Use email as much as you can for legitimate, helpful, one-to-one contact and support of customers or prospects. Sometimes you can offer services or content online that requires a registration. As part of that registration process, consider asking your customers if they want to receive more information on any of your products. If they opt-in, you can be sure that they'll value your follow-up emails.

Sending out an email to a list rather than an individual is also possible, but ensure that you have a clear purpose that benefits those people on the list.

Also make sure that your list only includes people who've indicated they're happy to be communicated with so you stay within the law and don't anger people. Never attempt to contact people who've opted-out of contact with you.

Understanding email etiquette

Goodwill is a valuable asset, so don't destroy it with your emails! The following list provides some rules for good mass emailing. Our inspiration for these rules comes from the Direct Marketing Association's guidelines for responsible use of email. We also bear the legal restrictions in mind.

- ✓ **Send emails only to those people who ask for them:** Your bulk emails should go only to those people who give you permission to contact them. The law (the Privacy and Electronic Communications Regulations) requires that no emails are sent without prior consent. What does that mean? It means that everyone you send an email to should have 'opted- in' to receiving emails from you, and each time you contact them, you must give them an option to reply and be taken off the list.

   If you have a 'prior relationship' with that contact (such as them being a previous customer or requesting information from you), the rules are slightly softer. Consider asking visitors to your website to register for extra information; you can then get these requests by creating a useful e-newsletter and advertising it on the web as a free subscription. Those people who sign up really want it, and they're happy to see the next issue arrive.

- ✓ **Remove addresses from your list immediately when people ask for them to be removed:** Remember that refusing to allow people to opt out is illegal. Also, people have such widespread distrust of web marketers that you may consider writing the person a brief, individual email from you (identify yourself and your title for credibility), letting them know that you have eliminated them from the list and are sorry if you've inconvenienced them. You shouldn't say any more in the email. Don't try to make a sale – you just irritate the person even more. You generally make a positive impression by being so responsive to the person's complaint, so don't be surprised if your special attention to their request leads them to initiate a sale later on.

- ✓ **If you insist on buying email lists, test them before using them:** We're assuming that the list you buy is legal (check first that the people on it have agreed to being contacted by third-party advertisers, like yourself). Then try sending a very simple, short, non-irritating message to people on the list, such as an offer to send them a catalogue or free sample, and ask for a few pieces of qualifying information in return. See what happens. Cull all the bounce-backs and irritated people from the list. Now your list is a bit better quality than the raw original. Save those replies in a separate list – they're significantly better and more qualified and deserve a more elaborate email, mailing or (if the numbers aren't too high) personal contact.

✔ **Respect privacy:** People don't want to feel like someone's spying on them. Never send to a list if you'd be embarrassed to admit where you got the names from. You can develop an email list in plenty of legitimate ways (from customer data, from web ads, from enquiries at trade shows, from return postcards included in mailings, and so on), so don't do anything that your neighbors would consider irritating or sleazy.

✔ **Send out your bulk emails just like you send an individual one:** Use a real, live, reply-able email address. We hate it when we can't reply to an email – it makes us angry!

✔ **Make sure that the subject line isn't deceptive:** Good practice and good sense dictate that you make the subject line straightforward. In marketing, you want to know straight away if someone isn't a good prospect, instead of wasting your time or theirs when they have no interest in your offer. A whole other book could be written about creating snappy lines that ensure emails get opened, but just consider what makes you do so. Opening with a deception such as 'Free money for you!' just looks like spam and will be deleted.

✔ **Keep your email address lists up to date:** When you get a *hard bounce-back* (notice that a message was undeliverable) from an address, remove it immediately and update your email list for the next mailing.

A *soft bounce-back* is an undeliverable message resulting from some kind of temporary problem. Track it to see if the email eventually goes through. If not, eliminate this address from your list, too.

People change their email addresses and switch servers. You can have bounce-backs on your list who may still be good customers or prospects. At least once a year, check these inactive names and try to contact them by phone or mail to update their email addresses. Some of these people are still interested and don't need to be cut from your list; they just need their email addresses updated.

If you're emailing an in-house list of people who've bought from you, gone to your seminar or asked for information in the past, remind them of your relationship in the email – they may have forgotten.

We hate *spam* – junk emails that clog up our mailboxes. We bet you feel the same way. So don't let your web marketing make you part of this problem. Use good quality lists, be polite and respectful, and integrate email into your broader web strategy so that you don't have to rely too heavily on email. Real people live at the end of those email addresses. Treat them as such!

Getting Mobile with Your Marketing

A staggering 6.5 billion text messages were sent in the UK during May 2008. According to the Mobile Data Association, 16.43 million mobile Internet (WAP) users were evident in the UK in the same month, and the latest Ofcom Communications Market Report showed that 12.5 million 3G (the fastest mobile speed) connections existed in the UK in August 2008.

Of course, you can also use a mobile phone as the launchpad for a whole host of marketing wonderment. MMS, WAP, Bluetooth, 3G – the terminology is almost as impenetrable as the average marketer's ability to take advantage of it. For the time being we suggest that, if you're interested in trying out mobile marketing, stick to the tried and tested methods (or at least as tried and tested as a less than ten-year-old method can be).

For now, we suggest leaving the development of Apple iPhone applications or Google Phone services to the larger brands, as new advertising eco-systems like these have multiple pitfalls. Letting someone else discover them before you take on this type of sophisticated mobile advertising is probably best.

Knowing How Much to Budget

If you're in a business-to-business (B2B) marketing situation, we strongly urge you to put at least 10 per cent of your marketing budget into digital marketing, both for maintaining a strong website and for doing some web advertising and search-engine placement purchases. If you add an e-newsletter, web distribution of press releases and occasional announcements to your email list, you may need to make set aside as much as 20 per cent of your budget. These figures are only a guide, however, and if the web is your main sales channel, dedicating more budget to the medium is probably worthwhile.

In 2010, the UK Internet advertising spend grew to £4 billion. This equates to a 25 per cent share of the entire advertising market; £1 in every £4 is now spent on interactive media. The money follows the eyeballs in the advertising industry and, as such, digital advertising is becoming even more important as more people spend more time online.

We believe that digital marketing is great because you can turn it up or down depending on its performance. If you book a big outdoor campaign, you won't find out you've wasted your money until you've already paid for it. Online, you can see how things are going on a minute-by-minute basis and adjust your spend accordingly. If you find that your web ads, search engine listings or emails are pulling well for you and making a profit, try doubling your effort and spending on them and seeing what happens. Still working well? Double again. You may find that the web can do a lot more of your basic marketing work than you think. Many marketers hold web spending down to a small minority of their budget for no good reason other than tradition and fear of all things new. Why not dive in and reap the rewards?

One Final, Important Thought

The single most important point to remember about websites and digital marketing in general is that investing in it routinely is crucial so that you're always changing and improving your presence. Whether you're a do-it-yourself online marketer or are willing to hire a professional digital agency, your interactive marketing needs to be a living thing. Don't let parts of your site get old and stale. Don't continue to run a *banner ad* (an ad that appears at the top or side of a web page) or bid on a *keyword or phrase* (a word or phrase people use in searching for websites, which you can pay to have your message linked to – see Chapter 11) if you aren't getting results in clicks and sales. Do adapt and change all the time. The web is a dynamic marketing medium. Be dynamic!

Chapter 11

Using Search Engines

C hances are you use search engines every day of your life to navigate your way around the web and find the information you're looking for. In this chapter we tell you how you can use these same search engines as powerful tools to attract customers to your business. Search engine marketing can be one of the most effective tools in a marketer's armoury and is vital to success if you're running an online business. Paid search advertising accounts for around 60 per cent of all online advertising spend in the UK, with the vast majority going on those services offered by Internet giant Google. We thus use examples of how to use Google to get the best from your search efforts in this chapter.

Search marketing is one of the more complex skills that a web marketer can master, but with a little basic knowledge getting decent results is quite easy. Its relative low cost also means search marketing is a fantastic medium in which to experiment and learn from your mistakes. This chapter explains the basics of search marketing, both paid advertising and search engine optimisation – otherwise known as how to build your website so people can find it in search engines. We cover when to outsource operations and when to keep them in-house, how to pick an agency to help you with your efforts and when to join up search advertising with the rest of your marketing efforts.

Getting to Grips with How Search Engines Work

Search engines are now *the* way to find information online. The Internet carries so much data that these engines are indispensable for sifting through it and, as such, can make the difference between your website succeeding or failing. Consider booking a three-star hotel in London. In the past, you'd have flicked through guides in the bookshop; now, you just type 'three-star hotel, London' into Google.

Building and maintaining a website that features high in the listings on a search engine results page isn't an exact science, but you can follow guidelines to ensure that you do get listed towards the top of the results when someone searches using terms relevant to your business. If you want to know even more about this area and digital marketing in general, you can find more detail in *Digital Marketing for Dummies* by Greg Brooks and Ben Carter (Wiley).

The term *search engine optimisation (SEO)* covers a vast amount of different techniques that can be used to ensure that your website is found and indexed by a search engine, so that when consumers type in your name or the name of your products, they find you. An entire industry has sprung up alongside the SEO business. If you take into account the fact that paid search was worth over £2.3 billion in the UK in 2010, you can estimate that the SEO industry may be worth a comparable figure – the two services often go hand in hand. Indeed, mastering both, or finding an agency that can do so, will certainly turbo boost your marketing.

To understand how to fully optimise your website so that it features as high as possible in the rankings of search engines, you need to understand how search engines work.

Search engines, such as Google, use software agents known as *crawlers* or *spiders* that are sent out onto the web and automatically 'read' a site. They pick up not only the words on the pages, but also the special *metadata* information that web page creators encode in the page but can't be seen by the final viewer. This metadata contains information that describes the content of the page and is what the 'spiders' look at when deciding how to list the web page in the search engine's index. For example, if your web page is all about cookery, and specifically Italian cookery, the metadata will contain relevant terms such as 'pasta', 'lasagne', 'Italy', 'pizza' and so on. This information is then used to match the request someone types into the search engine with your web page. The spiders then follow the links from that site, and links to the site from other web pages, before returning the information to the central database, where the data is stored and then interrogated every time a search is made. These spiders return to pages every now and again to see if any of the 'metadata' information has changed.

A page ranking in the search engines listings is determined by the relevance of the metadata and visible web page text to the request, and also by the quality and number of links that link to that page. Every search engine has a slightly different algorithm it uses to determine its page ranking, so SEO can become a very complicated art. You can gain a good ranking on one engine but it won't guarantee you the same result on another.

As we're not all superbrains, sitting down and trying to work out the different search engines' algorithms would be foolish. Instead, you can follow a few simple steps to ensure that your website is optimised to a decent level. We outline these steps in the 'SEO Do's and Don'ts' section later in the chapter.

SEO involves a mixture of lots of different skills and only the real experts can be great at all of them. Sometimes going to an agency is your best bet. See the 'Choosing between In-House or Outsourcing' section later in this chapter on making this decision.

Link building – getting other relevant sites to link to your site to improve its relevancy in search listings – is vital. You can create links through deals with other sites, or an SEO company can organise them for you. Another great way to build links is to simply get out there and comment on things that are going on in your industry online. The golden rule is to keep things relevant – don't start commenting and leaving your URL on forums and chat rooms that have no relevance, but where you can add to the conversation, go for it.

If you haven't already built your website, you can build accessibility into it to improve the number of users that visit you online and, in turn, raise your search ranking. The 'Understanding SEO' section covers accessibility.

Finally, you can also use online public relations (PR) as part of your SEO campaign. If PR stories about your company are published online and linked to your site, you gain traffic. The stories can also be talked about by people who read them, who may then comment on them and also link to your website – all increasing your relevancy in the eyes of the search engines. Chapter 15 covers online PR.

However you choose to approach SEO, you need to have a firm understanding of the necessary skills, whether you undertake it yourself or bring in a specialist to help you.

Understanding SEO

Search engine optimisation falls under the wider banner of search engine marketing, which encompasses anything that you do to attract customers to your website through search engines. This process can involve a massive number of different techniques and processes, from paid search to website design. The combination of all of these different techniques forms your search marketing strategy, which is vitally important to your overall business – most people in the UK now use the Internet to find the information, businesses and services they want.

SEO specifically relates to how your website is read and ranked by search engine spiders. Unfortunately, talking about the mechanics is difficult without going into some technical detail, but we endeavour to keep it as simple as possible.

Good SEO should begin before you even build your website. Planning your site so it's as relevant and accessible as possible will help you maintain a good ranking in search engine results pages. As soon as you decide that you require a website, you need to ensure that the way that you design and then build your site makes it as accessible as possible. The World Wide Web Consortium (`www.w3.org/WAI/guid-tech`) carries a list of guidelines to follow to make your website accessible.

Obviously, a badly designed site is hard for people to navigate and the same is true for the search engine spiders that collect information and rank your site. A clear structure, with relevant content, keywords and easy navigation helps to improve your site visibility to search engines and so achieve a better ranking in their search results pages.

To see if your site is already well designed – or if you haven't built yours yet and want to see what works – look at competitors' sites. Note details such as speed of page loading, ease of navigation, whether links point to relevant information and what details they give on their home pages.

If you use a search engine to find the sites under a common keyword, also take note of your rivals' rankings in the results and try to work out the link between the sites with good design and good rankings. The Internet is an incredibly open environment. The more time you spend looking at the efforts of competitors and other relevant players in your market, the more you'll learn about what you should be doing. In the same way that you probably check the pricing structures of your rivals, you should also make regular checks to see what they're doing online, including how effectively they show up on search engines using keyword searches relevant to your business.

Creating an eye-catching website with the latest Flash technology and whizzy graphics is all very well, but search engine spiders can't appreciate these details. They're cold, calculating little creatures that simply apply their logic to your site to give it a ranking and then move on to the next site. So, when designing a site, focus on your customers, but also keep one eye on the spiders. Creating a site that everyone can find and that does a decent job is better than an amazing site which nobody can find unless they already know the URL.

Considering SEO Do's and Don'ts

SEO can be a dangerous world; fortunately, guidelines and rules are widely available online to help you navigate the minefield.

A good SEO strategy includes:

- ✔ Getting as many relevant links to your site as possible
- ✔ Designing the best possible experience for both visitors and spiders alike
- ✔ Gaining a good search engine ranking in the results under relevant keyword search terms

Crucially, though, using SEO doesn't mean undertaking practices that trick users or spiders into thinking that your website is something that it isn't just to get them through the door or improve your ranking. Doing so will definitely result in you being de-listed from a search engine's index. Being de-listed is the SEO equivalent of football's red card and incurs a nasty stigma, as we explain later in the chapter.

Good and bad SEO practices are known as White Hat and Black Hat practices, respectively. To further complicate matters, a continual argument rages between the two groups as to what constitutes unethical SEO. The aim of SEO is to try to rise up the rankings and Black Hatters argue that any means of doing so are justified since all SEO is an attempt to manipulate the rankings. You can see their point – it's the law of the wild – but we strongly advise you to avoid Black Hat practices. Search engines frown upon them, and if you're found out you'll be kicked off the index and be out in the cold.

The following sections give you the low-down on White Hat and Black Hat practices.

White Hat practices

To make sure you stick to White Hat practices:

- ✔ **Make searching the page easy:** On each page, use a unique and relevant title and name and do the same in metadata so spiders can easily read the page and its content.
- ✔ **Keep the content as relevant as possible:** When spiders read the page, the terminology they find should be relevant to the subject of the page. Make the content what a user expects to find after searching on specific keywords.

✓ **Add content:** Content is king in SEO, so add as much relevant content as possible to your site, but don't *scrape* it from elsewhere as doing so is frowned on. (Content scraping is when you copy wholesale content from another site.) Create your own unique content.

✓ **Make your metadata relevant:** Make sure that your metadata is relevant to your site and specific page content, but avoid the use of excessive repetition of words and over the top punctuation such as exclamation marks. If you repeat keywords, a search engine may believe that you're attempting to fool it – and visitors, too.

✓ **Avoid cookies:** Set up your site so that spiders can crawl through your pages without having to accept *cookies* – packages of text that get swapped between a site and its users – doing so allows them to do their job much faster and takes up less resource.

✓ **Develop linking strategies to entice links from other websites:** Create your own interesting content, as sites with useful or entertaining information tend to get linked to more than those without. This linking increases your ranking.

✓ **Join a *web ring* that's relevant to your business:** A web ring is a group of sites that have all linked to each other to form a ring. When someone visits a site in the ring, they're offered links to other relevant sites in the ring.

✓ **Increase your online PR:** Write interesting articles that can be offered to other sites in exchange for a link back to your own site alongside the article. This approach is sometimes called 'bog outreach'.

These are just a few basic White Hat practices. You need to take a whole host of other things into consideration, too, which is why getting guidance from professionals, or at least doing a lot of research before setting up your website, is so useful.

If you want an exhaustive look at White Hat practices, try this link: www. google.com/support/webmasters/bin/answer.py?answer=35769

Black Hat practices

Spamdexing is the big no-no in SEO. *Spamdexing*, a mixture of spamming and indexing, falls into two categories: content or link spam. We explain these terms below.

Content spam

This type of Black Hat practice is designed to alter the search engine spider's view of the website so that it's different from what the user will encounter when they click through on the search results. All of the techniques aim to boost the site's ranking in the results lists.

- ✔ **Gateway or doorway pages (also known as cloaking):** Particularly sneaky, these are low quality hastily built web pages that are stuffed with very similar keywords. These pages will then rank highly in the search results and have a link on them to the destination site.

- ✔ **Hidden or invisible text:** This is the act of disguising keywords and phrases by making them the same colour as the background, using a tiny font size or hiding them somewhere else on the page or in the HTML (metadata). This makes the site seem more relevant to the search engine spider, when in fact it will be less relevant to the user.

- ✔ **Content scraping:** These programs are designed to 'scrape' content from search engine results pages and websites and then dump it on a site that will probably be filled with unrelated adverts. The content is designed to fool the spiders and attract users who see and also may click on the ads, meaning the site owner can generate income from advertising.

- ✔ **Meta tag stuffing:** This is the act of 'stuffing' keywords in the meta tags – which the spiders use to decide what the page is about – and then repeating them over and over. Often words unrelated to the content of the web page are also used to fool the spiders.

Link spam

Link spam is specifically targeted at search engines' web page ranking systems, which are partly based on the quality and quantity of links from other similar quality websites to the destination site.

- ✔ **Hidden links:** The act of hiding links where they won't be found by web surfers, but where they will be found by spiders, in order to increase the web page ranking.

- ✔ **Link farms:** These farms are created by designing a group of web pages that all link to each other over and over and over. This practice is also carried out with blogs.

- ✔ **Spam in blogs:** Since blogs became popular they've been targeted by Black Hatters who place links in any comment sections of the blog, linking back to a specific site. This practice has even become automated, with computers posting links all over the Internet.

- ✔ **Google bombing:** This happens when a large number of sites combine to link to one site and drive it to the top of the search listings. It works as a result of the nature of Google's search algorithm, but is usually only used for malicious non-commercial purposes. A Google bomb was used, for example, to promote a joke 'File Not Found' page that was returned top of the list when searching for the phrase 'weapons of mass destruction'.

If you follow the search engines' own rules and the White Hat rules that we outline above, you should have no problem creating a site that's visible to search engines and useful for visitors, too. But, in a nod to Star Wars: 'Do not underestimate the power of the dark side.' The draw of the quick fix that Black Hat practices offer can be alluring, but remember, Luke Skywalker – the good guy – got the girl and saved the galaxy in the end. Following the righteous path is always better. May the SEO force be with you!

Choosing between In-house or Outsourcing

SEO isn't a simple process and you may need to have quite a bit of experience in dealing with its subtle nuances to succeed. Luckily, help is at hand. A huge number of SEO agencies have sprung up all over the UK to feed the growing market for specialist search skills, and most reputable web design agencies offer these services as part of their build fee.

However, as with outsourcing any work to an agency, you need to go through the correct processes to choose an agency that fits well with your business and will be able to offer you all the services that you require. As search engine marketing covers a very wide set of skills, you may want to shop around before you decide on a search partner and you should certainly be prepared to ask a lot of questions in the search for your perfect match.

Hiring an agency that can handle both your SEO and your paid search needs is the best way to go. A number of agencies can provide this dual service, so do your homework and make sure that you find a partner that meets your needs.

So do you need to hire an SEO agency? Well, if you read all of the advice in this chapter you may feel well equipped and educated enough in the market to go it alone. But for the majority of people, an agency or at least some individual expertise is required to implement an SEO strategy.

If you decide that you don't have the skills to take on the project yourself, you need to investigate the agencies in the market. Below is a basic checklist to help you choose the right agency for your business. While it's not exhaustive, it should be enough to point you in the right direction and weed out some of the more undesirable agencies and SEO 'professionals' operating out there.

Score each agency in relation to the following points:

 ✔ **Do they appear on the first page of Google when you search under the terms 'search engine optimisation' and 'SEO'?** The agencies that come up top have obviously got their act together and should be worth a look.

✔ **Does their website provide details of for work they' have done, which clients they work for and any case studies and customer recommendations?** Any decent agency will carry information on previous projects and you could even ask for recommendations based on the agency's client list.

✔ **Are you able to request a site review?** Any decent agency will provide one free of charge. A review will show you how well they operate and can be an interesting gauge if you get a few of them to compare.

✔ **Do they spend a lot of time talking about paid services?** If this is the case, they may not have the expertise that you want in SEO.

✔ **Are they willing to settle on a set price for the work?** It's your money, so whichever agency you choose, insist on a set price and also set some targets to achieve, too. You can even see if you can set up a 'payment on results' business model.

✔ **Will they answer questions about the White Hat / Black Hat practices, as described earlier in this chapter?** You need to check that you won't be working with an unethical company.

✔ **Do they explain exactly what work needs doing?** Make sure that the agency explains to you exactly what they'll be doing. Don't let them bamboozle you – you're paying them, so make sure they explain things satisfactorily to you.

✔ **Do they make grandiose claims?** Beware of anyone offering to get you to number one in the Google rankings or making other wild promises; they won't be true, certainly not by any White Hat practices and without substantial investment.

✔ **Can you protect yourself legally?** Will the agency agree to a money-back guarantee or sign a document indemnifying your brand from damage.

✔ **Will they work with your other marketing efforts?** Any decent agency will want to know the whole marketing picture and really understand your company so it can achieve the best results.

Seek answers to these questions to ensure that you don't end up with the John Wayne of the SEO world. While you don't have to get pedantic, it's sometimes worth going down to the level of asking for meetings in the agency's office – just to make sure they actually have one.

Understanding What Paid Search Is

Put simply, paid search is the service offered by search engines that allows a business to advertise next to search results that have been requested by a user. For example, you're searching for an Apple iPod. The search listings may bring up Apple's own website but the paid results down the side of the page show adverts from retailers stocking the iPod, such as Amazon.

The system works on an auction basis using keyword bidding, meaning that a business can bid on relevant keywords that are entered into the search engine by users. The keywords that someone uses determine what results they're shown. If you can find out what your potential customers are searching for, you can make sure that you're prominent in the paid listings by bidding on those keywords.

Paid listings are found on the right-hand side of search results pages (and at the top) and are marked out separately from the 'natural' results that make up the main bulk of the page. The paid results comprise a link to your site and small ad blurb underneath describing what a company offers or high-lighting a special promotion. Writing these ads in such a small amount of space can be a skill in itself!

The difference between paid listings and natural listings is that you can't buy your way to the top of the natural listings; this can only be achieved by building a good website, generating lots of links and most probably, employing a reputable SEO agency.

One of the benefits of paid listings is that you can jump the queue and go to the head of the class by outbidding competitors on your chosen keywords. This approach can be very useful if you want to get some instant traffic to your website; for example, if you're running a specific campaign or special offer but don't have the time to undergo extensive SEO, which will take much longer. When a website visitor sees your ad and clicks the link, he's delivered to your home page or a specific page you've chosen for the campaign (it's at this point that you pay, not before).

Another benefit of paid search is that if you have chosen your keywords wisely you'll be advertising to consumers who are already interested in the product or service that you offer as they've made the effort to look for information on your chosen keywords using the search engine. This is one reason why, in 2010, the UK paid search industry was worth £2.3 billion (around 60 per cent of the total online ad market).

The Internet is a great place for marketing as you can try out lots of things at a relatively low cost. And the best of all these things is research, which is free! A good test to see if you should be doing any paid search marketing is to type in keywords relevant to your business and see who's advertising. If lots of your competitors are coming up, then you need to do some paid search work. Every time a user clicks on one of your competitors' ads, you're losing a potential customer.

In a worst case scenario, even though you've followed all the rules and made sure that your website is optimised for search engines and has a good natural listings rating, a competitor can still come in and steal potential business by having a good paid search strategy that places them at the top of the paid listings. Bidding on other companies' keywords is rife and, if nothing else, you should protect your SEO investment by carrying out some limited paid search marketing.

Paid search isn't a technique that can be set up and left to run because it's in a constant state of flux. Competitors can upweight their bids on certain keywords around promotions or products or simply try to price other competitors out of the market. So if you decide to undertake paid search marketing, ensure that someone within your company is keeping an eye on your keyword bids to make sure that they're working as hard as they can for you.

Keyword bidding can become complicated if you decide to use paid search on more than one search engine. Unfortunately, each search engine has its own service and interface for paid search, meaning that if you bid across a wide range of keywords and across a number of search engineers, it can become very time consuming and complicated. If this is the case, consider using a search marketing agency – see the 'Deciding between In-House or Agency' section later in this chapter.

Taking a Look at Google

Google has an almost unassailable lead in the search market in the UK at present, so if you're going to carry out any search marketing, you must use Google's service AdWords or you'll miss out on almost the entire market.

The other search players, Yahoo! and Microsoft, which operates the Bing search engine, each have their own systems that you can use to conduct paid search marketing. Yahoo!'s offering is called Yahoo! Advertising Solutions and Microsoft's is accessed through the Microsoft adCenter, which allows you to advertise across all of Microsoft's web businesses, including the search service. Interestingly, Yahoo! and Microsoft have recently joined forces to offer advertisers the chance to advertise across their combined search engines, in order to try to combat Google's market domination.

Although the array of services looks daunting at first, each company offers in-depth tutorials on paid search marketing and how their particular tools can be used.

For a brief introduction to each engine, visit these sites:

- **Yahoo! Advertiser Solutions:** advertisingcentral.yahoo.com/en_GB
- **Microsoft adCenter:** adcenter.microsoft.com
- **Google AdWords:** adwords.google.co.uk

Discovering How to Bid on Keywords

With paid search, the devil's in the detail; in this case, the detail is keyword bidding. Each search engine has its own service to guide you through the bidding process, but before you get to this stage, you need to decide what keywords are best suited to your business.

A few basic rules exist when it comes to choosing your keywords for your paid search marketing. Ensuring that the words you decide upon match the product or services you offer is the main rule. This may sound obvious, but if you trick users into clicking through to your site from an ad and they discover when they get there that the products you sell aren't relevant to that ad, you're losing money as they'll only be disappointed when they get there. Keep it simple and truthful.

Start by talking with colleagues and employees to find out what people most associate with your business and which words are most commonly used about your products. For example, if you sell books, you may find that some people search for 'books' but they also choose 'good reads' or 'stories' or particular author names.

Once you have your list – don't worry, it may look long at the moment – you can whittle it down to the keywords that you think are most relevant. Unfortunately, at this point you may discover that although a certain word is most relevant to your website, it's also the most relevant word to thousands of other sites. Under the auction system used by search engines, this means that unless you have deep marketing pockets, you may want to shy away from these popular keywords.

If you're using Google, use the keyword matching options (support.google. com/adwords/bin/answer.py?hl=en&answer=6100), which can improve results and lower potential costs. Using the service you can 'broadmatch' your keywords, meaning that if you use the phrase 'running shoes' your ads will appear when someone's query contains 'running' and 'shoes', in any order and even if other terms appear. You can also enter your keyword in quotation marks, as in 'running shoes', and your ad will appear when a user searches on the exact phrase 'running shoes', in this order, and possibly with other terms in the query, but not when the words are out of order. You can even use a negative keyword match, which means that if your keyword is 'running shoes', you can add a negative keyword such as 'blue' so your ad won't appear when a user searches for blue running shoes.

When you've settled on your main keywords, you can get help from sources online that will give you more keywords on the periphery, but linked to your own.

Try out these for a start:

- ✔ www.wordtracker.com
- ✔ http://adwords.google.com/select/KeywordToolExternal

When you've selected your search engine and chosen your keywords, you're ready to get started.

For ease of use, we explain the Google AdWords sign-up process as it currently covers most of the UK market. Follow these steps:

1. **Go to** www.google.co.uk/ads. Click on the get started with adWords Express link. The next page asks you to either sign in on your existing Google account, if you have one, or create a new one.

2. **Find your business.** Google will now want to link your business to your account. It does this by asking you for the country your business operates in and the main phone number of the business. If it can't find the business, it asks you to enter your business details.

3. **Create your ad.** Follow the steps outlined on the page, which cover the headline, description, where you want people who click your ad to go to (to your website, most likely) and your budget.

4. **Checkout.** You're then asked to enter your payment details in order to complete the advert and start your search marketing.

Congratulations, you're now a paid search advertiser!

Deciding between In-House or Agency

One of the biggest decisions you have to make is whether to carry out your paid search in-house or to outsource to a specialist search marketing agency.

Pros and cons exist for both options. If you carry out your paid search marketing in-house, you have more control over what's happening, but you may not necessarily have expert skills. Employing a specialist agency may cost you more money than handling it in-house, but the agency may make your marketing budget work harder for you and save you money in the long run.

We've mulled over the pros and cons of employing an agency versus going it alone and come to the conclusion that it boils down to one judgement.

Think of it like this: if you don't carry out much paid search marketing, then you can comfortably handle it in-house. If you carry out masses of paid search marketing, do you have the skills and resources to handle it in-house when it takes up a lot of time? If not, then outsource.

If you make the decision to handle your paid search marketing in-house, then you must get at least a couple of people up to speed with the ins and outs of the process. Unlike many other marketing disciplines that you may have undertaken, paid search is a fast-moving and constantly changing medium. If you're not on the ball, you'll lose out to the competition, and if you don't know what you're doing, you can easily get things wrong and end up costing yourself valuable time and money. Making sure at least two people know how your paid search marketing works is important in case one leaves or is unable to carry out his duties. Continuity in your search marketing is vital.

These two members of staff need to liaise with your other employees who carry out marketing to ensure that they know exactly what activity is taking place and can change the paid search strategy accordingly.

This detail is important as people's searches are often impacted by other marketing channels. For example, if someone sees a TV, press or billboard ad for a detergent, they may not remember anything more than the name or the tagline of the ad. One of the first places they'll look for more information is through a search engine. If your paid search team knows that ads carrying these taglines are running, they can spend more on those search terms and catch customers who have seen the ads when they search.

As long as you keep your paid search team up to date with your marketing plans, ensure they're taking advice and learning from the search engines and are aware of developments in the paid search market – such as new products and techniques – no reason exists why you shouldn't carry out successful paid search marketing.

If your paid search needs are greater than this and you have decided to use an agency to carry out your search marketing, you need to choose wisely. Since paid search marketing leapt onto the scene a few years ago, hundreds of small agencies have sprung up to provide services to the industry. Not all of them are good and not all of them are competent, but there are those that can make a real difference to your paid search marketing.

A good starting point is looking at some resources online to get a feel for a few different agencies. You can try the Search Engine Marketing Professional Organisation (www.sempo.org) a US-based organisation with international, including UK, membership. Another good resource is www.semlist.com, which gives a list of companies offering paid listing management, or www.nmamarketingservicesguide.co.uk, which includes a list of top search agencies in the UK and a brief introduction to each one.

To help you choose your shortlist of agencies, bear these points in mind:

- ✔ **Dedication to your account:** Make sure that your business will be high on the priority list of the agency.

- ✔ **Client list and case studies:** Check out what the agency has done in the past and how it's regarded.

- ✔ **Membership of associations:** This will ensure that the agency has a good working relationship with the key search players.

- ✔ **Press cuttings:** Look at the cuttings on the agency's site and also check out its profile online. Try a few searches on the Google News site and see what comes up.

When you've checked out the basics, you can move on with your shortlist and chat to your chosen agencies about what they can offer you and how they'll work with you to get the most out of your paid search.

Optimising Your Paid Search Campaign

When you're signed up with a search engine (or your new search agency has done it for you), you gain access to your account control panel, which allows you to control your paid search campaign. In this section you can add keywords, manage the cost of how much you pay per click and change the locality of where and who sees your ads.

How you optimise your paid search campaign will determine how effective your paid search budget will be. A number of different ways of optimising your campaign exist, with both the agencies and the search engines offering their own services and technologies.

Google allows you to optimise your campaign from your adWords account, letting you choose daily budgets, delete, pause or resume campaigns. It even allows you to schedule your adWords campaign so that your ads will only be seen at certain times and in particular places. Every search engine has its own optimisation tools but they all let you do pretty much the same things – control your prices, keywords and distribution.

Going through a third party that's developed software to manage all of your paid search campaigns through one interface is a great way to optimise your campaign. Ask any agency you employ about this capability.

Access to third-party software is handy as you get some of the expertise of the agencies without necessarily having to hand over your entire paid search strategy to them. As a hybrid between in-house or going to an agency, it's a good compromise.

When you begin optimising your paid search campaigns, you'll begin to see what strategies work best for you. There's no right or wrong way to optimise as every business is different and has different customers. Luckily, paid search is a very versatile medium and you learn very quickly what works and what doesn't.

The best advice we can give you is to keep it simple to begin with. Think about your customers and what their behaviour is. Analyse your target audience – your potential customers (see Chapter 4) – and use your findings together with information from your website analysis to decide on your paid search strategy. Armed with this information and the optimisation tools at your disposal, either through the search engines or a third party, you're well on your way to a successful paid search campaign.

Integrating Paid Search with other Channels

Once your paid search campaign is up and running and you've got to grips with optimisation, you can go to the next level by integrating your paid search campaigns with other marketing channels.

This is one area where paid search really excels. Search engines are *the* place to go for information. This means that your other marketing channels can now receive a boost from paid search.

Here's an example: You sell cars and a consumer is interested in buying a car. He's done some research online; possibly he's even seen your ad in the paid listings. Then he's sitting in a cinema waiting for a film to start and he sees your ad for the latest model. He likes the look of it, but can't do anything about it as he's sitting in the dark at that moment. So he watches the film. Later, when he's driving home, he hears a radio ad for the car, but only catches the tagline, 'the faster the better'. When he gets home, he wants to find out more information about the car, but can't remember the name of it; only the jingle stays in his mind.

So he goes online, types 'the faster the better' into a search engine and, because you've integrated your paid search into the rest of your marketing, hey presto! Your bidding on that keyword means your ad comes out top of the paid listings. The consumer can now get the information he wants and possibly even buy the car or arrange a test drive. Without integrating the paid search into the rest of your marketing, you'd have lost that potential lead – the consumer would have had nowhere to go for the information or could have ended up at a more web-savvy competitor's site.

That's just a simple example of how easy integrating paid search into your wider marketing mix is. In order to make this approach work, you must ensure that your paid search team or agency is fully up to date with your marketing department so that everything can work together.

As well as making other marketing channels work harder, paid search can also get a serious lift from other channels. The perfect example of this is the US TV event of the year, the Superbowl, and specifically the one that took place in 2006: Superbowl XL. The event, where traditionally the most expensive new adverts are aired during half time, had TV viewing figures rocketing. For the same event, Yahoo reported that searches on the phrase 'Super Bowl XL Commercials' increased by roughly 800 per cent in the day after the game was played and advertisers including Cadillac, Honda and Dove all bid on the phrase and took advantage of the resulting increased search traffic. Amusingly other search terms that rocketed around the event were 'Appetiser Recipes' (up 336 per cent), Chicken Wings (up 97 per cent) and Salsa Recipes (a spicy 76 per cent rise).

Although amusing, this demonstrates perfectly how the spikes of traffic that can be found online are created offline by other channels and events. The lessons learnt online in the US are not necessarily only applicable in that market.

Chapter 12

Tapping into Networking Sites

In This Chapter

▶ Defining social media

▶ Taking a look at Facebook, Twitter and LinkedIn

▶ Establishing your online profile

▶ Knowing your customers

▶ Keeping online conversations flowing

*T*he Internet isn't just a business tool. You're probably already using it to enhance your own life by searching for things that interest you or staying in touch with friends and family.

You must have noticed the rise of social networks online and we bet that you're a member of at least one social network, be it Facebook, Twitter, LinkedIn or any of the other hundreds of networks online. Known collectively as 'social media', these communication and interactive tools and services aren't only great for your social life, they're also powerful marketing tools. Also referred to as 'Web 2.0', social media are one of the most exciting and important areas of the Internet for a modern web marketer to get to grips with and in the following pages help you do just that.

Understanding Web 2.0

The term *Web 2.0* is often bandied around by Internet marketing professionals, but what does it actually mean? Well, in simple terms, it refers to the evolution of the Internet and what people do on it.

Following this logic, Web 1.0 thus represents the early days of the Internet, dominated by advances in technology. In Web 1.0, the Internet was a text-based service and was monopolised by companies selling their goods to people. You might see this period as the Internet's childhood, when it could only do a limited range of things and wasn't always the best communicator.

In contrast, Web 2.0 is all about how people use the Internet – the web has become a vital part of everybody's lives. It's shifted away from just text to become a place where pictures and video are widely viewed and shared with other people. Companies in the Web 2.0 world aren't just using technology to sell things but also to build their brands and create a two-way dialogue with consumers. The Internet is now a young, funky adult that likes chatting with friends, sharing things among groups and getting creative. That's our explanation of it anyway.

Web 2.0, or *social media* as we prefer to call it, has three key factors that you need to understand. They explain how people are now using the Internet – community, communication and content:

- **Community:** Refers to using the web to manage your friendships and social and professional networks, and expressing your likes and dislikes via websites. Millions of people do this on Facebook, Twitter and other social networks around the world every day.

- **Communication:** People have been using the Internet to communicate since the very early days of the web – in chat rooms, for example – but now, thanks to the widespread use of broadband, it's enabling more advanced participation. For example, people can make free calls over the Internet on services like Skype. Or they can share video and photos through photo service Flickr and networking websites like Facebook. The increased communication between friends, people with similar interests, family members, lovers, business colleagues and so on is leading to a world where everyone likes to feel constantly connected to people they know and those things that matter to them.

- **Content:** This term covers pretty much everything that's fun, interesting or informative online. A TV show, photo or song is a piece of content. While content isn't new to the web, more services than ever are now allowing users to create and share their own content online. YouTube has sought to harness user-generated content (UGC) by asking people to send in videos of themselves doing some funny (and some not-so-funny) things, which people then invite others to view in their thousands – and sometimes millions! People also regularly share their favourite TV or film clips with friends – often whether doing so breaks copyright laws or not.

This chapter explains how, as a business, you can get involved in this new social media world and gives you a few pointers to get your feet on the bottom rung of the social ladder.

Introducing Social Networks: Facebook, Twitter and LinkedIn

A *social network* is just a fancy name for a very simple idea. It means websites that combine lots of services that allow people to stay in touch with each other, swap messages and photos, play games and lots more.

Three social networks dominate in the UK: Facebook, Twitter and LinkedIn. Each has a slightly different target audience and slightly different rules on what you can and can't do as an advertiser. Twitter was just a small website when we wrote the last edition of this book – now it has more than 100 million users.

For many years, MySpace was the largest social network in the world, but it's now been overtaken by Facebook and Twitter – although this situation could change again in the future as the social space moves very quickly. Numerous specific social networks exist out there, too. If you're operating in the gaming industry, for example, you may want to visit GamerDNA. But the biggest player in the professional or business-to-business social networking world is LinkedIn; here, you can meet other people in your sector, make referrals, search for employees and generally do business.

When thinking about social networks, getting hung up on trying to reach everyone all over the world is a waste of time. In Brazil, India or Japan, you might find people on the social network, Orkut. Meanwhile, in the US, people might be trying out the Google+ network. In the UK, photography enthusiasts might be on picture-sharing site, Instagram.

So don't even start worrying about getting your business out there on every social network. Not all of these websites will be right for you anyway. And understanding the area properly before getting involved is a better approach. Let's look first at the big three social network brands in the UK that could benefit you: Facebook, Twitter and LinkedIn.

All of these sites offer a different set of tools and services for their users as they appeal to people for different reasons. This fact is important when you're thinking about who to target with your social media advertising.

Ensuring that you understand the differences between the social networks will help you to better decide where to concentrate your social media advertising efforts. For example, if you want to set up a transactional store within a social network, Facebook is the best network. If you're keen simply to have a conversation with your customers, Twitter could be right for you. A bit of research beforehand – even simply having a look around the sites to see what companies similar to yours are doing – will pay dividends when you come to launch your own efforts.

Marketing with Pull not Push Strategies

Social media marketing represents a difference from advertising as people usually perceive it. A lot of the usual forms of advertising on other media, such as radio, TV and outdoors, can be summed up as 'push' advertising. The marketer pushes (or shouts) out the message to people and they passively accept (or ignore) the communication.

This method doesn't work very well online. The social space is about building conversations with people, and allowing your message to be 'pulled' by the consumer and becoming a useful part of their online experience.

You can best approach or understand any sort of social marketing by first considering how your message would work in a traditional social setting. Imagine you're at a dinner party at a friend's house. He's in the building business and you meet one of his business partners for the first time. What would you think of his partner if, before even shaking your hand, he said:

'My business is better than any of my competitors. It is better quality, better value and better for the environment. I've won loads of awards and been recognised by the industry I work in as one of its leading practitioners. In fact, you'd be mad to hire anyone else but me.'

We suspect that, like us, you'd try your best to get as far away from him as possible and make a beeline for the opposite end of the table!

Now, what would your impression of this man be if, instead, he said:

'Welcome, can I get you a drink?'

You'd say 'thanks very much' and then proceed to have a nice chat with him and probably ask him what he does for a living.

These two approaches sum up the difference between most offline advertising and online social media advertising. Facebook and Twitter are used by consumers as part of their daily lives; people aren't there to be sold to in a 'shouty' way. Companies need to pull off the trick of making themselves useful to people in a social context and, if possible, starting a mutually interesting conversation.

British Gas has recently been using social network Twitter to respond to customer concerns and promote its messages in a more humanised way.

Why? The British energy market is rarely popular with customers. With energy prices almost always on the rise, it can be difficult for companies to either convince customers to stick with them or switch to them. British Gas says that as many as 98 per cent of the mentions of its brand online are now on Twitter, so it represents the biggest discussion forum available to the company.

So, how does this work? Well, Twitter allows users to post 140-character updates. Users 'follow' other people on the site and these chosen people's updates appear on the user's page. Essentially, they see a constantly updating list of 140-character messages from people or companies that they're interested in.

Typically, when a piece of news is released about British Gas, such as a price rise, the brand sees lots of negative mentions in Twitter updates. For example, it might see 19 per cent of positive comments, 23 per cent of overtly negative comments and 58 per cent of neutral comments. The neutral comments are often re-tweets (people reposting other people's comments), which tend to have a negative slant.

Rather than simply sending everybody a standard statement or trying to engage in a complex argument about gas prices, the British Gas team typically posts links to a video featuring managing director Ian Peters explaining why the price rise has occurred, in his own words. Or it sends the video direct to those people questioning the price rises.

This method has garnered results, claims British Gas. A typical percentage breakdown following the brand reaching out to customers might see 42 per cent of positive comments, 12 per cent of overtly negative comments and 46 per cent of neutral comments, an improvement in sentiment compared with the usual response to price rises. Third parties, such as the consumer action group Which?, also link to the videos, offering them more credibility with customers.

By talking to customers in a non-pushy, conversational way in the place where they're already discussing the brand – Twitter – British Gas has found a way of communicating that sets it apart from faceless corporate businesses.

Setting Up Your Own Brand or Professional Profile

To take your first steps into social advertising, you can create your own social network profile page for your company. But don't expect people to flock to this page as soon as you publish it; if only the process was that simple! A profile page for your business is the bottom rung of the social ladder, but it does establish your organisation in the social world online and gives you a spot to send people looking for information on your business to and a place where you can interact with customers.

Each of the social networks has their own systems for signing up, as described in the following sections.

Signing up to Facebook

Before you begin your social journey, creating your own personal page and using the service for a while is sensible, so you get the hang of how people use Facebook and discover what they find important. Always read the terms and conditions of social networking sites so you know what you are and aren't allowed to do. Surf the site and find out what you like and what you don't – doing so will help you to decide what should go on your own profile page.

Follow these steps:

1. **Create your page.** At the bottom of the home page, click on the 'Create a Page' link. This link takes you to the section where people representing a business, celebrity or band can create their page on the network. Choose what you do from the following options: local business or place; company, organisation or institution; brand or product. Make further entries from the drop-down menus to refine your choice. For example, you might choose 'health/beauty' as your industry and then enter your business name.

2. **Sign up for Facebook.** You need to indicate whether you already have a Facebook account or if you're signing up for the first time. Enter your login or registration details.

3. **Add content.** You can choose to add photos, logos, videos, reviews, business information, event information and pretty much anything else that you think best represents your organisation. At this point, your initial surfing will come in handy. Did you like pages that had lots of videos to watch? Is the product you sell best explained by a video – does it need lots of explaining in text otherwise? Depending on your company or product, each business profile will be slightly different. Simply follow the easy to use guidelines to add different details to the page.

Signing up to Twitter

Before you set up a profile on Twitter, first make sure that it will be relevant to your audience. While a wide range of people do use Twitter, it's less a community in the sense of Facebook, where people gather on your page to discuss their opinions, and more a place to take part in conversations or listen to how people feel about your brand. People often update their Twitter account with every thought that passes through their mind, so it can be an excellent way to carry out some free research.

As with Facebook, we suggest first checking out how other companies and brands are using Twitter, having registered a personal profile page on the network. Then follow these steps:

1. **Register your profile:** Go to www.twitter.com and click the 'sign up' button on in the top right hand corner of the homepage. You will then be prompted to set up an account on the social network and be asked to supply some information such as your email address and a login name.

2. **Add further details to your profile.** Consider a small photo and a short piece of biographical information. For example, Coca-Cola uses a picture of an iconic Coke bottle and the biography 'Official tweets of Coke & the Coca-Cola Company'. Choose something that fits your brand.

3. **Personalise your account.** Start off by following people who either talk a lot about your brand (you can search for such details on the site) or whose Twitter updates you admire. You can create lists of similar Twitter users to make following their updates more manageable. For example, you can make lists entitled 'loyal customers' or 'inspiration'. The updates from these people will then not appear in your main stream of information on your profile but will only be seen when you choose to access that list. Explore and have fun.

Signing up to LinkedIn

LinkedIn is different from Facebook and MySpace as it focuses purely on the professional sector. LinkedIn isn't the site to advertise on if you want to sell products – unless you're selling Ferraris and Rolex watches and want to target very wealthy individuals. Instead, join LinkedIn so that you can connect with professionals in your own industry, look for jobs and network with other business people who may be helpful to you in the future. Signing up to LinkedIn is just as easy as signing up for other social networks. Follow these steps:

1. **Go to** www.linkedin.com **and read the 'user agreement' at the bottom of the page.** This tells you what you can and can't do on the site. Once you're happy, you can return to the home page.

2. **Fill in your information in the boxes provided.** Add the relevant details to the First Name, Last Name and Email boxes. Next, click 'continue'. You enter a fuller registration page that prompts you to add your personal information.

3. **Fill in your personal information.** As this is a professional network, it doesn't ask for your favourite football team or what type of food you enjoy most. It asks what company you work for, what position you hold and what industry you work in. Once you've filled in this information, click 'join LinkedIn' at the bottom of the page.

4. **Complete your profile.** You can say as much or as little as you want on your LinkedIn profile. The details you provide will obviously differ depending on whether you're creating a personal profile or a profile for your company. You can add everything from previous workplaces to recommendations from former colleagues. You can post status updates, a little like Facebook and Twitter. And you can indicate why you're using LinkedIn – choose from everything from networking to career opportunities.

You're now a member of the LinkedIn community. On your home page, you can search for and connect with former colleagues and classmates, create a presentation about yourself and your company, join relevant groups and flesh out your profile and work history. The beauty of LinkedIn is that people are eager to connect with you because the site becomes more useful the more you use it, so you don't have to worry about making contacts. Start by adding your existing work contacts and you'll soon find that their colleagues or customers want to connect with you as well. Used properly, LinkedIn can gradually build into a powerful marketing tool for you and your business.

Use of LinkedIn has rocketed since the advent of the global recession in 2008. By June 2011, it had reached more than 33 million users. This has been driven by people needing to leverage their contacts much harder in order to continually generate business, keep their jobs, ensure that more orders for products and services are in the pipeline and generally stay active in what is a very tricky market. So now it's even more important for you to know about LinkedIn and understand what it does – even if you're not ready to use it yet.

Attracting Visitors to Your Page or Profile

For an organisation, the whole point of social networking is to continue a conversation with existing and potential customers in an environment that's comfortable for them. 'Push' advertising by getting in people's faces is totally inappropriate on networking sites, but you can do some things that will grab attention – as long as you're offering people something in return for their time.

First, remember to tell people about your social networking efforts. You wouldn't set up a website and then not tell anyone the web address, would you? Nor would you create a new product and put it on the shelves without letting anyone know what it does. The same needs to apply to your social media efforts. You can't expect consumers to be instantly excited by the fact that you've created a social network page for your business without telling them that it exists. Ask people to become a 'fan' or 'like' you on Facebook, follow you on Twitter or link with you on LinkedIn.

Creating interesting content

When you're creating your social network profile, put something up there that's worth visiting and won't just disappoint people. If they visit your page on a website that's primarily about them having a good time with friends and family, you need to make it worth their while.

Imagine how you'd feel if you were driving in your car on a family trip and saw a sign advertising 'free petrol – turn left', but then discovered when you got to the garage that you had to spend £50 on new tyres first to get a free £5 worth of petrol. You'd be pretty unhappy at having wasted your time, we reckon.

The same applies in social media. Users in social networks are having a good time by themselves. You need to create a reason for them to come to your site and the payoff has to be immediate and very obvious. If you don't sell products online, satisfying visitors can be tricky, which is why many brands have started to create their own content and applications (see the 'Unleashing the Power of Applications in Online Advertising' section later in this chapter) in order to create deeper relationships with users.

But for examples of what you can do on Facebook, check out these pages via the website's search function:

- ✔ **'Coca-Cola Store':** A shop that sells all things Coca-Cola related. The Facebook page contains product information but also an interesting and amusing video showing how plastic bottles are being recycled by Coca-Cola to create new items.

- ✔ **'Royal Opera House':** Not necessarily the first organisation that you'd expect to see on Facebook, but the ROH is posting behind-the-scenes footage, photos and trailers of upcoming performances on its Facebook page. The ROH has also held specific nights for fans of its Facebook page.

- ✔ **'ASOSOfficial':** This is the transactional store for fashion retailer ASOS on Facebook. Relatively few brands are using Facebook as a sales platform at the moment, so it's worth checking out what companies like ASOS are doing in case their approach is appropriate for you or your company.

Advertising your presence

Once you've created something useful for your potential customers to visit, you need to alert people to the fact that you're in their social world.

Social networks operate by keeping friends up-to-date with each other's lives. So if someone likes your Facebook page and becomes a 'fan' of it, this fact shows up on their home page in the 'news feed' that catalogues what everyone they know is up to. Their fan status will also be highlighted to their network of friends, who, upon seeing this situation, may want to check out what all the fuss is about. If they become fans after checking out your page, this fact will be highlighted to all their friends, and so on. If you have something interesting on your page, the effect can snowball and you could potentially quickly find yourself with literally millions of fans (although most brands will probably have a few hundred to a thousand fans rather than unmanageable millions).

The simplest way to start attracting fans is to highlight your Facebook page's existence on your existing marketing material; doing so will drive users to your Facebook efforts and start the ball rolling in terms of virally distributing your efforts through the social network. You can speed up this process by using Facebook's proprietary advertising system Facebook Ads.

Signing up to Facebook Ads, through the 'advertising' tab at the bottom of your homepage, allows your ads to be displayed to social network users who might have an interest in your product or service. The social stories, such as a friend becoming a fan of your Facebook page, make your ad both more interesting and more relevant. Facebook Ads are placed in highly visible parts of the site without interrupting the user's experience on Facebook.

Follow these steps to utilise Facebook Ads:

1. **Click on the 'Advertising' button on the bottom of the homepage on** `www.facebook.com`**.** You go straight to the advertising homepage.

2. **Click on the 'Create an Advert' button on the page (or click the link to contact the sales team).** You're asked if you want to create a 'sponsored story' or a 'Facebook ad'.

3. **Choose the type of ad you want.** Different ads show up in different parts of the site, so take time to read about the various ad types.

4. **Design your ad.** Add any photos and URLs you want to use. Think carefully about where you want to drive anyone who clicks on the ad – to your website, for example?

5. **Choose who you want to see your ad.** This decision is very important. You have the option to target different groups, so think carefully – are you trying to target existing customers or people who don't know about your products?

You can also choose to target your ad at a specific gender or age group. Facebook allows you to target the ad against certain keywords, so that it's shown to people to whom it's relevant. For example, if you're advertising football boots, relevant keywords are probably 'football', 'goal', 'sports' and 'Premiership'.

As you choose your targeting options, remember that each time you refine an option by gender, age or keyword, it changes the number of people that your ad could reach. You need to make your ad as targeted as possible but not so specific that only three people in the whole of the UK can see it – you won't bring in much business that way!

6. **Select the amount you want to spend on Facebook advertising.** Doing so will determine the eventual marketing solution the site offers you. You can set either a limit on how much you're willing to spend per day or a lifetime value for a marketing campaign.

    We can't advise you which is the better option for your organisation as your decision depends on your business objectives. By playing around with the service, however, you'll soon find which option works best for you.

7. **Review Facebook's 'guide to Facebook for Business' at** www.facebook.com/business**.** Check that your ad adheres to Facebook rules. Tweak any details, if necessary.

8. **Complete the ad ordering process.** Read the terms and conditions, fill in the payment information and press the 'place order' button. Congratulations – you're now running social advertising across Facebook.

Unleashing the Power of Applications in Online Advertising

Possibly, you're already a member of a social network and a good chance exists that you're already using applications. Do you listen to music service Spotify through Facebook? Or play the Farmville game with your friends on the network? If you do, you're using applications – or apps.

Essentially, apps are the little tools, services and games created by third parties that can be downloaded and sit on your Facebook profile. In Facebook, you can access them through the 'Applications' tab on your homepage.

However, apps can also be added to blogs, homepages, desktops or any other place on the web where people control the content. Apps are also called widgets or gadgets, depending on where they're found online or on mobile phones such as the iPhone. In fact, mobile phones are now the main place for finding apps (check out Chapter 13 for more details).

Don't let this language confuse you. Generally, these apps all do pretty much the same thing – they provide the consumer with a specific service or content inside another platform or web page. (Technically, a slight difference exists between them, but we'll leave that to the techies to worry about. For our purposes, we refer to these apps as one group.)

Spotify is an example of a successful app. As well as being a website in its own right, this service lets users of Facebook listen to music from the Spotify library of millions of songs. It currently has nearly 8 million users on Facebook. .The secret of Spotify's success is that, not only can you choose songs for yourself, you can also share tracks with others. If you share a track with someone, they may well download the app themselves.

But how do people developing apps know what to create? You may have a great idea for an app that would appeal to your target audience (an interactive race calendar if you're a betting shop owner, for example), but how do you know if enough of your target audience would use it? Well, Facebook's two-way dialogue works in your favour here. Facebook has become such a popular place to host apps because it's able to give developers access to information about its users. As a result, developers can create engaging apps that are more useful to people at relatively low cost.

Apps can achieve two distinctly different things depending on how you use them. First, if you create your own apps, you can create content or services that mean consumers spend time with your brand. Doing so will generate a positive feeling about your company with the users of the app, which will help you to market to them and hopefully sell them products or services.

Second, you can use other people's apps to advertise your services or products. Application/widget advertising networks have sprung up everywhere in the last couple of years. It's a young but growing market. Application advertising networks are regarded as great places to advertise because research show that Internet users spend a lot of time using these apps and are very engaged when they do so. This situation means they'll hopefully spend longer looking at one of your ads.

You can, of course, create an app yourself and then allow others to advertise through your efforts, generating some additional revenue for yourself. However, think about whether you want to have other brands occupying a space in which you're trying to develop a deeper relationship with your customers. Most apps are developed either by a brand and take no advertising or are created by a third party with the express purpose of attracting advertising. Decide which approach suits you best.

If you're interested in finding out more about advertising inside apps, take a look at these companies' websites: www.adknowledge.com, and www.clearspring.com for some useful advice.

Creating Your Own Apps

If you decide that the best route is to create your own app to enable you to spend a little more time with your customers, you probably need to hire an agency to do so. You can have a go yourself if you're very technically savvy, but at the end of the day, the app space is competitive and creating an engaging app is harder than you think. Getting expert help is probably best.

All social networks that use apps have released tools to help people create services that use the best parts of their social network platforms. However, these *software development toolkits* (*SDKs*) don't really help you if you have no experience in writing code for the Internet. If you have no in-house capability to write code, you need to employ an agency to do it for you.

We can't recommend an agency to you – hundreds, if not thousands, operate in the UK, ranging from one-person outfits to big international players, and singling any one out would be unfair. We can, however, help you to get the selection process underway.

Step 1

First, you need to decide on a brief. Essentially, what is it that you want to achieve? Do you want to give your customers something fun to play with – a game; or a useful tool – a tracking app for deliveries; or simply a window into your inventory so they can buy products through the app?

What you offer is your call, but most people will use an app if it gives them something in return for spending their time using it. So your app should be engaging and useful – whether that's in creating entertainment or in a way that helps them enjoy or deal with their daily lives.

Step 2

When you've decided roughly what you want to offer, create an RFP – a Request for Pitch – document. An *RFP* is an outline (no more than two sides of A4) of what you want to achieve that you can send out to a number of selected agencies. Agencies will use the RFP to come up with ideas to meet your needs. The RFP needs to outline who you are, what your business is, whom your target audience is and what you want to achieve. It might also be useful at this stage to indicate the size of your project, so that nobody's time is wasted if it's too big or too small for a particular agency to handle.

Step 3

Choose and contact a few agencies. We recommend contacting somewhere between five and ten to begin with. You can select your agencies to contact in a number of ways:

- ✔ Ask your industry contacts to recommend some agencies – this is particularly easy to do through LinkedIn.
- ✔ Go through the list of member agencies at organisations such as the Internet Advertising Bureau (IAB), the UK's interactive advertising trade body (www.iabuk.net).
- ✔ Look for agencies via your local business organisations and in local directories.
- ✔ Discover which companies made your favourite apps.
- ✔ Use a search engine to look for digital agencies in your area.

Step 4

Now undertake the selection process. When you've contacted agencies and those that are interested have indicated a desire to talk further, you should be able to decide on the five that you'd like to invite to a beauty parade. Choose five agencies to come to your office and present their ideas to you.

Don't invite more than five agencies, as making them put in a lot of effort if they have to compete against ten others for the business is unfair. If less competition is encountered, they may put more effort into meeting your brief requirements, too, as they'll feel they have more of a chance to win the business. After you've met all five (avoid letting them meet each other in the process, to keep things above board), then select the two you like best for whatever reason (price/chemistry/locality) and invite them back for a second round to iron out any last issues that you have. At the end of this process, you should be able to make a decision on the right agency for you.

Maintaining Your Conversations and Adding Value

When you've entered the social space via the creation of social network profile pages for your company, social advertising, the creation of an app and maybe some app advertising, consider the dinner party analogy we use in the 'Marketing with Pull not Push Strategies' section earlier in this chapter.

In that section, you were aiming to be the genial guest, not the bore who only talks about himself. But what about when you're the host? Well, you serve the drinks and canapes and have a nice chat with your guests. But what would happen next if you just shut up and ignored all the guests at your party? They'd pretty quickly leave. The same thing will happen if you begin to talk to your customers in the social space and then stop just as speedily.

Chances are that some kind of community already exists inside a social network or using social media elsewhere online that you can tap into. They could be talking directly about your products and services or be interested in content that's related to what you do.

By entering the social space and offering these people something, you've made the first step in becoming part of that community and added a bit of value to their discussion.

The worst thing you can do, but something that we see happen all too often, is to start a conversation with customers only to stop it when the 'campaign' comes to an end. Customers are still customers after a campaign has ended and you've sold them something. So why would you stop offering them value and listening to them? If you act in this way, you're not reaping the full benefits of the marketing you've done so far and you're not setting yourself up to be someone who they'll talk to in the future.

To be a successful social media advertiser, you need to continually add value to people's experiences and this means throwing away your 'campaign' short-term marketing mentality and entering into social media with a long-term commitment to helping your customers.

You can maintain the conversation with your customers in several ways and none of them need to be prohibitively expensive:

✔ If you have existing assets such as articles, photos or anything else that's generated in the course of your business, allow your customers to access and use it in a useful way. Anything that's not sensitive to your business can be useful to the consumer. Your openness will make you look like a more trustworthy and interesting company. (For example, if your company's a building firm and you take photos and videos of your new developments as they're created – for health and safety purposes – why not let the online audiences play with them? Providing them online costs you very little as you're taking these photos anyway and you'll create some interest around your company.)

✔ Once you've created an environment in which people can interact with your company – either by posting comments online or any other method – continue to respond to them. Nothing is more frustrating for a customer than finding nobody at the end of an email or blog post.

- ✔ If you start a blog or social network profile page, keep it up. An out-of-date profile page that only has one or two postings is shoddy. It looks exactly what it is – a half-hearted effort – and people will form that impression of your company

- ✔ If you decide to reinvent yourself in some way, remove any earlier social media efforts so that people don't find them and start interacting with your company in the wrong place. This advice sounds obvious, but leaving incorrect or misleading information online can cause real business problems.

Another way to continue your conversations is to employ online PR (public relations) to create a buzz around events at your company such as product launches or anniversaries. We talk more about online PR and word of mouth in Chapter 15.

Benefitting from Others' Success

Congratulations, you're now a successful social media advertiser. But the education process for digital advertisers is continuous and, as social media is currently at the cutting edge of digital marketing, you have more to learn here than in any other area.

Always answer the following questions in relation to your social advertising efforts in order to give them the best chance of success:

- ✔ Does it add value to the user?

- ✔ Is it engaging?

- ✔ Would you interact with it?

- ✔ Have you been honest and open?

The last of these points is very important. Advertising in the social space is a relatively new phenomenon, but people have been interacting with each other online for some time, so they often view it as a personal space. Many companies have decided the best way to market in this personal medium is to disguise who they are and their intentions, rather than trying to add value by being up-front and adding value to the user's existing experience.

These companies have been found out in very embarrassing ways – which we detail in Chapter 15, along with new laws that exist in the UK covering the illegality of disguising advertising online. For more info now, visit the Office of Fair Trading website, www.oft.gov.uk, where you can find it under the 'Business Advice' heading and the 'Competing Fairly' section.

To avoid encountering problems and making mistakes using social networking you can learn a lot by looking at those companies who are getting it right. Below are a few case studies and reports into brands using social media:

```
http://tinyurl.com/4lhgncr
```

```
www.casestudiesonline.com/
```

```
http://wearesocial.net/blog/2009/05/buy-social-media-
case-study/
```

If so many other companies can get it right, so can you!

Chapter 13

Embracing Mobile Marketing

*T*his chapter talks about mobile marketing. To our US cousins the vehicle for this marketing approach is a cell phone, in the UK a mobile phone and in Finland a kännykkä, which literally means 'an extension of the hand'. The Nordic region is one of the world's most sophisticated mobile markets, primarily because of companies such as Nokia and Ericsson that make the handsets used by many people. The word kännykkä shows how the mobile phone has become our most intimate communication device.

For a marketer, this is great news. If you can communicate with customers on their most intimate device – and the one they nearly always keep on them – you stand a great chance of success. However, with this great opportunity comes great danger. The same intimacy means that people aren't likely to want to be bombarded with messages on their phones. So, as you read this chapter, keep in mind the mantra 'would I want this on my own phone?' It will serve you well.

The mobile marketing world can be very complex and is dominated by ever-evolving technology, different handsets and operating systems (the software on phones such as iPhone, Blackberry and Android phones – collectively referred to as smartphones). We do our best to cut out the jargon and bring you a relevant guide to mobile marketing.

We discuss various techniques you can use to engage your customers using mobile technology. A lot of the guidelines and best practices we talk about are provided by the leading trade body for mobile marketing, the Mobile Marketing Association (MMA), whose website is a great resource for mobile-related marketing information (www.mmaglobal.com).

Texting for Success

More than 4.3 billion mobile phones exist in the world, according to the GSMA, the organisation representing the interests of mobile operators world-wide. Of these, 3.4 billion are GSM phones (not smartphones). This means that over three-quarters of the world's mobile phones are being used for reasonably basic functions, such as making calls and sending text messages.

Whilst it's true that many of these mobile phone owners are in developing markets, this fact certainly makes you wonder whether the simplest of marketing techniques may sometimes be the best. The majority of phones aren't being used for apps or to surf the Internet whilst on the move, even if the trend is towards this type of use. So, while this chapter does cover this style of mobile marketing, you first need to consider whether you're using the basics well enough.

Nowadays when you make an appointment with the dentist, you can ask for a reminder to be sent to your phone the day before – just in case you forget. A simple text message does just the job and it could be just the job to let your customers know about special offers you have, too.

The MMA defines SMS as follows:

Short Message Service (SMS) is a communications service that allows the exchange of short text messages, limited to 160 characters, between mobile phones. It is also referred to as 'text messaging' or 'texting'. SMS messages can be sent and received between virtually all operator networks. Virtually every mobile phone in the world supports SMS, creating a ubiquitous market for SMS-based advertising campaigns. SMS supports messages sent from one user to another, as well as messages sent from a machine, such as a PC, application or server, to a user.

Clearly, then, the huge benefit of using SMS to talk to your customers is that every mobile phone can receive your messages!

SMS also offers the following advantages:

✔ Mobile phones are very personal, so messages received on them can have great power.

✔ A mobile phone is nearly always within three feet of its owner.

✔ People tend to read every text they get – unlike direct mail through their door.

The disadvantages are:

- You only have 160 characters to get your message across.
- People can respond negatively to unwanted texts.
- Lots of spam and phishing SMS texts are delivered, so people can be wary of an unknown sender.

Getting started with SMS

First things first, you need a message for your existing or potential customers.

SMS marketing works best if your message is clear and concise; remember, you only have 160 characters to play with – so no waffle allowed! Offering an incentive for the customer to do something – get more information, get a coupon or take advantage of a time-sensitive offer are all good ideas. An SMS won't achieve a complex goal; it's purpose is really to move the customer along to the next step of your marketing.

When you've created your message, you then need to send it out – and to do so you need your customers' mobile phone numbers. Always ensure that you take this detail when you ask a new or potential customer for contact information.

Fitness First, a gym company, was keen to find young adults who might be interested in joining up. The company decided that the best way to encourage people to take up a membership was to get them to trial the gym first. The idea was that, once someone tried going to the gym, they could see it becoming part of their regular routine.

Fitness First partnered with mobile operator O2 and defined various areas in London where it wanted to gain customers. All O2 customers passing through these areas were then sent an SMS offer of a free two-day pass for Fitness First.

More than 1100 people signed up as new members of Fitness First on four- and 12-month contracts, netting the gym brand an extra £385,000. This worked out as a return on investment of 2690 per cent!

As well as the new customers, the campaign showed that the most responsive recipients of the offer were single people aged between 18 and 35. So not only did Fitness First find a relatively low-cost way of attracting new members, it also found out which demographic it could target more often in future.

If you engage in SMS marketing, you must ensure that those people you contact have opted-in to receiving communication from you via this channel. You can check out the Information Commissioner's Office Guide to the Privacy and Electronic Communications Regulations (`www.ico.gov.uk/for_organisations/privacy_and_electronic_communications/the_guide.aspx`) before you start to make sure you do things by the book.

Partnering with a mobile marketing agency

Once you have your message and your target list (see the preceding sections), you need to employ a mobile marketing agency to send out the texts for you. Prices for this service vary, depending on the number of texts you wish to send.

You can, of course, also buy or rent a list of mobile phone numbers to send your message to. However, if the recipients aren't already your customers, your success rate using mobile marketing to target these 'cold' prospects will be really low. You need to use less personal forms of communication, such as email, to approach new prospects – although, as you will have seen from the Fitness First campaign earlier in this chapter, sometimes if your offer is good enough cold prospects can be warmed up!

Companies tend to price their services by package – so check their delivery rates, try before you buy and make sure the support services are satisfactory. Just type 'SMS Gateway' into Google and compare the prices and services of the leading companies. These services often include a certain amount of analytical information on your SMS campaign as part of their offering too – be sure to check out what they can tell you about the SMS campaign once you have pressed the 'go' button. Look for data on aspects such as delivery and open rates.

Taking a Look at the Mobile Web

Whilst SMS marketing can reach every mobile phone in the UK if you really want to, the mobile web is slightly less accessible as it requires a phone with a mobile browser. The good news is that over a quarter of all adults (27 per cent) and almost half of all teenagers (47 per cent) now own a smartphone. And according to the latest Ofcom report, smartphones are very user friendly for accessing the Internet.

Even better than that, 28 per cent of adults in the UK use their mobile phones for Internet access. And according to the Mobile Entertainment Forum's Global Consumer Survey, of everyone accessing the Internet, 18 per cent do so via mobile devices rather than desktop computers.

So, a very large number of British adults, and increasingly teenagers too, have access to the Internet wherever they are and whatever time it is. This reality has huge implications for businesses that sell goods and services – a simple price comparison when out shopping is never more than a few clicks away. In the past, many customers had to 'buy blind' and hope they were getting the best deal.

To take advantage of this new market, you need to make sure that your website is as user friendly on a mobile phone as it is on a PC. Chapter 10 covers building a great website but, depending on the complexity of your business, the number of products you sell or the amount of information you want to convey, you may need to consider creating a shorter, more concise mobile website to take advantage of this trend for mobile Internet access.

Many websites work perfectly fine on mobile web browsers already. Access your own website via smartphone to check out how easy it is to navigate and find information on; if it's not user friendly, you're a prime candidate for a mobile website.

If a mobile website appears to be a necessity, don't panic! You either already have many of the skills you need from building your main website (as described in Chapter 10) or you can hire a designer. Select a specialist mobile web design agency for this job; your existing web agency may be able to help you directly or at least provide you with a list of good companies to talk to. Alternatively, go to www.nmamarketingservicesguide.co.uk for a list of mobile agencies to get yourself started.

Make sure that whoever you choose to build your mobile website follows the World Wide Web Consortium (W3C) guidelines. Check out www.w3.org/standards/webdesign/mobilweb for details.

A mobile website should present those people who are accessing the Internet via a mobile phone with the same great experience as they'd get from your main website.

To understand the significance of mobile websites from a brand perspective, check out the MMA's wisdom on the matter at www.mmaglobal.com.

When your mobile website is up and running, you can then promote it using SMS marketing, giving people the chance to simply click a link and be taken straight to your digital showroom. You can also take advantage of a better return on your other digital marketing efforts, because search marketing (see Chapter 11) will direct people using search engines on their phones to your mobile site, which will deliver a better experience than your main website and thus, increase your chance of a sale.

This logic also applies when potential customers are out shopping and use their phones to compare a rival's product on price. If you have a great mobile website and a good search strategy, you stand a good chance of stealing that customer away.

Realising There's an App for That!

On 10 July 2008, Apple opened the Apple App Store and the world went crazy for apps. Mobile apps were originally designed to help us out with our daily lives and included calculators, maps, calendars and other useful tools. Nowadays apps are created for just about any reason you can think of and brands are heavily involved.

Since Apple launched the Apple App Store, every other smartphone provider and some third parties have followed suit and now thousands of apps are available.

Smartphone owners can download apps from the following sites:

- ✔ Android Market
- ✔ App Catalog
- ✔ Apple App Store
- ✔ App World
- ✔ Ovi Store
- ✔ Windows Phone Marketplace
- ✔ Amazon App Store

We bet that, if you own a smartphone, you've downloaded at least three apps in the last year, and probably many, many more. However, we're also willing to bet that you only regularly use a small number of the apps on your phone and most simply sit there untouched. Unfortunately for brands, this is what happens to the majority of apps that are created with marketing in mind.

At the advent of a new technology, brands always seem drawn to use it in an attempt to appear cool and cutting edge. Sadly, this has resulted in a lot of rather useless apps that offer no real value to the consumer. If an app provides no benefits, not only will it not be used, it will also probably create a negative view of that brand in the consumer's mind.

Some good examples of apps created by brands do exist, but these mostly fit into one category – service-based apps.

Addison Lee is a car service based in London. As the company already operates a telephone and website booking service, it wasn't a great leap to take advantage of the rise in consumers' use of apps by creating one of its own.

Addison Lee's app uses the company logo as its screen icon, and offers the user the opportunity to book a car whenever he needs it. It also provides details such as journey time and price. If the user is an existing customer, he can use his account or pay by credit card. A new customer can arrange to pay in cash. The customer receives a series of text messages telling him when the car is booked, when it's on its way and when it arrives ready for pick-up. Simple. Effective.

You can also create apps with just entertainment in mind. Consider devising a game that's linked to your brand – think of a car-based game if you are a car dealership or a fun shopkeeper game if you're a convenience store. Just bear in mind that creating game apps is a bit of an art form and will require significant investment if you want to do it right.

Your final option in relation to this form of marketing is to advertise on popular apps rather than create one of your own. A number of companies offer in-app advertising and the process is just the same as buying web banners on websites.

Try either of these companies for a start:

- ✔ http://advertising.apple.com
- ✔ www.admob.com

Reviewing Other Mobile Marketing Technologies

The lack of consistency in mobile marketing technology is its biggest drawback; everyone's using different phones, operating systems and providers.

Replicating your marketing efforts to make them work on each different device and operating system means your effectiveness in reaching the desired number of people may be compromised. This confusing ecosystem has been created by years of fierce competition between different handset manufacturers and mobile operators (the Vodafone, O2 and Everything Everywheres of the world).

As well as these incompatibilities, and just to confuse you further, another layer of mobile technology exists that isn't directly related to the inner workings of the mobile phone, to make calls or surf the web, but rather is used to enable different forms of mobile advertising.

Below we list some of these technologies and explain their various uses. It's hugely unlikely that all of these will appeal – or be useful – to you and the list is in no way exhaustive. However, it is representative of the options available to you if you become a fully-fledged mobile marketer.

- ✔ **MMS – multimedia messaging service:** The multimedia version of SMS, MMS messages can contain images, text, audio and video.

- ✔ **QR code – quick response code:** A barcode that can be scanned by a mobile device with the right software to direct the user to any website or mobile website page desired. QR codes were originally used to track car parts by manufacturers, but are now used by marketers to bring consumers to information online.

- ✔ **Bluetooth:** An open wireless technology used to send data over short distances. Most mobile phones can receive Bluetooth communication and this technology is often used by advertisers who want to make an out of home advert (billboard or bus stop advert) interactive by sending data to a consumer's mobile phone. The data is often a short film or other visual communication. Interestingly, this technology is named after Harald I of Denmark and parts of Norway who united dissonant Danish tribes into a single kingdom. The implication is that Bluetooth does the same with communications protocols, uniting them into one universal standard!

- ✔ **LBS – location-based services:** An information or entertainment service accessible through mobile devices, which uses the mobile network and GPS to determine the location of the user and tailor information/entertainment accordingly. Businesses such as cinema chains use LBS to let people in the vicinity know what's on at particular cinemas at certain times.

- ✔ **NFC – near field communication:** Allows for simplified transactions, data exchange and wireless connections between two devices in close proximity to each other, usually by no more than a few centimetres. This technology represents the future as it enables your mobile phone to become your mobile wallet and buy everything from your train ticket to your cup of coffee in the local cafe. NFC is already being used in some cities, with the technology linked to debit or credit cards.

- ✔ **Shortcodes:** These are phone numbers – significantly shorter than full phone numbers – that can be used to address SMS and MMS messages from brands to consumers. For example, if you want to get a consumer to visit your website but the only advertising you're doing is on a big billboard, the consumer is unlikely to stop, write down your web address and then wait until he gets home to look up your website.

> With a shortcode, people can simply text a keyword you decide upon, such as 'web', to a specified number (codes are five digits in length, mostly starting with 6 or 8; codes starting with 7 are used by charities in the UK) and receive a message back with a link to the website. To encourage more people to use them, shortcodes are usually paid for by the advertiser with no cost to the consumer.

All of these technologies are being used to varying degrees in the UK today, but not all of them will be relevant to you. However, knowledge of what's out there will enable you to make the best decision for your brand. As a hard and fast rule, the newer a technology is, the more you'll probably be drawn to it; but it's also more expensive and less likely to generate significant results for you. Much better to be on the leading edge than the 'bleeding' edge, so let others make the mistakes and you can learn from them.

Following Privacy and Best Practice Guidelines

Mobile marketing is a relatively new discipline and, as such, people are still finding out what works and what doesn't.

In an effort to tackle the complexity of this new form of marketing, the mobile marketing industry has compiled a series of good conduct guidelines. The MMA provides a Global Code of Conduct for its mobile marketing members. This code, together with the legal rules concerning privacy, should be your guiding light when engaging in any mobile marketing activity.

The five key tenets of the MMA Global Code of Conduct are outlined in the following list. To access all of the MMA's guideline documents, and to get the crucial detail on these guidelines, go to http://mmaglobal.com/policies/education.

- ✔ **Notice**: Mobile marketers must give users *notice*, describing the terms and conditions of a marketing programme clearly and accessibly. Notice should include the marketer's identity (or the products and services offered), and the key terms and conditions that govern contact between the marketer and the mobile device user.

- ✔ **Choice and consent:** Mobile marketers must respect the right of the user to control which messages they receive.

- ✔ **Customisation and constraint:** Marketing must be targeted appropriately, and should reflect what the customer expects to see, and what can genuinely bring them added value. User information collected by the marketer must be used responsibly, and users should not be targeted with excessive messages.

✔ **Security:** Mobile marketers must protect the user information collected in connection with mobile marketing programmes from use, alteration, disclosure, distribution or access, unless authorised by the user.

✔ **Enforcement and accountability:** The MMA expects its members to comply with the MMA Global Code of Conduct (see the weblink earlier in this section for further details). At the moment, self-regulation is the name of the game, but regulation by a third party in the future is a possibility.

If you're operating in the UK, you must also comply with the Data Protection Act, which is designed to protect consumers against the misuse of their personal data held by companies. This includes mobile telephone numbers. To access information on the Data Protection Act, including a guide to its principles, visit the Information Commissioner's Office website: www.ico.gov.uk.

If these guidelines look a bit scary, don't panic! Chances are you'll just want to engage in some pretty basic mobile marketing, and most of it will be conducted with people who are already your customers. This approach is called customer relationship management (CRM), and mobile is a fantastic channel for keeping existing customers up to date with your company news or letting them know about their orders, for example – so don't be afraid to use it. Just make sure you have their permission first!

Chapter 14

Direct Marketing and Telemarketing

● ●

In This Chapter

▶ Boosting response rates and sales with direct marketing

▶ Designing effective direct-response ads

▶ Setting up a call centre to service your direct customers

▶ Using telemarketing

▶ Understanding direct marketing and the law

● ●

Direct marketing is easy to do, but difficult to do well. You have to master direct marketing to the degree that you can beat the odds and obtain higher-than-average response rates. We share multiple ways to achieve this goal in this chapter as we help you review the varied problems and practices of direct marketing. This chapter focuses on conventional media – print ads, conventional mail (versus email, which is covered in Chapter 10) and the telephone. Remember these media can be integrated with (or sometimes replaced by) digital marketing, which we discuss in Chapters 10, 11, 12 and 13.

Beating the Odds with Your Direct Marketing

Direct marketing, relationship marketing, one-to-one marketing: they're all the same thing at heart, so we don't care what term you use. To us, direct marketing occurs whenever you, the marketer, take it upon yourself to create and manage customer transactions through one or more media.

The importance of civility in direct marketing

Many marketers rush to direct marketing in the often-mistaken belief that they can handle their customers better than any intermediaries can. But if you aren't accustomed to dealing directly with customers, you're likely to mess up your attempt at direct marketing. Being too direct is the most common way to mess up marketing. If you're in your customers' faces, you're probably getting on their nerves as well. Direct marketing should build a bridge between you and the customer. No matter what direct marketing you do, keeping it civil and polite gets much better results. Avoid impolite calls, errors on address labels and anything else that may offend the average person. Cull lists to eliminate duplications and errors. Doing direct marketing well costs a bit more, but you get far better results.

You have to make a positive impression if you want to achieve high response rates. Here's the most important principle of direct marketing. Please repeat after us: Contacting a hundred people well is better than contacting a thousand people poorly!

The odds of success in direct marketing aren't particularly good. The average direct appeal to consumers or businesses goes unanswered. Yet if you can up the response rate even a little bit over the average, you can make some serious money using direct marketing.

Perfecting your performance

Practice makes perfect in direct marketing if you make sure to keep records of what you do and track the responses. That way, you can tell when a change improves response rates. Even if you have little or no experience in direct marketing, have faith that a small initiative can generate enough information for you to get a grip on how to direct market better and on a larger scale. The best way to become good at direct marketing is to start doing it.

Ease into direct marketing with a modest campaign to minimise your risk and start growing from there. This principle is true whether you're big or small, a retailer or wholesaler, a for-profit or not-for-profit business. When Levi Strauss & Co. started a direct-marketing initiative, it started simply, by including a registration card with each pair of jeans it sold. As cards came back, Levi Strauss & Co. built up a database of customers that it could use in its direct marketing.

Developing benchmarks for your campaign

Because your goal is to stimulate consumers to respond to you, your direct marketing has a fairly difficult task to accomplish. You need to understand that most of the interactions between your ad and your prospects fail to stimulate the response you want. Failure is the most common outcome of direct marketing! So your real goal is to minimise failure. Look at the statistics if you don't believe us:

- ✔ A direct-mail letter, individually addressed, typically gets a response from 6.7 per cent of the names you mailed to. So you can expect, at most, 67 responses per thousand from an average letter.

- ✔ The average response from a direct-mail campaign to consumers (as opposed to a *business-to-business* (B2B) campaign) is 7.1 per cent. For business campaigns you can expect a 6.2 per cent response rate.

- ✔ A *door drop*, where your message is delivered to home addresses but is not individually addressed, has an even lower hit rate – typically 5.0 per cent.

- ✔ Of all direct mail, 40 per cent goes into customers' bins unopened. Of the 60 per cent that does get opened, a further 20 per cent doesn't get read.

- ✔ A telemarketing call centre making *outbound* calls to a qualified list can typically achieve responses from up to 5 per cent of the households called for a consumer product, but can get as high as 10 per cent for some B2B sales efforts. However, telemarketing generates far more failures than successes and its cost per thousand is often higher than direct mail because it's more labour intensive.

In short, direct marketing doesn't generate very high response rates, and you have to make realistic projections before deciding to embark on any activity. However, before you despair, know that good direct-marketing campaigns beat these odds and can be highly profitable – campaigns with more than 50 per cent response rates aren't unknown. So don't be discouraged; just be dedicated to doing direct marketing better than average.

Boosting sales from your offers

Here are a few starting tips to help you get focused on the goal of generating high responses to your direct marketing:

- ✔ Send out a letter, special announcement or brochure by first-class post once in a while to find out how well your customer list responds.

Regularly update your mailing list. Not only will doing so keep your postage costs down, it is also your legal responsibility since the introduction of the Data Protection Act (see the 'Keeping It Legal (and Decent)' section later in this chapter). The Royal Mail's Postcode Address File, or PAF, is the most accurate and up-to-date address database in the UK. It lists more than 28 million addresses. You can license it direct for prices starting at £85 or go through one of the many licensed resellers and *list brokers*.

✔ Run a very small display ad because they're the least expensive. Limit yourself to 15 words or less. Describe in a simple headline and one or two brief phrases what you have to sell and then ask people to contact you by post or phone for more information. (Include a simple black-and-white photo of the product to eliminate the need for wordy description.)

✔ Replace your existing advertising copy (your words) with *testimonials* (quotes praising your product or firm) from happy customers or with quotes from news coverage of your firm or product. These comments attract more buyers because they seem more believable than positive things you say about yourself.

✔ Give away a simple, useful or fun gift in exchange for placing an order. People love to receive gifts!

✔ Swap customer lists with another business to boost your list size for free. Before you do so, make sure you're trading contact addresses for people who've given their consent to be contacted. See the 'Observing the Data Protection Act' section later in this chapter.

✔ Send a thank-you note or card to customers by mail or email after they make a purchase. This polite gesture often wins a repurchase. This gesture also lets you test your contact information and gets the customer used to reading your messages so that they're more likely to pay attention to a sales-orientated message later on. In addition, this approach helps to reduce perceived risk and encourage word of mouth.

✔ Send out birthday or holiday greetings in the form of cards or gifts to your in-house list. If you consider someone a valuable customer, let them know it. You may be surprised by how many people contact you afterward to place a new order, even though your mailing to them was non-commercial. (Don't know their birthdays? Send cards on your company's birthday, instead.)

✔ Change the medium or form of your communication every now and then. If you always send out a sales letter, try a colour postcard or an emailed newsletter. Variations like this can increase customer interest, and you may also find that different customers respond best to different forms of communication.

✔ Use a photograph of a person's face, looking directly at the reader with a friendly expression. The person should represent a user or an expert on the product, or relate to the product or offer in some other way. A face attracts attention and increases sales for most direct-response ads and direct-mail letters.

✔ Use a clear, appealing photo of the product. Showing what you have to sell attracts appropriate customers simply and effectively. And if some details don't show up in the photo, add close-up photos. Seeing is believing, and believing is a prerequisite for buying! Few businesses use largely visual direct-response ads, though we can't tell you why. Visual direct-response ads can outsell wordy ones by a wide margin.

✔ Try a radio ad asking people to call a free number or visit a website. Radio ads can be fun and people really listen to them when they grab their attention.

✔ Run your direct-response ad in the *Yellow Pages*. Get a local number for each directory you list your ad in (you can have the calls forwarded to your central office; ask your phone company for details).

And remember that behind every effective direct-marketing campaign stands a well-managed database of customer and prospect names.

Designing Direct-Response Ads

Direct-response ads are ads that stimulate people to respond with an enquiry or purchase, for example 'call this number for your free credit check'. You see direct-response ads most commonly in print media such as magazines and newspapers, and in online advertising. You can also hear and see direct-response ads on radio and TV.

The people who respond to direct-response advertising have self-selected themselves as customers or prospects. You need to do two things with these people:

✔ Try your best to close the sale by getting them to buy something.

✔ Find out as much as you can about them and put the information in your database for future direct marketing efforts.

Many businesses build a direct-marketing capacity through this very process. These businesses place ads in front of what they hope is an appropriate target market and wait to see who responds. Then these businesses attempt to build long-term direct-marketing relationships with those who respond (for example, by sending them brochures or direct-mail letters). Over time, these businesses add respondents to their direct-marketing databases, information about the respondents builds up and many of those respondents become regular direct purchasers.

You can stimulate responses in ways other than direct-response advertising. We show you how to use direct mail and telemarketing in the same way in the 'Delivering Direct Mail' and 'Tuning in to Telemarketing' sections later in this chapter (and don't forget the web's capabilities in this area, too!). Both print and television advertising also have successful track records in this area. Radio may work, too, but you have to innovate to overcome the problem of people rarely writing down what they hear on it. You need to make the otherwise passive radio an action-orientated medium by making your call to action easy to remember. A memorable website address, such as www.elephant. co.uk, may do the trick – as well as repeating it numerous times in the advert.

A direct-response ad must do more than the typical image-building or brand-orientated ad. A direct-response ad has to create enough enthusiasm to get people to close the sale, on their own initiative, right now. How do you accomplish this goal? Make sure that your direct-response ad does the following:

- ✔ **Targets likely readers:** Your ad's readership dramatically affects your response rate. In fact, the same ad, placed in two different publications, can produce response rates at both ends of the range. So the better you define your target consumers, the easier it becomes to find publications relevant to those target consumers, and the better your ad performs.

  Highly selective publications work better for direct-response advertising. A special-interest magazine may deliver a readership far richer in targets than a general-interest magazine or newspaper. For instance, if you have a gardening product that you're trying to sell to women, select a publication read by them. *Good Housekeeping* reaches more than 430,000 women readers, or you could choose *BBC Gardeners' World*, which has a readership of more than 265,000, all of whom are gardeners and, apparently, 60 per cent of whom are women.

- ✔ **Appeals to target readers:** A good story or a character that target readers can identify with and want to be more like – these factors make up the timeless elements of true appeal.

- ✔ **Supports your main claim about the product fully:** Because the ad must not only initiate interest but also close the sale, it has to give sufficient evidence to overcome any reasonable objections on the reader's part. If you think the product's virtues are obvious, show those virtues in a close-up visual of the product. If the appeal isn't so obvious (as in the case of a service), then use testimonials, a compelling story or statistics from objective product tests – in short, some form of evidence that's logically or emotionally convincing, or better still, both.

- ✔ **Speaks to readers in conversational, personal language:** Your ad must be natural and comfortable for readers. Don't get fancy! Write well, yes. Polish and condense, yes. Seek better, catchier, clearer expressions, yes. But don't be stiff or formal.

- ✔ **Makes responding easy:** If readers can make a purchase easily, ask them to do so. If the process is complicated or the product difficult to buy (because it's technical, for example), just ask people to contact you for more information and try to close the sale when they do so. Sometimes, you need an intermediate step. When in doubt, try two versions of your ad – one with an intermediate step and one that tries to make the sale on the spot. Then see which one produces the most sales in the long run.

Delivering Direct Mail

Direct mail is the classic form of direct marketing – in fact, the whole field used to be called direct mail until the experts changed the term. *Direct mail* is the use of personalised sales letters, and it has a long tradition of its own. Direct mail is really no more than a form of print advertising. So before you design, or hire someone to design, a direct-mail piece think about it in the context of being an ad (see Chapters 7, 8 and 9 on designing ads).

Actually, a direct-mail piece isn't like a print ad – it resembles two print ads:

✔ **The first ad is the one the target sees when the mail arrives.** An envelope, usually. And that ad has to accomplish a difficult action goal: getting the target to open the envelope rather than recycling it. Most direct mail ends up in the recycling pile or the bin, without ever getting opened or read! Keep this fact in mind. Devote extra care to making your envelope:

   • Stand out – it needs to be noticeable and different.

   • Provide readers with a reason to open it (sell the benefits or engage their curiosity or, even better, promise a reward!).

   Or send a colour brochure with a stunning front and back cover readers can't resist. Make sure the recipient can see the brochure's exterior by using a clear plastic wrap – don't hide it under a dull envelope.

✔ **The second ad goes to work only if the first succeeds.** The second ad is what's inside, and it needs to get the reader to respond with a purchase or enquiry. In that respect, this ad is much the same as any other direct-response ad. The same rules of persuasive communication apply – plus a few unique ones that we discuss in the following section.

Unlocking the secrets of great direct mail

A great many so-called formulas exist for successful direct-mail letters. None of them work. Instead, your letter must represent creative copywriting and design at its best; don't make anything about your letter formulaic. Your direct-mail letter needs to use the secrets of direct-response advertising design (as described in the 'Designing Direct-Response Ads' section earlier in this chapter) and to employ the principles of creative marketing and good communications, which you can find in Chapters 5 and 7. However, certain strategies can help you employ these principles of good design in a direct-mail piece.

The most effective direct-mail letters generally include several elements, each with its own clear role:

- **Bait:** Include some sort of bait that catches the reader's eye and attention, getting her to read the letter in the first place. Visuals work well as do time-limited offers.

- **Argument:** You then need to provide a sound argument – logical, emotional or both – as to why your great product can solve some specific problem for the reader. Marketers devote the bulk of many letters to making this case as persuasively as possible and you need to keep this sound practice in mind when drafting your direct-mail letter.

- **Call to action:** Finally, you should make an appeal to immediate action; some sort of hook that gets readers to call you, send for a sample, sign up for a contest, place an order or whatever. As long as the readers act, you can consider the letter a success. So this hook is really the climax of the letter, and you need to design everything to ensure that it works.

These three essential elements can be described in various ways. One favourite of many copywriters is the star, chain and hook approach. If you can't find and mark all three of these elements in your own letter, it isn't any good:

- **The star (aka the bait):** A lively opening to your letter. It attracts attention and generates interest.

- **The chain (aka the argument):** This part of the letter presents your argument – the benefits of the product and your claim about what it can do to make the reader's life better.

- **The hook (aka the call to action):** This part ends your letter and it asks the reader to do something immediately. If the letter doesn't make a purchase request, then it should offer an incentive for readers to send in their name or call for more information.

Do these principles apply to email? Yes, but think screens not pages. You have to provide the bait in the subject line in order for the email to be opened. When writing the body copy of an email sales letter, you need to hold the reader's attention and remember to provide the chain and hook as well or your email won't pull as well as the same letter in printed form.

These formulas refer specifically to the text of your letter itself. Remember to think hard about what else goes into your mailing as well.

Enticing envelopes

The outside of the envelope needs to entice readers and get them to open your letter in the first place. The following are some techniques to make your envelope enticing enough to open:

✓ **The stealth approach envelope:** You disguise your letter so that it looks like a bill or personal correspondence – or just cannot be identified at all. You're hoping the reader will open the envelope just to find out what's inside and like what they see enough to respond. Use this approach cautiously, if at all; after all, it's a bit sneaky, and you don't want to annoy the recipient as doing so may ruin your chances forever more. Also, nowadays people often resent being sent unasked-for post because of concerns about environmental waste – some councils actually charge for anything thrown away and not recycled – so be careful with this technique.

✓ **The benefits approach envelope:** You include a headline, perhaps a little supporting copy, even some artwork, to let people know what the mailing is about and summarise why you think your offer is worthy of their attention. We like this approach best because it's honest and direct – and this is direct marketing, after all! Furthermore, this method ensures that those who do open the envelope have self-selected themselves based on interest in your offer. But this technique only works if you have a clear benefit or point of difference to advertise on your envelope. If you can't say 'Open immediately for the lowest price on the XYZ product ranked highest by *Which?*', this method may not work.

✓ **The special offer envelope:** By letting consumers know that they can enter a competition to win a country cottage or get free samples or find valuable coupons enclosed, this envelope gives them a reason to read the letter inside. But the envelope itself doesn't try to sell the product – it leaves that to the carefully crafted letter inside.

✓ **The creative envelope:** If your mailing is unique enough, everyone wants to open it just to find out who you are and what you're up to. Consider an oversized package in an unexpected colour, an envelope with a funny cartoon or quote on the back or a window teasing readers with a view of something interesting inside. You can make your envelope the most exciting thing in someone's letterbox by using any number of creative ideas. Yet this strategy is the least common, probably because creative envelopes cost more. But don't make false economies. If you spend 25 per cent more to double or triple the response rate, then you've saved your company a great deal of money on the mailing by spending more on the envelope!

If you fancy doing something really creative with direct mail and you've got a decent budget or exciting product, consider trying the Royal Mail's Matter service. The service gets consumers to sign up to receive special boxes. Called 'Matter', these boxes contain relevant products and offers. For example, a box which was sent out to affluent men on the database included everything from samples of Original Source shower gel to a special metal badge from Stolichnaya Vodka. The creative box and its interesting contents are intended to create a greater impact than an envelope. Because people choose to sign up, you know they're open to the marketing they'll receive. Visit www.matterbox.co.uk for more details.

Persuasive letters and reply forms

What else should go into your mailing? In general, a letter combined with a simple catalogue of your product(s) pulls more strongly than a letter alone. Catalogues don't work for all products (don't bother for magazine subscriptions), but do work well for any product or service the consumer sees as expensive or complex. And make the catalogue more elaborate, glossy, colourful and large where involvement should be higher – big catalogues for big-ticket items, little ones for simple items.

Your catalogue doesn't need to be as big as the Argos catalogue to succeed. It just needs to show your product range in the best possible way. Even a few pages can make your product come alive and give you greater success.

Also include reply forms. Allow readers to easily get in touch with you in multiple ways. Give readers some choices about what offers they want to respond to, if possible. Postage-free (or prepaid) reply forms generally ensure a higher response rate and thus justify their cost many times over. Don't skimp on the form because, after all, getting that response is the whole point of your mailing.

Getting your letter mailed

How to send your letter is the first question to resolve. Royal Mail? Or another supplier? Should you use an overnight air service for an offer to business customers? Or maybe send the letter by email or fax? In general, the postal service is still best. And, as direct mail is such a big revenue earner for Royal Mail, it offers many different mailing systems and services for businesses of all sizes (check out www.mmc.co.uk, the Royal Mail's Mail Media Centre, which has lots of information on the complexity of direct mail and different services).

One little detail often puzzles first-time direct mailers – how to actually get your mailing printed, folded, stuffed and mailed. If you don't know, you should probably hire someone who does. Google some companies that do this kind of work under 'mailing' or 'marketing'. Commercial printers often do this type of work as well. Printers can often handle anything from a small envelope to a major full-colour catalogue. Talk to various printers to get an idea of the range of services and prices.

If you're planning small-scale mailings – say, less than 2000 at a pop – then you may find doing the work in-house offers you a cheaper and quicker route. Many local businesses and not-for-profit organisations do small-scale mailings and they'd be throwing away money by hiring printers. If you want to set up this in-house capability, talk to your local post office to find out how to handle metered mail. Consider purchasing mailing equipment, such as the following (all these items can process standard-format mailings): feeders, sealers, scales to weigh the mailings and a franking machine to frank the post before mailing. Combine this equipment with your local photocopy shop's ability to produce, fold and stuff a mailing and you have an efficient small-scale direct-mail centre.

Purchasing mailing lists

When you don't have a database of your own, or you want to expand the one you do have quickly, you can use purchased lists to prospect for leads. Don't expect the purchased lists to work very well – response rates can be low, and you may get high returns or undeliverables. But that situation's okay because you're using these purchased lists just to build up your own higher-quality in-house list of customers. So, plan to send out relatively inexpensive mailings with easy-to-say-yes-to offers and then focus on the replies. If you get any calls, emails or postcards from these purchased lists, qualify them as leads or customers, and move them to your own list.

We recommend buying one-time rights to mailing lists, with phone numbers (plus email addresses, if they're offered) to make replying to a response easier for you. One-time use means that you don't own the list, just rent it. But you do own the replies. As soon as someone contacts you from that mailing and you begin to interact with and gather information about them, you can add that person to your own list.

You can buy lists from list owners (those who first developed the list and rent it out), list managers (who manage it on an owner's behalf), list compilers (whose business it is to create bespoke lists from a wide range of sources) or list brokers (who can point you in the direction of the right list for your purposes and advise you how best to use them). You can find hundreds of list brokers through the Direct Marketing Association (DMA) website, at www.dma.org.uk.

No matter how good your direct mail is, some people simply don't want to receive it. The Mailing Preference Service, or MPS, is a suppression file that exists for those people. You aren't legally required to screen any of your mailings against the MPS (though you are for some other preference services, so we cover both in the 'Keeping it Legal (and Decent)' section later in this chapter) – but industry codes of practice say you should when renting third-party lists. Using the DMA directory to source lists will ensure you get ones that are regularly checked against the MPS. Most importantly, you won't be aggrieving potential customers or wasting money. A preference service exists for phone, fax and email – so whichever direct channel you use, think about those people who don't want to hear from companies, full stop.

List suppliers usually have minimums. We recommend buying the minimum (it comes on sticky mailing labels or in a database, depending on what's easiest and cheapest for you to use in your business). Then test the list with a mailing and see what happens. If you get some good customers out of the list, go back and buy a larger number of names, excluding the ones you already used. Or if you're disappointed in the response, buy a different list next time. (And if your mailing is too expensive to test on the minimum – which is often 1000 names – just mail to the first 250. That's enough names to find out how the list performs.)

You have so many lists to choose from that you can keep shopping until you find one that works for you. But remember the basic principle of list-buying: the best indicator of future purchase is past purchase.

So try to find lists of people who've purchased something similar to what you're selling, preferably through the mail, rather than people who fit your customer profile in other ways.

If you're new at the list-buying game, be prepared for some list sellers to refuse to send their names to you. These list sellers worry that they'll rent a one-time use of a list, but users won't honour the agreement, so they sometimes want to work through a supplier they trust, like a graphic designer, ad agency or printer in your area. You probably use the services of someone they do trust, so if you run into this problem, network with your contacts until you find someone the list-seller will send the lists to.

Establishing and Running a Call Centre

A *call centre* is the place where telephone calls from your customers are answered. A call centre can be a real, physical place – a big room full of phones staffed by your employees, or it can be a virtual place – a telephone number that rings to whatever subcontractor you're currently using to handle telemarketing for you.

If you don't want to set up a call centre yourself, you can hire a consultant to design one for you or simply use a service firm to perform the function for you. *Marketing Week* magazine publishes features and supplements each year relating to the top agencies in this area. These agencies range in size from Vertex, with 12,000 employees and offices in 80 countries around the world, to Price Direct, with a 50-seat call centre. Many telemarketing agencies are members of the Customer Contact Association; access details through its website: www.cca.org.uk.

Every business is a call centre, but most don't realise it. If you have telephones and people calling in and out on them, you need to manage this point of customer contact very carefully. Small businesses may not operate on a big enough scale to hire or build a dedicated call centre, but they still must manage this function wisely if they want to win customers, rather than lose them, on the phone. So please, read and apply the principles of this section, no matter how large or small your business may be!

Being accessible to desirable customers when they want to call you

If you service businesses, you can use business hours to answer business calls. If you service consumers, however, be prepared to take calls at odd hours. Some of the best customers for clothing catalogues do their shopping late at night – just before bed, for example.

And remember, being accessible means more than just having staff by the phones. You need to make sure that nobody gets a busy signal (your phone company will have a variety of services to help solve this problem – ask them for details). If you answer your phone faster than the competition does, you can gain some market share from them.

You need to measure and minimise customer waiting time. Don't leave people sitting on hold for more than what they perceive to be a moderate amount of time. Depending upon the nature of your product and customer, that time limit is probably less than two perceived minutes. A *perceived minute* is the time period a customer on hold thinks she's waited for a minute – and that time typically is more like 40 seconds when you measure it on the clock. To appreciate the customer's perspective, you have to convert actual wait times to perceived wait times.

Capturing useful information about each call and caller

Fielding enquiries or orders from new customers as they respond to your various direct-response advertisements – such as magazine ads, letters to purchased lists and your website – is one of the most important functions of your call centre. This function is known as *inbound telemarketing* and these callers are hot leads. You don't want these customers' orders as much as you want their data. Don't let these customers escape from your call centre. Make sure that your operators ask every caller for her full name and contact details, including her mobile phone number and email address, how she heard of your company and perhaps a few other qualifying questions as well.

To capture call-ins for your customer database, have your operators online so that they can enter the data directly into your database as they obtain it. At the very least, give your operators a printed information form they can fill in – or, if you're the one answering those customer calls, make yourself a form so you don't forget to capture useful information about the prospects, their needs and how they found your number.

Recognising – and taking care of – repeat customers

Accepted wisdom has it that acquiring a new customer costs a lot more than keeping an existing one. If you can find a way of identifying your most valuable customers (those that spend more with you over a long period of time), you're on to a gold mine (see Chapter 4 for more on researching your customers). So how do you know when the person calling you is a new customer or an old and valued one? In smaller organisations with a few regular customers, knowing your best customers, what they regularly buy from you and what their business requirements are, is just good business. The same is true for bigger companies, but keeping track of all those different customers is harder. We recommend you keep customer records, even if only a name, address and list of transactions held on a paper form. You can quickly identify who your loyal consumers are and treat them accordingly – doing so makes good business sense and will win you even more repeat customers. Keeping records on a computer database is even better, so when a customer rings you, you can call up their data instantly.

Putting your operators online also solves the related problem of recognising repeat customers. Repeat customers' names pop up on-screen for the operator's reference. That way, the operators don't have to ask stupid questions and they can surprise customers with their knowledge about past purchases or interactions with your company.

These services fall under the collective name of customer relationship management (CRM) systems. You can find lots of providers through a quick search on Google; one of the best known is www.salesforce.com.

Gathering data on the effectiveness of direct-response ads and direct mail

We're often amazed by how little information marketers gather about the effectiveness of their own work. What you don't know does hurt you when it comes to marketing! You can easily find out which direct-response ads, call scripts or mailings work best. And by doing so, you make your direct-marketing campaigns more effective over time. You only need to tell your operators to ask every caller where she heard about you (or ask repeat customers what prompted this latest call).

Consider this more rigorous way of tracking the effectiveness of each marketing effort: use a unique code number on each mailing to help trace each call or other customer response. You can also broaden this technique to include all written promotions – even those on the web. An identifying code links calls and sales to specific ads, allowing easy analysis of their effectiveness.

You can also use codes for each ad to support customised sales promotions. For example, one mailing may offer a special two-for-one price over a two-month period – with the code, your operator can quickly display the terms of this offer on screen. And because you've associated an offer with this code, you motivate the customer to give you this information.

Tuning in to Telemarketing

In the UK, a company with an 0800 freefone number generates around three times as many calls as a business without one. With a free, or at least very cheap, phone number you're inviting customers to call you rather than giving them a reason not to. Telemarketing has gained a poor reputation in recent years, as many people think it just means unsolicited sales calls by companies they don't want to hear from. Those people don't think of the calls they make to companies as telemarketing, but it is. In fact, *inbound telemarketing* – where the customer is invited to call the business – can be one of the most effective sales channels, as you're not wasting resources on people who don't want to do business with you and are simply making yourself available to those who do.

Using inbound and outbound telemarketing

Inbound and outbound telemarketing are completely different things, requiring totally different approaches. While customers make the choice to contact you in the former, they may be less than pleased to receive a call from your sales rep in the latter. The next sections give you tips on maximising the returns from each approach.

Inbound

Inbound telemarketing means the customer phones you. Although telemarketing requires nothing but a telephone, combining it with free, or at least low-cost, inbound calling usually makes it most effective. You can offer free calling to your customers and prospects with all 0800 or 0808 numbers. You, the marketer, get to pick up the cost of the customer's telephone call so that you can remove a possible objection to calling. By using an 0800/0808 number, you can provide customers and prospects with a single, memorable and free route to contact you. These numbers also mean you can direct all calls to a centralised call centre, which is why many marketers prefer freefone to other types of numbers.

Other types of phone numbers exist that keep down the cost of calling for customers and also allow you to route all calls through a single call centre. The following freefone or low-cost numbers are useful in inbound telemarketing, in which customers call you in response to direct-response advertising:

- ✔ **0800/0808:** Freefone is a zero-cost way to encourage customers to call. At its most basic, freefone can route all calls to a specific telephone line or can be linked to a call management monitoring program to improve the way your business handles calls.

- ✔ **0845:** Lo-call allows customers to contact you from anywhere in the country, but they pay only the cost of the local call while you pick up the difference in price. The advantage is a single number for customers to remember and a single call-routing system for you.

- ✔ **0870:** NationalCall means customers pay a single national-rate call from anywhere in the country. While your customers pay a 'fair' price for the call, this type of number can actually be a revenue-earner. The advantage of a single, memorable number for your business still applies.

- ✔ **09xx:** ValueCall is a premium-rate phone number, charged at various rates to your customers, depending on the service being offered. While it is a single business number, customers associate 09xx numbers with higher-cost calls, so they're best used for competitions or advice lines.

While these easy-to-remember numbers can simplify things for your business and customers alike, some telephone packages and mobile operators don't include them in their 'free landline calls' packages. As a result, people can get a heftier charge than expected for calling what they consider to be a cheap number. If you're producing a large piece of marketing material, considering printing a normal local number for your headquarters or call centre for those people who wish to avoid 0870 or 0845 numbers is worthwhile. Check here for a full list of BT's small business tariffs: http://business.bt.com. .

Every direct-response ad should have a phone number as one of the contact options – with a trained telemarketing sales force or an eager entrepreneur at the other end. (We recommend posting a freefone number prominently on your website and printing it on packaging, brochures, business cards and so on, in case someone prefers to talk to you, rather than email or mail you. Even add a free fax number, too, if customers in your industry like to fax in orders.)

Everything you send out that could have your phone number and web address on it, should have it displayed prominently. We're amazed by how often we find ourselves staring at a catalogue page, package, product, website or memo trying to find a phone number that just isn't there. Then what? We may just call the competition instead. The solution? Audit and order!

- ✔ First, *audit* your mailings and other customer communications to find those holes where you've accidentally left out contact information.

✔ Next, *order* up some simple contact information stickers with your brand or business name, phone numbers, address(es), website and email information. Pop those stickers on folders, boxes, cards, products, scribbled notes or anywhere else anyone may conceivably look when thinking of calling you with a question or order.

Outbound

Outbound telemarketing involves salespeople making calls to get prospects on the phone – and then pitching to them to make a sale; see Chapter 20 for how to design a good sales presentation. You can do a little bit of outbound telemarketing informally as part of a broader routine of contacting customers and following up on leads, or you may have a full-blown outbound telemarketing campaign set up in a call centre that you either run yourself or contract with (the bureaus are the same as for inbound telemarketing, covered in the preceding section).

One way or the other, though, every marketer makes some calls to customers and prospects and must be prepared for the reality that outbound telemarketing yields plenty of rejections. In fact, we don't generally recommend outbound telemarketing for *cold call* lists, or lists of strangers who've never done business with you before. You can buy such lists from list brokers easily, but expect lower response rates than from lists you build yourself.

You can improve the success rate of outbound telemarketing dramatically by developing a good list before you start calling. Preferably, this list is of people who've had some contact with you before (they've purchased, returned an enquiry card, tried a sample or responded to a print ad or web banner ad). With a good list, you can afford to put competent salespeople on the phones so that your company puts its best face forward. We don't know why most telemarketers haven't worked out that the first contact between their company and a prospective customer shouldn't be in the hands of a temp worker who can't even pronounce the name of the product correctly. To avoid such problems, you need to develop lists and a calling style that give your callers at least a 15 per cent success rate – more than ten times the average for typical unfiltered consumer telemarketing operations.

Being truthful and decent in your telemarketing

The pressure's on in telemarketing. Selling anything over the phone is much harder than it used to be. People (and businesses) are getting sick and tired of these sales calls and adding their names to *preference services* (meaning they opt out of receiving marketing communications) by the thousands. So marketers are experimenting with stealth techniques, and these techniques lead them into dangerous ethical and legal territory.

A formerly new distribution channel, the telephone, has matured. Many desirable consumers became jaded to direct mail, print ads, billboards and radio and television ads decades ago. But the rise of telemarketing in the 1980s gave marketers something new and different to experiment with. Telemarketing was great fun – for a while. But now, most prospects have received hundreds, if not thousands, of telemarketing calls.

So today's telemarketers have only two choices: one, they can go on doing what they've always done, which can only lead to increasingly desperate and shady practices as their medium matures and their industry shakes out; or, two, they can wake up and realise that a new dawn has arrived. Telemarketers need to find new strategies for their newly mature medium. Some of these strategies include:

- ✔ **Use the phone to follow up on leads, not to find them:** Whenever possible, use your web marketing activities (see Chapters 10, 11, 12 and 13), events and advertising to generate telephone or personal sales call leads. When you generate enquiries about your product or service, you have permission to call. The prospect takes your call gladly in 99 per cent of these cases, and you close a sale in many of them.

- ✔ **Don't overuse the phone:** Save calls for issues that really deserve personal contact from the prospect's perspective, and try to call people who actually know you or your firm. You want to speak to people who will welcome the call for some other good reason. If you have something truly important to talk about, then you don't need a misleading hook to keep people on the phone. Remember that every marketing campaign should use a balanced mix of media and methods. You can't do all jobs with one tool. And also remember that even where telephoning is appropriate, your customers and prospects don't want you to call constantly – give them a little breathing room.

- ✔ **Be respectful:** Remember that you're interrupting anyone you reach by phone. Be especially wary of calling in evenings and at weekends unless you know for sure that this is exactly when people actively wish to be contacted.

- ✔ **Be human:** Some experts waste a lot of time debating whether or not outbound calls should be scripted. As long as what your caller says sounds warm and natural, whether it's written down or not doesn't matter. Get your callers to say 'you'll' not 'you will'. If the script is written in perfect English but still doesn't sound right, then throw the grammar book out of the window. *Never* use automated calling systems which start off silent and kick in a few seconds after the consumer has picked up the phone. These calls do nothing but scare people and put them off.

- ✔ **Compensate telemarketers for building relationships, not destroying them:** If telemarketers are paid only by the *kill* (commission on sales), they can become frustrated and start berating and hanging up on your prospects and customers.

✔ **Guard existing customers from bad telemarketing:** Deceptive, high-pressure or irritating phone sales tactics may produce a good-looking end-of-day sales report, but they're guaranteed to increase customer turnover. Why? These tactics bring in deal-prone customers, who can be taken away by the next telemarketer, and they irritate your loyal customers rather than reward them. At the very least, use two different strategies and scripts: one for existing customers and one for deal-prone prospects. At best, focus your telemarketing on building existing customer loyalty; for example, by really calling to see if you can improve the product or service quality.

✔ **Gain insight from other media:** Holding someone's attention long enough to deliver a marketing message is a major problem in every medium, not just telemarketing. And marketers have developed clever solutions in other media. Why not try some of them in telemarketing? You can write a script that includes entertainment; a very short story, a good joke, a warm and pleasant manner or another engaging opener may build interest far better than a deceptive claim about the purpose of the call. Similarly, a sales promotion tie-in can hold attention. For example, your script can start with the offer of a contest or free sample giveaway and then go on to a pitch for the product. Get creative!

Keeping it Legal (and Decent)

A host of new laws has recently been introduced to protect consumers and any data about them – and that affects a lot of what marketers do day to day. Whether you're storing or using customer data, mailing, emailing or phoning customers (new or old), these laws make a difference to how you should be doing it. And abiding by the law isn't your only concern. Industry codes of practice and preference services (which allow people to opt out of receiving many communications) also need to be borne in mind – they're not legally binding, but we explain later why adhering to them makes good sense.

The following sections cover the basics on new laws and codes that restrict what you can do when trying to contact your customers. We urge you not to treat these restrictions as the enemy – in many cases, making sure you're only using *clean* data and aren't trying to contact consumers who don't want to hear from any businesses (not just yours) makes sense and will actually save you money in the long term.

Observing the Data Protection Act

So, do you process personal data? The answer to this simple question will determine whether the Data Protection Act (or DPA) affects what you do – and in most cases, the answer is yes. Processing personal data covers almost any activity you can think of. A person's name and address stored in a marketing database is personal data, never mind consulting it, disclosing it, transferring it or even deleting it. If you've got personal data, assuming you're processing it is safest, even if it doesn't feel like you are.

Before you can do anything with the data you hold, you need to formally notify the Information Commissioner's Office of who you are and what you're planning to do. This notification costs £35 per year. The Information Commissioner (www.ico.gov.uk) is the office responsible for administering the DPA, and as well as registering there, you can find more detailed guidance on the Act.

The DPA is based on eight principles (actually they're enforceable but this term makes them sound nicer) of good information handling practice. They state that data must be:

✔ Fairly and lawfully processed

✔ Processed for limited purposes

✔ Adequate, relevant and not excessive

✔ Accurate and up to date

✔ Not kept longer than necessary

✔ Processed in accordance with the individual's rights

✔ Secure

✔ Not transferred to other countries without adequate protection for the individual

The good news is that, while the DPA may look like a legal minefield, you can easily navigate it if you're only using the data for advertising and marketing purposes and if you've obtained the consent of the customers you plan to contact.

The 'fair and lawfully processed' principle in the DPA is the one that most relates to you and your direct marketing, because here is where you must be able to prove 'prior informed consent' before contacting customers. 'Prior' means that you've obtained consent before you begin mailing or calling them, and 'informed' means you haven't buried the consent clause somewhere in the small print.

Always try to be honest and upfront, not just legal. While allowing your customers and prospects to easily opt out of further advertising from you may pain you, the fact that you've weeded out those customers from the ones that are happy to hear from you means your marketing campaigns will become much more efficient.

As long as you're clear in your communications, you can give customers the chance to *opt out* of or *opt in* to your information – worded properly, both count as informed consent. You have to give customers this choice every time you communicate with them. You'll have seen tick boxes, of the opt-in or opt-out variety, on a lot of the mailings and emails you get from companies – and similar, easily understood devices should be on all materials you send out to your customers (for email, you must make sure the tick box actually works or you're in breach of the DPA).

Always use opt-in boxes when designing new forms or web pages. While opt-out boxes have always been popular with marketers because they mean people have to actively choose not to receive ads or promotional material, this approach is a pretty poor idea. Having people signed up who are genuinely interested in receiving your messages is better, so always choose opt-in boxes to ensure this happens.

You can be sued if you're in breach of the DPA. That means that you need to make sure you've got consent to contact your customers, but also that your suppliers have, too. Again, if you're buying or renting a list, use a reputable source such as the Direct Marketing Association directory , or make sure you have legal cover to indemnify you against bought-in data.

Understanding preference services

You need to know about the existence of five preference services, which allow individuals (and in some cases companies) to register to opt out of receiving certain types of communication from you. (Don't take it personally; these people have chosen not to receive *any* marketing communications.) These services are the Mailing Preference Service (MPS), Baby MPS, Telephone Preference Service (TPS), Facsimile Preference Service (FPS) and Email Preference Service (EMPS).

You also need to know that not all preference services are created equal. No legal requirement exists for you to check your mailing lists for people that may be registered with MPS or Baby MPS (for bereaved parents to register not to receive baby-related mailings), but it pays not to contact people who don't want to hear from you, and most reputable list brokers and mailing houses respect the MPS lists.

The other three preference services – TPS, FPS and EMPS – fall under the Privacy and Electronic Communications (EC Directive) Regulations 2003, but, again, the same rules don't apply for each. Calling or faxing individuals or companies who've registered with TPS or FPS is prohibited by these regulations, so you need to check your database against both of these registers. Check regularly, as a 'for the time being' clause means those who have registered can change their mind (to receive or not to receive) whenever they like. You're also responsible for making sure that any subcontractors using your lists to make calls aren't phoning or faxing those names on the TPS or FPS registers.

In terms of whom you can and can't contact using email, the Regulations introduce two new rules. The first rule is that you, as the sender of email, must not conceal your identity and must provide a valid address for opt-out requests. The second rule is that you cannot send unsolicited email marketing messages to individuals without their prior consent. This means that accordance with EMPS and this rule are slightly more relaxed if you have

- Obtained an email address 'in the course of a sale or negotiations for a sale'.

- Only sent promotional messages relating to 'similar products and services'.

- Given the recipient the opportunity to opt out when the address was collected, and have given the opportunity to opt out with every subsequent message.

Adhering to consumer protection Distance Selling Regulations

When you enter into an agreement with a consumer (not another business) to supply your product or service without having met face to face, you enter into a distance contract. Contracts formed by mail order, digital television, over the phone, by fax or on the Internet are all distance contracts and are subject to these *Distance Selling Regulations* (*DSRs*).

DSRs do not apply in some sectors, so if your business is in financial services, travel or leisure (plane, train, concert or sports event tickets or hotel accommodation), you can breathe easy. Otherwise, play it safe and assume that any direct business you do with customers is affected by DSRs and supply the following information – in writing or by email – before a distance contract is formed:

- Your business name.

- Your address – if you're seeking payment in advance.

- A description of the goods or services you're offering.

- The full price – including any taxes.

- For how long the price or any special offers remain valid.

- Details of any delivery costs.

- Details of how payment can be made.

- The arrangements for delivery or performance – when customers can expect delivery, for example.

- Information about your customers' right to cancel.

You'll need to supply this information again, plus more detail on cancellation conditions, after-sales service or guarantees, before the items are delivered or the services are completed. If you fail to do this step, your customer has longer to cancel – generally seven days from the time this *follow-up disclosure* is given. Persistent offenders of serious non-compliance with the DFRs could receive a court order to comply from the Office of Fair Trading (www.oft.gov.uk).

Chapter 15

Public Relations and Word of Mouth

....

....

*W*hen people bump into reminders of your company name, brand, product or service, they're more likely to buy. And if those exposures to your identity create a strongly positive impression, they can have a big impact on sales. So far, so simple.

But while advertising does work, most people who are affected by it don't like to admit to it. Plenty of people will deny ever having bought anything as a result of seeing an ad for it. However, we'll bet you've never come across anyone who says the same about a magazine article or something a relative or friend recommends to them.

Independent endorsements for your product or service can be so much more powerful than 'pure' advertising, for the simple reason that consumers are more sceptical about a message that's been paid for and is self-serving.

In this chapter, we discuss the two key ways of gaining independent endorsement for your business: *public relations* (when exposure to or mention of your company, service or product becomes part of the news or an editorial feature) and *word of mouth* (what people say about you to others). Each endorsement can make a positive impression in a low-key, polite manner and can do so – if managed well – for surprisingly low cost.

Public relations and word of mouth have traditionally been vastly underrated techniques for communicating with your customers but, these days, companies are realising their power. The ease with which information can be passed between people on the Internet means that your messages can be spread further and more quickly than ever before. These endorsements belong in the front line of your marketing plan because of their ease of use, simplicity, low cost and potential.

Using Publicity to Your Advantage

Publicity is coverage of your product or business in the editorial portion of any news medium. Why would journalists cover a product as a story? One reason is that the product is better or worse than expected. If, for example, *Which?* magazine runs an article praising your product as best in a particular category, that's publicity. Good publicity. If, in contrast, the evening television news programmes run a story saying that experts suspect your product caused numerous accidents, that's publicity, too. Bad publicity.

Obviously, any marketer aims for good publicity. But if you do find yourself facing bad publicity, don't despair. Good public relations (PR) can be turned to an organisation's advantage. For example, in 2005, when someone claimed to have poisoned Snickers and Mars bars in Australia, the confectionary company made a big show of recalling all the bars and creating a hotline for concerned consumers. The company then launched a campaign giving away free bars, running ads and reminding everyone how much they'd miss the brands if they weren't around. The bad publicity cost the confectionary business some money in the short term but overall the response improved its image in the country. Compare this outcome to when Perrier found benzene in its water in 1990. The company had little choice but to withdraw the water from shop shelves but didn't back up doing so with enough information. Consumers were confused and worried, and the brand suffered. Perrier did set up a customer care line in the UK to try to deal with the anxious public but it failed to realise that the issue had become global. Its market share never fully recovered.

In both cases, product quality was the key factor to both stories reaching the news in the first place. Keep this fact in mind.

When you use publicity, remember the all-important factor – the quality of your product innovation and production/delivery. You can gain positive publicity simply by designing and making a truly superior product. If you want to generate negative publicity, just make your product shoddy or carry out your service poorly. *Good publicity starts with the pursuit of quality in your own business!*

How do you go about getting the PR machine started in the first place? The following sections list ways that you can take advantage of good publicity (and, if the need arises, neutralise bad publicity) in your marketing materials.

Tackling public relations

Public relations (PR) is the active pursuit of publicity for marketing purposes. You use PR to generate good publicity and to try to minimise bad publicity. Generally, marketers have the responsibility of generating good publicity. If marketers create good stories and communicate them to the media effectively (see the 'Creating a good story' and 'Communicating your story to the media' sections later in this chapter), the media pick them up and turn them into news or entertainment content. Good publicity.

Although marketers or general managers wear the PR hat in smaller organisations, large companies generally have a PR person or department whose sole job is to manage its reputation – generating good news but also reacting promptly and effectively to publicity crises. Also, many businesses hire *PR consultancies* – agencies that can work for a number of clients, planning and delivering messages to the press or reacting to incoming enquiries.

If you need help writing a good press release and placing the story, enlisting this professional help is worthwhile – you may not get any coverage without it.

PR consultancies vary in size from international groups employing thousands to single owner-operator PR professionals. You can also find specialists who have expertise in particular industry sectors, such as IT or healthcare. Around 3000 PR consultancies operate in the UK, so you'll need help narrowing down your search. If you're serious about hiring one, the Public Relations Consultants Association (PRCA) offers a free online service (www.prca.org.uk), which matches your needs with the member consultancies that most closely match them.

Creating a good story

To a journalist, a *good story* is anything that has enough public interest to attract readers, viewers or listeners and hold their attention. For example, a good story for a journalist covering the plastics industry must hold the attention of people in that industry.

We're sorry to say that most of what you want to communicate to your market doesn't fall into the category of a good story. For that reason, you need to develop your story (by collecting the right facts and quotes and writing them down clearly and well) to a level that may qualify as good editorial content. And when you think of good editorial content, think like a journalist would.

Finding the hook

The *hook* is what it sounds like: the compelling bit of information that snags your reader's interest and draws him to the story.

Here's a simple exercise to help you understand how hooks work. Scan today's newspaper (whichever one you like to read) and rank the top five stories based on your interest in them. Now analyse each one in turn to identify the one thing that made that story interesting enough to hold your attention. The hooks, the things that made each story interesting to you, differ. But every story has a hook, and all hooks have certain elements in common:

✔ Hooks often give you new information (information you didn't know or weren't sure of).

✔ Hooks make that new information relevant to your activities or interests.

✔ Hooks catch your attention, often by surprising you with something you hadn't expected.

✔ Hooks promise some benefit to you – although the benefit may be indirect – by helping you understand your world better, avoid something undesirable or simply enjoy yourself as you read the paper.

Combining the hook with your marketing message

You need to design hooks to make your marketing message into stories that appeal to journalists. Your hooks need to be just like the ones that attracted your attention to those newspaper stories, with one exception: *you need to somehow tie them to your marketing information.* You have to make sure that at least a thin line exists connecting the hook to your brand identity, the news that you've just introduced a new product or whatever else you want the public to know. That way, when journalists use your hook in their own work, they end up including some of your marketing information in their stories as an almost accidental side effect.

Journalists don't want to help you communicate with your target market but they'll happily use any good stories that you're willing to write for them. If your product gets mentioned or you get quoted as a result, they don't have a problem giving you the reference. So what's the secret, the key or the essence of good publicity? Develop stories with effective hooks and give those stories to overworked journalists with empty pages to fill.

Communicating your story to the media: Press releases

For communicating a news story the most basic format is the press release. Unfortunately, journalists don't like press releases. We know this because we are journalists. We get hundreds of press releases emailed and posted to us every day. Most of them are rubbish, which is exactly where they end up. At the head of every magazine, covering every imaginable professional or consumer interest, is the equivalent of us – a stressed-out editor with the next deadline looming. So look on your challenge as getting past us, or at least the equivalent of us.

When we say that journalists don't like press releases, we mean that we don't like admitting to being influenced by them – a bit like consumers with advertising, really. Now we're not going to attempt to hold back the tide of press releases that flood into our inbox, but we shall give some insider advice about how to get on the right side of journalists by giving them what they need and not troubling them with what they don't.

A list of do's

Here's a list of ways that you can get a positive response from the journalists you contact:

- ✔ **Do offer exclusives:** Offering the news as an *exclusive* is the best way to make a journalist feel better about a press release (but remember, it still has to be a relevant story). An exclusive means that the journalist you're dealing with gets the story before it appears anywhere else, the story gets a more prominent position in the newspaper or magazine and the journalist scores points with their editor. Everybody's happy.

   You, or your PR consultancy, need to get close to the journalists that are most relevant to your business – this usually means calling them with the story first to discuss it and then sending the press release if they've shown an interest. Most companies do it the other way round, or worse, simply blanket email to every journalist on their database.

- ✔ **Do make it relevant and timely:** Target the right media and contacts. The food critic doesn't need a release about a new robotics manufacturing facility. And the business correspondent doesn't either, if the facility opened two months ago, because now that story's old news.

   Read the paper or magazine and be familiar with its content before making contact with its journalists. Don't pitch a story without having knowledge of the media you're targeting or you risk making a fool of yourself.

- ✔ **Do build up a list of media contacts:** You need to create an accurate database of journalists, with all contact details so you can get in touch with them quickly. Emailing your release can be sensible because journalists work on tight deadlines, so include fields for email addresses in your database. Think about developing a list identifying which journalists write articles that may be similar to stories related to your business. Now you have a smaller list that's a much tighter match with your content and target audience. You can get commercial lists and information on journalists from PR directories and list-sellers such as Gorkana (`www.gorkana.com`) or Cision (`www.uk.cision.com`).

- ✔ **Do think creatively:** Journalists need stories; you need some positive PR – so think up a story idea that serves both needs. A common but effective PR tactic is to carry out a piece of consumer research that's relevant to your business and let a newspaper publish the results. For example, a DVD rental company might research a list of people's favourite films.

Include something helpful, such as tips, rules or principles, which the media can quote. (An osteopath's practice may send out a release that includes five tips for a healthier back; a management consultant may offer five tips for avoiding cash-flow crises; a home inspection firm may offer five tips to avoid costly surprises when buying a home.)

✔ **Do offer yourself as an expert commentator on industry-related matters, in case they need a quote for another article:** A journalist may just include one sentence from you, but if they mention your company name, you just got some good publicity. For example, an article on how to shop for a used car in the Sunday magazine of a newspaper may quote the owner of a large car dealership as saying, 'If you don't have an independent mechanic evaluate a used car before buying it, I guarantee you'll be in for some unpleasant surprises.' The article may also mention that this dealership's repair department does free evaluations for car buyers. The combination of a quote and a bit of information about the free service is going to attract many new customers, some of whom will become steady users of the dealership's repair service, and some of whom will become buyers of new or used cars from the dealership.

✔ **Do keep it brief:** Journalists are quick on the uptake and work fast, so let them call or email if they need more information.

✔ **Do post your press releases on your website:** Even if you've given your story as an 'exclusive', your press releases can do double duty on the web, providing information for journalists to follow up once the exclusive story becomes public. Remember to provide a phone number, email address and, if possible, more than one relevant contact in case reporters want more information on a story.

✔ **Do send releases to every local editor in your area, no matter how small their publication or station:** You can get local coverage more easily than regional or national coverage and that local coverage can be surprisingly helpful.

And a few don'ts

The do's must be balanced by a few helpful don'ts that will help your information stand out from the junk that flies into every journalist's inbox:

✔ **Don't make a nuisance of yourself:** One of the worst pieces of advice that's seemingly given to every aspiring PR practitioner is to make a follow-up call. If your media contacts database is accurate, the journalist will have received your press release: if it's a good story, they'll use it; if it isn't, they won't. You can't do anything to change your press release after the event, so make sure that what you send is as carefully crafted as it can be.

✔ **Don't ask for clippings:** Journalists don't want to send you clippings of the articles they write, so don't bother asking. Nor do they care to discuss with you why they didn't run a story, or why they cut off part of a quote when they did run a story. They're busy with the next story. Forget about it. You should focus on the next story, too. If you want a clipping, most publications keep an online database of all their published stories.

✔ **Don't make any errors:** Typos throw the facts into question. Don't include any inaccurate facts, either. You want the journalist to have trust in the information you're providing. Prove that you're worthy of that confidence.

✔ **Don't give incomplete contact information:** Make sure you include up-to-date names, postal and email addresses and phone numbers on the press release. Let the contacts know when they should be available if reporters need to speak to them and brief them properly about what they should say so that the journalist finds them helpful and co-operative.

✔ **Don't ignore the journalists' research needs:** The more support you give a journalist, the easier he'll find it to cover your story. Remember to send over a high-resolution photograph of your product or a quoted expert with your press release. Some story slots in magazines or newspapers require images; if you send one over, you're a little bit closer to being chosen, with very little effort. Don't overload emails with lots of pictures, though – you don't want to make reporters' inboxes crash – but do offer in the release to provide more images, if they're wanted. Also consider offering tours of any venues mentioned, interview times, sample products or whatever else may help journalists cover your story.

✔ **Don't forget that journalists work on a faster clock than you do:** When a journalist calls about your release, return the call (or make sure that somebody else does) in minutes or hours, not days. If you handle media requests slowly, a journalist will just find another source or write another story by the time you've returned the call.

pressdispensary.co.uk and businesswire.co.uk

For easy access to a cheap way of distributing releases, check out www.pressdispensary.co.uk where you can access information on prices charged for distributing press releases. At time of writing, the site offers to create and send a release to targeted, relevant media outlets for prices from £260. Not bad, but we recommend using this service alongside making key journalistic contacts because you can't beat the personal touch. A similar service is offered at www.businesswire.co.uk.

Considering video and electronic releases

You can get a story out to the media in ways other than press releases. Consider generating a video release, with useful footage that a television producer may decide to run as part of a news story. Or put a written press release on the PR Newswire (see below) or any other such service that distributes hard copy or electronic releases to its media clients – for a fee from the source of the release, of course. You can also pitch your stories to the Associated Press, Reuters and other newswires (but we recommend hiring a major PR firm before trying to contact a newswire).

Being interviewed for TV and radio

So now you've got a hook or a reputation for expertise within your sector (see earlier sections in this chapter), the requests for interviews will come flooding in. Okay, usually the process isn't that simple; you need to be prepared for when a broadcast interview does come your way. A few people are naturally confident and gifted when speaking publicly or on radio or TV – but they're not normal! You will feel nervous the first time you're in an unusual interview situation. Professional media training is available, where you'll be put into mock interviews in front of real cameras and microphones and put through your paces by professional journalists. Or you can prepare yourself by simply following these basic (and much cheaper) tips:

- ✓ **Give no more than three key messages:** If you're tempted to blurt out everything you know about your subject, your main messages will get lost and people won't remember anything. Prepare in advance what you want to say and then say it.

- ✓ **Know your audience:** Find out as much as you can about the interview, the programme and its audience. Is it live or pre-recorded? Light-hearted chat or serious comment? For business experts or housewives?

- ✓ **Be positive:** State your main messages in positive terms, and provide examples rather than go on the defensive. Whatever you do, don't say 'no comment' – the interviewer and audience will assume you've got something to hide. Watch how politicians manage this scenario when they're being interviewed. They repeat their key message and studiously ignore the question.

- ✓ **What not to wear:** Avoid patterns when on TV as sometimes the cameras can't cope and viewers get a disturbing strobe effect. Small checks and herringbone are obviously out, but also avoid bold patterns as they'll detract attention from what you're trying to say. Keep your attire simple and light – dark clothes can drain colour from your face.

✔ **Speak like a normal human being:** After all, normal people are watching or listening, so thinking about what they may or may not know about the subject and tailoring your message to them pays. Imagine you're speaking to someone who's bright, but knows nothing about the topic. Don't patronise, but definitely don't overwhelm them with jargon and abbreviations.

Making the Most of Word of Mouth

Word of mouth (WOM) gives a consumer (or a marketer) the most credible source of information about products, aside from actual personal experience with those products. What consumers tell each other about your products has a huge impact on your efforts to recruit new customers. WOM also has a secondary, but still significant, impact on your efforts to retain old customers.

If you survey customers to identify the source of positive attitudes toward new products, you generally find that answers such as 'my friend told me about it' outnumber answers like 'I saw an ad' by ten to one. WOM communications about your product don't actually outnumber advertising messages; but when customers talk, other customers listen.

How can you control what people say about your product? You can't easily encourage customers to say only nice things about your product and actually prevent them from criticising it. But you can influence WOM – and you have to try. Making your product special is the most obvious way to influence WOM. A product that surprises people because of its unexpectedly good quality or service is special enough to talk about. A good product or a well-delivered service wins fans and turns your customers into your sales force. Other tactics for managing WOM about your business or product may not be so obvious. Fortunately, we discuss them in the following sections.

Doing good deeds

If no aspect of your product is itself particularly wonderful or surprising, do some attention-grabbing activity and associate that with your product. Consider these strategies for generating positive publicity and word of mouth:

✔ Get involved with a charity or not-for-profit organisation that operates in your area (see Chapter 16).

✔ Stage a fun event for kids.

✔ Let your employees take short sabbaticals to volunteer in community services.

Get creative. You can think of something worthwhile, some way of helping improve your world that surprises people and makes them take notice of the good you're doing in the name of your product. But bear in mind that any positive deeds you do are much more credible, memorable and impressive if they have some association with what your organisation does. For example, a washing powder business might offer to wash a football team's kit free for a year. Or a sports company could get its employees to do a fun run for charity.

Spicing up your sales promotions

A 20p-off coupon isn't worth talking about. But a competition in which the winners get to spend a day with the celebrity of their choice can get consumers excited – and can be cheaper, too. You can generate positive PR and a lot of word of mouth with such a premium (Chapter 16 on face-to-face marketing has more on running special events and promotions).

You can use special offers and competitions to get people to recommend a friend. For example, the mobile phone company T-Mobile has run offers giving subscribers £20 credit if they recommend the service to a friend who then signs up. The friend also gets £20 credit. Everyone wins and even those people who don't want to sign up immediately may remember this 'generosity' when considering a new mobile deal later on. You see, you can influence word of mouth.

Identifying and cultivating decision influencers

In many markets, some people's opinions matter a lot more than others. These people are *decision influencers*, and if you (hypothetically) trace back the flow of opinions in your industry, you may find that many of them originate with these people. In business-to-business (B2B) marketing, the decision influencers are often obvious. A handful of prominent executives, a few editors working for trade magazines and some of the staff at trade associations probably exert a strong influence over everybody else's opinions. You can find identifiable decision influencers in consumer markets, as well. Just think about chat show host Oprah Winfrey, in the US. If she recommends a book, the author sees an immediate spike in sales. She's so important to the publishing market that now any titles that Oprah picks for her special 'book club' are often marketed more heavily on that detail than their plot or author. The same has happened in the UK with TV presenters Richard and Judy's Book Club in association with newsagent WH Smith and sales of certain products named by celebrity chefs – Delia Smith's cake mix pack for Waitrose sold at a rate of one every seven seconds during Christmas 2010.

To take advantage of decision influencers, develop a list of who falls into that category for your product or service and then make a plan for cultivating them. Match these people with appropriate managers or salespeople who can take them to events or out to lunch, just for fun. You just need to make sure that people associated with your business are in the personal networks of these decision influencers. Consider developing a series of giveaways and mailshots to send to these decision influencers. If we wanted to sell a football boot to youth players, we'd send free samples of a new shoe to youth coaches. When you know who's talking and who's listening, you can easily focus your efforts on influencing the talkers.

Seizing control of the Internet

Okay, you can't actually take over the Internet, but you need to be aware of what people are saying about your product or service online. Weblogs, or blogs as they're commonly known, are an established part of the Internet age. What are blogs? The term _blogs_ refers to personal web publishing based on a topic or topics that attract a like-minded community of online participants. In other words, blogging is word of mouth on the web. Blogs exist dedicated to pretty much every subject you can imagine, from cars to politics to chocolate. You need to know about blogs because you can use them to your advantage in two key ways:

- ✔ **Getting in on the discussion:** If a website dedicated to your market exists, try to get your product mentioned or even establish a link between your site and the blog (blogs make extensive use of links to other sites). A survey among more than 600 blog publishers found that two-thirds would be happy to consider a direct public relations approach. Brands regularly send out new products to influential bloggers for them to test before they become widely available.

- ✔ **Creating your own blog:** Blogs are cheap and easy to set up, which is why they're blossoming on the web. You can use free blog sites such as `www.wordpress.com` or `www.blogger.com` and start publishing within the day. You can use your blog to promote your products and services and elicit feedback (bad as well as good) from potential and existing customers. Make sure you can moderate any feedback before it goes live to avoid libellous information but don't be tempted to ditch any negative comments – people won't use your service to give their views if they think you ignore anything but good news.

Not all blogs or their users are business friendly, and you need to remember this when making approaches or setting up your own blog. Blogs are run by enthusiasts and are usually independent of corporate ties: that's their point, as well as their appeal. While Microsoft attracted a lot of attention for sending laptops to bloggers for review, it also received criticism as some people considered it too close to paying for publicity.

Controlling what people say about you on blogs is also difficult. You can't and you shouldn't try to. If a comment about your product or service is incorrect, identifying yourself and responding is the best approach. Or just leave it be: you need to accept that not everyone will like what you do but that situation's alright.

Regulations now exist to control corporate blogging. These regulations ensure that consumers aren't fooled into thinking that corporate remarks are those made by ordinary people.

In 2005, people working on behalf of household cleaner Cillit Bang made the mistake of commenting on some blogs in the guise of the brand's fictional spokesperson Barry Scott. This deceit was uncovered by a blogger and the clumsy marketing attempt made online headlines around the world.

Now posting on blogs on behalf of businesses without revealing your identity as representing that organisation is banned. The Consumer Protection from Unfair Trading 2008 regulation aims to stamp out this practice. Read up on this regulation if you plan to comment on other people's blogs or start your own. Visit the Office of Fair Trading's website (www.oft.gov.uk), where you can find the relevant information under 'Business Advice' in the 'Competing Fairly' section.

Blogs aren't the only online means of promoting your messages or WOM these days. As described in Chapter 12, social media networks are also very important. Twitter can also be a great way to spread WOM. Topshop uses Twitter to promote its products and build its brand identity. People who follow @topshop get early information about new clothing collections, can access help with customer service issues and are able to chat to the brand about fashion. At the time of writing, the company has nearly a quarter of a million followers and its tweets are often passed on from friend to friend. Virtually free publicity!

Lots of companies have their own Facebook page dedicated to their product or service, too.

Chapter 16

Face-to-Face Marketing

*I*n this chapter, we use the term *face-to-face marketing* to describe the way your business can have a personal impact on individuals and groups. Of course, you want that impact to lead to a sale, but the effect isn't usually that immediate or direct, which is why an important distinction exists between face-to-face marketing and selling. When you set up a stand and display your wares at an exhibition, you're doing face-to-face marketing. Many potential buyers walk past that stand and some will come in to examine and ask questions. That stand is a powerful opportunity to do good marketing.

Face-to-face marketing's personal, warm and human element gives it special marketing leverage. We should say, however, that sometimes a special event may be a bit less personal than this – perhaps you sponsor a local football team, for example, in which case the individuals who play, and their families and fans, do certainly have a high level of involvement but probably not with you or other representatives of your company. Still, that human contact and sense of bringing people together in some sort of community makes sports team sponsorship especially effective, so we think considering it a form of face-to-face marketing too is fair.

Face-to-face marketing serves many purposes and can take a number of forms. You can sponsor someone else's event or stage your own. You can buy exhibitor space in a trade show – a special kind of face-to-face marketing designed to put you in front of a lot of prospects in a hurry. And with the web at your command, you can inexpensively connect people via virtual face-to-face marketing.

Whatever the exact nature of the face-to-face marketing, the approach gives you a temporary way to make a special connection with a large number of customers or prospects.

We recommend every marketer consider face-to-face marketing and every marketing plan have a section devoted to it. In this chapter, we show you how to bottle up the face-to-face marketing magic and put it to work in your marketing campaign.

Harnessing the Power of Face-to-Face Marketing

Face-to-face marketing has to have considerable drawing power. Think of this approach as theatre – a performance that entertains or stimulates people in a satisfying way (and sometimes includes people as participants, not just as an audience). At an exhibition or trade show, you may need to add interactive activities to your stand or invite a team of massage therapists to do their thing at specified hours to attract your target audience. In a store, appealing to your audience can mean bringing in an expert to give a weekend workshop. For a consulting firm, it may mean offering a special one-hour seminar led by your directors, accessible to all clients and prospects over the web.

Face-to-face marketing is a great example of the real-world marketing principle that you should give away as much as you can. Facing stiff competition, you often have to give potential customers an interesting performance to win their attention. Here are more ideas for face-to-face marketing that you may want to promote:

- A client-appreciation event (what used to be called a party).

- A musical performance.

- A weekend at a golf resort for your top customers, along with prizes for the winning golfers – and everyone else, too.

- A fundraising dinner for an important charity.

- A community event, such as a fair or children's workshop.

- An exhibit or hospitality suite at a major trade show for people in your industry.

- A workshop in which you share your expertise or solve problems for participants.

Endless and varied possibilities exist. You know best what your customers or potential customers will find valuable. But they all attract people and hold their attention. And you need that attention to communicate and persuade as a marketer.

Planning it yourself or piggybacking

You have a great deal of choice – not only over the type of face-to-face opportunity you can participate in, but also about the level and nature of your participation. At the highest level of commitment, you can plan and manage your own events. Depending on the scale of the event, that process can be costly and difficult, but sometimes organising it yourself is the best solution; especially if you want to have enough control to keep any other marketers from using the audience attention that the event generates. But you may also choose an event that others are organising and sign on as a sponsor. Doing so is easier, and often cheaper, but may be less powerful in terms of marketing impact.

Energy drink Red Bull provides a good example of a brand that has successfully created its own event. The Red Bull Flugtag competition – which started in 1991 – involves people attempting to fly their own homemade planes. The machines are normally launched off a pier over water and draw massive crowds of spectators. The entries are judged on three criteria: distance flown, creativity and showmanship.

The annual event has now been held in more than 35 cities worldwide; the British version in 2011 drew crowds of 15,000 people in pouring rain. This example shows how a company can go beyond sponsorship; the brand has actually created its own sport. People who attend the Flugtag or watch footage of the flights on TV, realise that an energy drink company is hoping to promote its products but also appreciate that without the corporate involvement, the sport itself wouldn't exist. Red Bull demonstrates how to do event sponsorship and creation on a large, exciting scale.

Using business and industry opportunities

Turn first to your professional groups and industry trade associations for appropriate business-to-business (B2B) marketing. These venues differ for each industry but have the benefit of collecting your prospective customers altogether in one place in common. Attend conferences and trade shows if your budget is small and do plenty of informal networking. If you can afford to, also rent display space at trade shows, present at conferences and sponsor industry events. The more visible you are at your own industry events, the more customer attention and credibility you can generate.

Trade shows are great because they draw people who are wearing their business hats, ready to make purchase decisions for their companies. You can also put on special events for your own customers or employees. (In fact, employee events often provide that extra motivating power that you need to get your people fully behind your marketing plan.)

Whatever the business-orientated opportunity, remember that you're still trying to attract and hold the attention of people, not businesses. You're interested in the people in any business who make the purchase decisions.

Getting stuffy and businesslike is very easy, but do people really want to sit through two days of lectures or PowerPoint slides on the impact of new technologies in their industry? Offering them optional, one-hour panel discussions on the topic, with a backbone of outdoor sports and recreation events or a visit to a nearby golf course is a much better idea.

Sponsoring a Special Event

Some people assume that special events are only useful in special circumstances, when you can justify a major effort and expense. Not so. Staging small-scale events or (as we discuss in this section) riding on the coat-tails of somebody else's event can work, too. (You should also think of this strategy as piggybacking on others' investments in events, a helpful term in visualising the benefits.)

After all, why create your own event when so many wonderful events already exist? But if you're becoming involved with someone else's event, make sure you get a clear, detailed agreement in writing about where, how and how often it identifies your brand name. That identification is the return on your sponsorship investment. Too often, sponsors end up complaining that they didn't get as much good exposure as they expected, so make sure you and the event directors understand the exposure level up-front.

You can find local organisations by following the events notices in local papers and on regional radio stations. A number of web-based companies now help you locate possible events to sponsor. For example, check out www.uksponsorship.com for hundreds of possibilities in everything from sports to the arts. You can find an exciting new event sponsorship out there that fits both your budget and your customers.

Finding cause-related events

You can attract a lot of positive attention from the media and your local community by sponsoring a fundraising event for a charity. This event sponsorship is, for obvious reasons, called *cause-related event sponsorship*.

You can generate extremely valuable goodwill through cause sponsorship if the cause and event are appropriate to your target market. For information about funding for this type of project, check out the advice offered by Sport England's funding body at www.sportsmatch.co.uk.

Too much money is thrown away on events that appeal to somebody at the sponsoring company but don't appeal to its customers. Be careful to pick causes that appeal not only to you and your associates, but also to your target customers. The biggest and best-known events aren't always the most effective for your business – try looking for something smaller and more local.

Donations to controversial causes or to political campaigns are likely to offend people. Stay away from anything contentious. Causes related to health, children, preventing diseases and drug abuse, helping animals and conserving the natural world generally pass the controversy test – unless the particular organisation takes an overly offbeat approach.

If you don't have the marketing budget to sponsor a local charity, consider donating your time instead. You can join the board of a charity and offer your energy and business savvy. Or give your employees two hours off on a Friday to donate their time and effort to a local cause.

Be careful to examine the charity's books and tax-exempt status before offering sponsorship or running an event to benefit it. Make sure it has full charitable status (you can check registered charities with the Charity Commission, at www.charitycommission.gov.uk). Make sure that its audited financial statements show it has relatively low overheads and moderate-looking executive salaries. You don't want to support a charity that turns out to be poorly or dishonestly run. Some charities are more effective and well run than others and you never really know until you look. Their records and financials should be available for public inspection, so just ask. If an organisation hesitates to share this information, don't get involved with it.

Running the numbers on an event

Be careful to pick a cause-related or other event that reaches your target customers efficiently. Like any marketing communication, an event sponsorship needs to deliver reach at a reasonable cost. So ask yourself how many people will come to the event or hear of your sponsorship of it. Then ask yourself what percentage of this total is likely to be in your target market. That figure's your *reach*. Divide your cost by this figure, multiply it by 1000 and you have the cost of your reach per thousand. You can compare this cost with cost figures for other kinds of reach, such as a direct mailing or print or radio ads.

If you think the event sponsorship is more credible and convincing than an ad because of its affiliation with an appealing cause, you can adjust your cost figure to compensate. Doing so is called *weighting the exposure*. For example, say you decide one exposure to your company or brand through a cause sponsorship is twice as powerful as exposure to one of your ads. Then multiply the number of people the event reaches by 2 before calculating the cost. That way, you compare the cost of reaching 2000 people through the sponsorship to the cost of reaching 1000 people through advertising, which adjusts for the greater value you attach to the cause-related exposure.

In our experience, the right special event is often many times more effective than an advertisement. But the event has to be appropriate for its target market or is worthless. Also, make sure you publicise the event well.

Evaluating the options for sponsorship

If you're considering event sponsorship, you're in good company. The UK sports sponsorship market will grow to a value of £1.92 billion by 2015, up from a current £1.59 billion, according to research forecasts by specialist company Key Note. But sports aren't the only option for sponsorship – consider arts initiatives or even TV and radio programmes (see Chapter 9 for more details on using these media).

Sport sponsorship is generally judged to be the most effective approach as it attracts the largest sums of money. But what's right for your particular firm may be very different. If your product, service or customer base is related to the arts, or if you happen to be particularly involved in this area, you may want to ignore sports events and sponsor the arts exclusively. Let your own particular interests and talents focus how you market.

To decide on the best approach for your company, use the three-step selection process discussed in the following sections.

You can apply this three-step process to other forms of event, too. You need to design all events by examining your options, running the numbers and screening for relevance.

Step 1: Explore the options

You can find sponsorship opportunities all over the place, so take time to explore all the available options – and, as you do with any other aspect of your marketing, employ a little creativity. Visit Business in the Community's site at www.bitc.org.uk for examples of what other companies are doing with charities in their local areas.

Step 2: Run the numbers

Carefully analyse the marketing impact of each candidate for sponsorship. Cut any from your list if their audiences aren't a good match with your target market. Chop out any that may be controversial and likely to generate negative as well as positive publicity. Ditch any that don't seem to present strong, positive images – sponsoring something that your customers don't feel passionate about is pointless. Now compare the remaining options by calculating your cost per thousand exposures for each one.

Don't be afraid to negotiate. If a sponsorship opportunity appeals to you but is priced too high, show the team there your comparative numbers and ask if they can cut you a deal!

This process may lead you away from the most popular types of sponsorship. A big event (like a World Cup football match) certainly exposes you to millions of people. But how many are really in your target market? And what's the cost of reaching them this way? Big sports and entertainment events often charge a premium because of their popularity and size. But they aren't worth that premium if you can buy similar reach for less by sponsoring several smaller events.

Step 3: Screen for relevance

Relevance is how closely the event relates to your product and its usage by customers and, oddly, is the most important, but least considered, factor. Let us give you an example to illustrate the importance of relevance.

A few years ago, the world football body FIFA lifted the sponsorship ban on referees, suddenly and unusually opening up a new sponsorship 'space' in a high-profile sport; who would be first to take it? Step forward the optical retailer Specsavers. The relevance, and humour, of having an optical retailer sponsoring football referees is obvious but inspired. Specsavers gained high-value media coverage (especially after offering free eye tests to referees after some controversial decisions) and sales went up significantly – all because the company had the 'vision' to sign a highly relevant sponsorship deal.

Putting on a Public Event

Sometimes, you have no alternative but to stage the event yourself. None of the sponsorship options fit your requirements. Or you really need the exclusivity of your own event – a forum in which no competitors' messages can interfere with your own.

Increasingly companies are staging their own events so they can tailor them to their own products and customers. We mentioned Red Bull's Flugtag earlier in this chapter but this is just one of the company's events; it has also staged 'The Art of Can', a competition involving customers making sculptures out of the product's packaging. Meanwhile, ice cream brand Ben & Jerry's has run 'bog snorkelling' events.

Starting your own event may seem like a great idea but if you don't have the expertise to run such experiences within your own business (why would a florist or a car dealer necessarily know how to organise an event?), leaving it to the experts is wiser. Otherwise you risk not only alienating potential customers by doing everything badly but you may also cause problems for yourself and any employees by expecting people to do activities they're not trained for. Remember, setting yourself a challenge is good but tackling something out of your league is just irresponsible.

Selling sponsorship rights

Finding other companies that want to help sponsor your event is a good way of making it pay for itself. Not your competitors, of course. Many companies may have an interest in the same event as you do, but for different reasons, and these firms make good co-sponsors. Basically, if the event is relevant, novel and likely to draw in their target audience, then you have a good pitch. Now you just need to go out and make sales calls to potential sponsors. Or consider hiring an event management firm that can sell sponsorships as well as help to organise and run events.

Getting help managing your event

Some people specialise in managing special events; they work on a consulting basis, from conception through completion, to make sure that everyone comes and everything goes just right. Many such specialists exist, from independent experts to major companies. We recommend bringing in a specialist of some sort to help you design and manage any event that involves a lot of people, shows, speeches or activities, meals, conference and hotel room reservations, security and transportation. To avoid disaster, you must get these details right.

You can find event management companies through the Association of Event Organisers (AEO) at `www.aeo.org.uk`. The AEO has a listing of all suppliers to trade and consumer exhibitions through its sister associations, the Event Supplier and Services Association (ESSA; `www.essa.uk.com`) and the Association of Event Venues (AEV; `www.aev.org.uk`).

Exhibiting at Shows and Exhibitions

Do you need to exhibit at trade shows? If you're in a B2B selling situation, we assume that you do. Exhibiting is almost always necessary, even if you only do so to keep competitors from stealing your customers at the show! Some sources suggest that trade shows generate 18 per cent of all sales leads, on average. As a way to control your own trade show spending, why not compare per cent of budget and per cent of leads, adjusting the per cent of budget figure until you find the spending level that yields the best return in leads? If you spend 20 per cent of your budget on trade shows, you need to beat the average and get more than 20 per cent of your leads from them. That means being a savvy event manager – selecting appropriate shows and staging excellent booths at them.

Some retail or consumer industries also hold major shows. Boat manufacturers use boat shows as an important way to expose consumers to their products. County fairs attract exhibitors of arts and crafts, gourmet foods and gardening supplies. Computer shows showcase new equipment. If your industry has a major show for the public, we highly recommend that you exhibit there. Send your in-house list of customers and friends an invitation, too – the more traffic you can get to your stand, the better. (In fact, begin direct marketing to announce the event and give people incentives to come starting at least two months before the show!)

Knowing what trade shows can accomplish for you

You can generate leads, find new customers and maintain or improve your current customers' perceptions of you at trade shows. You can also use them to introduce a new product or launch a new strategy. Trade shows also give you great opportunities to introduce back-office people (like the sales support staff or even the chairperson) to your customers face to face.

Use trade shows to network in your industry. You usually find the best manufacturers' representatives and salespeople by making connections at trade shows. If you're secretly hoping to find a better employer, a little mingling may yield an offer at the next big trade show. Also, be sure to talk with a lot of attendees and non-competitive exhibitors in order to find out about the newest trends and what your competitors are doing in the market. The information a good networker gleans from a trade show is often worth more than the price of attendance. Never mind selling – just get out there and chat.

In short, you should see trade shows as essential to your marketing for many reasons. Even if you think you may lose money on the project, a trade show can be worthwhile in the long run. A well-designed exhibit, well promoted in advance and staffed with people who are prepared to find leads and close sales, usually produces an almost immediate return on investment.

Building the foundations for a good stand

Marketers focus on the stand when they think about how to handle a trade show. But you should consider the stand just a part of your overall marketing strategy for the show. And you don't have a show strategy until you've written something intelligent in response to each of these questions:

- ✔ How do we attract the right people to the show and to our stand?
- ✔ What do we want visitors to our stand to do at the show?
- ✔ How can we communicate with visitors when they get to the stand?
- ✔ How can we figure out who visitors are and how to handle them?
- ✔ How can we capture information about them, their interests and needs?
- ✔ How can we follow up to build or maintain our relationship with them?

The strategy has to start by attracting a lot of prospects and customers, and the easiest way to do so is to just go with the flow by picking a show that potential customers already plan to attend. Ask yourself what shows your customers are going to attend. For example, if you import gift items and your customers include the buyers from retail gift stores, then where do they go to make their purchases?

Can you cover enough of the market by exhibiting at the Ideal Home Show or do you need to specialise, by going to the Baby Show for example? You can ask the sponsoring organisations for data on last year's attendees and who's registered for this year's show and use this information to help you decide. You need to see high numbers of your target customers; otherwise the show wastes your company's time and money.

You can also ask a sampling of customers for their opinions about your stand. You may want to use the simplest research method, which researchers call informal *qualitative interviews* – what real people refer to as conversations. Just talk to some customers, preferably at the show because their memory of your stand is still clear in their minds. See what they think. Or you can do some *intercept interviews* at the show. You conduct an intercept interview when you walk up to people as they pass by your stand and ask them if they'll answer a few questions, such as 'Do you like the such-and-such stand?' and 'How exciting is this stand's design?'

Locating compatible trade shows

How do you find out about possible trade shows? We thought you'd never ask! If you subscribe to trade magazines, the shows in your industry find you because the magazines sell their lists to the show sponsors. But don't go just by what gets sent to you because you may overlook something important. Go to www.exhibitions.co.uk for a list of pending shows; you can search by category. For international listings, try www.eventseye.com.

You do have another source, one that we find much more reliable than any other – your customers. The whole point of exhibiting at a trade show is to reach customers, so why don't you just ask them where you should exhibit? Call or drop by a selection of your best customers and ask them for advice on where and when to exhibit. They know what's hot right now and what's not.

Renting the perfect stand

You need to select a location and stand size. Aim for a spot near a major entrance, food stands, bathrooms or any other place where groups of people are likely to be concentrated. Being on the end of an aisle can help you, too. And bigger is better – in general, you should get the biggest stand you can afford.

But even if you end up with a miniature booth in the middle of an aisle, don't despair. Many shoppers try to walk all the aisles of a show, and these locations can work, too, provided the show draws enough of the right kind of customers for you. In fact, smart buyers often look at the smallest, cheapest booths in the hope of discovering something hot and new from a struggling entrepreneurial supplier.

Setting up other kinds of displays

Companies that make trade show stands often also produce many other kinds of displays, such as those designed for the lobby, conference room and tabletop. These smaller-scale displays can be effective in the right spot and often cost you less than a trade show booth, so explore all the options before you decide what fits your marketing campaign and budget best.

Experts can help you design and build your stand or other display, manage the trade show activity and handle the sales leads that result from it – consult business directories at a library or search the Internet for leads, starting with the members list at the Association of Event Organisers (www.aeo.org.uk).

We recommend getting opinions and quotes from multiple vendors (and asking for credit references and the contact names of some recent clients) before choosing the right company for your job. We also recommend sharing your budget constraints up-front to find out if the company you're talking to is appropriate for you. Some can do very economical, small-scale projects with ease, and others are more orientated to large-scale corporate accounts.

Don't overlook the drawing power of simple details, such as fresh flowers or food. A simple gesture like this can be remarkably effective at drawing traffic to your stand and putting visitors in a positive mood! Alternatively, try using comfort as your draw by setting up some sofas in the stand. People are on their feet for hours at these shows, so they appreciate a chance to rest. Of course, if someone sits there too long, you can launch into your hard sell and either win an order or politely drive them from the stand to open the seat to someone else. A massage chair or bottles of cold water can also draw weary visitors to your booth. The current trend at business trade shows is offering cupcakes and setting up ice cream machines at stands – be creative.

Doing Demonstrations

Seeing is believing: if you think a demonstration is applicable to your goods or services, you should definitely consider giving one. A demonstration is often the most effective way to introduce a new product, or even to introduce an old product to new customers. This area of marketing falls under what the experts call *field marketing* or, even worse, *experiential marketing*. To you and us, this approach simply means getting your product in front of the people who might buy it, and giving them a reason to do just that.

You can do a demonstration anywhere. Really. Even when you sponsor someone else's event, if you ask early on, they can often find a time and place for you to stage a demonstration. And when you control the event or a part of it, you have considerable freedom to design demonstrations. Let us show you some specifics.

In a shop, retail park or other consumer-orientated location, a demonstration is often the most persuasive form of promotion. You can see run-of-the-mill *sampling* take place at supermarkets nearly every day – often a bored member of staff handing out bite-size pieces of cheese or a thimble full of wine from a temporary table. Give us a break. A proper retail demo should be:

- **Realistic:** Show the product in a natural use context – and that includes normal portions of foods. (*Natural use* means how the customer would normally use it. If you eat a food product for dinner, find a way to demonstrate it on a table with real place settings, for example.)

- **Wonderful:** The event should be worthy of attention, with real entertainment value that adds excitement to the product. Try a cooking demonstration with a lot of action, not just a one-bite taste. What about getting a well-known chef to cook it for you? Or make the demonstration a taste test in which the product wins a contest and the tasters get the prizes. Imagine you're creating a skit for a TV show – that's the sort of entertainment people pay attention to.

✔ **A marketing priority:** Here's your chance to sell your product directly to customers. Think of a political candidate going out to shake hands (notice the candidate always wears her best suit and biggest smile). Too often, companies put poorly qualified temps in charge of demonstrations. Who do you really want out there selling on your behalf – someone who makes the product look good or someone who doesn't actually know anything about it?

When you follow these three rules, you create great demonstrations. But note that these demonstrations are more expensive than the lame ones we usually encounter. That extra expense is okay because they're more effective. Use these demonstrations more sparingly, but put more into each one, and they can reward you with a surprisingly high level of customer enthusiasm.

Giving Gifts

Premium items, *promotional items*, *incentives*; however the industry refers to them, these are simply gifts you give to your customers, clients, prospects or employees. Not bribes – gifts. We recommend sending your regular customers some kind of premium they'll appreciate at least once a year. Another approach is to distribute them in ways that spread the good word about your firm or product, making the premiums, and those who receive them, your ambassadors.

Giving out a free pen at the checkout is as simple as putting a FREE PENS sign on a container, but when choosing a gift for your good customers, put more care into the selection and presentation of the premium to make sure they appreciate the gesture. Think of gift giving as a form of theatre, as a special option among special events, and you can avoid the standard stupidities. You may even gain customer attention and goodwill. If pens don't float your boat, lots of other items exist out there that you can give away to customers.

Note that you need to provide giveaways at trade shows. We recommend giving a fun or interesting gift (a puzzle, joke book or toy, for example) as a token of appreciation for filling in a registration form. You need to focus your marketing resources on finding and qualifying leads, so make everything you do, from advance mailings and emailings to booth design and signs, count towards this goal.

Giving everyone who wanders by your booth a gift is silly and requires such a large volume of gifts that you can't afford something nice. But exceptions to this rule do exist. Free bottles of cold water or other draws can be offered to everyone as a way of attracting people to your stand. Then add a more durable premium gift as a thank you when you give out brochures and collect information from serious leads.

If you're selecting premium items for a trade show or other event, stick to easy-to-carry items. Keep gifts small, durable and able to pass airport security checks. Also make an effort to keep your marketing materials (brochures, for example) compact and durable enough that they won't be left in the hotel room or ruined in someone's luggage.

As with all face-to-face marketing opportunities, you want to make a positive impact that customers remember down the road, so choose your gifts with this end in mind.

Part V
Connecting With Your Customers

In this part . . .

1f you can design a great product, give it an appropriate brand name, package it well and then turn it over to a good salesperson, you may be able to dispense with everything else discussed in this book. The combination of an appealing product or brand, plus good sales and service, can make a business successful, all on its own. And so it seems fitting to devote an entire part to these topics.

We have an interesting story to illustrate this. A consultant was hired to consult with the chief executive of a speciality chemicals company. They wanted him to evaluate the overall business plan and suggest ways of making the business grow. After poking around the premises for a few hours and interviewing a bunch of the people, he discovered a startling thing: the chemicals business apparently did no marketing at all. They had no marketing department, and the company had no brochures, no ads, no publicity, and no web site. So, how had they got this far, and where in the world did their customers come from?

In this part, we explain the secrets of companies like this one. We show you how to maximise the impact of your product and its packaging, tell you how to price your products and services, keep you from underselling yourself by making common mistakes associated with distribution and pricing, and help you approach sales and service like an old pro.

Chapter 17

Branding, Managing and Packaging a Product

. . . .

In This Chapter

▶ Designing and developing hot new products

▶ Fitting your products into product lines

▶ Finding the right name

▶ Creating strong identities under trademark law

▶ Packaging and labelling to boost sales

▶ Knowing when and how to improve or eliminate a product

. . . .

The product is the heart and soul of any marketing plan. If the product is good, then that marketing plan has a decent chance of success. But if the product is nothing special in the customer's eyes, no marketing plan can make that product a winner in the long run. We call this the 'lipstick on the gorilla' effect.

Many people in the field of marketing, and in business in general, don't understand this point about quality. These people underestimate their customers and overestimate the persuasive power of marketing. Something of real value has to be at the core of any marketing plan; it should be about emphasising a tangible benefit for the consumer, not pretending something without merit is worthwhile. The product needs to have some notable advantages from the consumer's perspective.

This chapter shows you how to develop winning products, how to manage them as part of a product line and how to select your products' names to amplify their natural strengths and communicate those strengths to the target customer.

We use 'product' as an umbrella term that means a product, service or anything else your company wants to sell. A product can be a tin of beans, an insurance policy or a new piece of Internet software. If you're selling it, it's your product.

Finding Simple Ways to Leverage Your Product

Taking small steps to keep a product fresh and to boost its visibility and appeal is one of the first and most important things you can do. Product management is a lot like gardening. You occasionally plant a whole new crop but you tend the existing plants routinely, too.

Here's a list of simple and quick things you can do to build customer loyalty and grow sales by working on your product:

- ✔ **Update the appearance:** Many companies present good products to the world in poorly designed exteriors that don't dress for success. Look at the product itself (colours, attractiveness and visibility of any brand names). Mobile phones exist that have more technical features than Apple's iPhones but the latter outstrips all its competitors because it has a distinct, intuitive and desirable design.

- ✔ **Update the packaging:** A consumer product that sits on a shelf waiting for someone to pick it up should be highly visible and appealing (remember, in-store buying decisions are made in seconds or less). Can you add a brighter colour to the packaging to attract the eye? Can you mention key features on the outside? Or perhaps you can add a clear window on the pack to show the actual product inside.

- ✔ **Make sure the product is attractive and easy to use:** Your product should also feel nice – smooth, polished, soft or whatever texture is appropriate to the product's use. In some instances, the smell and sound of your product matters, too. This doesn't just apply to food products; cars are deliberately given that special 'new leather' smell inside to help them sell. Many car manufacturers also tune car doors so that they make a distinctive 'clunk'. Even very minor changes in a product's look, feel, smell and function can improve customer satisfaction and appeal.

- ✔ **Improve any printed materials that come with the product:** Can you enhance their appearance? Dress them up? Make them clearer or more useful? Make sure they instil pride of ownership in the product.

- ✔ **Choose your product's best quality:** Coin a short phrase to communicate this best quality to the consumer and put that phrase on the product, its packaging and its literature in prominent places. Make up simple (but attractive) colour-printed stickers for this purpose – these are the quickest and cheapest way to add a marketing message.

- ✔ **Eliminate confusion about which product does what for whom:** Clarify the differences and uses of your products, if you have more than one, by pricing and naming them distinctly (to make them obviously different). Most product lines look confusing to the average buyer.

✔ **Make your logo beautiful:** Apple Inc. switched from a somewhat dated-looking rainbow-coloured version of its distinctive apple-shaped logo to a beautiful, sophisticated version made of a clear plastic panel backlit with diffused white light. This logo sits on the top of all its newer laptops, giving those computers a more sophisticated appeal. Can you upgrade your image by improving the appearance of your logo on your products?

✔ **Purchase a related but non-competing product from another company, then repackage and distribute it as part of your product line:** Adding another good product your customers like can increase the average purchase size significantly. We recommend using distributor-style arrangements that eliminate the investment of product development, giving you a good way to expand your product line in a hurry. Selling a new (or new to you) product to an existing customer is often easier than finding a new customer for an existing product.

We hope this list of simple ideas for action has your marketing blood pumping! You can still do a lot with and for your existing products, even if you don't have the cash or time right now to develop and introduce an entirely new one.

You're only as good as your products, so try to update, upgrade or perhaps even replace your current line of products. Doing so is a long-term but vital activity that most marketing plans need to include, just as gardeners have to remember to plan the next planting session along with their more routine weeding and watering duties.

Identifying When and How to Introduce a New Product

We wish we could say that you don't need to worry about new product development very often. But if your market is like most, innovations give you a major source of competitive advantage. A rival's major new product introduction probably changes the face of your market – and upsets your sales projections and profit margins – at least once every few years. So you can't afford to ignore new product development, ever. You need to introduce new products as often as you can afford to develop them.

Coming up with the next great thing

Okay, you think you need a hot new product. But where do you get the idea? First, check out the basic creativity skills covered in Chapter 5. That chapter offers a host of brainstorming and idea-generating techniques that you can use. If you and your fellow marketers are stale, bring in salespeople from the field, production, repair or service call centre. Even try bringing in some customers for a brainstorming session. Your approach hardly matters, as long as what you try is new and different. New ideas come from novel thought processes, which come from adopting different approaches to thinking. Do something new to produce something new!

Also consider two cheap but valuable sources of new product ideas: old ideas and other people's ideas.

Rediscovering old products

Old ideas are any product concepts that you or another company have previously abandoned. These concepts may have been considered but rejected without being marketed, or they could even be old products that have fallen out of use but could be revived with a new twist.

Because people have been struggling to develop new product concepts for decades in most markets, a great many abandoned ideas and old products are around. Often, companies fail even to keep good records, so you have to interview longstanding employees and poke through faded files or archived catalogues to discover those old ideas. But old ideas may be a treasure trove, because technological or marketing developments may have made the original objections less serious than when marketers originally scrapped the idea. Technical advances or changing customer taste may make yesterday's wild ideas practical today. Even if you can't use any of the old ideas you find, they may lead you to fresh ways of thinking about the problem – perhaps they suggest a customer need that you hadn't considered before.

Also note that old products in one market may be new products in another. Old-fashioned, hand-cranked cash registers sell well in some countries, even though they've been replaced by electronic cash registers in others. The use of electronic cash registers depends upon the nature of the local economy and the availability and reliability of the local electrical service. You may be able to turn your dead products into winners in other countries, if you can partner with local distributors.

One product strategy or multiple strategies?

Do you sell into one market or more? How you answer this question determines whether you need to have one product line and one strategy or multiple lines and strategies. Many businesses sell into multiple markets. PepsiCo sells into the beverage and snack markets. Car manufacturers sell to consumers and to fleet buyers. Small companies use this strategy, too: a local cleaning service may have both homeowners and businesses as customers and the marketing (and specifically the product offering) needs to be different for each.

Stealing – er, borrowing – ideas

You can often pursue the second source, other people's ideas, through licences. A private inventor may have a great new product concept and a patent for it, but may lack the marketing muscle and capital to introduce the product. You can provide that missing muscle and pay the inventor 5 or 10 per cent of your net revenues as reward for their inspiration.

Many companies generate inventions that fall outside of their marketing and sales focus. They don't want to take their eyes off their core activities. These companies are often willing to license to someone specialising in the target market.

Licensing is the official way to use other people's ideas; however, an unofficial way exists that's probably more common and certainly more important for most marketers. You simply steal ideas. Now, by steal, we don't mean to take anything that isn't yours. A *patent* protects a design, a *trademark* protects a name or logo and a *copyright* protects writing, artwork, performances and software. You must respect these legal rights that protect other people's expressions of their ideas. But legally protecting underlying ideas in many countries where you're likely to do business isn't possible.

If an idea makes it to your ears or eyes through a legitimate public channel of communication, you can use it. (Just don't bug your competitors' head-quarters, go through their rubbish bins or get their engineers drunk – doing so may violate *trade secrecy laws* – ask your lawyer before planning any questionable research.)

Although a competitor may be upset to see you knocking off or improving upon its latest idea, nothing can stop you as long as your source was public (not secret) and you aren't violating a patent, trademark or copyright. In most markets, competitors steal ideas as a matter of routine. You can also look at other industries for inspirations that you can apply in your own. The good idea hunter has to be open-minded – you never know where you may find something worth stealing!

Note that you're less likely to violate these legal protections if you just take a public idea and develop it all on your own, but you may still want to have a lawyer (preferably one who specialises in intellectual property law) review what you've done before going public with it.

By the way, we call this activity 'stealing' in humour – it isn't really, if you do it legally. Some people call it *benchmarking*; some call it 'being inspired by others'. Whatever you call this borrowing of ideas, try to be aware of new concepts and keep your product offerings up to date with them. For example, most dating services have taken inspiration from social networking websites such as Facebook. Many dating sites mimic the look and feel of social networking profile pages, offering 'walls' where other users can leave messages or the means to announce your mood to the whole service. Because many people now feel comfortable with the way that Facebook works, dating sites have incorporated these elements to help encourage people to spend more time on their services and minimise any stigma connected to using an online dating service.

Picking your customers' brains

A final source of new product ideas is your customers – although often they don't know it. Ask a customer to describe a brilliant new product you should provide for them and you get a blank stare – or worse. Yet frustrations with your existing products and all sorts of dissatisfactions, needs and wants lurk in the back of every customer's mind. And you may be able to help them with these gripes.

How do you mine this treasure trove of needs, many of them latent or unrecognised? Collecting the customers' words helps you gain insight into how they think – so talk to them and take notes or record their comments (with their permission). Get customers chatting, and let them wander a bit so that you have a chance to encounter the unexpected. Also watch customers as they buy and use your product. Observation may reveal wasted time and effort, inefficiencies or other problems that the customer takes for granted – issues that the customer may happily say good-bye to if you point them out and remove them.

Using the significant difference strategy

New product development has a downside: almost all new products fail. Every expert seems to have his own statistic, but most suggest that eight out of ten new product ideas fail and that half of line extensions fail. Before you give up and turn to another chapter, here's a different statistic to keep you reading: industry-wide research shows that line extensions account for 62 per cent of total revenue but contribute just 39 per cent of profits, while 'real' innovation represents 38 per cent of revenue and 61 per cent of profits.

The odds aren't great but the potential rewards are. Make sure your new product beats the odds by being much better than the typical new product. How?

Common sense and a large pile of research reports say that new products do better – make more money, for a longer amount of time – when customers see something strikingly new about them. Walk down the aisle of your supermarket and notice the number of packages proclaiming something 'new'. Without the word splashed across them, you may never have been able to tell they were new. We experience the same trouble seeing what's really new in the services industry, too. For example, take a look at the brochures and posters in your bank and see whether the 'new' services really seem more like repackaged old services with fancy new names and pricing.

To achieve real success, you have to introduce something that's not only new but also looks new and different to the market. The product needs a radical distinction and a clear point of difference. Innovations that consumers recognise more quickly and easily provide the marketer with a greater return. Researchers who study new product success use the term *intensity* to describe this phenomenon – the more intense the difference between your new product and old products, the more likely the new product will succeed.

Branding and Naming Your Product

Once you've got your product, everything you do to it and everything the customer sees, counts as *branding*. What do you call your new product? Should you launch it under a brand identity your business already owns or give it a new one? Should you attempt to add value (and raise the price) by promoting a positive brand identity, or should you save your marketing budget and just get the product out to point of purchase? You have to make all these difficult decisions. Let us show you how to make them well.

Designing a product line

A *product line* is any logical grouping of products offered to customers. (Remember, products can be goods, services, ideas or even people such as political candidates or celebrities.) You usually identify product lines by an umbrella brand name, with individual brand identities falling under that umbrella.

The Apple computer line includes many different products, called different things, from the MacBook to the iPhone but they all bear the same brand logo (a trademarked asset of Apple Computer). The company has made each product distinct enough from each other that together they give the customer a wide range of choices yet are all recognisable as being related to one another. You can think of product lines like this one as families of products – and, like families, their relationship needs to be close and clear.

You need to consider two key issues when designing your product lines:

✔ **Depth:** How many alternatives should you give the customer within any single category? For example, should you make a single T-shirt design in a range of sizes? How about offering the design in a variety of colours? All these options increase depth because they give a customer more options. Depth gives you an advantage because it increases the likelihood of a good fit between an interested customer and your product. You don't want to miss a sale because somebody was too big to wear a size large.

Increase depth when you're losing customers because you don't have a product for them. Increasing your depth of choice reduces the chance of disappointing a prospective customer.

✔ **Breadth:** This option allows you to generate new sales. For example, if you sell one popular T-shirt design, you can increase breadth by offering more T-shirt designs in your product line. When you add anything that the customer views as a separate choice, not a variant of the same choice, you're adding breadth to the product line. A broad line of T-shirts includes dozens of different designs. A broad and deep product line offers each of those designs in many sizes, different colours and forms of T-shirt.

Increase breadth whenever you can think of a new product that seems to fit in the line. By *fit*, we mean that customers can see the new product's obvious relationship to the line. Don't mix unrelated products – that's not a product line, because it doesn't have a clear, logical identity to customers. But keep stretching a successful line as much as you can. Doing so makes sense for one simple reason: you sell new products to old customers. Of course, the line may also reach new customers, which is great. But you can sell to your old customers more easily (and more cheaply), so you definitely want to do more business with them in the future. Offering them a greater breadth of products is a great way to do this.

Maintaining your product line: When to change

'Don't leave well enough alone' is the secret to good product management. But if you keep growing your lines, you can obviously bump into some practical limits after a while. How do you know when the pendulum is going to swing the other way – when you need to do some spring-cleaning?

If your distribution channels can't display the full product line to customers, you need to decrease your depth or breadth (or both). Often, distribution becomes a bottleneck, imposing practical limits on how big a product line you can bring to the customer's attention.

Potatoes with pedigree

You'd be forgiven for thinking that you can do only so much with the humble potato crisp. After all, in how many ways can you slice up and fry a potato? The market is already saturated with big brands such as Walkers or Pringles, backed by big companies.

Well, fortunately not everyone thinks like that – particularly the people at Chiltern Snacks, who created Salty Dog crisps. A lot of good marketing exists behind Salty Dog (although the owners would be first to admit they're no experts). The product's significant difference feeds into its name, which feeds into its packaging.

Every packet of Salty Dog carries the line 'The hand-cooked crisps that bite back', together with a cartoon of a dog on the distinctive silver-foil bags. The dog is based on the owner's real terrier puppy and the 'bite back' phrase is also based in truth. The company only uses the biggest and best potatoes, hand fries them in sunflower oil for extra crunch and gives them powerful natural flavours such as Jalapeno & Coriander or Ham & Wholegrain Mustard. So, you see, even for fairly ordinary product areas in oversupplied markets, you can succeed if you create something that's different from its competitors and which tells its story in a powerful way.

The household and personal products giant Unilever decided to cut back its 1600 brands to 400 as part of a five-year plan. Not all of the 1200 products it wanted to lose were failing; they just didn't fit with what Unilever was best at doing. Of the 400 chosen products left, the company then identified 40 *star brands* on which to focus its main marketing efforts. This focus didn't necessarily mean each line had fewer products within it; some, like Dove and Lynx, have since expanded into new and different areas.

But what Unilever wanted to do was concentrate its resources around fewer, well-thought-out product lines – making things easier for retailers and ultimately consumers. Too many choices frustrate customers and lead to confusion between products. Brand identities start to overlap, and you make customer decisions harder rather than easier.

Always calibrate your product line to your distribution channels and your customers. Don't overwhelm or underwhelm. Keep talking to all your customers and watching how they behave with your product to see if you need to shrink or grow your product line.

Naming a product or product line

Naming a new product isn't simple – that's why so many brand agencies exist out there charging a fortune for the service – but you can use a number of effective methods. You can choose a word, or combination of words, that tells people about the exact character of your product – such as Salty Dog crisps, which uses the slogan 'The hand-cooked crisps that bite back' (see the nearby sidebar). This approach resembles giving a new puppy a name. You want to get a feel for its personality first and then give it a name that fits. A stand-offish poodle can be Fifi, but that name doesn't fit a playful mutt!

The Ford Mustang, an extremely successful brand since 1964, used the strategy of matching the name to the product's characteristics. When it started out, the car's marketers presented it as simply having the personality of the small, hardy horse of the American plains from which the car took its name. Those marketers hoped that the driver saw himself as a modern-day cowboy, akin to the real cowboys who broke and used the mustangs for their work. This strategy has a powerful effect because it uses existing terms whose meaning marketers apply to their product. Forty years or so later, people think of the car long before the horse when hearing the word 'mustang'.

You can also name your product by making up a brand-new word that has no prior meaning. This approach gives you something you can more easily protect in a court of law, but it isn't necessarily effective at communicating the character of your product. You have to invest considerable time and money in creating a meaning for the new name in consumers' minds, but when you get it right, it can be very powerful. The name 'Google' is now synonymous with searching for information online. The name itself is a mis-spelling of the word 'Googol' – the mathematical name for a '1' followed by a hundred zeros. Now, however, Google is not only the name of a search engine, it has also made it into the *Oxford English Dictionary* as a verb, 'to Google'.

Legally protecting your product's name and identity

You can gain legal protection by using, and getting legal recognition for, a unique identifier for your product, a line of products or even your entire company. This protection can apply to names, short verbal descriptions and visual symbols. All these forms of identification are marks that can represent the identity of the thing you apply them to. A tangible product's name and/or visual symbol is a *trademark*. A business name is a *word mark* – again, offering similar protection under the law.

You establish and protect your rights to exclusive use of any unique trademark by registering it and then by using it. UK and European trademark law has seen many improvements in recent years. For starters, the definition of trademark has become very broad, giving companies better protection for all aspects of their brand than previously. Trademarks can now be words (including personal names), designs, letters, numerals or the shape of goods or their packaging. This last point is particularly important to products that come in distinctive packaging (think of the classic contoured bottle of Coca-Cola, which is now a protected trademark).

Recognising what you should trademark

Consider registering as many different aspects of your product's identity as you think are important to its commercial success (you can even register colours and smells, though companies have had mixed success with this). Don't go overboard, though. You could register everything about your brand, if someone hasn't got there first – but don't register elements of your name or design that don't regularly feature. In trademark law, you need to follow a simple rule of thumb: use it or lose it. For the law to apply, you have to register the trademark (and keep it registered, as registrations usually run out after ten years) and then you have to use it – regularly.

Registering trademarks in the UK and Europe

If you want to register a trademark of any kind in the UK, contact the UK Intellectual Property Office at www.ipo.gov.uk or by calling their Enquiry Unit on 0300 300 2000. A wealth of information is offered on the Intellectual Property Office website, including information on copyright, designs and patents. You can even use the site to help you in your name search, by typing in your desired product or company name and seeing whether another company in the same or similar line of business is already using it.

Registering your trademark for the main foreign territories is also now relatively easy. You can cover the whole of the European Community by applying for a community trademark (CTM). For information on how to do this, contact the Office for Harmonization in the Internal Market, at www.oami. europa.eu. Or to cover an even wider international area, including the United States, you can have your trademark protected under the 'Madrid system'. Visit the website of the World Intellectual Property Organization at www.wipo.int for a list of member countries. Check first, however, if the whole registering process can be done through the UK Intellectual Property Office. You may eliminate the need for an expensive army of international lawyers (unless, of course, your application is challenged).

Packaging and Labelling: Dressing Products for Success

At some point in every marketing plan, the product has to take over and market itself. You reach that point when the customer and product meet and the customer makes a purchase decision – for or against your product. A customer enters a shop, glances over the shelves, pulls a package down and carries it to the cashdesk. A customer opens a catalogue or brochure, flips through its pages, selects an item and dials the freefone number. A customer goes online to purchase plane tickets and make a hotel reservation. The product must sell itself. But to do so, your product must be noticeable, enticing and appear to be better than (and better value than) the competition.

To prepare your product for its solo role at this vital point-of-purchase stage, you need to give careful thought to how you display and present it. You can't play this all-important role for your product, but you can select the stage and design the set and costume. The *stage* is made up of the shop, catalogue or other meeting place; the *set* includes the shelving, signs, display or other point-of-purchase designs; and the *costume* is the exterior wrapping you give your product. Together, these elements make up what marketers refer to as the *packaging*.

Every product has a package! If you work in banking or property, sell wind-screen gaskets to car manufacturers or distribute your products by mail order rather than in a shop, you may be wondering if you can skip this chapter. But, sorry, you can't. Remember, the package is the product as the customer first sees it. So marketers must give careful thought to package design, regardless of the product. Services, ideas and even people (such as musicians, job seekers and political candidates) are included because they can all be products in the right context.

Appreciating the importance of packaging

In spite of the vast sums of money and attention lavished elsewhere – on advertising, marketing research and other activities – success finally comes down to the package. Does the prospective customer see the package and choose it over others? Studies of the purchase process reveal that people rarely know just what they'll buy before the *point of purchase* (*POP*) – the time and place at which they actually buy something. The majority of consumers are ready and willing for your product to sway them at point of purchase, as the findings in Table 17-1 (from a study by the Point-of-Purchase Advertising Institute) reveal.

Table 17-1   The Point-of-purchase Decision-making Process

Nature of Consumer's Purchase Decision	Percentage of Purchases, Supermarket (%)	Percentage of Purchases, Mass Merchandise Shops (%)
Unplanned	60	53
Substitute	4	3
Generally planned	6	18
Total = Product selection made at point of purchase	70	74

As Table 17-1 shows, unplanned purchases make up the biggest category. Furthermore, specifically planned purchases (those purchases not included in the table) are less than a third of all purchases – all the rest can be influenced at least partially by the packaging and other point-of-purchase communications. (The study is for packaged goods in shops, but we find that service purchases can also be strongly influenced by the brochure, sales presentation or website that packages the service.)

If more than half of final decisions about what to buy are made at point of purchase – where the customer is interacting with the product and its packaging – then the packaging may be more important than any other element of the marketing plan. Wow! In fact, you may want to stop and ask yourself whether you can dispense with all other forms of marketing communication and invest only in packaging and point-of-purchase promotions and displays. Well, if your target customer is open to a point-of-purchase decision, then this extreme is at least a possibility. And by focusing 90–100 per cent of your marketing attention on the point of purchase, you can handle this stage better than less focused competitors. You may want to at least think about this option, if for no other reason than its radical nature means your competition probably won't think of it. But this strategy won't work for every product – remember all those people who do plan what to buy before entering a shop – so think carefully about such drastic action.

Working out if your packaging can make the sale

The packaging makes the sale in the majority of purchase decisions (along with any additional point-of-purchase influences to draw attention to the product – but you can look at those eye-catchers in Chapter 19). Here are some ways to make sure your packaging makes the sale:

✔ **Bump up the visibility of the packaging:** Increasing the size of the brand name, the brightness or boldness of the colours and layout or the size of the package itself helps make your product more visible, as does arranging (or paying) to have shops display it more prominently. Look at the cover of this book for a good example. The *For Dummies* series is an amazing marketing success, partly because the books' bold, clear cover designs mean you can easily find them in the bookshop.

✔ **Choose a colour that contrasts with competitors' products:** Consider easyJet's bright orange colour scheme, which stands out among the typically staid corporate liveries of the bigger airlines. Orange is a colour that shouts 'good value', a quality that worked well for the easy brand as it extended into hire cars, Internet cafes and male toiletries. The colour only became a problem when easy moved into the mobile phone market, where it became embroiled in a legal battle with mobile network operator, Orange. Colour can be very important to a business.

✔ **Improve the information on the packaging:** In terms of clarity, less is more, so can you cut down on the number of words you use? Alternatively, ask yourself if the shopper may find any additional information useful when making a purchase decision. For example, on food products a nutritional breakdown is necessary but Walkers crisps have gone as far as telling people about their carbon footprint (how much energy was expended on the products) because it believes that this information is proving important to its customers.

✔ **Use the web to package a product in information:** Many products are too technologically complicated to communicate any information of value on their actual packaging, so the websites for these businesses have become important 'packages' in their own right – think mobile phones and computers. You can use websites for more simple brands, too.

Innocent makes fruit smoothies and juices – hardly complex products that need further explanation, you'd think. But like its packaging, the website contains loads of useful and entertaining information about the recipes and ingredients used in its products.

✔ **Let the packaging sell the replacement, too:** Make some aspect of your packaging (if only a label on the bottom) necessary for reordering, perhaps by offering a phone number or sending the user to your web page.

✔ **Give your packaging or label emotional appeal:** Warm colours, a friendly message, a smiling person, appealing language and a photo of children playing are all ways to make the buyer feel good when he looks at your product. Purchases are about feelings, not just logic, so give your packaging a winning personality.

✔ **Add some excitement to the packaging:** You can learn a lot about what's hot in packaging on a simple trip to the local supermarket. Let us direct you down some of the aisles. Visit the bread section and look for stock cubes – see the Oxo display, with single, bold letters filling the side of the box? Products that stand out, sell well. Can you break away from category conventions with your product?

✔ **Increase the functionality or workability of the packaging:** Can you make your packaging protect the product better? Can you make it easier to open, useful for storage or easier to recycle? Packages have functional roles, and improving functionality can help increase the product's appeal.

Use these ideas or your own to improve sales by upgrading your packaging. Whatever you do, do something. Packaging can be a significant cost in the manufacture of any product, so make sure it pays its own way by becoming a powerful marketing tool.

We can't do full justice to packaging in this book. That subject is big enough to justify a book of its own. But we can direct you to some of the leading resources out there for marketers looking to make their packaging work harder in the marketing mix:

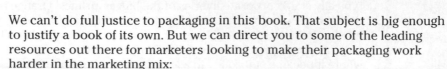

✔ **The Packaging Society** (www.iom3.org/packaging): The main UK trade association for packaging professionals, it organises qualifications, conferences and events, including the Starpack Awards.

✔ *Packaging News* (www.packagingnews.co.uk): This magazine tells you the latest product news and makes case studies available through its website.

✔ **The Design Council** (www.designcouncil.org.uk): This website contains useful information and case studies on all aspects of packaging design.

✔ **The easyFairs Packaging Innovations event** (www.easyfairs.com): This event covers all areas of packaging and innovation relating to brand, retail and consumer needs.

Modifying an Existing Product: When and How

Some products are so perfect that they fit naturally with their customers and you should just leave them alone. For example . . . well, we can't actually think of an example at the moment. Our inability to name the perfect product tells you something important about product management: you'd better modify your products to improve performance, value and quality with each new season and each new marketing plan.

You're competing on a changing playing field. Your competitors are trying hard to make their products better, and you have to do the same. Always seek insights into how to improve your product. Always look for early indicators of improvements your competitors plan to make and be prepared to go one step farther in your response. And always go to your marketing oracle – the customer – for insights into how you can improve your product.

The following two sections describe tests that a product must pass to remain viable. If it doesn't pass, you need to improve or alter your product somehow.

When it's no longer special

At the point of purchase – that place or time when customers make their actual buying decisions – your product needs to have something special. Your product has to reach out to at least a portion of the market; it needs to be better than its competition on certain criteria because of inherent design features; or it needs to be as good as the rest, but better value, which gives you a sustainable cost advantage. (Do you have such a cost advantage?

Marketers generally underestimate their rarity!) Or your product needs to be the best option by virtue of a lack of other options.

For example, if you sell sewing needles, your product may be about as good as most of the competition – but not noticeably better. But if you happen to be the company that a major retail chain uses to single-source needles for its small sewing section, then you have a distribution advantage at point of sale.

Don't assume your lack of special features means that your product isn't special. You can be special just by being there when customers need the product. You can justify keeping a product alive just by having a way of maintaining your distribution advantage. But a product at point of sale has to have at least something special about it if you expect it to generate a good return in the future – otherwise, it gets lost.

If your customers don't think your product is unique in any way, you may need to kill that product. But don't set up the noose too quickly. First, see if you can work to differentiate your product in some important way.

When it lacks champions

Champions are those customers who really love your product, who insist on buying it over others and who tell their friends or associates to do the same. But such loyal champions are rare. Does your product have champions?

The championship test is tougher than the differentiation test. Many products lack champions. But when a product does achieve this special status – when some customers anywhere in the distribution channel really love it – then that product is assured an unusually long and profitable life. Such high customer commitment needs to be your constant goal as you manage the life cycle of your product.

Products with champions get great word of mouth, and their sales and market shares grow because of it. Even better, champions faithfully repurchase the products they rave about. This repeat business provides your company with high-profit sales, compared with the higher costs associated with finding new customers. Check out the principles of good marketing in Chapter 1.

The hook? The repeat buyer must want to repeat the purchase. He needs to be a convert, a true believer or an advocate – whatever you call him, he's worth winning and keeping.

How do you know if you have champions rather than regular, ordinary customers? Because when you ask them about the product, they sound excited and enthusiastic. 'I'd never drive anything but a Volvo. They're comfortable and safe, they don't break down and they last longer than other cars.' Some customers say just that when asked about their Volvos, so the company has an excellent base of repeat buyers. They can even convince their friends and families to buy the same products that they rave about. The existence of customer champions gives Volvo the luxury of selling virtually the same car to people time after time, while competitors are madly retooling their factories every year or two.

Killing a Product

Unlike people and companies, products don't die on their own. Products never had a pulse anyway and product bankruptcy just doesn't exist. Consequently, the marketer needs to have the good sense to know when an old product has no more life in it and to keep it going just wastes resources that ought to go to new products instead.

Yet often you see weak products hanging around. Companies keep these products on the market despite gradually declining sales because everybody, from manufacturer to retailer, hates to face reality. Even worse, you sometimes see marketers investing treasured resources in trying to boost sales of declining brands through renewed advertising or sales promotions. If the product has one foot in the grave anyway, you need to put those resources into introducing a radically improved version or a replacement product.

When to kill a product

You need to face facts: many products are better off being put out of their misery and replaced with something fresh and innovative. 'But,' you rightly object, 'how do I know when my particular product reaches that point of no return?'

In the following sections, we discuss the warning signs to which you must pay attention.

A weak/falling market share

Saturation means that you and your competitors are selling replacement products. You don't have many new customers around to convert. Growth slows, limited by the replacement rate for the product, plus whatever basic growth occurs in the size of the target market.

Saturation alone is no reason to give up on a product – most markets are saturated. An obviously saturated market is that for the car. You find very few adults who don't already own a car if they have the means to buy one and the need for one. So manufacturers and dealerships fight for replacement sales and first-time sales to young drivers; this tactic can still be profitable for some of the competitors – but usually not all of them. If you have a product that has a share of less than, say, 75 per cent of the leading product's market share, and if your share is falling relative to the leader, then you're on a long, slow, downward slide. (Market share means the percentage of all product sales in a defined market that one company captures for itself.)

Better to introduce a replacement and kill the old product than to wait it out. You have to replace the product eventually, and the sooner you do, the less your share and reputation suffer. Whatever else happens, you can't afford for customers to see you as a has-been in a saturated market!

We use the term *product*, in the marketing sense, to include whatever you're offering, whether goods, services, ideas or people. Remember, too, that services, ideas and even people sometimes need to be withdrawn from the market, just as goods do.

A series of improvements fails to create momentum

Often, companies try a series of 'new and improved' versions, new packages, fancy coupon schemes, contests and point-of-purchase promotions to breathe life into products after they stop generating year-to-year sales growth. Sometimes these ploys work and help to renew growth; sometimes they don't.

Something is wrong with your product

All too often, marketers discover some flaw in a product that threatens to hurt their company's reputation or puts its customers at risk. If your engineers think that the fuel tank in one of your vehicles can explode during accidents, should you pull the model immediately and introduce a safer version or keep selling it and put the technical report in your paper shredder? A major car manufacturer chose the second option. In the long run, the faulty fuel tank killed some of its customers, and the company had to stage an extremely unprofitable recall, along with a repair-the-damage publicity campaign, topped by several lawsuits.

Brand equity and profits take a licking whenever your customers do. But many marketers lack the stomach or the internal political clout to kill a bad product, even when the product may kill customers.

We don't know why some marketers keep making these mistakes but we hope that you don't. Pull the product if you find out it may cause cancer, give people electric shocks, choke a baby or even just not work as well as you say it does. Pull the product immediately. Ask questions later.

Pulling the product may seem an incredibly tough decision but it can work in your favour if you take quick, decisive action for the good of your customers. For example, you could write a press release announcing that you're acting on behalf of your consumers, just in case the rumours are true. By taking this step immediately, you let the market know that you have a great deal more integrity than most – and that can only make your brand equity stronger, not weaker. Trust us – pulling a product takes courage but is always the best option, when the dust settles. And if you follow our advice and always invest creative energy and funds in your product development efforts, you should have something better to offer as a replacement.

How to kill or replace a product

Getting rid of old products – those that aren't faulty in any way – is the least of your troubles, because *liquidators* are happy to sell your inventory below cost to various vendors. Contact some of your distributors or your trade association for referrals.

If you want to use a more elegant strategy that avoids the negativity of customers seeing your old products offered for a tenth of their normal price, you could try staging some kind of sales promotion to move the old inventory to customers through your normal distribution channels. We much prefer this option, especially if it also introduces consumers to the new product. You can make customers feel like you're doing them a favour. But this method only works if you get started before the old product loses its appeal. So you have to aggressively replace your products. Don't wait for the market to kill your product; do the deed yourself. The following sections discuss more strategies for bowing out gracefully.

The coat-tails strategy

The *coat-tails strategy* uses the old product to introduce the new. Only your imagination limits the variety of ways in which you can put this strategy to use. You can offer a free sample coupon for the new product to buyers of the old product. You can package the two products together in a special two-for-one promotion. You can do special mailings or make personal or telephone sales calls to old customers.

If the two products are reasonably similar from a functional perspective, you can call the new product by the old product's name and try to merge it into the old identity as if you wanted to introduce an upgrade rather than something brand new. In other words, you can dress the new product in the old product's coat instead of just attaching it to the coat-tails. You need to be able to defend this stealth strategy from a common-sense perspective or your customers get angry. If you can make the argument that customers are getting a 'more and better' version of the same product, then the strategy should work.

The coat-tails strategy is a great promotional device for replacing an old product with a new one. Use it whenever you want to kill an old product in order to make room for a new one. *Room* can mean room in the customer's mind, room on the shop shelf, room in the distributor's catalogue or room in your own product line. Products take up space, and physical or mental space can give you an important resource. But you do take a big risk with this strategy. When you make room for your new product, competing products can try to take that space instead. Why? Any customers still faithful to the old product have to reconsider their purchase patterns, and they may choose a competitor over your new option. The choice may make them wake up and realise that they don't need to buy only your brand. Similarly, retailers, distributors or other channel members may give your space to another product. So you need to hold on to your space, even as you eliminate your product. Avoid any gaps in the availability of your products.

The product line place-holding strategy

You can use *product lines* to create clear product niches and hold them for replacement products. Keep pricing consistent with product positions in your product line, too – a practice called *price lining*.

For example, a bank may offer a selection of different savings options to its retail customers – a mix of straight savings accounts, easy access accounts, fixed rate bonds and mini cash ISAs. If the bank organises these options into a coherent range of named products and lists them in a single brochure in order from lowest-risk/lowest-return to highest-risk/highest-return, then it creates a clear product line with well-defined places for these products. (The bank must be sure, however, that each product sits in a unique place on that spectrum – no overlaps, please!)

In future, when the bank wants to introduce a new product, it can substitute the new one for an old one and consumers accept that this new product fills the same spot in the product line. The bank can also extend the product line in either direction or fill gaps in it with new products. Whatever the bank does, the product line can act as a place-holder to ease the entry of new products. (See the 'Branding and Naming Your Product' section, earlier in this chapter, for more information on product lines.)

But we bet that your bank doesn't use this strategy – few do. As a result, you're always confused when you try to get your mind around your bank's offerings, and it therefore loses some business that it should have won. The fact is that, although product lines are a very important part of any marketing strategy, marketers often neglect them.

Make sure your offerings fall into a clear product line with an obvious logic to it and clear points of difference anyone can understand at a glance. What can you do – right now – to clarify the options you give your customers and make sure your branding and product offerings make good sense to everyone?

Chapter 18

Using Price and Promotions

Some marketers believe that businesses fail most often for two simple reasons: their prices are too high or their prices are too low! Getting the price just right is the hardest task marketers face, but finding the right pricing approach makes success a lot easier to achieve.

The bottom line of all marketing activity is that the customer needs to pay – willingly and, you hope, rapidly – for your products or services. But how much will they pay? Should you drop your prices to grow your market? Or would raising the price and maximising profits be better? What about discounts and special promotional pricing? It can be especially hard to work out what pricing strategies you should use when the economic outlook is bad. And then which ones to adopt when things pick up. Getting the price part of your marketing plan right is hard – but the following pages help you through it.

Understanding the Facts of Pricing

Most companies fall prey to the myth that customers only choose a product based on its price. As a result, they set their prices lower than they need to. Or when companies need to boost sales, they do so by offering discounts or free units or the infamous BOGOF – Buy One Get One Free. If you insist on selling on the basis of price alone, your customers buy on the basis of price.

But alternatives always exist. To raise or maintain your price and still sell more, you can:

- ✔ **Build brand equity:** Better-known brands command a premium price.

- ✔ **Increase quality:** People spread the word about a good product, and that can earn the product a 5 to 10 per cent higher price than the competition.

- ✔ **Use prestige pricing:** Giving your product a high-class image can boost your price by 20 to 100 per cent. See the 'Using Discounts and Other Special Offers' section later in this chapter for details on how prestige pricing works.

- ✔ **Create extra value through time and place advantages:** Customers consider the available product worth a lot more than one they can't get when they need it. (That's why a cup of coffee costs more at the airport – are you really going to leave the terminal, get in a taxi and go somewhere else to save a pound?)

Price is important, but it doesn't have to be customers' only consideration.

Avoiding underpricing

Lowering prices is always easier than raising prices. In general, you want to set a price a bit high in relation to the competition and see what happens. If your product sells the way you want it to, great! If not, you can take back any price increase with a subsequent price cut.

Customers may not be as price sensitive as you fear. They may tolerate an increase better than you think and they may not respond to a decrease in price as enthusiastically as you need them to in order to make that decrease profitable. Customers may even assume that price correlates with quality – in which case, they don't buy your product unless the price is high enough. Instead of assuming that you need a price cut whenever you want to boost profits, start by experimenting with a price increase. Be a contrarian. They often succeed!

Exploring the impact of pricing on customers' purchases

Price sensitivity is the degree to which purchases are affected by price level – that is, how willing are customers to pay the price you're asking? You need to estimate how price sensitive your customers are in relation to your product or service.

To check price sensitivity, you need good data to look through. The following checklist is a series of *qualitative indicators* (clues we can guess from) of price sensitivity. You have to ask yourself a set of questions about your customer, product and market, ticking the box next to each question that you can answer with 'yes'. Then you add up the number of ticked boxes to see which way they lean. This study isn't scientific, but is better than ignoring the problem altogether!

❑ **Does the customer view the price as reasonable?** If you're operating within an expected price range, customers aren't very price sensitive. (Outside of the expected price range, they become more so.)

❑ **Is the product valuable at (almost) any price?** Some products are unique and customers know that they may have a hard time finding a cheaper substitute. That fact lowers price sensitivity.

❑ **Is the product desperately needed?** Customers generally don't care how much fixing a burst pipe on a Sunday costs – certainly not if their homes are filling up with water! And they're not too price sensitive about the cost of treatment by a dentist when their teeth hurt. These products meet essential needs. (But if your product is a *non-essential* – something that customers want but don't have to have right now – the customer is more price sensitive.)

❑ **Are substitutes unavailable?** If the customer purchases in a context where substitute products aren't readily available, price sensitivity is lower. (Shopping for price requires that substitutes at different prices be available. For example, if you're the only company offering emergency plumbing repairs on weekends in your town, your customers will pay a high price for your services.)

❑ **Is the customer unaware of substitutes?** Shopping is a complex, information-dependent behaviour. Customers can find the cheapest price available by comparing products and retailers if they have the time and access to the Internet. But not everyone does. You don't have to charge the least if your customers are unable or unwilling to shop around or they are unaware of substitute products.

❑ **Does the customer find comparing options difficult?** Even where options exist, the consumer can have problems comparing products in some product categories. What makes one dentist better than another? Most people don't know. The technical complexity of their work, plus the fact that you can't consume dental care until after you make the purchase decision, makes comparing options hard. As a result, that difficulty makes dental care consumers less price sensitive – and dentists richer.

❑ **Does the product seem inexpensive to customers?** Customers don't worry too much about price when they feel they're getting good value. However, if customers feel the pinch in their purses when they make purchases, they pay close attention to prices. That's why you negotiate so hard when you buy a car or a house. Even products that cost far less can seem expensive if they're at the high end of a price range. For example, you're more price sensitive if you shop for a fancy, high-performance laptop than for a simple, basic desktop computer because the former probably costs 50 to 100 per cent more than the latter, making the laptop expensive by comparison.

The more boxes you ticked, the less price sensitive your customer is. If you ticked multiple boxes, you probably can raise your prices without hurting sales significantly – great news!

You can supplement your estimate of price sensitivity (from the checklist) with actual tests. For example, if you think a 5 per cent increase in prices won't affect sales, try that increase in a test market or for a short period of time, holding the rest of your marketing constant. Were you right? If so, roll out the increase to your whole market.

Finding profits without raising prices

When you think about profits, you may assume that your focus should be on the price. But many factors drive your company's cash flow and profits, not just the list price of your products. If your manager tells you to work out how to raise prices because profits are too low, don't assume that raising prices is the only or right solution. Here are some ways to boost profits *without* raising prices:

✔ Check to see how quickly you're making collections – are vendors paying within 45 days? If so, cutting that time by 15 days may make up the needed profits without any price increase.

✔ Look at the discounts and allowances your company offers. These can affect revenue and profits. Are customers taking advantage of quantity discounts to stock up inexpensively and then not buying between the discount periods? If so, you have a problem with your sales promotions, not your list prices.

✔ If you're in a service business that charges a base price, plus fees for special services and extras, look hard at the way in which you assess fees. Perhaps your company is failing to collect the appropriate fees in some cases.

✔ Evaluate whether your fee structure is out of date and doesn't reflect your cost structure accurately. For example, an independent financial adviser who's making profits solely on commission from the products she sells may find profits stagnating if more and more of her time is spent offering complex investment advice. In such a case, the problem isn't with the commission percentage rate, which may be capped anyway. Switching to an annual retainer or charging for advice may even be more popular with higher value customers.

Following Five Easy Steps to Setting Prices

If you need to establish a price, you're facing one of the toughest decisions in business. Surveys of managers indicate they suffer from a high degree of price anxiety. So let's take you through the process logically, step by step. Price setting doesn't have to be a high-anxiety task if you do it right! Figure 18-1 illustrates the process that we describe in the following sections.

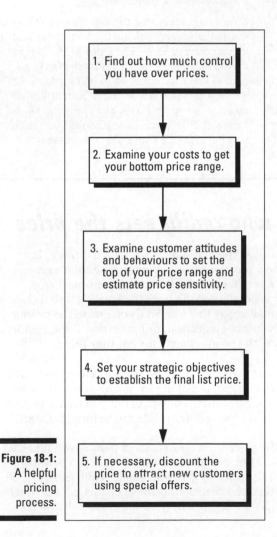

1. Find out how much control you have over prices.

2. Examine your costs to get your bottom price range.

3. Examine customer attitudes and behaviours to set the top of your price range and estimate price sensitivity.

4. Set your strategic objectives to establish the final list price.

5. If necessary, discount the price to attract new customers using special offers.

Figure 18-1:
A helpful pricing process.

Calculating discount structures

Confused? Let's show you how to calculate prices and discounts in a complex distribution channel. Say that you discover the typical discount structure in the market where you want to introduce your product is 30/10/5. What does that mean? If you start with a £100 list price, the retailer pays at a discount of 30 per cent off the list price (0.30 × £100 = £70). The retailer, who pays £70 for the product, marks it up to (approximately) £100 and makes about £30 in gross profit.

Now, the discount structure figures tell you that other intermediaries exist – one for each discount listed. The distributor, who sells the product to the retailer, has a discount of 10 per cent off the price that she charges the retailer (that's 0.10 × £70 = £7 of gross profit for the distributor).

And this distributor must have paid £70 – £7, or £63, for the product to another intermediary (probably a manufacturer's representative or wholesaler). The marketer sells to this intermediary. And the 30/10/5 formula shows that this intermediary receives a 5 per cent discount: 0.05 × £63 = £3.15 in profit for her.

Subtracting again, you can also determine that the marketer must sell the product to this first intermediary at £63 – £3.15, or £59.85. You, as the marketer, must give away more than 40 per cent of that £100 list price to intermediaries if you use this 30/10/5 discount structure. And so you have to calculate any profit you make from a £100 list price as costs subtracted from your net of £59.85. That's all you ever see of that £100!

Step 1: Find out who really sets the price

This first step isn't obvious. You, as the marketer, can set a list price. But the consumer may not ultimately pay your price. You may encounter a distributor or wholesaler and a retailer, all of whom take their mark-ups. Furthermore, the manufacturer generally doesn't have the legal right to dictate the ultimate selling price. The retailer gets that job. So if you create the product yourself your list price is really just a suggestion, not an order. If the retailer doesn't like the suggested price, the product sells for another price.

So you need to start by determining who else may be setting prices along with you. Involve these parties in your decision making by asking some of them what they think about pricing your product. They may tell you that you have constraints to consider. Know what those constraints are before you start.

For example, if you're setting the price for a new range of paints, you find that the big DIY chains expect a 40–50 per cent discount off the list price. Knowing that, you can set a high enough list price to give you some profit, even at a 50 per cent discount rate. But if you don't realise that these chains expect much higher discounts than smaller DIY shops, you may be blind-sided by their requirement.

Marketers who operate in or through a *multilevel distribution channel* (meaning that they have distributors, wholesalers, retailers, agents or other sorts of intermediaries) need to establish the *trade discount structure*. Trade discounts (also called *functional discounts*) are what you give these intermediaries. These discounts are a form of cost to the marketer, so make sure that you know the discount structure for your product before you move on. Usually, marketers state the discount structure as a series of numbers, representing what each of the intermediaries gets as a discount. But you take each discount off the price left over from the discount before it, not off the list price.

Step 2: Examine all your costs

How do you know your costs? In theory, that part's easy: your company's excellent cost accounting system captures all your costs and a man in a pinstripe suit with a calculator can simply give you the figure.

In practice, you may not have good, accurate information on the true costs of a specific product or service. Take some time to try to estimate what you're actually spending, and remember to include some value for expensive inventories if they sit around for a month or more (assume you're paying interest on the money tied up in those products to account for the loss of capital wasting away in inventory).

After you examine your costs carefully, you should have a fairly accurate idea of the least amount you can charge. That charge is, at a bare minimum, your actual costs. (Although, occasionally, you may want to give away a product for less than cost in order to introduce people to it – what's known as a *loss leader*. This approach is often used by retailers to get people into stores so they then go on to buy more products and make up for the one loss leader product.) More often, you need a price that includes the cost plus a profit margin – say, 20 or 30 per cent. So that means you have to treat your cost as 70 or 80 per cent of the price, adding in that 20 or 30 per cent margin your company requires.

This cost-plus-profit figure is the bottom of your pricing range (see Figure 18-2). Now you need to see if customers permit you to charge this price – or perhaps even allow you to charge a higher one!

Step 3: Evaluate customer perception of price

Your costs and profit requirements determine a lower limit on price. But your customers' perceptions determine an upper limit. You need to define both of these limits to know your possible price range. So you need to work out what price customers are willing to pay.

In Figure 18-2, we show the price that customers favour as the *customers' preference*. Note that customer preference may not be the upper limit. If customers aren't too price sensitive, they may not notice or care if you set your price somewhat higher than their preferred price. (See the 'Understanding how customers perceive and remember prices' section later in this chapter.)

Pricing experts sometimes call the difference between the customer's desired price and a noticeably higher price the *indifference zone*. Within the indifference zone, customers are indifferent to both price increases and price decreases. However, the zone gets smaller (on a percentage basis) as the price of a product increases. How big or small is the zone of indifference in your product's case? Go back to the price sensitivity checklist. The zone is small if your customers are highly price sensitive, and large if they aren't that price sensitive. Just make some assumptions that seem reasonable for now. We know this process involves some guesswork, but still, breaking down the pricing decision into a series of smaller, educated guesses is better than plucking a number out of thin air! At worst, your errors on all those little guesses may be random, in which case they should cancel each other out.

You can also uncover customer preference by looking at the current pricing structure in your market. What are people paying for comparable products? Does a downward or upward trend exist in the prices of comparable products, or are they stable? Go shopping to get a grasp of the existing price structure; you'll get excellent clues as to how customers may react to different prices for your product.

Through these sorts of activities, you can at least get back-of-the-envelope figures for the customers' preferred price and an idea of how much higher you can price without drawing the wrong sort of attention. This knowledge means you've established the top of your price range.

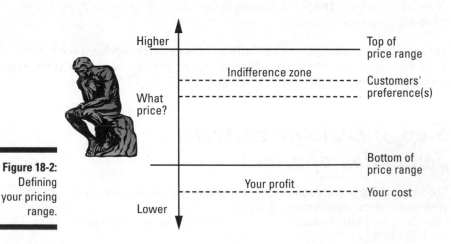

Figure 18-2:
Defining
your pricing
range.

Setting your price at the top of the range is the simplest approach to pricing. As long as the price range is above the bottom limit (your preferred price plus the indifference zone is equal to or greater than your cost plus your required profit), you're okay.

But you can't always set your price at the top of the range. In the next step of the pricing process, we show you how to calculate what your final price should be.

Step 4: Examine secondary influences

Your two primary considerations are your costs and the customers' upper price limits. They set a price range but you also need to consider many other factors. These factors may influence your decision by forcing you to price in the middle or bottom of the price range rather than at the top, for example.

Consider competitive issues. Do you need to gain market share from a close competitor? If so, either keep price at parity and do aggressive marketing, or adjust your price to be slightly (but noticeably) below the competitor's price. Also consider likely future price trends. Are prices falling in this market? Then you need to adjust your figures down a bit to stay in synch with your market.

Similarly, currency fluctuations may affect your costs and, thus, your pricing options. If you're concerned that you may take a hit from the exchange rate, better to be safe and price at the high end of the range. The overall economy is also a big factor, especially if you sell relatively expensive items – take into consideration both the current economic situation and the spending power of your customers. If a recession is in full swing, rising prices without obvious and understandable reason will be unpopular, to say the least!

Finally, product line management may dictate a slightly lower or higher price. For example, you may need to price a top-of-the-range product significantly higher than others in its line just to make it clear to the customer that this product is a step above standard alternatives.

Step 5: Set your strategic objectives

You may have objectives other than revenues and profit maximisation. Many marketers price near the bottom of their price range to increase their market share. (They price so low because a high market share later on will probably give them more profits – so they're applying an investment strategy; see Chapter 2 for details.)

This low-price strategy only makes sense if the customer is fairly price sensitive! If not, you're throwing away possible revenues without any real gain in market share. You should be pricing at the top of the range and using the extra revenues to invest in quality and brand-building marketing promotions in order to increase market share (see Chapter 2 for details on these and other strategy options).

In other cases, marketers have certain volume goals they need to reach – such as when they need to run a factory near its capacity level. So they may price in the low end of the range in order to maximise unit sales, even if doing so doesn't maximise net profits per unit.

Sometimes, marketers even want to minimise unit volume – for example, when introducing a new product. They may not have the capacity to sell the product to a mass market and so decide to *skim the market* by selling the product at such a high price that only the very wealthy or least price-sensitive customers can buy it. Then they lower prices later on, when they've made maximum profits from the high-end customers and have added production capacity. Video game consoles and mobile phones are all examples of products that use the skimming strategy, entering the market at significantly higher prices than they settle down at later in the product life cycle.

Don't use a skimming strategy unless you're sure that you're safe from aggressive competition in the short term.

Understanding how customers perceive and remember prices

Pricing involves more than just finding the highest price that most customers are willing to pay. You have to pick a pricing strategy that works for the context of your business and the market in which it operates. Do you need to beat your competitors on price? Do you have a vertical range of different quality products? The following list gives you an idea of how to pick a pricing strategy that works for you and your customers.

Whichever of the following strategies you use, remember: in pricing services, set a price that's consistent with your quality. Don't accidentally cheapen the perceived quality of your service by setting your price too low.

Odd–even pricing

In this strategy you use a price that ends with the number 9. Why? Because people perceive prices ending in 9 as cheaper – generally 3 to 6 per cent cheaper in their memories than the rounded-up price. You can take advantage of this perception about price. For example, if the top of your price range for a new child's toy is £10, you probably want to drop it down to £9.99 or £9.89

for the simple reason that this price seems much cheaper to most consumers. Assuming they're price sensitive at all, they buy considerably more of the lower-priced product, even though the price difference amounts to only pennies.

The only downside to using prices ending in 9 is that customers sometimes associate this pricing with cheap, low-quality products. So don't use odd–even pricing when your customers are more quality than price sensitive. For example, odd–even pricing may cheapen the image of an original work of art for sale in an art gallery. But, in general, the strategy seems to work. Also be aware of other outside factors that can affect the odd–even price strategy. The 2011 rise in VAT to 20 per cent (after a cut in 2008 to 15 per cent and for many years previously resting at 17.5 per cent) threw many pricing strategies into confusion. If you have a price ending in 9, this may appear not to have gone up (or down) and confuse customers. Make sure you're always clear about any pricing changes where VAT rate changes are involved.

Price lining

You may also want to adjust your price to make it fit into your product line, or into the range of products sold by your retailers or distributors. The idea is to fit your product into a range of alternatives, giving the product a logical spot in customers' minds. Marketers know this common and generally effective strategy as *price lining*.

Competitive pricing

You may want to price relative to an important competitor or set of competitors. Marketers call this practice *competitive pricing*, for obvious reasons. If you're in a highly competitive market, you need to exercise competitive pricing. Decide which competing products the customers may view as closest to yours and then make your price sufficiently higher or lower to differentiate your product.

How much difference is enough depends upon the size of the customers' indifference zone (see the 'Step 3: Evaluate customer perception of price' section earlier in this chapter to find out about this).

Should you price above or below that tough competitor? That decision depends on whether you offer more or fewer benefits and higher or lower quality. If you offer your customer less or about the same, you need to make your price significantly lower so that your product looks like better value. If you offer greater benefits, you can make your price a little higher to signal this fact – but not too high because you want to be sure that your product seems like better value than the competition.

Sometimes you should just price exactly at a competitor's price. You may want to match prices if you plan to differentiate your product on the basis of some subtle difference. This way, customers focus their attention on the difference rather than on the price.

In setting price, trying to anticipate the likely reaction to any price changes is important. A drop in price may be matched by the major player who may have deep enough pockets to match or better your price reductions. Tesco dominates the UK food market with more than 30 per cent share and has recently implemented a number of price reductions under the banner, the 'Big Price Drop'. Asda, with the backing of Walmart, also tries to keep prices low and, with the arrival of the European low-cost chains Aldi and Lidl on the British high street, all the supermarkets are keeping a close eye on how much they charge. In retail, discounting is the order of the day, so remember that pricing is affected by nationwide behaviours as much as by the outcome you'd like to achieve.

Finally, some competitors try to convince customers that their product is better but costs less than the competitors' products. Nobody believes this claim – unless you present evidence. If you do, customers will love you – we all hope to get more for less, after all. For example, a computer with a new, faster chip may really be better but cost less. A new anti-wrinkle cream may work better but cost less if you've discovered a new formula. And a retailer may be able to sell the same brands for a cheaper price because it has larger stores that do more volume of business. As long as you have – and can communicate to the customer – a believable argument, you can undercut competitors' prices at the same time as claiming superior benefits. But make sure that you back up the claim, or the customer assumes that your lower price means the product is inferior.

Using Discounts and Other Special Offers

Special offers are temporary inducements to make customers buy on the basis of price or price-related factors. Special offers play with the price, giving consumers (or intermediaries) a way to get the product for less – at least while the offer lasts.

You may wonder, why play with the price? If you think the price should be lower, why not just cut the price permanently? The answer is because a price cut is easy to do, but hard to undo. A special offer, on the other hand, allows you to temporarily discount the price while still maintaining the list price at its old level. When the offer ends, the list price is the same – you haven't given anything away permanently. Here are some cases in which maintaining your list price and offering a discount is a good strategy:

- When you have a short-term reason for wanting to cut the price, such as aiming to counter a competitor's special offer or responding to a new product introduction.

- When you want to experiment with the price (to find out about customer price sensitivity) without committing to a permanent price cut until you see the data.

✔ When you want to stimulate consumers to try your product, and you believe that, after they try it, they may like the product well enough to buy it again at full price.

✔ When your list price needs to stay high in order to signal quality (prestige pricing) or be consistent with other prices in your product line (price lining strategy); see the earlier section 'Understanding how customers perceive and remember prices' for details on these pricing strategies.

✔ When your competitors are all offering special lower prices and you think you have no choice because consumers have come to expect special offers.

Don't try to fool your customers with sneaky pricing tactics. In 2011, the TV show *Panorama* revealed that UK supermarkets were carrying out a number of underhand tactics. One retailer was claiming that it had amazing deals on various products in its marketing, yet *Panorama* researchers found that eleven items had been for sale at the same price for at least six months and four items were actually more expensive than they were previously. Meanwhile, other supermarkets were putting up the price of products for a couple of months and then dropping them with a big marketing push about the amazing 'discount'. These tactics will be discovered and may leave your business on the end of some very annoyed customers and bad press.

What happens when competitors become too focused on making and matching each other's special offers? They flood the customers with price-based promotions. Discounts and other freebies begin to outweigh brand-building marketing messages, focusing consumer attention on price over brand and benefit considerations. Special promotions can and do increase customer sensitivity to price. They attract *price switchers*, people who aren't loyal to any brand but shop on the basis of price alone. Special promotions encourage people to become price switchers, thus reducing the size of the core customer base and increasing the number of fringe customers. So remember that special offers have the potential to erode brand equity, reduce customer loyalty and cut deeply into your profits. You can easily lose your footing on this slippery slope!

Despite these potential pitfalls, you still may have legitimate reasons to use special offers (see the preceding bullet list). Or you may not have the power to change practices in your market and so have to go with the flow. If you have good reason to use discounts and deals, several options are available to you.

You can offer coupons, refunds, premiums (or gifts), extra products for free, free trial-sized samples, event-orientated premium plans and any other special offer you can think up.

Because a large (and growing) majority of all special offers take the form of *coupons*, we focus on them in explaining how to design special offers.

As you decide on a promotion strategy, be sure to check that the promotion is legal. Legal constraints do exist. You can't mislead consumers about what they get. And a sweepstake or contest has to be open to all, not tied to product purchase. The Institute of Promotional Marketing (IPM) offers legal advice covering the basics of most types of promotional device. You can access it for free at www.theipm.org.uk, but if you really want a guarantee that your promotion is legally watertight, you have to become a member to use the IPM's full legal advice service.

Designing coupons and figuring out how much to offer

Any certificate entitling the holder to a reduced price is a coupon, which is a pretty broad definition – and that means you have a lot of room for creativity in this field. Collect a handful of recent coupons from your own and other industries to get an idea of available options and how they're utilised.

How much of a deal should you offer customers in a coupon or other special offer? The answer depends on how much attention you want. Most offers fail to motivate the vast majority of customers, so keep in mind that the typical special offer in your industry probably isn't particularly effective. A good ad campaign probably reaches more customers.

But you can greatly increase the reach of your special offer simply by making the offer more generous (the higher the price sensitivity, the more notice you generate). In consumer non-durables, whether toothpaste or tinned soup, research shows that you have to offer at least 50p off your list price to attract much attention. All but the most dedicated coupon clippers ignore the smaller offers. But when offers get over the 50p level, attractiveness grows rapidly – sometimes even reaching the 80 per cent level! You can find within this larger percentage of interested consumers many brand-loyal, core customers – both yours and your competitors'. And you should find these core customers far more attractive than the coupon clippers who flock to smaller offers.

So we think (and we disagree with many marketers on this point) that you do better to use fewer, bigger offers than to run endless pennies-off coupons. Too much noise exists already, so why add to the clutter of messages when you can focus your efforts on fewer, more effective coupons?

Forecasting redemption rates

Designing a coupon isn't the hard part – guessing the *redemption rate* (or percentage of people who use the coupon) is. And you raise the stakes when you use big offers, making them riskier to forecast.

We can tell you that, on average, customers redeem a little over 3 per cent of coupons (and the average coupon offers 25p off the list price). So you can use that figure as a good starting point for your estimate. But the range is wide – some offers are so appealing, and so easy to use, that customers redeem 50 per cent of those coupons. For others, the redemption rate can be close to zero. So how do you find out if your coupon will have a high or low redemption rate?

You can refine your redemption estimate by comparing your offer with others. Are you offering something more generous or easy to redeem than you have in the past? Than your competitors do? If so, you can expect significantly higher than average redemption rates – maybe twice as high or higher.

Also, look at your past data for clues. If you've used coupons before, your company should have rich information about response rates. Just be sure that you examine past offers carefully to pick those that truly match the current offer before assuming the same response rate can be repeated.

Think about price sensitivity – again (see the earlier section 'Exploring the impact of pricing on customers' purchases'). A lower price isn't always better. Your offer really just shifts the price on a temporary basis – at some cost to the customer because of the trouble she needs to go to in order to redeem the coupon. So the real new price is something less than the discount you offer on the coupon – adjust it a little to reflect how much the customer thinks it costs her to redeem it. Now ask yourself whether this real price is sufficiently lower than the list price to alter demand. Does the price fall outside of most customers' indifference zones or not?

Many coupons don't shift the price very far beyond the indifference zone. For this reason, they generally attract those fringe customers who buy on price but don't attract the core customers of other brands, which is why redemption rates are only a few per cent, on average. However, if your coupon does shift the price well beyond the indifference zone, you're likely to see a much higher redemption rate than usual – which will erode your profit margin considerably. A happy medium does exist, and your goal is to find out what level of discount is high enough to encourage trial of your brand without losing money.

Coupon deals gone wild is a reason for marketers to lose their jobs. Back in 1992, the British arm of Hoover ran a marketing promotion offering free flights to anyone spending more than £100 on its products. So many people took up the offer that the company was overwhelmed, and estimates put the resulting cost of fulfilling so many flights at £50 million. Always check the offer against what you know of customer perception and price sensitivity to make sure that you aren't accidentally shifting the price so far that everyone and her brother want to redeem coupons.

Also, if you're distributing coupons via the Internet or email, make sure you explicitly state who can use the coupon and whether it can be used once or multiple times. Christmas 2007 saw off-licence chain Threshers email a 40 per cent discount coupon to their business partners; it was quickly forwarded on to friends nationwide. Unfortunately, Threshers hadn't specified that the email coupon could only be used by business partners and ended up with thousands of consumers asking for a 40 per cent discount as they stocked up on Christmas cheer.

Beware of getting involved with 'daily deal' email coupon providers like Groupon, too, unless you have a very tight grip on how this relationship will affect your business. The email voucher offer arrives in people's inboxes every day with great money-off deals from local companies in their area. The lure for local businesses is an enormous amount of business from new customers, some of whom will likely shop again at full price if they enjoy the product or service on offer.

For some, the email coupon approach can open up a whole new market. For others, such as Rachel Brown, it can be a less positive story. Brown's bakery Need A Cake signed up to Groupon with a 75 per cent discount offer for cupcakes. While the bakery was prepared for less than 1000 orders, the email saw more than 8,500 sign up for her products. Brown was forced to hire more staff to help with the extra work, fearing that she'd produce a lower quality product that would put off any new customers. She lost between £2.50 and £3 for every batch she sold and also had to pay out £12,500 in extra staff and postage costs – a full year of profits.

Predicting the cost of special offers

Okay, you've thought about the redemption rate. Following the advice in the preceding section, you believe, for example, that 4 per cent of customers will redeem a coupon offering a 10 per cent discount on your product. To estimate the cost of your coupon programme, you must first decide whether this 4 per cent of consumers accounts for just 4 per cent of your product's sales over the period in which the coupon applies. Probably not; customers may stock up in order to take advantage of the special offer. And so you have to estimate how much more than usual consumers will buy (unless you've limited the number of products that any one customer can buy with the coupon).

If you think customers will buy twice as much as usual (that's a pretty high figure, but it makes for a simple illustration), just double the average purchase size. Four per cent of customers, buying twice what they usually do in a month (if that's the term of the offer), can produce how much in sales? Now, apply the discount rate to that sales figure to find out how much the special offer may cost you. Can you afford it? Is the promotion worth the money? You need to make that judgement call; the numbers can't tell you.

Some marketers have their cake and eat it too when it comes to special offers. These marketers use what they call *self-liquidating premiums*, which don't cost them any money at all in the long run. A *premium* is any product that you give away to customers or sell at a discount as a reward for doing business with you (see Chapter 16 for ideas on how to use premiums). A self-liquidating premium is one that customers end up paying for – or at least covering your costs on that product. Say you run a contest in which some of the customers who open your packaging are instant winners, able to send away for a special premium by enclosing their winning ticket plus £3.95. If your direct costs for the premium you send them are £3.95, you don't have to pay out of pocket for what the customer may see as a fun and valuable benefit.

Staying Out of Trouble with the Law

You don't have to be a legal whiz to know when pricing is illegal. Whenever a customer or competitor can make a good case for unfair or deceptive pricing, you run the risk of legal action. However, just to keep legal eagles happy, we provide a short list of some of the more common and serious illegal pricing practices. Make sure that you read this list correctly – these are things you should *not* do!

- **Price fixing:** Don't agree to (or even talk about) prices with other companies. The exception is a company you sell to, of course – but note that you cannot force them to resell your product at a specific price.

- **Price fixing in disguise:** Shady marketers have tried many ideas – they don't work. If your competitors want you to require the same amount of down payment, start your negotiations from the same list prices as theirs, use a standard contract for extending credit or form a joint venture to distribute all your products (at the same price) – realise that these friendly suggestions are all forms of price fixing. Just say no. And in future, refuse even to take phone calls from marketers who offer you such deals.

- **Exchanging price information:** You can't talk to your competitors about prices. Ever. If it ever comes to light that anyone in your company gives out information about pricing and receives some in return, you're in big trouble, even if you don't feel you acted on that information. Take this warning seriously. (By the way, *price signalling* – announcing a planned price increase – is sometimes seen as an unfair exchange of price information because competitors may use such announcements to signal to others that everyone should make a price increase.)

- **Bid rigging:** If you're bidding for a contract, the preceding point applies. Don't share any information with anyone. Don't compare notes with another bidder. Don't agree to make an identical bid. Don't *split* by agreeing not to bid on one job if the competitor doesn't bid on another. Don't mess with the bidding process in any manner or you're guilty of *bid rigging*.

✔ **Parallel pricing:** In some cases, you could actually be charged with price fixing even if you didn't talk to competitors – just because you have similar price structures. After all, the result may be the same – to boost prices unfairly. In other cases, the law considers similar prices as natural. Here's a rule that makes good sense: don't mirror competitors' prices, unless everyone can see that you selected those prices on your own – especially if your price change involves a price increase.

✔ **Don't fall foul of Breaching the 2010 Bribery Act:** This Act is designed to clamp down on business corruption. You can read more about it by going to www.justice.gov.uk, clicking on 'Guidance', then 'Legislation Guidance' then 'Bribery'.

Some people throw up their hands in despair because so many pricing techniques are illegal. Let us just add that trying to influence prices in certain ways is okay. You can offer volume discounts to encourage larger purchases. And, although you can't force a retailer to charge a certain price for your product, you can encourage them to by advertising the suggested retail price and by listing it as such on your product.

Also, you can always offer an effective price cut to consumers through a consumer coupon or other special offer. Retailers usually agree to honour such offers. However, if you offer a discount to your retailers, you can't force them to pass that discount on to your customers. Retailers may just put the money in the bank and continue to charge customers full price.

Chapter 19

Distribution, Retail and Point of Purchase

Companies with a wide and efficient distribution network are often the most successful because it gives them access to so many potential customers.

Of course, reaching out into the world of your customers with your distribution doesn't guarantee success; it only makes success possible. The customers still have to know and like your product (which, we remind you, can be a service as well as a tangible good). And customers have to view your product as affordable, too. So distribution isn't the only important matter in marketing, but it is a big one.

In developing a marketing strategy (see Chapter 1), we encourage you to treat distribution as one of the key factors, or seven Ps, of marketing. For the purposes of fitting distribution into this list of marketing Ps, it's referred to as *place* – along with *product*, *price*, *promotion*, *people*, *process* and *physical presence* – but the idea is the same. What you're doing in distribution is placing your offering when, where and how prospective customers need and want it.

Offering Distributing Advice

This book's distribution is a simple example of how powerful the right distribution channels can be. This book receives good placement on the shelves of bookshops, where it's placed in the marketing area of the business section, making it easy to find. *Marketing For Dummies* is also placed conveniently by topic, title and author on searchable Internet bookshops like Amazon (www. amazon.co.uk). These two main distribution channels provide broad reach into the market of people who are looking for helpful advice and information about how to market their businesses and sell their products or services. Without this broad distribution, you may never have encountered this book, regardless of how well written, packaged or priced it may be.

Keep these points in mind when considering your distribution strategies:

✔ If you can add distributors or expand your distribution network, your product may become available to more people and sales could rise as a result. (If not, consider the web, direct-response marketing and events as three alternatives because they bypass distributors and reach out directly to customers; see Chapters 10 to 16 for more details.)

✔ Boost sales by improving the visibility of your product within its current distribution channel; for example, by making sure it's better displayed (a product) or better communicated (a service). Or perhaps you can find a way to shift your distribution slightly so as to give you access to more desirable or larger customers.

✔ Increasing the availability of products in your distribution channel can also help boost sales and profits. Can you find ways to get more inventory out there? Or can you speed up the movement of products out to customers so that they feel better able to find your product when they need it? These sorts of improvements can have a dramatic impact on sales by making finding what they want, when and where they want it easier for more customers.

✔ We urge you to make a list of every company that has a hand of any sort in making your sales and servicing your customers and then to think about ways to strengthen your business relationship with them. Consider doing something simple, like sending them a gift at Christmas. Do something to invest in these relationships – they're very important to most businesses but too easily taken for granted.

✔ Using distributors is a low-cost way to keep expanding. Almost every business can sell through distributors if they're open minded and creative about cutting deals. If you already sell through distributors, find some more.

✔ Even if you have to give a distributor a deeper discount than you want in order to motivate them, consider doing it if you believe that your business hasn't achieved its potential until your products are readily available everywhere within your industry.

Getting Distributors on Your Side

Distributors want items that are easy to sell because customers want to buy them. Making sure your product is appealing is thus the first step in getting distributors on your side. A brilliant product and a clear way of presenting it so that its brilliance shines through is a great investment for growing any distribution system. You may still have to go out and tell distributors about it and work to support them, but if you start with a product whose unique qualities shine through, expanding your distribution is a lot easier.

When you're confident that you have something worth selling, ask yourself which distributors may be successful at selling it. Who's willing and able to distribute for you? Will wholesalers or other intermediaries be helpful? If so, who are they and how many of them can you locate? Try these sources:

- **Local business telephone directories or an online equivalent such as Yell** (www.yell.co.uk): These directories often reference the category of intermediary you're looking for.

- **Trade associations and trade shows specialising in distributors in specific industries:** If you don't already know which trade associations serve your industry, you can search the Trade Association Forum at www.taforum.org.

- **Google (google.co.uk/) or any other search engine:** Go online and search for products like yours. Once you find them, work out who's selling them. Maybe they'll sell yours, too!

- **Major conventions in your industry:** These are the best places to find distributors. Take along product samples and literature, put on comfortable shoes and walk around the convention hall until you find the right distributors.

- **Retail outlets:** Use an Internet search engine to find shops operating in your local area, grouped by the types of products they sell. (You can also search for some shops in your local area using the Google Maps function, which helps show you where they are.) These shops also have their own trade associations, such as the Association of Convenience Stores, at www.acs.org.uk. Consult any directory of associations for extensive listings, or consider wearing out a little shoe leather and tyre rubber to discover the leading retailers in any specific geographic market. Just visit high-traffic areas and see what shops are prominent and successful to identify the leading retailers in the area.

Understanding Marketing Channel Structure and Design

Efficiency is the driving principle behind *distribution channel* design. (*Channel* refers to the pathways you create to get your product out there and into customers' hands.) Traditionally, channels have evolved to minimise the number of transactions because the fewer the transactions, the more efficient the channel.

As Figure 19-1 shows, a channel in which four producers and four customers do business directly has 16 (4 x 4) possible transactions. In reality, the numbers get much higher when you have markets with dozens or hundreds of producers and thousands or millions of customers – diagrams can become very complicated when you consider the distribution channels offered by the Internet.

You lower the number of transactions greatly when you introduce an intermediary, because now you only have to do simple addition rather than multiplication. In the example shown in Figure 19-1, you only need 8 (4 + 4) transactions to connect all four customers with all four producers through the intermediary. Each producer or customer has only to deal with the intermediary, who links him to all the producers or customers he may want to do business with.

Although intermediaries add their mark-up to the price, they often reduce overall costs of distribution because of their effect on the number of transactions. Adding a level of intermediaries to a channel reduces the total number of transactions that all producers and customers need to do business with each other.

This example is simplistic, but you can see how the logic applies to more complex and larger distribution channels. Introduce a lot of customers and producers, link them through multiple intermediaries (perhaps adding a second or third layer of intermediaries), and you have a classic indirect marketing channel. Odds are that you have some channels like this in your industry.

We have to warn you that we're suspicious of these traditional, multi-level channels. The longer and more complex they grow, the more types of intermediaries they have. The more times a product is handed from intermediary to intermediary, the less we like the channel. We prefer to see only one layer between you and your customers, if possible.

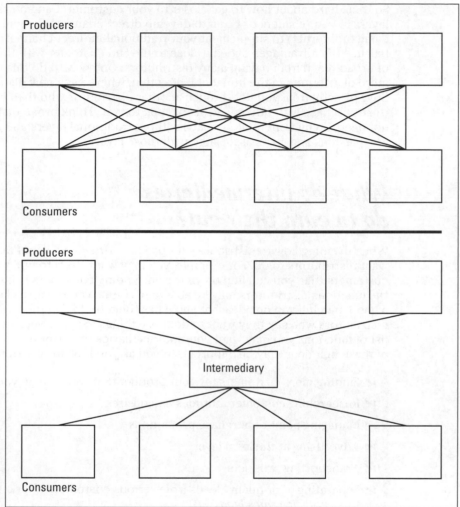

Figure 19-1:
Reducing
transactions
through
intermed-
iaries.

Why? We don't like traditional, many-layered channels because they separate you too much from the end consumer. We think that improved transportation; computerised links between channel members; the creation of just-in-time inventory systems in which suppliers bring only what you need, when you need it; and the emergence of direct marketing technologies and practices all make running lean and mean channels much easier. Just as big companies are de-layering to become more efficient and get closer to their customers, the big distribution channels in many industries are trying to do the same thing.

The trend is toward simpler, more direct channels and marketers need to be prepared to handle a large number of customer transactions on their own without as much help from intermediaries. Database management techniques alone do much to make this future possible.

So think hard about how to get closer to your customer. Can you reduce the layers in your channel or begin to develop direct channels (by mail, phone, email or Internet) to supplement your traditional indirect channels? If so, balance the advantages of being close to the end customer with the benefits of broad reach from having many distributors. One way to do this is to add more distributors in the horizontal direction, where each new distributor buys directly from you not through another distributor who then bundles their purchase with others and sends it on to you. Think broad distribution, not deep, if you want modern reach without traditional layers and all of the complexities and costs associated with those layers.

What do intermediaries do to earn their cut?

When deciding how to distribute your product, draw up a list of tasks you want distributors to do. For example, you may want them to find you more customers than you can find on your own. Finding customers is just one of the functions distributors may be able to perform. You're more likely to get a good match if you decide what you'd like them to do and then seek out distributors who say they want to do those things for you. Here's a starting list of functions you may want your intermediaries to perform. One or more of these functions may be important to you as you look for distributors:

- Finding more customers for your product than you can on your own
- Researching customer attitudes and desires
- Managing point-of-purchase promotions
- Advertising at the local level
- Transporting products
- Separating poor-quality leads from serious customers (marketers call this *qualifying sales leads*)
- Providing customer service and support
- Sharing the risks of doing business
- Combining your products with others to offer appropriate assortments

Channel design considerations

Your intermediaries can do several useful things for you, as the preceding section indicates. You need to decide who can do which of these things. But in addition to thinking about those various functions and who should perform them, you may want to consider the following sections, listing strategic issues. How you set up and manage your distribution channel or channels affects each issue.

Market coverage

How well does your channel reach your target customers? If you go direct, doing everything yourself, you may be unable to cover the market as intensely as you want to. By adding even one layer of intermediaries, you suddenly have many more warm bodies or shopfronts out there. As you add more intermediaries, the bottom of the channel grows ever larger, allowing you to achieve increasingly good market coverage.

In short, market coverage increases as you add intermediaries to your distribution channel. As you increase market coverage, you increase your availability to customers, which in turn maximises your sales and market share. You can't fight that logic – so sometimes building a channel, rather than de-layering it, makes sense. Just make sure that you really do get better coverage and that the coverage translates into increased sales. Otherwise, those intermediaries aren't pulling their weight. Also remember not to add in too many layers, which separate you too far from your customers. You need to identify the optimum balance between gaining market coverage and being in contact with consumers.

Level of intensity

Thinking about the issue of market coverage in terms of *intensity*, defined as the extent of your geographic coverage of the market, can help you work out how many and what types of distributors to use. Conventional wisdom identifies three practical strategies:

- **Intensive distribution strategy:** Here, you attempt to put every customer within reach of your products by using as many intermediaries and layers as needed to create maximum coverage. You should use this strategy in mature markets where your competitors are trying to do the same thing, or in markets where the customer makes a convenience purchase – because intensive distribution makes your product convenient. Keep in mind that this strategy is expensive, and you may not need it in other circumstances.

- **Selective distribution strategy:** Here, you target the most desirable areas or members of your market. For example, the business-to-business (B2B) marketer may decide to target a geographic region where many users of his technology are based. The consumer products marketer may decide to market to areas by postcode or counties where he finds heavy users of his product.

- **Exclusive distribution:** Here, you cherry-pick to find the best intermediaries and customers. This strategy is appropriate when you don't have any really serious competition and you have a speciality product that you want to keep providing at the same profitable level. This method doesn't grow your market or boost share significantly, but it does maximise profit margins, which is no bad thing!

Exclusive distribution is also appropriate if you introduce an innovative new product or service. You find a limited number of early adopters – people who are quick to use your products or services in any market. Start with exclusive distribution to find those customers most interested in trying new ideas and then work up to selective distribution as competition builds and the product goes mainstream. Finally, push toward intensive distribution as the market matures and your emphasis shifts from finding first-time users to fighting over repeat business.

Speed to market

The longer the channel, the slower the product's trip from producer to customer. A relay team can never beat an individual runner in a sprint. If your customers need or want faster delivery and service, you have to prune the distribution channel until you make it fast enough to satisfy the consumers. You may even need to replace physical distributors with a website, where everything can be ordered immediately for next-day delivery.

Think about the trend toward online home-shopping in the clothing industry. Customers can obtain their choice of style and size from a large assortment and the company can deliver it within a few days or even the next day. You may think that you can shop in a department store even more quickly because you can walk out with your purchase. But the busy consumer may not have time to visit a department store for days or weeks, whereas he can take care of a late-night click of the mouse on a store's website in seconds when it suits him. Instead of spending days wandering round different shops to find what you need, you can look through a few websites in a flash. In the early days of the Internet, shops thought that people wouldn't buy clothes online because they wouldn't be able to try them on. Now every high-street shop tends to have a comprehensive website because they've realised just how many people prefer the convenience of using the mouse rather than shoe leather.

Reviewing Retail Strategies and Tactics

If you decide to improve sales at a shop and you bring in a specialised retail consultant, you may soon be drawing *planograms* of your shelves (diagrams showing how to lay out and display a shop's merchandise) and counting *SKUs* (stock-keeping units – a unique inventory code for each item you stock). You may also examine the statistics on sales volume from end-of-aisle displays (higher sales) versus middle of the aisle (lower sales), and from eye-level displays (higher sales) versus bottom or top of the shelf (lower sales). Great. However, we have to warn you that, although a technical approach has its place, you can't use this method to create a retail success story.

The real winners in retail are the result of creative thinking and good site selection – in that order. Those elements are the two big-picture issues that determine whether your shop is a low or high performer: a creative, appealing shop concept, in a spot that has the right sort of traffic, and a lot of it.

Traffic is a flow of target customers near enough to the shop for its external displays and local advertising to draw them in. You want a great deal of traffic, whether that means foot traffic on a pavement, car traffic on a road or virtual traffic on a website. Retailers need to have people walking, driving or surfing into their shops ('virtual' shops on websites need to have traffic in the form of lots of clicks and visitors; see Chapter 10). Customers don't come into a shop or onto a site in big numbers unless you have plenty of people to draw from, so you need to work out where high traffic is located and find a way to get some of it into your shop.

An old joke about retailing goes like this: 'The retail business has three secrets of success – location, location and location.' Not very funny, really, unless you've tried to market a shop in a poor location. And then you laugh pretty hard over the joke, but with a certain hysteria! Pick a store location carefully, making sure that you have an excess of the right sort of traffic nearby. Think of designing a shop like digging a pond. You wouldn't dig a pond unless running water was nearby to fill it. Yet people often dig their retail ponds in deserts or up steep hills, far from the nearest flow of traffic. You also wouldn't dig a huge reservoir beside a small stream. You must suit your shop to the amount and kind of traffic in its area, or move to find more appropriate traffic.

Developing merchandising strategies

Whether you retail services or goods, you need to think about your merchandising strategy. You do have one, whether you know it or not – and if you don't know it, then your strategy is based on conventions in your industry and needs a kick to make it more distinctive. *Merchandising strategy*, the selection and assortment of products offered, tends to be the most important source of competitive advantage or disadvantage for retailers.

What's your merchandising strategy? To answer this question, you need to recognise your own brilliance – what makes you especially notable – and make sure you translate that brilliance into visible, attractive aspects in both exterior and interior shop design.

We want to encourage a creative approach to merchandising. The majority of success stories in retailing come about because of innovations in merchandising. So you should be thinking of new merchandising options daily – and trying out the most promising ones as often as you can afford to. The following sections describe some existing strategies, which may give you ideas for your business. Perhaps no one has tried these strategies in your industry or region, or perhaps they suggest novel variations to you.

General merchandise retailing

This strategy works because it brings together a wide and deep assortment of products, thus allowing customers to easily find what they want – regardless of what the product may be. Department stores and general merchandisers fall into this category, but so too do the large out-of-town supermarkets, which have expanded from groceries into non-food sales. In the UK, Tesco is leader in this area because it offers more variety (and often better prices) than nearby competitors. The warehouse store (such as Costco and Matalan) is another example of general merchandise retailing.

Limited-line retailing

This strategy emphasises depth over variety. London's Planet Organic chain of grocery stores specialises in natural and organic food products; as a result, the chain can offer far greater choice in this specialised area than the average supermarket (and it picks locations with a high concentration of wealthy households). Similarly, a bakery can offer more and better varieties of baked goods because a bakery sells only those goods.

Limited-line retailing is especially common in professional and personal services. Most accounting firms, chiropractic offices and law firms offer just the one service.

Perhaps you can combine several complementary services into a less limited line than your competitors. If you can expand your line without sacrificing quality or depth of offerings, you can offer customers greater convenience – and that convenience should make you a winner.

Mixing and matching

Can you think of the perfect new combination of shops? How about a gym and a launderette, so people can work out while washing their clothes? Or a 'connections' shop that offers the combined services of a flower shop, jeweller's and gift shop, card and stationery shop, email/Internet access service, gift-wrapping and shipping service and even a computerised dating/introduction service? With all these services under one roof, the shop can serve any and all needs having to do with making or maintaining personal relationships. See? Coming up with novel combinations isn't hard – give it a try!

After all, the limited-line strategy only makes sense to customers if they gain something in quality or selection in exchange for the lack of convenience. Regrettably, many limited-line retailers fail to make good on this implied promise – and they're easily run over when a business introduces a less-limited line nearby. What makes, say, the local chemist's or butcher's selection better than what a Boots or Tesco offers in a more convenient setting? If you own a small business, make sure that you have plenty of good answers to that question! Know what makes your merchandise selection, concept or location different and better than that of your monster competitors.

Scrambled merchandising

Consumers have preconceived notions about what product lines and categories belong together. Looking for fresh produce in a grocery shop makes sense these days because dry goods and fresh produce have been combined by so many retailers. But 50 years ago, the idea would seem radical because specialised limited-line retailers used to sell fresh produce. When grocery shops combined these two categories, they were using a *scrambled merchandising* strategy, in which the merchant uses unconventional combinations of product lines. Today, the meat department, bakery, deli section, seafood department and many other sections combine naturally in a modern supermarket. And many supermarkets are adding other products and services, such as a coffee bar, bank, bookshop, dry cleaners, shoe repair service, hair salon, photographer, flower shop, post office and so on. In the same way, petrol stations combine with fast-food restaurants and convenience stores to offer pit stops for both car and driver. These scrambled merchandising concepts are now widely accepted.

You can use scrambling as a great way to innovate. Scrambling gets at the essence of creativity because many people define creativity as the search for unexpected but pleasing combinations of things or ideas.

Never employ the scrambling strategy just for your convenience as a marketer. Too often, retailers add a novel product line just because doing so is easy – they know someone in another industry who can handle the line for them, or they have a chance to buy a failed business for very little cash. Those reasons don't justify scrambling.

Scrambling only works if you approach it from the customer's point of view by seeking new combinations that may have special consumer appeal. For example, several innovators around the world have stumbled independently upon the concept of combining a coffee shop and an Internet access service into one venue. The result is a coffee shop where you can enjoy your espresso while cruising the Internet or flirting with another customer online. This new combination adds up to more than the sum of its parts, giving customers a pleasurable new retail experience.

Creating atmosphere

A shop's atmosphere, or *physical presence*, is the image that it projects based on how you decorate and design it. Atmosphere is an intangible – you can't easily measure or define it. But you can feel it. And when the atmosphere is comforting, exciting or enticing, this feeling draws people into the shop and enhances their shopping experience. So you need to pay close attention to this detail.

Sophisticated retailers hire specialist architects and interior designers to create the right atmosphere and then spend far too much on fancy lighting, new carpets and racks to implement their plans. Sometimes this approach works, but sometimes it doesn't. And at any point in time, most of the professional designers agree about what shops should look and feel like, which means your shop is like everyone else's.

Develop the concept for your shop yourself. If you think a tropical forest provides the right atmosphere, then hire some artists and designers to turn your shop into just that! Rainforest Cafe did so a few years ago by creating a fantasy environment they call 'a wild place to shop and eat' with themed menu items like 'Snappy Salmon Fishcakes'.

Maybe you really like old-fashioned steam engines. Great. Make trains the theme of your children's toy shop or men's clothing boutique. Run model train tracks around the shop, put up huge posters of oncoming steam engines and incorporate the occasional train whistle into your background music. Some people will love it; others will think you're nuts. But nobody will forget your shop.

Atmospherics are important because consumers increasingly seek more from shopping than just finding specific products. Surveys suggest that less than a quarter of shoppers in shopping centres go there in search of a specific item. Consumers often use shopping to alleviate boredom and loneliness, avoid dealing with chores or problems in their lives, seek fulfilment of their fantasies or simply to entertain themselves. If that's what motivates many shoppers, you need to take such motivations into consideration when you design your shop.

Perhaps you can honestly and simply provide some entertainment for your customers. Just as a humorous ad entertains people and thereby attracts their attention long enough to communicate a message, a shop can entertain for long enough to expose shoppers to its merchandise.

The Apple store provides a great example of an entertaining retail concept. All around the world, Apple shops allow people to listen to music and play on computers, and some even offer lessons in how to best use the products. The entertaining atmosphere draws in people who have a reason to linger and buy. Likewise, mobile phone brands such as o2offer outlets where you can recharge your phone and receive training on how to make use of all the available functions on it – a form of entertainment. And some bookshops create comfortable, enclosed children's book sections with places to play and read or be read to, so that families with young kids can stay and enjoy the experience.

Building price and quality strategies

Retail stores generally have a distinct place in the range of possible price and quality combinations. Some shops are obviously upscale boutiques, specialising in the finest merchandise – for the highest prices. Other shops are middle class in their positioning, and still others offer the worst junk from liquidators but sell it for so little that almost anybody can afford it. In this way, retailing still maintains the old distinctions of social class, even though the people who shop there may not.

As a retailer, this distinction means that customers can get confused about who you are unless you let them know where you stand on the class scale. Does your shop have an upper-class pedigree, or is it upper-middle, middle or lower-middle class?

 After you make a decision about how to place your shop, you're ready to decide what price strategy to pursue. Don't forget that building-in upmarket appeal can be an effective strategy for attracting the mass market – because you've built in desirability. In general, the higher class the shop's image, the higher the prices that the shop can charge. But the real secret to success is to price just a step below your image. That way, customers feel like they're buying first-class products for second-class prices – which makes them very happy indeed.

Pursuing retail sales

Many retailers take a passive approach. These retailers put the products on the shelves or display racks and wait for customers to pick them up and bring them to the counter. Other retailers are a bit more proactive: their staff walk the aisles or floors, looking for customers who may need some help. But few retailers go all the way and actually put trained salespeople on the floor to work the customers.

Apparently, less than 20 per cent of retailers make active efforts to close a sale. We think the actual number is probably much lower. Even approaching customers to ask whether they need help is rare these days.

Sometimes that hands-off approach makes sense. But, in general, if people walk into a shop they're considering making a purchase, which makes them likely prospects. To us, that means that somebody should find out what their wants or needs are and try to meet them! The effort doesn't need to be pushy – in fact, it shouldn't or you reduce return visits – but you do need to make a friendly effort to be helpful. Find out what customers are looking for, offer them whatever you have that seems relevant and ask them if they want to make a purchase. The last part, asking them for the purchase, is especially important. In selling, you call that question the *close*, and when you attempt to close sales, you usually up the sales rate. See Chapter 20 for more details.

If you want to get plugged into a wide variety of publications, conferences and other events of interest to retailers, get in touch with the British Retail Consortium (BRC) at www.brc.org.uk. The BRC is the leading retail trade association in the UK, but you can also find specialist associations covering everything from bike shops to DIY centres. And if you need to find out more about shop planning or track down experienced shop planners, try the Shop & Display Equipment Association, at www.shopdisplay.org.uk.

Stimulating Sales at Point of Purchase

Point of purchase, or *POP*, is where customer meets product. It may be in the aisles of a shop, on a catalogue page or computer monitor, but wherever this encounter takes place, the principles of POP advertising apply. Table 19-1 gives you percentage figures relevant to retail design and POP marketing, according to Point of Purchase Advertising International or POPAI (whose members are professionals working on POP displays and advertising, so the Institute does a fair amount of research on shopping patterns and how to affect those patterns at points of purchase).

Table 19-1	Nature of Consumer's Purchase Decision	
	Supermarkets' Percentage of Purchases	*Mass Merchandise Shops' Percentage of Purchases*
Unplanned	60	53
Substitute	4	3
Generally planned	6	18
Specifically planned	30	26

Customers plan some purchases outside of the shop – 30 per cent of supermarket purchases and 26 per cent of mass merchandise purchases fall into this category. In these cases, customers make a rational decision about what shops to go to in order to buy what they want. Because they have a clear idea of what they want to buy, these customers' purchases aren't highly subject to marketing influence. Even so, the right merchandise selection, location, atmosphere and price strategy can help get customers to choose your shop for their planned purchases rather than a competing shop. And the right shop layout and POP displays help customers find what they want quickly and easily. So even with so-called specifically planned purchases, you do have an influence over what happens.

Furthermore (and this news is really good for marketers), you have a far greater influence over the majority of purchases than you probably realise. All the studies that we've seen, including the one from which we took the statistics in Table 19-1 (and also the oft-quoted statistic that 75 per cent of decisions are made at the point of purchase), all add up to the startling conclusion that . . .

Shoppers are remarkably aimless and suggestible!

The fact that customers don't plan between a half and three-quarters of all retail purchases is really incredible. What happened to the venerable shopping list? How do consumers get their bank accounts to balance with all that impulse buying? And why do they wander aimlessly through shops in the first place – don't they have jobs, families or hobbies to keep them busy? Evidently not.

We don't pretend to understand our consumer society, we just write about it. Although we can't explain the fact that the modern retail shopper is in some sort of zombie-like state much of the time, we can tell you that this fact makes POP marketing incredibly important to all marketers of consumer goods and services. Whether you're a retailer, wholesaler or producer, you need to recognise that customers make an impulse decision – to buy your product or not to buy it – in the majority of cases. You should thus do what you can to sway that decision your way at point of purchase. Another advantage is that not many companies seem to understand the power of point of purchase – we can't think of another reason why only 5 per cent of marketing budgets in the UK are spent on POP advertising. Can you?

For more information about POP, a directory of POP designers and manufacturers, or a calendar of trade shows and events for the industry, contact Point of Purchase Advertising International at www.popai.co.uk. You can come up with your own winning POP or retail concepts by perusing the trade shows, such as the In-Store show (now part of MarketingWeekLive! at www.marketingweek live.co.uk). Finally, don't overlook the interactions between package design and labelling and POP.

Designing POP displays

Designing appealing displays from which consumers can pick your products can boost your sales. Free-standing floor displays have the biggest effect, but retailers don't often use them because they take up too much floor space. Rack, shelf and counter-based signs and displays aren't quite as powerful, but shops use these kinds of displays more often. Customers are likely to notice any really exciting and unusual display, which means that display works very well because it has a general impact on shop traffic and sales, as well as boosting sales of the products it's designed to promote. Exciting displays add to the shop's atmosphere or entertainment value, and store managers like that addition.

Because creativity is one of the keys to successful shop concepts, it also drives POP success.

When Procter & Gamble introduced a new formulation of its Vicks 44 cough syrup, it created a point-of-purchase display (that shop-owners could use as a free-standing display or as a wall rack) that featured a rotating frame in which two clear bottles were visible. Each bottle had some red syrup in it – one with Vicks 44, the other with a competing cough syrup. When customers rotated the frame to turn the bottles over, they could see that the Vicks 44 coated the inside of the bottle and the competition's syrup sloshed to the bottom. This interactive display was supposed to prove the unique selling proposition that Vicks 44 coats your throat better than the competition. We like this display because it's interactive – giving customers something interesting to do to build their involvement – and because it demonstrates the product's *USP* (its unique selling proposition – what makes it brilliantly different from all competitors). Like a good advertisement, this POP display attracts attention, builds involvement and then communicates a single, powerful point about the product.

Too often, POP displays don't do everything that the Vicks 44 display does. POP displays don't work well unless they:

- **Attract attention:** Make them novel, entertaining or puzzling to draw people to them.

- **Build involvement:** Give people something to think about or do in order to create their involvement in the display.

- **Sell the product:** Make sure that the display tells viewers what's so great about the product. The display must communicate the positioning and USP (make sure you have one!). Simply putting the product on display isn't enough. You have to sell the product, too, or the retailer doesn't see the point. Retailers can put products on display without marketers' help. Shopkeepers want help in selling those products.

You may have noticed that we keep worrying about whether retailers like and use POPs. This concern is a major issue for marketers because between 50 and 60 per cent of marketers' POPs never reach the sales floor. If you're a product marketer who's trying to get a POP display into shops, you face an uphill battle. According to the statistics, your display or sign needs to be twice as good as average or the retailer simply throws it away.

Answering questions about POP

The following sections give you some information to help you develop and implement your own POP campaign.

Who should design and pay for POPs – marketers or retailers?

In some cases, marketers design POPs and offer them to retailers as part of their marketing campaigns. In other cases, retailers develop their own POPs. Point of Purchase Advertising International (POPAI; www.popai.co.uk) reports that the industry is equally divided. In other words, retailers directly purchase half of all POP displays and marketers who offer their materials to retailers make up the other half. So the answer is a bit of both.

What kinds of POPs do marketers use?

POPAI is a helpful source of data. POPAI surveys reveal that salespeople spend most on POPs for permanent displays (generally, retailers make these purchases). Next in popularity (based on spending) are in-store media and sign options. And temporary displays come in third. Yet marketers generally think about temporary displays first when talking about POP. Maybe marketers need to rethink their approach and redesign their POP campaigns to emphasise permanent displays and signs first and temporary displays second.

How much can POP lift your sales?

Lift is the increase in sales of a product attributable to POP marketing. Researchers compare sales with and without POP to calculate lift (which is the difference between the two). You need to estimate lift in order to work out what return you can get for any particular investment in POP. First, we can tell you that, in general, accessories and routine repurchases have the highest lifts. Also, significantly, new products have high lifts if their POPs effectively educate consumers about their benefits. Table 19-2 shows you a range of lift statistics based on a detailed study of the question by POPAI.

Table 19-2	Lift Statistics
POP Displays/Signs For	*Typical Lift (%)*
Film/photo-finishing	48
Socks/underwear/tights	29
Dishwasher powder	22
Biscuits and crackers	18
DVDs	12
Butter/margarine	6
Pet supplies	6
Stationery	5
Salty snacks	4
Salad dressing	3

How much of your marketing budget should you allocate to POP?

We can't answer this question with any certainty because every campaign has to be shaped by its unique circumstances. But we can tell you that POP advertising accounts for only 5 per cent of UK advertising expenditure (and don't forget 75 per cent of buying decisions are made at point of purchase). Partly because retailers, distributors, wholesalers and producers spread this spending out broadly between them, POP doesn't get the attention that other media do in most marketing plans. Big mistake. Try to identify who in your distribution channel is involved in POPs that affect your sales and work toward an integrated strategy and plan so that you can bring this hidden medium into the spotlight and make it work more effectively for your marketing campaign.

POP is just one example of what we consider to be proactive marketing. Getting a distributor to agree to sell your product isn't enough. Now you have to get to work making sure that your product moves faster than others so that you win the enthusiastic reorders and loyalty that make for durable, profitable distribution channels. Channel management is an important part of most marketers' jobs and requires attention and a generous share of marketing imagination. Offering a selection of good point-of-purchase options to help your distributors succeed in selling your product is one effective channel management strategy.

Chapter 20

Sales and Service Essentials

In This Chapter

▶ Improving sales effectiveness with a strategic focus

▶ Looking at personal selling and your sales performance

▶ Managing the sales and service process

▶ Organising and compensating a sales force and finding sales representatives

▶ Delivering great service recovery to retain unhappy customers

Making a sale is the whole point of marketing. Nothing else can happen in business without that. But do you need to be involved in personal sales and service, in which you interact with people directly as part of your marketing? The answer is always yes. Whether you have a formal sales role or not, selling should be a natural, everyday part of business life. Selling is something you do whether you're interacting with clients, ringing sales at a checkout, meeting other professionals or taking a phone call. So this chapter may be the most important one in the book.

Providing Strategic Leadership in Sales

The sales process is a journey for the buyer. Sometimes, Mr or Ms Buyer just takes a quick trip down the block, but often has to make a difficult, even lengthy, journey – and then needs the leadership of a good salesperson.

Some people think that the topic of leadership is not related to the topic of sales and marketing. Not at all! Many similarities exist between great leadership and great salesmanship. As a salesperson (or an entrepreneur, consultant or other professional who needs to wear a sales hat sometimes), you need to be prepared to help and guide your prospects toward purchase. You can't force your prospects to buy, but you can guide and facilitate their journey. To paraphrase the old saying, you can lead your customers to water, but you can't make them drink. You can't close their sales. Instead, your customers have to be prepared to close their sales with you, and that won't happen until they arrive at the end of their purchase journeys.

Every purchase of any consequence involves the whole human being – *including* their thoughts and feelings. You need to address the prospect's cognitive and rational thoughts, but you also need to address their irrational, emotional feelings. Think about buying a car, for example. You want it to be well designed, in good repair and unlikely to break down. Those details are the rational side of the purchase. But even if you know the vehicle works well, you don't want to buy a car if you find it ugly. The vehicle has to appeal aesthetically to you, which is the emotional side of the purchase journey.

Most people tend to focus on one or the other appeal when they sell – they orient their sales pitch more toward information and logical argument (that's the first dimension), or they focus it on emotional elements in their approach (which is the second dimension). Advertising – and selling – needs to appeal to *both* the rational and the emotional dimensions of this journey, as we point out in Chapter 7. The sales process also involves a third dimension – after-sales support – which will ease repeat sales. Delivering this multidimensional appeal well, and at the appropriate times, can be hard without some special training and practice.

Describing sales strategies in a nutshell

Below are the four sales strategies that you should use as the basic framework for all your sales challenges. Remember to ask yourself (or the potential customer) what emotional (feelings) and informational (facts) barriers exist, and then choose a strategy to fit the strategic context. A great salesperson possesses and uses this core skill.

Appealing to your customers' feelings

The classic example of the feelings-orientated or intuitive approach is the super-friendly salesperson who knows people well, remembers their birthdays, entertains them and brings them considerate gifts. This individual is a strong relationship builder and may do reasonably well in sales.

If you focus solely on building relationships you are, in essence, just a well-connected order taker. You run the risk of leaving the logical side of the purchase process to the prospect and not giving enough information and problem-solving support. This approach is best combined with one that addresses the cognitive side of selling, as explained in the next section.

Appealing to your customers' logical side

Some people naturally tend to emphasise the cognitive side of selling: they prepare by researching the prospect's needs, they present a lot of factual information, and they anticipate and refute objections. These people can be effective at selling, too. But sometimes their prospects balk – they refuse to complete the journey, even though all the evidence seems to point that way.

Why do people sometimes fail to purchase when the purchase seems perfectly suited to them? Maybe the problems aren't rational or cognitive, but emotional. For example, you don't make a major purchase if you're feeling uncomfortable or uncertain – you postpone it or back out entirely. If you describe yourself as a logical, fact-orientated salesperson, be sure to pair this strength with the characteristics of the intuitive approach to maximise your effectiveness.

Coaching your customer through the purchase

Perhaps you're one of the rare people who naturally combine both facts and feelings in their efforts to help a prospect move toward purchase. When the prospect has both factual- and feelings-orientated issues or barriers, you need to use this strategy by encouraging her to take small steps with plenty of support from you. For example, you may break the purchase decision down to make saying 'yes' to a small thing possible today. Positive results from a trial or test purchase or a small use of a service can reinforce both the factual and emotional dimensions of the prospect's journey, allowing her to reach the next level.

Think about selling in terms of being a sporting coach, patiently improving the performance of an athlete. What can you get the prospect to do today to increase her comfort and move her closer to a major commitment? Try to do something with the prospect each time you interact, even if you're only warming that person up to the big purchase. Salespeople achieve most success using the coaching-orientated style, especially with complex purchases, so if you don't use this style already, make a point of using it in the future.

Delegating the sale to the prospect

Delegating means trusting the prospect to take the initiative and make the purchase. Delegators set up the opportunity for a purchase, and then step back and wait to see who buys. Many people overuse this delegate strategy and assume that, if the customer needs something, they ask for it. That strategy isn't necessarily a good way to approach sales, because many prospects don't complete their purchase journeys without help.

Normally, you want to check on your prospects and assess their level of factual- and feelings-based readiness for purchase – and then step in, using one of the three strategies listed in the previous sections. Otherwise, if you delegate and leave the final step up to the prospect, she may not make it to the end of her purchase journey. However, you can use the delegate sales strategy effectively when your prospect is really committed and ready on the emotional dimension, and also has all the information needed to decide what to do. In this situation, try a simple closing strategy, such as asking if she wants to place an order or what kind of purchase she wants to make.

When the time's right, you need to trust your prospect to make a sound decision that's to her (and thus your) benefit. Try to close in several low-key ways until you secure the sale. Then make a flow of business occur easily by providing continuing access and service support.

Following up with customer support

Don't forget this all-important element of maintaining a flow of business through good customer support. If you ignore the customer after the order comes in, you'll probably lose her and have to start all over again with another prospect – a much harder task than retaining a good customer would have been.

Knowing When to Emphasise Personal Selling

Sometimes you need *personal selling* – that is, selling face to face – as a part of the marketing process. In that case, you need to make sales the main focus of marketing plans and activities. Any advertising, direct mail, telemarketing, event sponsorships, public relations, or anything else you may think of, has to take a back seat to sales. To find out if your business should rely on sales, take the sales-needs quiz in Table 20-1.

Table 20-1		Are Personal Sales and Service the Key to Your Marketing Plan?
❏ yes	❏ no	Our typical customer makes many small purchases and/or at least a few very large ones in a year.
❏ yes	❏ no	Our typical customer usually needs help figuring out what to buy and/or how to use the product.
❏ yes	❏ no	Our typical customer's business is highly complex and imposes unique requirements on our products/services.
❏ yes	❏ no	Our products/services are an important part of the customer's overall business process.
❏ yes	❏ no	Our customer is accustomed to working with salespeople and expects personal attention and assistance.
❏ yes	❏ no	Our competitors make regular sales calls on our customers and/or prospects.
❏ yes	❏ no	We have to provide customised service to retain a customer.

If you gave multiple 'yes' answers to the questions in the previous table, then you can probably use personal sales (one-to-one with prospects) effectively, and you should make them an important part of your marketing plan and budget. You need to focus your marketing plan on personal selling and good follow-up service. Although you certainly also want to employ many other marketing methods, be sure to think of the rest of your marketing activities as support for the personal sales process. That personal sales process is going to be the key to your success – or failure. And that means you need to give careful thought to how you hire, manage, organise, support and motivate salespeople. Your salespeople's performance determines whether your marketing succeeds or fails.

Figuring Out Whether You Have What It Takes

Some people seem born to sell, and others are doomed to fail. But most of the population muddles along, struggling to improve their sales ability and wondering if they really have the right stuff. You can't categorise most people as either sales stars or no-hopers; they sit somewhere in the middle – capable of great performances but not so gifted that the performances come naturally. These potential salespeople can figure out how to do better by practising the strategic approach that we outline with the three-dimensional sales process in the preceding section. You probably fall in this middle range and can increase your performance, too. We recommend that you check your sales talent in order to decide whether you should find someone else to do this challenging task for you, whether you're a natural sales star or if you're somewhere in-between and can easily improve with study and practice.

Table 20-2 is a simple version of a test of sales ability. Take five minutes to answer the questions and then another couple of minutes to score them. At the end, you have some useful feedback about your overall sales ability right now, plus an idea about the areas you need to focus on if you want to improve your overall score in the future.

Employers take note. Tests like this one don't guarantee someone's success – your management and the rest of your marketing plan affect an employee's performance as much as their sales ability does. Also, ability alone doesn't give you much without appropriate training and technique. But anyone who you think ranks low on this test probably shouldn't take over an important sales territory.

Table 20-2		Measure Your Sales Ability
❏	1.	I feel good about myself much of the time.
❏	2.	I usually say the right thing at the right time.
❏	3.	People seek out my company.
❏	4.	I don't get discouraged, even if I fail repeatedly.
❏	5.	I'm an excellent listener.
❏	6.	I can read people's moods and body language with ease.
❏	7.	I project warmth and enthusiasm when I first meet people.
❏	8.	I'm good at sensing and bringing out the real reasons behind a negative answer.
❏	9.	I can see many ways to define a problem and understand its causes.
❏	10.	I'm skilled at drawing out other people's concerns and problems.
❏	11.	I know enough about business to help others solve their problems with ease.
❏	12.	I'm so trustworthy and helpful that I quickly convince people to work with me in true collaborations.
❏	13.	I manage my time so well that I'm able to get to everything that's important in a workday.
❏	14.	I focus on the big-picture goals that matter most to me and my company instead of always reacting to the latest crisis or chore.
❏	15.	I can balance the need for finding new customers with the demands of maintaining and strengthening all existing customer relationships.
❏	16.	I keep looking for and finding ways to be more effective and efficient.
❏	17.	I find that, for me, a sense of accomplishment is even more rewarding than money.
❏	18.	My internal standards and expectations are higher than any imposed on me by others.
❏	19.	I don't care how long it takes to succeed at a task – I know I can succeed, in the end.
❏	20.	I feel I deserve the respect and admiration of my customers and associates.

Score your sales ability like this:

A. Positive Personality?

Total number of ticks on statements 1 to 4:

Less than three ticks means that you need improvement on personal attitude, emotional resiliency and self-confidence.

B. Interpersonal Skills?

Total number of ticks on statements 5 to 8:

Less than three ticks means that you need improvement on communication and listening skills, including your ability to control your own non-verbal communications and read others' body language.

C. Solution-finding Skills?

Total number of ticks on statements 9 to 12:

Less than three ticks means that you need improvement on problem-finding, creative problem-solving and collaborative negotiating skills.

D. Self-management Skills?

Total number of ticks on statements 13 to 16:

Less than three ticks means that you need improvement on organisation, strategy and focus skills.

E. Self-motivation?

Total number of ticks on statements 17 to 20:

Less than three ticks means that you need to build your personal motivation and figure out how to find rewards in the pleasures of doing a job well and accomplishing a goal.

F. Overall Level of Sales Ability?

Total up the number of ticks on all statements (1 to 20). Check your results on Table 20-3.

Table 20-3	Checking Your Score
Total Number of Ticks	*Score*
0–5	Guaranteed to fail. Sorry, but you should let somebody else do the selling!
6–9	Low sales ability. Not likely to succeed.
10–12	Low sales ability, but with practice and study, may become moderately capable.
13–15	Moderate sales ability. Capable of improvement.
16–18	High sales ability. Capable of rapid improvement.
19–20	Guaranteed to succeed. Superstar potential!

If you ticked a total of 13 or more, you have enough ability to be out there on the road making sales calls right now. However, this score doesn't mean that you're perfect. If you ticked fewer than 19 or 20 boxes, you need to work on your weak areas – and when you do, your sales success rate should go up. (But be aware that rating yourself on such tests can be difficult and inaccurate. How do you think your customers would rate you on each item? Finding out may be useful!)

Technique can and often does trump natural ability. The salesperson who starts with high-quality prospects and then uses the right strategy at the right time with them doesn't have as tough a sales task as the one who starts with less. You can close a sale far more easily when you start with good-quality leads and use the right strategy. These factors can make even someone with little natural talent perform like a star!

Making the Sale

The sales process can sometimes be painful but if you think of sales in the following way, you can divide and conquer. You can divide sales into multiple steps and then focus on one step at a time as you prepare a sales plan or look for ways to improve your sales effectiveness. As with any complex process, a weak link always exists. When you look at the steps in your own sales process, try to find the one you perform most poorly right now. And focus on that one!

Figure 20-1 displays the sales and service process as a flow chart. Note that the chart doesn't flow automatically from beginning to end. You may be forced to cycle back to an earlier stage if things go wrong. But, ideally, you never lose a prospect or customer forever – they just recycle into sales leads and then you can mount a new effort to win them over. (By the way, the strategies we describe in the 'Providing Strategic Leadership in Sales' section earlier in this chapter can apply at multiple stages of this flow chart. The strategy gives you an overall approach and the steps give you a narrow tactical focus.)

Figure 20-1 emphasises the need to integrate the sales and service processes. That's real-world selling – you can't stop when you close a sale and write the order. Your competitors certainly don't stop trying to win that client or account. So you need to think of a completed sale as the *beginning* of a relationship-building process. More sales calls, further presentations and efforts to find new ways to serve the customer – you need to focus on these points after you close a sale.

You also have to anticipate problems. You always do have a problem at some point – something goes wrong that upsets, disappoints or even angers your customer. Trust us – problems happen, no matter how good your company is.

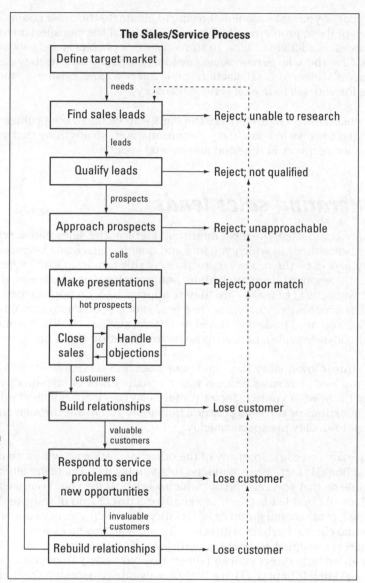

The Sales/Service Process

Define target market

↓ needs

Find sales leads → Reject; unable to research

↓ leads

Qualify leads → Reject; not qualified

↓ prospects

Approach prospects → Reject; unapproachable

↓ calls

Make presentations → Reject; poor match

↓ hot prospects

Close sales ←or→ Handle objections

↓ customers

Build relationships → Lose customer

↓ valuable customers

Respond to service problems and new opportunities → Lose customer

↓ invaluable customers

Rebuild relationships → Lose customer

Figure 20-1: This flow chart shows you the process behind sales and service — try it!

How well can the salesperson respond to a problem? If the salesperson finds that she's overscheduled with sales calls, she can't take the time to solve problems. So budget, say, one in ten sales calls as *service recovery time* to prepare for this contingency. (Over time, you should be able to drive down the need for recoveries; perhaps you only need to budget one in 20 calls next year, if you make a point of trying to eliminate the most common root causes of these problems.) And keep in mind that the salesperson needs some resources, in addition to time, to solve customer problems and rebuild relationships. Give the salesperson some spending authority so that they can turn the customer's anger into satisfaction (or, if you're a small business, budget some funds for yourself to use on service recovery).

The most faithful customers are the ones who've had a big problem that you managed to solve in a fair and generous manner, so anything that you invest in service recovery is time and money well spent!

Generating sales leads

In many companies, the most important steps in the sales and service process are those in which you find and qualify sales leads because – as in any process – the *rubbish in, rubbish out* rule applies. *Qualifying* means gathering enough information about someone (or some business, if that's what you sell to) to make sure they're appropriate. By appropriate, we mean that the prospective customer fits a profile of a good customer. What is this profile? You need to decide, based on criteria such as wealth, age and interests (for a consumer sale), or size, industry and location (for a business sale).

Don't throw low-quality leads into your sales and service process. Make sure that you feed your sales process with a constant flow of high-quality sales leads. Know what your customer profile is and seek out qualified prospects with questions or screening criteria that allow you to sift through and eliminate poor-quality prospects quickly.

Sales leads can come from any of the other marketing activities we describe in this book. In fact, we recommend that you try using as many alternatives as possible so that you can find out which work best for you. Your website may produce the best leads (see Chapter 10 for a discussion of website design). Or joining a professional group or association may help you network and meet potential clients. Perhaps a direct-mail campaign produces leads. And many marketers use direct-response advertising to find their sales leads. (Chapter 14 talks about both direct mail and direct-response ads.) Then you can consider telemarketing (Chapter 14), trade shows, event sponsorship (both discussed in Chapter 16) and so on.

You get the idea. You can use almost any kind of marketing to produce leads. You just have to find a good way to communicate with people who seem like good prospects for you and ask whether they're interested in your product or service. You also need to begin to ask for factual information: who your prospects are, how to contact them, what they've bought or used in the past and what their current needs are. Getting even a bit of information and an indication that someone is interested means that you have yourself a lead!

Here's a very simple way to generate leads:

1. **Select a magazine, newsletter, e-newsletter or newspaper that the kind of people who should be interested in what you sell or do are likely to read.**

2. **Find the smallest, cheapest display ad in that publication and buy that ad space for the shortest possible time – one insertion, if you can.**

3. **Write a very simple, short description of what you do or sell, keeping it clear and factual.**

   Include a clear, simple photo, if you have a relevant one (you can show the product, if you're in a product business), or use your name and logo to illustrate the ad.

4. **End the ad with the following sentence: Please contact us to find out more about our offerings by calling 0800 xxx yyyy, or by using the enquiry form on our website at** `www.mywebsite.com`.

You run a no-nonsense direct-response ad if you use the preceding method. This ad is designed to generate some sales leads. This method may or may not work well – you always have to experiment to get your lead-producing formulas down – but it certainly gives you a good start. (If you already use some good lead generation techniques, why not test something simple in a new medium? Everyone should be experimenting in marketing or they can't improve.)

Purchasing lists for lead generation

You can, of course, buy or rent names from list brokers. Mailing and call lists are widely available (you could start with researching 'lists' under the Directory section of the Direct Marketing Association website at `www.dma.org.uk`). Don't make the mistake of thinking that lists are leads in and of themselves. Nobody can sell you leads; you have to create them. Write a letter or email describing your offer and what you do and make sure your brilliance – what you're especially good at and want to be known for – is clearly and persuasively described. Send the communication out to a purchased list and ask recipients to contact you if they want more information.

To increase the response rate, try including a special short-term offer and a prepaid postcard or fax form for recipients' replies – unless you're using email, of course. Try following up with a telephone call to the recipient. You may have to make two or more contacts to sort out the real leads from the rest of the list.

After you get some responses and capture their names and other information, you can call them leads. You own these leads and have the opportunity to follow up on them and see how many actually turn into customers. Good luck!

Remember, telemarketers are the first people from your company to talk with these prospective customers, so make sure that they're well spoken and polite. Better yet, have your salespeople select and train your telemarketers (or do it yourself, if you have a smaller business) so that you have plenty of control over that vital first impression.

Forgetting cold calling on households

The stereotypical retail salesperson walks around a suburban housing estate, ringing doorbells to pitch brooms, encyclopaedias and various household products.

Forget that approach. For most businesses, door-to-door selling isn't worth the effort that goes into it. Nobody's home at most houses in the daytime anymore, and the few people who do stay home are afraid to admit a stranger carrying a large suitcase – or should be. Some charities canvas door-to-door in the early evening, enjoying moderate success if they pick areas where their name is well known and their cause popular. But this tactic doesn't work for most salespeople. Cold calling door-to-door is dead.

So how do you use personal selling to reach households? At *Encyclopaedia Britannica*, which eliminated its traditional sales force 20 years ago, salespeople generate leads through advertising and referrals. They then follow up by tele-marketing, or in person if absolutely necessary. To eliminate cold calling, you need to get really good at generating sales leads – and to use many other marketing communication components for the purpose of getting leads.

You can also use a web page or online newsletter to reach out for prospects and generate visits and enquiries that you can turn into leads. See Chapter 10 for more ideas on how to use the web to supply your salespeople with better leads. Another idea is to ask your current customers to supply you with referrals, and thanking them or even rewarding them with gifts or discounts for the information. Current customers often can find you good quality leads through their personal networks.

If you do consumer marketing, also consider following the lead of one of the most successful cosmetics companies. At Avon, the salespeople reach households by *networking*, using personal and professional contacts, in order to set up appointments – usually after working hours. This strategy overcomes people's natural suspicions and doesn't interfere with their busy schedules. Around the world, Avon has five million salespeople – evidence that person-to-person selling isn't dead in the retail industry. You just have to do it differently, and with a bit more finesse, than previously.

Developing great sales presentations and consultations

At the sales presentation, the salesperson must convince the prospect to become a customer, which can be a challenge. Only the truly great sales presentation has a high rate of success in persuading prospects to become customers.

What makes a sales presentation great? Success. Any presentation that works, that gets customers to say 'yes' quickly and often, is an exceptional presentation. Be prepared to experiment and think creatively about this task. And make sure that you designed the presentation to cover both basic fact needs and basic feelings needs. Your presentation needs to inform while also making the prospect comfortable (see the 'Providing Strategic Leadership in Sales' section earlier in this chapter for details). Sometimes, the right approach to sales presentations is to be consultative, meaning that you first ask a lot of questions to work out what the customer needs, and then propose a somewhat customised solution and not just a generic purchase. This tactic is good in some cases – especially if you sell complex services. But consultative selling may not be right for your company. Maybe you can't see any obvious ways to sell customised services along with your product. You just want to deliver an excellent product and let the customer worry about what to do with it. If so, pretending they're consultants is the last thing that you want your salespeople to do.

Or – and this problem is increasingly common – perhaps you have the ability to solve customers' problems, but customers don't give you the time. Bringing a salesperson up to speed about a business so that they can solve the company's problems takes considerable time. In many markets, the buyers can't be bothered, so you can forget consultative selling. In that case, you need a good old-fashioned *canned approach* – which means you write a detailed, specific, script that you (or your sales force if you have one) follow every time you give a sales presentation.

You can use a simple, canned approach as effectively as a sophisticated consultative approach, if the customer just wants an easy way to evaluate your offering. Be sure to tailor your sales style to accommodate your customers' needs, purchase preferences and habits.

Organising Your Sales Force

If you have a large enough sales operation that you need to think about bigger-picture sales force management issues, look over this section.

Who does what, when and where? Such organisational questions plague many sales or marketing managers, and the answers can make a big difference to sales force productivity. Should your salespeople work out of local, regional or national offices? Should you base your salespeople in offices where staff provide daily support and their boss can supervise their activities closely? Or should you set salespeople free to operate on the road, maximising the number of calls they can make – and communicating with the company through laptops or smartphones rather than through regional offices? Or – if you have a small business – should the owner do all the selling, or does bringing in a salesperson on commission make sense? We don't know. Honestly. These decisions depend on your situation. But we can help you decide by giving you an idea of the options available – several exist – and by sharing some conventional wisdom to help you assess your particular situation.

Determining how many salespeople you need

If you have an existing sales force, you can examine the performance of each territory to decide whether more salespeople can help, or if perhaps you can do with less. Are some territories rich in prospects that salespeople just don't get to? Consider splitting those territories. Also consider splitting territories, or adding a second person to create a sales team, if you're experiencing high customer turnover in one area. Turnover probably indicates a lack of service and follow-up visits. Alternatively, if you realise that some territories have little potential, you may be able to merge them with other areas. (Similarly, if time and travel constraints make covering all prospects adequately impossible, the small-business owner could consider employing commissioned salespeople.)

Hiring your own or using reps?

You have to make the most basic choice of whether to do it yourself or to subcontract. Good sales companies exist in most industries that take on the job of hiring and managing salespeople for you. Called *sales representatives* (or reps), they usually work for a straight commission of between 10 and 20 per cent, depending on the industry and how much room you have in your pricing structure for their commission. Also, in areas where you need more work done – customer support through consultative selling and customised service – reps earn, and deserve, a higher commission.

If you have a small company or a short product line, we recommend using sales reps. Reps are the best option whenever you have *scale problems* that make justifying the cost of hiring your own dedicated salespeople somewhat difficult. Scale problems arise when you have a too-short product line, which means that salespeople don't have very much to sell to customers. Each sales call produces such small total orders that those sales don't cover the cost of the call. Reps usually handle many companies' product lines so that they have more products to show prospects when they call than your own independent salesperson would. Many product lines spread the cost of that sales call over more products, which may make the sales call more valuable for the buyer, as well. If you sell too few products, a busy buyer may not be willing to take the time to listen to your salesperson's presentation – so again, the rep has a scale advantage.

However, if you can possibly justify hiring and running your own dedicated salespeople, by all means do so! You'll have much more control and better feedback from the market. You'll also find that a dedicated sales force generally outsells a sales rep by between two and ten times as much. Why? The dedicated salesperson is focused and dependent on your product. Often, the rep doesn't care what she sells, as long as the client buys something. As a result, reps tend to make the easy sales, which may not be yours!

Finding good sales reps

How do you find sales reps? The obvious doesn't work – you can't find them listed in a directory. We don't know why, but rep firms prefer that you find them by networking. Doing so may avoid a lot of requests from companies that don't know the industry and don't have decent products. But if you want to find reps, you have to do it on the reps' terms, which means getting word-of-mouth referrals or meeting them at a trade show or industry conference. Or, even simpler, asking the buyers of products such as the one you sell for names of reps who currently call on them.

For word-of-mouth referrals, we recommend asking the companies that reps sell to for their opinions about the best rep firms. After all, you need the reps to sell your product to these customers, so their opinions are the most important! You can also get referrals from other companies that sell (non-competing) products through the same kinds of reps.

We also highly recommend networking for reps at trade shows in your industry. Reps attend the trade shows, and many of them rent booths to represent their products. You can find reps just by wandering around the exhibition hall, using your eyes and nose and asking occasional questions.

Managing your reps – with an iron glove!

When you have reps lined up for each territory, your work has only just begun. You must, absolutely must, monitor your reps' sales efforts on a regular basis. Which rep firms sell the best (and worst)? Usually 10 or 15 per cent of the reps make almost all your sales. If you notice such a pattern developing, you can quickly put the others on notice. And if the other reps don't heat up in a hurry, replace them.

Renting a salesperson

Temporary salespeople are also an option. Temp agencies have been providing telemarketers on a temporary basis for years. Businesses often use those temporary telemarketers for a few weeks in conjunction with any special project that requires telephone prospecting or follow-up – such as generating leads for a new product or new territory.

Temp agencies can fill a short-term need for experienced telemarketers, salespeople, trade show staff and other marketing people. You can do a search online; check out Reed (`www.reed.co.uk`), Kelly Services (`www.kelly services.co.uk`) or Manpower (`www.manpower.co.uk`).

Businesses don't use temporary salespeople that often, but we think they're a great alternative because they allow you to put a lot of salespeople on the street quickly without making a long-term financial commitment. Use temps to help you open up a new territory, introduce a new product or follow up on a backlog of sales leads from that big trade show you exhibited at last month. You probably want to hire these sorts of temps on a monthly basis to give them time to develop some continuity. And consider teaming temps with your full-time salespeople (if you have any) to ease the transition for new accounts when the temporary service period ends.

Compensating Your Sales Force

Figuring out how to compensate your salespeople is one of the toughest and most important management decisions you face in marketing. Compensation has a significant impact on the sales staff's motivation and performance, and (of course) salespeople's performance has a big effect on sales. The issue becomes difficult because compensation's effect on motivation isn't always obvious.

An important issue to consider is how to make sure that you have relationship-orientated salespeople, not people who just go after the maximum number of transactions. Make sure that you aim your commissions and also your non-financial incentives (recognition, praise and so on) at both finding and *keeping* good customers, not just attracting the most new business.

If you want to recruit special salespeople, you may need to offer them a special compensation plan. Do something sufficiently different from the norm in your industry to make your job openings really stand out. For example, what if you want to make sure that your salespeople take a highly consultative, service-orientated approach, with long-term support and relationship building? You need people with patience and dedication, people who are looking for a stable situation and can build business over the long term. So try offering them less commission than they would earn elsewhere. Make your compensation salary based. If you give your salespeople sales incentives, consider bonuses linked to long-term customer retention or to building sales with existing customers. Your compensation plan stands out from your competitors and sends a clear signal about the kind of sales behaviour you expect. Similarly, if you want the hottest, most self-motivated salespeople, offer more commission than the competition.

Retaining Customers through Great Service

Sales and service go hand in hand. When your business relies on personal selling you can bet that you also need great customer service. Why? Although personal selling produces new customers, personal service keeps them. If you don't know how to keep new customers, don't waste your time seeking them. You'll just lose them.

Measuring the quality of customer service

Do you know your *customer turnover rate* (the percentage of customers who leave each year)? If your turnover goes over 5 per cent in most industries, you need to build retention to lower that percentage (this advice doesn't apply to highly commoditised industries such as mobile phones, insurance or utilities where 'churn' of customers – another name for customer turnover rate – is high). You probably have a customer service problem. If you don't already calculate customer turnover (churn rate), we tell you how in the following steps. Find out your customer turnover rate by comparing customer lists from two consecutive years – or asking your salespeople to gather the data if you can't do so easily from your central customer database or billing records.

Sometimes companies define a lost customer as one whose business has fallen by more than half, which gives you a more conservative measure than one based only on customers who've stopped ordering entirely.

To work out your churn rate or rate of customer turnover, follow these steps:

1. **Compare last year's and this year's customer lists to find out how many customers you lost during the year.**

   Ignore new customers for this calculation.

2. **Count the total number of customers on the first of the two lists, the list from the previous year.**

   That number gives you your *base*, or where you started.

3. **Divide the number of lost customers (from Step 1) by the total number of customers (from Step 2) to get your turnover or churn rate.**

If you started the year with 1500 customers and lost 250, your turnover rate is 250 ÷ 1500, or nearly 17 per cent. If you find yourself in that situation, you fail our 5 per cent test and need to get to the bottom of your problem with customer service!

Delivering service recovery

Service recovery starts with recognising when service isn't going well. What makes your customers unhappy? Which customers are stressed or frustrated? Talking and thinking about these questions can lead to a list of the five top warning signs of an unhappy customer. We're not going to write your list for you because every company has a different one. Whatever your top warning signs, educate everyone in your company to recognise them and to leap into action whenever they see one.

Service recovery needs empathy and polite sensitivity. Make the starting point just paying polite attention to someone. In fact, sometimes that action can be enough to turn the customer around.

You can practise service strategically, in the same way as sales (like we describe in the section 'Providing Strategic Leadership in Sales' earlier in this chapter), with the goal of winning back the customer by solving her problem or helping her feel better. Usually, you have to start with the feelings of the unhappy customer. Use your emotional intelligence to empathise with her. Let her vent or complain, and don't argue with her. The unhappy customer is always right.

After a customer has calmed down a bit and is ready to listen to you and look to you for help, you can ask factual questions and give information in return. But remember, every service recovery starts with working on the (hurt) feelings of the disgruntled customer, not on the facts. That important insight can save a lot of customer relationships and help you build a reputation as a great company to buy from. If you make sure that you fix whatever problems a customer has experienced, he may even be more motivated to buy from you in future as you've turned a bad experience into a memorably good one.

Part VI
The Part of Tens

'A great advertising gimmick, George, but who's going to see it up here on top of Everest?'

In this part . . .

We could give you ten good reasons to read this part, but why bother – it already contains more than 30.

In this part, we warn you how to avoid many of the common mistakes and causes of failures that have torpedoed other marketers and their programmes in the past. We suggest you re-read this section once a month, just to make sure that your marketing innoculations are up-to-date. It's easy to get infected by bad habits if you don't pay attention!

We bet you want to save as much money as you can on marketing. Believe me, almost every marketer shares this wish. But few accomplish it, at least not without ruining next year's revenues and profits and sending customers away angry. So please consult this part of the book to find out how to save money by being an economical marketer. Given unlimited funds, any idiot can sell something, but doing it for less is a true art form.

Chapter 21

Ten Common Marketing Mistakes to Avoid

. . . .

In This Chapter

▶ Keeping customers happy through great service

▶ Keeping up your marketing momentum

. . . .

*O*ver many years, people have honed relevant and useful marketing techniques that you can benefit from. However, they've also made lots of mistakes along the way. Take a couple of minutes to find out about the all-too-common mistakes that so often derail sales and marketing efforts and then avoid them!

Don't Sell to the Wrong People

We regularly get sent a catalogue from a company specialising in maternity clothes and have done for several years. As we've never ordered anything from them, you'd think they'd give up sending out the expensive catalogues. At the very least, you'd hope someone at the company would realise that none of its customers can be pregnant all of the time. At work we get sent all kinds of letters from office equipment suppliers and magazine publishers – none of which are relevant to our jobs. What a waste of paper, time and money, not to mention the effect on the environmental.

You can sort people easily by profession or gender, thus eliminating some of the more obvious mismatches. Face it, most people are the wrong people – meaning that they probably don't want to buy from you – and if you pull out the obvious mismatches, you can eliminate lost-cause prospects and not waste your money on them.

Don't Give Away Money

Many marketers devote half or more of their budgets to price-orientated promotions, and we can't tell you the number of times we've heard managers say things like, 'Sales seem to be off this month. Why don't we cut prices and see if that helps?' Discounts and price cuts have their role, certainly – but you should never use them unless you have clear evidence that the net result can be profitable. And it usually isn't, as we demonstrate in Chapter 18. Sometimes, customers are highly price sensitive, competitors undercut you and you have no choice but to slash your prices too. But, in general, avoid competing on price. You'll find making a profit (and staying in business) far easier when you compete on the elements that make you different and better.

Don't Forget to Edit Before You Print

People will notice and remember if your letter, email, web page, print ad, sign or poster contains a spelling error. We often see signs outside businesses or on vehicles with obvious typos and a fair number of business cards feature them too. Talk about making a bad first impression!

Don't Keep Repeating Yourself

If you send someone a mailing or email once, they can chuck it or act on it quickly, no harm done either way. But what if they get the same communication two or three more times in rapid succession? Now they're going to respond in a third way – by getting irritated with you for bothering them.

Avoiding this error can be difficult. Check every list before you use it, looking for duplications that may slip by and end up causing irritation at the other end. We don't need to get three copies of a sales letter addressed to us with three different mis-spellings of our names, but we often do (and you probably do, too).

Don't Fall into the Wish-We-Could Trap

Every business has its core speciality and does best when it stays close to it. Sometimes you should expand into a new market area or try a new kind of product or service – but carry out this expansion with a careful, well-researched and funded strategic thrust (see Part I of this book). Otherwise, trying to play on someone else's patch is a big mistake. To fool around in an area that you aren't expert in just invites disaster. The grass may look greener on the other side of the fence, but someone erected that fence for good reason. Make sure that you're prepared to fight with the dog that lives next door before you jump over it.

Don't Dole Out Impersonal Treatment

Every single one of your customers is a person, and they like to be treated as such. Yet sometimes, businesses send out generic bills or mailings that have mis-spellings of customers' names. And perhaps the person who answers the phone doesn't know that the caller is an old customer. You can make these easy, casual mistakes often without even noticing that you make them. But put yourself in the customer's shoes and take a hard look at all your customer interactions. Are they as personal as they should be? If not, invest in better list-checking, a central list or software database of customers, training in how to pronounce people's names or whatever else it takes to allow your business to treat good customers like important individuals.

Don't Blame the Customer

We recently received an overdue notice on an invoice from a cleaning and maintenance company that we'd used many months ago. Our accountant was puzzled because she thought that she remembered paying the bill when it first came in. Reviewing her records, she called the company and gave them the cheque number, date and amount of our payment and asked them to correct their records. This company met her polite efforts to correct this error with sullen irritation on the other end of the phone. A manager at the company told her off for 'sending a misleading cheque' and 'not making it completely clear which account it applied to' (even though she'd returned their invoice with the cheque). In short, instead of apologising for the confusion, this contractor blamed us for the error. He may have felt better after letting off steam on the phone, but he just lost these customers forever. Don't make the same mistake with your customers.

Don't Avoid Upset Customers

You naturally want to avoid someone who's irritated with you – but don't. Customers can get unpleasant or abusive if they feel that they've been poorly treated – even if you don't think they really have been. Treat the unhappy customer as your top marketing priority. And don't stop working on them until they're happy again. If you win them back, they're especially loyal and will bring you new business. If you let them walk away fuming, they become an anti-marketer, actively trying to drive others away from your business. The choice is yours.

Don't Forget to Change

You can easily fall into the trap of doing the same thing with your marketing communications every year – many companies do. If you're spending the same proportion of your budget on direct mail, telemarketing and point-of-purchase materials every year, you've probably fallen into the trap of letting processes get in the way of effective change.

Don't throw out the marketing that does work, but at least find out which aspects work best and adjust your spending accordingly. New communications ideas are coming along all the time, too. You can't test out whether a blog or mobile marketing will work for you if your entire budget is tied up in local press advertising.

Don't Stop Marketing

When things go well, you may be tempted to relax and let marketing costs slip down while you enjoy higher margin sales. If you have a loyal following and a recognised brand name, you can probably stop active marketing for a while without noticing any significant drop in sales. But whether you notice it straight away or not, this slip undermines sales and erodes your customer base. Keep up your marketing momentum at all times!

When things aren't going so well in an economic depression or recession, maintaining communication with customers is even more important. Study after study shows that in a downturn, those companies that keep advertising through the hard times do much better than their competitors when business picks up.

We think this little saying sums up the situation nicely: 'The man who tries to save money by cutting spend on advertising is the same man who tries to save time by stopping the clock.'

Chapter 22

Ten (Or So) Ways to Save Money in Marketing

. . . .

In This Chapter

▶ Cutting costs and being creative

▶ Staying close to home

▶ Adding value to your product without adding cost

. . . .

*E*veryone wants to know how to do marketing on the cheap. Generally, you can only find worthless advice on this topic. Yes, you can place photocopied fliers under people's windscreen wipers for very little cash but will that really appeal to the people you want to reach? When you compare the impact of a cheap flier with a well-produced TV spot, you can easily justify the difference in price. As a rule, you get what you pay for in marketing. The cheapest consultants, designers and researchers may be professionals on their way up – but they usually aren't. And free exposures usually don't reach your target market or, if they do, don't make a favourable impression on that market. The real money-saving techniques aren't as obvious or easy as some people try to tell you, but these techniques can really work. Usually, they involve doing real marketing, rather than substituting some cheap alternative. If you want an approach that really saves money you need to do the right things – better. This chapter gives you ideas for saving money without reducing your effectiveness or embarrassing yourself.

Planning Your Expenditure

We estimate that businesses don't plan half of their marketing expenses, meaning they spend the money without thinking about how it fits into the big picture of their marketing plan. Companies often reprint their brochures, renew their sales reps' contracts, buy expensive display ads in phone directories and trade magazines, inventory large quantities of poor-selling products or spend money on fancy packaging without any idea of whether they're making good marketing investments. If you and your organisation make a commitment to spend nothing on marketing without knowing why – and without considering alternatives – you can avoid wasting money on marketing activities that don't have much impact on sales. The more time you spend on developing strategy and designing your plan, the more cost-effective and economical your marketing becomes.

Thinking Small in a Big Way

Grand gestures aren't necessary – you can make lots of small tweaks to your marketing budget. The following list provides ideas to help you be more focused on your target market and thus save money:

- **Targeting your audience narrowly.** Most marketing campaigns waste much of their effort on people or organisations who can never become good customers because they aren't in the target market. Think about the waste involved in running an ad that thousands or millions view, when only a small fraction of that audience is your target, or direct marketing to a list that generates a 1 per cent response rate. Look for the narrowest, most specific, way to talk to your customers and prospects. If you switch from a list with 75 per cent wasted names to a list with only 25 per cent, you can have the same impact with a mailing that costs half as much but still reaches the same number of prospects!

- **Narrowing your territory.** Think small by focusing your resources on a smaller market area. In essence, you become a bigger fish in a smaller pond. Many entrepreneurs use this strategy successfully by marketing (at first) in a single area. After they gain significant market share in a small area, they can afford to roll out to other areas.

  Understanding the effects of *scale* in your business is the trick to this strategy. Most industries have a minimum profitable market size, and that size varies dramatically. So, do some quick calculations. Can a 10 or 20 per cent share of the market in a single region, county or city cover your fixed as well as variable costs and get you significantly above your break-even point? If your fixed costs aren't too high for that market, it can. Businesses with high fixed costs – a factory, for example – usually have to think bigger when choosing a market. Consultants can think very small because they have minimal overheads. Consultants can best boost consulting sales by focusing a local marketing effort on the members of just one chamber of commerce.

✔ **Concentrating your resources.** Don't spread yourself too thinly. Concentrate your salespeople, your shops, your direct marketing or whatever you do in your plan into certain areas or periods of time so that you can cash in on economies of scale. *Economies of scale* means that your costs per ad or other marketing efforts go down as you do more. Make sure that you do each marketing activity on a large enough scale to make it economical. Take advantage of discounts from printers, mailing list houses and the media that sell ad time and space. If you print and mail 50,000 copies of your catalogue rather than 5000 copies, your costs fall to less than half per copy. However, apply this advice only to aspects of your marketing that you know will work well enough to pay their own way, like mailing a catalogue that you have already tested and found to be profitable. Otherwise, be careful of over-committing.

You can concentrate your resources by rolling out sequentially. Even the biggest consumer marketers often use this strategy to concentrate their resources. Introduce your new product in one market at a time, and make a big impact in that area before going to the next one. This strategy works for more than just new product introductions. You can roll out an expensive advertising campaign in one or two markets and then wait for your returns from this investment before funding the campaign in additional markets. If you're patient, you can fund a much higher level of advertising and achieve far higher impact than you may think your annual budget permits.

✔ **Holding your target's attention.** Sometimes, you can make a big impact in marketing media by being smaller than anybody else. A little print ad sometimes out-pulls a big one – not usually to be sure, but sometimes. And that means you should be able to develop a great small ad of your own if you work at it hard enough.

The same holds true in other media, especially those where the ad is measured in time. Most radio spots run 30 seconds. And most of the time, radio ad writers struggle to hold the listener's attention for the full 30 seconds. Why not give up that battle and just make a ten-second radio ad?

Integrating Your Efforts

In the Japanese approach to total quality management, you sometimes hear the expression 'too many rabbits' to describe the situation in which a business has a lot of initiatives under way without sufficient co-ordination. Marketing plans usually have too many rabbits when they really want one big rabbit. To avoid the multiple rabbits scenario, you need to integrate all your marketing communications by doing the following:

1. **Identify all the channels of communication with your market.**

2. **Design an overall message strategy that says what your organisation should communicate through any and all channels and defines a general feel or style for all communications.**

You communicate far more effectively using integrated marketing communications, and you may find that you can cut back your budget and still get your point across. Have one (just one) way to display your name and logo, plus one (just one) key point you want to make to sell people on your benefits. Then be consistent in all your communications.

Spending Money Wisely and Cutting Judiciously

Well-designed marketing plans are an investment in future sales. You can most obviously save money on marketing by cutting the marketing budget, but across-the-board cuts rarely work. These cuts save money this year but hurt sales and profits disproportionately next year. If you don't reach out to customers, they don't reach out to you! So remember to view marketing as an investment in future revenues and profits. Follow these tips:

- **Make smarter investments.** You can save money by making smarter investments, not by stopping the investments entirely. Take a look at your results from the past year (or month, or even week if you're looking at web marketing, where you can get reports immediately) and figure out which investments are working best. Then cut out low-return investments and shift the spending into the best-performing marketing activities. If you keep a vigilant eye on your activities, your returns keep growing from your marketing spending, but it is still relatively rare to find marketers benefiting from their experience in this way.

- **Cut your fixed costs.** Consider cutting your *fixed costs* (those costs that you incur regularly, like rent, regardless of what you do or don't sell). Although this advice sounds more like accounting or operations management than marketing, you can use it as an incredibly powerful strategy! Apply your marketing imagination to cost management and see if you can find a smaller-scale way to produce that product or perform that business process. If so, you can do small-scale and local marketing activities that you can benefit from but your competitors can't.

  If you're trying to work out how to introduce a new product on a shoe-string budget, consider searching for a low-cost supplier who can make the product for you in small batches. Even if you end up with slightly higher total costs, you have much lower fixed costs because you don't have to order large quantities in advance or find storage for extra units. And so you can *bootstrap* (or grow your own cash flow) by making and marketing a small batch in a small market and then reinvesting your profits into a slightly bigger second batch.

✔ **Cut back where customers can't see.** To a customer, many of the line items in a company's budget seem unimportant. Yet nobody asks the customers what they think about the company's budget. Customers may tell you to cut back on many expenses that don't affect the product's quality or availability in ways that matter to them. From the customer's perspective, the landscaping outside the headquarters building doesn't matter (and many people inside that building feel the same way!). Most consumers couldn't care less whether you print the department's letterhead in two colours or one, or whether salespeople drive new or used cars. Put money where customers will see it, not where they won't.

Focusing on Your Bottleneck

Many marketers spend their money on raising awareness of their brands when they don't actually have a problem in that area. If consumers already know about the brand, exposing them to it more often may not help sales – or, at least, not very much. Marketing more likely needs to work on the brand's image so that more of those people who do know about the brand decide that they *like* it.

Or you may have the problem that a lot of people try your brand, but too many of those people give up on the product without becoming regular users. Then the problem may lie in the product itself, and marketing money should go towards an upgrade rather than on expensive sales or advertising. A weak distribution system poses another common problem that makes finding your product when a person wants it difficult. If you don't know where your bottleneck is, you aren't spending your money wisely. Make sure that you focus hard on the most important bottleneck. Spend your marketing money there, and you'll see the biggest return on your marketing investment, in the form of increasing sales and profits.

Giving Your Product or Service Away

You're in business to make money from sales, but sometimes making a sale involves giving would-be customers a taster of your product and service – for free. This idea works on at least a couple of levels. First, giving freebies encourages trial, which encourages purchase, which encourages repeat purchase. Second, this idea shows your prospective customers that you believe in your own product enough to let them have some of it now and they can return for more later.

You can find ways to give away samples of your product or service no matter what business you're in. Consultants and professional advisers can provide basic documents and advice on their websites to pull customers in, food and drink manufacturers can give away samples in supermarket car parks and software and video games manufacturers can build in limited-time free usage. Let your product find you more customers. Give some of it away!

Rewarding Your Customers

Give your customers a treat as a reward for their business. Send them a bottle of wine, a cake, flowers or some other treat you think they may like, along with a personal thank you note. This tip is very simple, but it does a lot to let people know that you care about their business. This idea is also worth its weight in gold because customers who feel you've treated them well always send new customers your way.

Using New Channels and Media

Whenever possible, find the up-and-coming thing and hop on for the ride. Or better still, create the new thing yourself. (Can you use an exciting new event with associated publicity instead of using advertising?) Your marketing money goes much farther when you do something novel, for three reasons:

- ✔ New means unproven and advertisers are charged lower prices as a result.

- ✔ New means smaller, so you can be a big fish in a little pond. You have much higher visibility in a new medium than in an overcrowded mature medium. Advertise where no competitor ads distract the consumer from yours. That way, you get to be the star cheaply and easily.

- ✔ Your originality catches eyes and impresses customers. Be a market leader, not a follower!

Do direct marketing on the Internet instead of by phone – this route's cheaper and more effective. Take advantage of that fact by shifting your marketing efforts to a new and better medium. Or switch from mailings to email for new product announcements. Or experiment with direct marketing as a replacement for the traditional intermediaries in your industry. How about a radio ad, accompanied by a text message appearing on the information panel on the front of DAB digital radios? Few marketers have used this medium so far.

Giving Solid Guarantees

If you really think that you have a good product or service, why not take the risk out of trying it? A money-back guarantee, without a lot of small print to qualify it, tends to get customer attention. And what's the cost? If you're right and they love it, the offer costs you nothing at all. If you're wrong occasionally, then you still have a pretty low cost and it isn't cash out of pocket. You can't lose on a guarantee unless you're selling a bad product – in which case, you need to upgrade it straight away because nothing is more expensive to market than a bad product!

Recognising your own excellence

The one thing customers find most attractive about you is . . .?

If you don't know how to finish this sentence in your sleep, you need to invest in understanding, polishing and communicating what it is your company excels at before doing any more marketing. You can't be all things to all people, and trying to be spreads your money and effort too thinly.

So, tell us, what *is* your most appealing quality? If you don't know the answer to this question, your marketing budget is poorly spent. Work out what your prime quality is, and then show and tell the story of what makes you special everywhere you do marketing.

Being creative

All things being equal, the more you spend on marketing, the more you sell. Competitors with the largest marketing campaigns get more attention and sales so it's no wonder that winning the marketing war can get pretty expensive. However, one of the wonderful things about marketing is that you can escape this spending war by being more creative than your competitors. A creative new product concept or package design, a clever approach to point-of-purchase advertising, a pop-up colour brochure with a musical chip – any such innovations can help you achieve big-money returns from small-time investments. You can get big results on a shoestring budget, but you need to apply some creativity!

Joining and participating

We call this approach the *J and P strategy*, and many entrepreneurs say that it's the foundation of their success.

The average marketer goes home in the evening and watches two hours of television. Well, you're not average, and you can use those ten perfectly good hours each week (plus some weekend time) for more productive activities. Join community and professional groups, sponsor or coach youth sports teams, volunteer at a local community service agency, help raise funds for a local museum or go to educational and cultural events (especially those at which you can mingle with other professionals, such as art gallery openings and ribbon-cutting ceremonies). Get out there and participate in these many fun and rewarding activities, and you'll find that your network will grow quite naturally. Although your participation in such activities is its own best reward, you may also be pleasantly surprised at how often you bump into leads for your sales and marketing or discover that prospective customers have heard about your good works and call you up to introduce themselves. This strategy can be supplemented by the many online social networking platforms available, both in the consumer world (Facebook, Twitter and so on) and in your professional life (LinkedIn). Check out Chapter 12 for more information on these sites.

Chapter 23

Ten (Or So) Ideas for Lower-Cost Advertising

. . . .

In This Chapter

▶ Getting more advertising benefits than those you pay for

▶ Pulling in help from other sources

. . . .

They say that 'you get what you pay for'. Well, they're missing the point. You want to get *more* than you pay for, and this book is all about how to achieve just that. In this section we give you 11 good ideas (for the price of 10!) on how to get free publicity, use your own 'media' space and pay less for advertising than you have to.

Never pass up free advertising opportunities and always think about ways to create them. Handing out a business card and shaking someone's hand costs almost nothing – yet done in the right context, it can be the most effective marketing activity in the known universe.

Creating Billboards on Wheels

The vast majority of company-owned vehicles and vehicles of company employees don't have any signs on them, yet these same businesses pay good money to buy expensive advertising space elsewhere. You can turn your vehicles into attention-grabbing business generators by being creative with them. Think vintage cars, full-livery paint jobs, giving each vehicle a separate name or identity (so kids can 'collect' them) or covering them in artificial grass. If you have the vehicles, you should make them earn their keep.

Using Free Advertising Space

Free advertising space exists all around you, but you can easily mistake it for a wall, window, envelope or email. If your customers or potential customers see your building, or you're sending something to them, look on it as an advertising opportunity. Use buildings (if you own them) and windows for signs and posters, packaging and envelopes for stickers and stamps, and make sure you end each and every email with a thought-provoking tag line such as 'Smart marketers read *Marketing For Dummies*'. Don't forget to add your contact details too.

Getting Others to Advertise for You

Pass out window- and bumper-sticker versions of your logo and company name (with web address). Give out premium items (pens, mugs, caps, shirts, notepads or whatever – but make sure that you've made them nice enough that people use them). This way, your customers and the people in their extended networks can all begin to promote your business for you.

Inviting a Customer to Lunch

You should have regular lunches with a customer. You can use this great way to stay in touch with someone actually buying your product or service and to keep your ears open for input and ideas. Often, this gesture also generates repeat or expanded business.

If you don't know your customers or how to reach them because you distribute through intermediaries, take those intermediaries to lunch instead. They're your immediate customers, and they deserve the same royal treatment that you want them to lavish on your end customers.

Taking Liberties with Launches

New magazines, papers, radio stations, websites – all kinds of media – are launching all the time. And they need advertisers. The first few months of any media launch is a perfect time to strike a good deal for advertising space. If anything, these media businesses need you more than you need them: they're untested as a sales lead, they need to demonstrate they have the confidence of advertisers (like you) and they need some revenue. Keep an eye open for media launches targeting your customers or area – they can offer great value for money.

Ignoring the Ratecard

A ratecard is a list of prices with some rates set out for advertising options. An ad salesperson uses the ratecard as a starting point for a negotiation, and so should you. If you like, a ratecard is a guide to how much of a rookie advertiser you are – and nothing makes an ad salesperson's day like someone who pays ratecard price. So, before you even think about buying media space anywhere, you need to know what the ratecard is – and then negotiate down. Any media owner will happily send you their ratecard, so take the time to familiarise yourself with who charges what, and why. If you absolutely must have a certain ad slot, at a certain time, then don't expect much leeway. If you express a nonchalant interest at possibly advertising sometime in the near future, they'll bend over backwards to accommodate you. Pretend that you're haggling in an open air market. Doing so shouldn't be too hard – you are.

Getting Publicity for Nothing

Magazines, newspapers, radio and TV stations need editorial as much as they need advertising. Getting your business on air or in print is easier than you think. All you need is a good story, or even a strong opinion, to get yourself into the pages of business-to-business (B2B) magazines, like *Marketing Week*, more often than your competitors. What has your company got that a local or specialist publication or TV channel might like to cover? Have you or one of your staff done something noteworthy? You can create 'good news' by doing some work in the local community, carrying out an original survey and publicising the results, or taking part in some sponsored event such as a marathon.

Standing Up and Saying Something

Most people hate public speaking and consequently pass up the chance to get their business in front of a highly relevant and captive audience. Don't make the same mistake. Look out for opportunities to talk about your product or service. If you're ever invited to speak on a conference platform, take it – few occasions exist where the audience is so self-selecting and where you get to talk about your business and expertise without being interrupted. Talking about your product will also help give focus to your speech. Public speaking may not feel like advertising but it can be one of your most effective marketing activities – and it's free.

Running a Training Course

At the Apple stores all over the world, not only can you buy an iPod or iPhone you can also attend free workshops on everything from how to use photography software to managing databases – using Apple products, of course! This strategy's brilliant. It appeals to everyone from real computer geeks to those just hoping to pick up a new skill. Not only are they more likely to buy more Apple products on which to practise their new skills but they'll probably want to upgrade older products sooner to use the new, more exciting functions seen in the workshops.

This idea works well for any kind of 'lifestyle' business, from wine-tasting to DIY, but with a little adaptation you can copy it and apply it to any product or service.

Borrowing Good Ad Ideas

A breed of marketing agency exists that specialises in *ambient* or *non-traditional* media. Marketers in big, cash-rich companies pay them good money to come up with original (and often very cheap) ways of advertising. You can follow their lead and look for original ways of advertising and then do them yourself. Try hiring a pavement artist to draw your ad on a busy pedestrian pavement. Doing so's legal (although some local authorities still don't approve of it) and you don't have to pay for the media space. Projecting your ad or logo onto a wall at night is a similar idea. For more ideas on unusual and cheap places to put your ad, see Chapter 15.

Creating Your Own Network

Look out for marketers in complementary businesses that you can work together with towards a common goal – finding and retaining more customers. Putting cards or flyers into retail outlets that serve your type of customers is one of the easiest ways of doing this. If you have a shop, consider using products from another store as props for your window display. Doing so will make your display more interesting and increase your exposure if the other shop does the same. In business to business, where the target market is relatively small and time is precious, marketing a combined offer can benefit everyone involved – we're amazed this approach isn't used more often.

Index

FOR DUMMIES

Making Everything Easier! ™

UK editions

BUSINESS

Bookkeeping For Dummies
978-0-470-97626-5

Persuasion & Influence For Dummies
978-0-470-74737-7

Starting & Running a Business All-In-One For Dummies
978-1-119-97527-4

REFERENCE

British Politics For Dummies
978-0-470-68637-9

DIY For Dummies
978-0-470-97450-6

Dad's Guide to Pregnancy For Dummies
978-1-119-97660-8

HOBBIES

Growing Your Own Fruit & Veg For Dummies
978-0-470-69960-7

Keeping Chickens For Dummies
978-1-119-99417-6

Beekeeping For Dummies
978-1-119-97250-1

Asperger's Syndrome For Dummies
978-0-470-66087-4

Basic Maths For Dummies
978-1-119-97452-9

Body Language For Dummies, 2nd Edition
978-1-119-95351-7

Boosting Self-Esteem For Dummies
978-0-470-74193-1

British Sign Language For Dummies
978-0-470-69477-0

Cricket For Dummies
978-0-470-03454-5

Diabetes For Dummies, 3rd Edition
978-0-470-97711-8

Electronics For Dummies
978-0-470-68178-7

English Grammar For Dummies
978-0-470-05752-0

Flirting For Dummies
978-0-470-74259-4

IBS For Dummies
978-0-470-51737-6

Improving Your Relationship For Dummies
978-0-470-68472-6

ITIL For Dummies
978-1-119-95013-4

Management For Dummies, 2nd Edition
978-0-470-97769-9

Neuro-linguistic Programming For Dummies, 2nd Edition
978-0-470-66543-5

Nutrition For Dummies, 2nd Edition
978-0-470-97276-2

Organic Gardening For Dummies
978-1-119-97706-3

Available wherever books are sold. For more information or to order direct go to www.wiley.com or call +44 (0) 1243 843291

FOR DUMMIES®

Making Everything Easier! ™

UK editions

SELF-HELP

978-0-470-66541-1

978-1-119-99264-6

Mindfulness FOR DUMMIES

978-0-470-66086-7

STUDENTS

978-0-470-68820-5

978-0-470-974711-7

978-1-119-99134-2

HISTORY

978-0-470-68792-5

978-0-470-74783-4

978-0-470-97819-1

Origami Kit For Dummies
978-0-470-75857-1

Overcoming Depression For Dummies
978-0-470-69430-5

Positive Psychology For Dummies
978-0-470-72136-0

PRINCE2 For Dummies, 2009 Edition
978-0-470-71025-8

Project Management For Dummies
978-0-470-71119-4

Psychometric Tests For Dummies
978-0-470-75366-8

Renting Out Your Property For Dummies, 3rd Edition
978-1-119-97640-0

Ruby Union For Dummies, 3rd Edition
978-1-119-99092-5

Sage One For Dummies
978-1-119-95236-7

Self-Hypnosis For Dummies
978-0-470-66073-7

Storing and Preserving Garden Produce For Dummies
978-1-119-95156-8

Study Skills For Dummies
978-0-470-74047-7

Teaching English as a Foreign Language For Dummies
978-0-470-74576-2

Time Management For Dummies
978-0-470-77765-7

Training Your Brain For Dummies
978-0-470-97449-0

Work-Life Balance For Dummies
978-0-470-71380-8